THE GLOBAL
DIFFUSION
OF EVANGELICALISM

A HISTORY
OF EVANGELICALISM

THE GLOBAL
DIFFUSION
OF EVANGELICALISM

THE AGE OF BILLY GRAHAM
AND JOHN STOTT

BRIAN STANLEY

ivp

INTER-VARSITY PRESS
Norton Street, Nottingham NG7 3HR, England
Email: ivp@ivpbooks.com
Website: www.ivpbooks.com

First published 2013

British Library Cataloguing in Publication Data
A catalogue record for this book is available from the British Library.

ISBN: 978-1-84474-621-7

Set in Garamond 11/13pt
Typeset in Great Britain by Servis Filmsetting Ltd, Stockport, Cheshire
Printed and bound in Great Britain by the MPG Books Group

Inter-Varsity Press publishes Christian books that are true to the Bible and that communicate the gospel, develop discipleship and strengthen the church for its mission in the world.

Inter-Varsity Press is closely linked with the Universities and Colleges Christian Fellowship, a student movement connecting Christian Unions in universities and colleges throughout Great Britain, and a member movement of the International Fellowship of Evangelical Students. Website: www.uccf.org.uk

CONTENTS

To

Rosey

ACKNOWLEDGMENTS

This book has been too many years in the making, and I must first express my gratitude to the series editors, Professors Mark Noll and David Bebbington, and to Philip Duce of Inter-Varsity Press, for being willing to wait so patiently for its appearance. Mark and David have been constant sources of gentle encouragement, constructive criticism and sound advice, and I am greatly in their debt. I am also grateful to Mark in the early stages of the book's production for generously making available one of his students at Wheaton College, Ethan Sanders, as a research student; Ethan went on to become a graduate student first of mine and then of Derek Peterson at the University of Cambridge, and his assistance in compiling American periodical sources was invaluable. Another of my graduate students, James Enns, opened my eyes through his doctoral work on American missions to post-war Germany to the significance of that topic for post-war Protestant concepts of mission. Many other people have enriched this book by sharing their knowledge, insights and memories. I must mention in particular Andrew Atherstone, Alister Chapman, Larry Eskridge, Leighton Ford, Robert Forrest, John Gatu, Tim Grass, Stephen Gregory, Graham Kings, Peter Lineham, Bruce Milne, Judy Powles, Ian Randall and Roger Shuff. I am old and fortunate enough to have known personally a number of those who feature in these pages, some of whom are no longer with us. Those who remain may not agree with all I have written about them, but I thank them nonetheless for the several contributions they have often unwittingly made to various stages of my life and to my personal experience and understanding of the evangelical tradition.

A version of some of chapter 6 will be published in the *Journal of Ecclesiastical History* 64:3, July 2013. I am most grateful to the editors for permission to reproduce it in expanded form here.

Finally, I must thank my wife, Rosey, for her unfailing support and love, and to her this book is dedicated.

ABBREVIATIONS

AEAM	Association of Evangelicals of Africa and Madagascar
AIM	Africa Inland Mission
BCMS	Bible Churchmen's Missionary Society
BDE	*Biographical Dictionary of Evangelicals*, ed. Timothy Larsen, David Bebbington and Mark A. Noll (Downers Grove: IVP Academic, 2003)
BGCA	Billy Graham Center Archives, Wheaton College, Illinois
BGEA	Billy Graham Evangelistic Association
BJRL	*Bulletin of the John Rylands University Library of Manchester*
CC	*Christian Century*
CEN	*Church of England Newspaper*
Chm	*Churchman*
CICCU	Cambridge Inter-Collegiate Christian Union
CLAME	Comunidad Latinoamericana de Ministerios Evangélicos
CMS	Church Missionary Society (Church Mission Society from 1995)
CSSM	Children's Special Service Mission
CT	*Christianity Today*
EA	Evangelical Alliance
EFI	Evangelical Fellowship of India
EFMA	Evangelical Foreign Missions Association
ETS	Evangelical Theological Society
EvQ	*Evangelical Quarterly*
FGBMFI	Full Gospel Businessmen's Fellowship International
IBR	Institute for Biblical Research
ICBI	International Council on Biblical Inerrancy
ICCC	International Council of Christian Churches
IFES	International Fellowship of Evangelical Students
IFMA	Interdenominational Foreign Missions Association
IMC	International Missionary Council

INFEMIT	International Fellowship of Evangelical Mission Theologians (from the Two-Thirds World)
IRM	*International Review of Mission(s)*
IVCF	Inter-Varsity Christian Fellowship
IVF	Inter-Varsity Fellowship
IVP	Inter-Varsity Press
JEH	*Journal of Ecclesiastical History*
LCCWE	Lausanne Continuation Committee for World Evangelization
LCWE	Lausanne Committee for World Evangelization
MM	*Moody Monthly*
NAE	National Association of Evangelicals
NEAC	National Evangelical Anglican Congress, Keele, 1967
OM	Operation Mobilisation
Pneuma	*Pneuma: Journal for the Society of Pentecostal Studies*
RTR	*Reformed Theological Review*
SCH	Studies in Church History
SCM	Student Christian Movement
SOMA	Sharing of Ministries Abroad
SST	*Sunday School Times*
SU	Scripture Union
TynB	*Tyndale Bulletin*
UCCF	Universities and Colleges Christian Fellowship
USQR	*Union Seminary Quarterly Review*
WCC	World Council of Churches
WEC	Worldwide Evangelization Crusade
WEF	World Evangelical Fellowship
YMCA	Young Men's Christian Association
YWAM	Youth With a Mission

1. EVANGELICAL CHRISTIANITY IN GLOBAL PERSPECTIVE

In the second half of the twentieth century the story of evangelical Christianity became more diverse in terms of geographical distribution, cultural orientation and theological emphasis than it had been in any previous era since the origins of the evangelical movement in the early eighteenth century. As a transnational and transdenominational movement evangelicalism had from the outset encompassed considerable and often problematic diversity, but this diversity had been held in check by the commonalities evangelicals on either side of the North Atlantic shared – most notably a clear consensus about the essential content of the gospel and a shared sense of the priority of awakening those who inhabited a broadly Christian environment to the urgent necessity of a conscious individual decision to turn to Christ in repentance and faith. Evangelicalism had maintained an ambiguous relationship with the structures of Christendom, whether those structures took the institutional form of a legal union between church and state, as in most of the United Kingdom, or the more elusive character that obtained in the United States, where the sharp constitutional separation between church and state masked an underlying set of shared assumptions about the Christian (and indeed Protestant) identity of the nation. Evangelicals had differed over whether the moral imperative of a national recognition of godly religion should also imply the national recognition of a particular church, but all had been agreed that being born or baptized within the boundaries of Christendom did not in itself make one a Christian. Evangelical identity had in a paradoxical way been dependent on the surrounding Christendom culture, whose all-pervasive influence constituted the need for individuals to differentiate their faith and commitment from the nominal forms of Christian adherence that were socially acceptable. It also supplied the very widespread familiarity with the bare rudiments of Christian doctrine and vocabulary that made possible the verbal proclamation of the gospel, whether from the pulpit or in the home, to crowds gathered in the streets or fields, in terms that were broadly comparable, whether the evangelist was Calvinist or Arminian, churchman or dissenter, and in a measure intelligible, whether the hearers were American or British, Canadian or Australian, socially respectable or from the ranks of the poor.

The evangelical dilemma: how to respond to a radically changing context

In the decades that followed the conclusion of the Second World War these commonalties of context and even of theological substance could no longer be taken for granted within the evangelical world. In Britain, Australia and Canada especially, the notion of Christendom began to disintegrate, as secular influences increasingly eroded the structures of diffusive Christianity that were the legacy of nineteenth-century piety. Bryan Green, vicar of Holy Trinity Church, Brompton, and a leading English evangelist, told a gathering of Anglican evangelicals on the eve of the Lambeth Conference in 1948 that, despite a recent denial of the point by the bishop of London, 'England is a pagan country in any ordinary sense of that term.'[1] The chairman of the meeting, the distinguished layman Sir Kenneth Grubb, also referred to pervasive secular influences in England, and noted the recent report of a commission chaired by the bishop of Rochester, with the striking title *Towards the Conversion of England.*[2] Evangelicals had, of course, always been enthusiastically committed to mission at home as well as overseas, but the dawning realization of the shocking extent of popular indifference to organized Christianity now began to provoke divergent responses: Was it enough, as those of a more Reformed inclination tended to affirm, simply to go on proclaiming the classic gospel verities in the expectation that God would

---

[1] *Evangelicals Affirm in the Year of the Lambeth Conference: The Proceedings of the Congress Held in London, April 13th–14th, 1948* (London: Church Book Room Press, 1948), 34.

[2] Ibid. 8. See Church of England, Archbishops' Commission on Evangelism, *Towards the Conversion of England* (Westminster: Press and Publications Board of the Church Assembly, 1945).

in his good time honour the preaching of his Word through the bestowal of a revival? Or, as more liberal evangelicals affirmed, did the seriousness of the situation call for more radical rethinking of how Christian doctrine should be presented to modern people? Even among those who were clearly conservative in their theology, divergences of strategy began to become more pronounced on both sides of the Atlantic: Was the combative and uncompromising stance of the fundamentalist battles with modernism in the pre-war years more than ever required, or was there rather a need for a less aggressive style of theological conservatism, one prepared to engage the liberals on their own intellectual ground, which meant taking the realm of the mind much more seriously, presenting a reasoned and scholarly case for biblical truth, and perhaps also participating in both denominational and ecumenical structures? On both sides of the Atlantic a significant proportion of evangelical leaders in the 1940s and 1950s opted for the latter course, as I shall discuss in chapters 2 and 4. That strategic decision, often taken in conjunction with a policy of focusing evangelistic efforts on university students who were likely to be the future leaders in both church and state, proved notably successful.

This period accordingly saw substantial growth in the numbers and, in many places, of the ecclesiastical influence of evangelicals in the English-speaking world. Expanding ecclesiastical influence was not, however, a guarantee of wider influence on culture and society: on both sides of the Atlantic, orthodox Christian values became increasingly marginal to mainstream culture from the 1960s onwards. In the United States the 'New Christian Right', a grouping that had more in common with classic fundamentalism than with the new evangelicalism of the post-war era, mounted a high-profile but ultimately fruitless rearguard political campaign against the encroachment of secular and liberal values. Radical and often avowedly 'secular' theologies attained a high public profile in the 1960s and 1970s, and retained some of their influence in academic circles thereafter, but versions of supposedly Christian radicalism that were scarcely distinguishable from secular humanism proved predictably unappealing beyond the walls of the academy, with the result that liberal congregations dwindled rapidly. As a result the 'conservative evangelicals', whose identity had been forged in the 1950s in contradistinction to fundamentalism on the one hand and 'liberal evangelicalism' on the other, by the 1980s or 1990s often found themselves in something approaching a majority position within their respective denominations. Inevitably, as a result the cohesiveness of conservative evangelicalism weakened, as its adherents found themselves to be no longer members of a despised minority party but rather representatives of a widely acceptable general tendency. Those Reformed or quasi-fundamentalist evangelicals who had from the beginning resisted the argument in favour of seeking broader influence were now inclined to answer, 'We told you so,' and sought to reassert their claims to be the true heirs of the evangelical tradition. Their concerns were heightened by the extent to which evangelicals from the late 1960s onwards were influenced, often unconsciously, by the cultural and philosophical assumptions of postmodernity, which questioned the meaningfulness of truth claims, reliance on textual authority, and privileged human experience instead. The study of the charismatic movement in chapter 7 will note the major consequences of charismatic renewal for the stability of evangelical identity and raises the question of how far the movement can be explained as the product of the encounter between Christianity and the cultural changes associated with postmodernity. The subtitle of this book, the 'global diffusion of evangelicalism' thus refers not simply to processes of growth and geographical expansion, but also to the difficulty evangelicals faced at various times in that period (notably so at both its beginning and its end) in defining the boundaries of their identity. Chapters 2 and 9 will explore these themes at greater length.

The growth of Christianity in the majority world[3]

Another primary reason for the weakening of the commonalities that had once been assumed within the evangelical family was because of the very success of the global missionary enterprise in which evangelicals had played such a prominent part. Missionaries from Europe or North America were never numerous enough to evangelize the world through their own agency, but in many cases their witness of life and word, and particularly their labours of Bible translation, had sown the seeds of later movements of conversion, in which indigenous evangelists took the gospel message in distinctive vernacular forms to their own and neighbouring peoples in Africa, Asia, Latin America and Australasia, and often found a ready response, especially from those groups oppressed or marginalized by existing social structures. Such group or people movements of conversion appeared in Protestant contexts

---

[3] The term 'majority world' is used in this book, following the practice of many scholars of world Christianity, to denote the majority of the world's population who live in the continents of Africa, Asia, Latin America and the less developed islands of Australasia. Previous terms, such as the 'Third World', the 'Two-Thirds World', the 'developing world' and (more recently) the 'Global South' are still to be found in use, though all have their drawbacks.

in Tirunelveli in South India as early as the end of the eighteenth century,[4] and surfaced sporadically during the nineteenth century in locations such as the Pacific islands and parts of West and East Africa. After 1914 they became much more widespread, profoundly affecting the north-eastern and tribal areas of India, taking deep root in Korea, touching parts of China and South-East Asia, and turning large swathes of Africa south of the Sahara into predominantly Christian regions. Rather later, in Latin America from the 1950s onwards powerful currents of religious and ideological change of a different kind swirled through the continent. Its religious landscape was reshaped from a vast but superficially grounded replica of Hispanic Catholic Christendom into an arena of contestation in which Marxism and traditional and liberationist styles of Roman Catholicism competed for the allegiance of the populace with an emerging folk Christian movement nobody had taken very seriously before the 1950s – Pentecostalism. The mid- and late twentieth century witnessed church growth in large parts of the majority world on a scale unparalleled in any previous period in history. Throughout the globe, women and men who were economically poor, politically oppressed and educationally disadvantaged were adopting a range of popular and broadly evangelical Christianities whose cultural and theological tone differed significantly from that which had formerly been common to most white Anglo-American evangelicalism, though it bore many similarities to the style of evangelical religion that had been characteristic of African-American churches in the United States ever since their origins in the era of slavery. This geographical and cultural diffusion inevitably posed further challenges for the maintenance of evangelical unity.

This series of five volumes has been conceived as a history of evangelicalism in the English-speaking world rather than as a history of global evangelicalism, so there is a sense in which such movements in the non-Western world, dependent as they were for their cultural and spiritual vitality on the translation of Christianity into vernacular languages and idioms, fall beyond the scope of this book. Certainly, this book is not intended to be a comprehensive world history of all evangelical forms of Christianity since 1945: that would be a much larger, more protracted and infinitely more complex enterprise, for the necessary regional component church histories are still in the making in many instances, with much of the requisite primary documentary and oral research still awaiting the attention of scholars. Nevertheless, there are at least three respects in which it has become necessary and entirely

---

[4] See R. E. Frykenberg, *Christianity in India from Beginnings to the Present* (Oxford: Oxford University Press, 2008), 163, 207–225.

appropriate for this book to range more widely in its geographical scope than any of the other four volumes in the series.

The communications revolution

First, the period after 1945 has been marked by an unprecedented revolution in international networks of transport, communication and economic relationships. Intercontinental air travel did not become established as the principal means of journeying between continents until the 1950s. The invention of the jet airliner in 1949, and especially the introduction of the Boeing 707 into airline service from late 1958, brought international air travel within the experience of many of the well-to-do in Europe and North America. Rapid air travel enabled the two-way transatlantic links that had been integral to evangelicalism ever since its eighteenth-century origins to be immeasurably strengthened. North American evangelists, Christian music and literature could now travel to Europe and beyond with greater facility and frequency. The flow was not all in one direction, however: prominent British Christian figures, such as John Stott in the 1970s and 1980s, were able to widen their influence, particularly among university students, through speaking and preaching tours in the United States without major disruption to the primary sphere of their ministry in their homeland. However, possibly even more significant was the role of air travel in narrowing what had been the large gap in space and therefore in time between the Western and non-Western worlds. The unique stature Billy Graham achieved from the 1960s as a Christian figure performing on a world, and not merely a transatlantic, stage, was dependent on the modern air transport that enabled him and his supporting team to conduct crusades in every continent, and not simply in North America or Europe, where his early campaigns from 1946 to 1958 had been located; the role of satellite television in relaying images of his mass meetings around the world was no less crucial in making him a figure of world renown. Chapter 3 will chart the remarkable geographical coverage of Graham's ministry. Through translation facilities, the use of modern satellite technology and rapid air transportation Graham became a major religious force, not simply, like some of his American predecessor evangelists, within Britain, but on a truly global stage, surpassing in the geographical reach of his influence even R. A. Torrey's ministry in the early twentieth century.

Short-term mission teams from North America or Europe, mainly comprising students and young people with only a few weeks or months to spare, have also become a pronounced feature of the contemporary mission scene in a way that was unthinkable in the days when missionaries sailed rather then flew to the mission field. Intercontinental air travel was, and remains, expensive, which meant that it did more to promote the export of well-funded American or European Christian influences to the rest of the globe than it did to carry indigenous spiritual movements in the reverse direction. Nevertheless, some important channels of 'reverse influence' can be traced: chapter 3 will pursue this theme with particular reference to the East African Revival movement. Moreover, the economically determined imbalance of influence in the relationship between North and South does not necessarily imply that Christianity in the South has become more and more homogeneous, increasingly conformed to an alien and 'northern' pattern of being Christian or understanding theology, although there are some commentators who tend to interpret contemporary trends in world Christianity broadly in these terms.[5] Christians in the South have in fact been adept at appropriating, remoulding and hybridizing styles of Christian worship and belief which, although they can often be traced, at least in part, to northern origins, have become distinctive and authentic in their own cultural contexts.[6] Chapter 7 will expand this theme with reference to the global spread of Pentecostal Christianity.

Air travel has also greatly facilitated the economically driven processes of human migration from South to North and from East to West, and in so doing has brought countless thousands of Asian, African and Latin American Christians to reside in North American and European cities. Korean, Chinese, Nigerian and Ghanaian churches especially are now highly visible and almost universal features of the religious scene in northern-hemisphere cities. Some recent commentators have hailed these northward flows of southern Christianity as a new missionary movement, and there is no doubt that impassioned missionary rhetoric about bringing light to the new 'dark continent' of Europe is widespread among the new churches of the African diaspora in

---

[5] For the most capable expositions of an interpretation of Pentecostal Christianity in Africa as a form of religious globalization see the books by Paul Gifford, *African Christianity: Its Public Role* (London: Hurst, 1998); *Ghana's New Christianity: Pentecostalism in a Globalising African Economy* (London: Hurst, 2004); *Christianity, Politics and Public Life in Kenya* (London: Hurst, 2009).

[6] For an excellent case study in support of this alternative view see David Maxwell, *African Gifts of the Spirit: Pentecostalism and the Rise of a Zimbabwean Transnational Religious Movement* (Oxford: James Currey; Harare: Weaver Press; Athens, Ohio: Ohio University Press, 2006). For a stimulating (though unfortunately error-ridden) broader survey of African Pentecostalism that insists on its essential indigeneity to the continent see Ogbu Kalu, *African Pentecostalism: An Introduction* (Oxford: Oxford University Press, 2008).

Europe.[7] Nevertheless, many of these migrant congregations continue to be primarily settler churches, no more successful in impacting the surrounding indigenous population than were the white settler churches of South Africa or Australasia in the nineteenth century.

The revolution in methods of travel was only one aspect of a whole complex of interlocking changes in communication and economic systems that sociologists describe as integral to the process of 'globalization', linking all parts of the globe 'in such a way that local happenings are shaped by events occurring many miles away and vice versa'.[8] First radio, and, increasingly from the 1960s, television, enabled preachers and evangelists both to expand and 'target' their audience by leapfrogging the barriers erected by geography or ideology; this was particularly significant during the years of the Cold War, when physical access to eastern Europe was generally impossible for missionaries from western Europe or North America. Successive new forms of digital reproduction of sounds and images – first reel-to-reel tape recordings, then cassette tapes, video tapes, CDs and DVDs – have all been eagerly taken up by churches and mission agencies, and placed in the service of the gospel, often being listened to or viewed in contexts far removed from their place of origin. Perhaps most transformative of all, American experimentation with electronic mail systems between computers ('email') in the early 1970s and their development for general public use from the early 1990s, supplemented by the British invention between 1989 and 1991 of the World Wide Web, have brought the whole of the globe, and a steadily increasing proportion of humanity, within a single network of instant communication and knowledge dissemination. Whereas in the early nineteenth century an exchange of missionary correspondence between India and Europe could take anything

---

[7] See Afe Adogame (ed.), *Who Is Afraid of the Holy Ghost? Pentecostalism and Globalization in Africa and Beyond* (Trenton, N.J.: Africa World, 2011; Afe Adogame and James Spickard (eds.), *Religion Crossing Boundaries: Transnational Religious and Social Dynamics in Africa and the New African Diaspora* (Leiden: E. J. Brill, 2010); Frieder Ludwig and J. Kwabena Asamoah-Gyadu (eds.), *African Christian Presence in the West: New Immigrant Congregations and Transnational Networks in North America and Europe* (Trenton, N.J.: Africa World, 2011); Jehu Hanciles, *Beyond Christendom: Globalization, African Migration, and the Transformation of the West* (Maryknoll: Orbis Books, 2008).

[8] Anthony Giddens, *The Consequences of Modernity* (Stanford: Stanford University Press, 1990), 64, cited by Donald M. Lewis, 'Globalization: The Problem of Definition and Future Areas of Historical Enquiry', in M. Hutchinson and O. Kalu (eds.), *A Global Faith: Essays on Evangelicalism and Globalization* (Sydney: Centre for the Study of Australian Christianity, 1998), 27.

between eighteen months and four years to complete its laborious ocean-borne route, back and forth around the Cape of Good Hope,[9] an exchange of emails between church or mission leaders in India and Europe or North America can now be accomplished within a couple of minutes.

Far-reaching innovatory trends in global communication during the period covered by this book have, therefore, relativized the concept of 'the English-speaking world', both extending its tentacles of cultural influence into regions where English is not the mother tongue and increasing the potential for events and spiritual movements outside the West to reshape the experience and re-define the horizons of Christians in the West, a theme to which I shall shortly return. In the course of the nineteenth and twentieth centuries Protestant fellowship became progressively global in its scope and structures, a develop-ment first partially exemplified in the mid-nineteenth century by the forma-tion of the Evangelical Alliance (1846) and World Alliance of YMCA's (1855). Only in the second half of the twentieth century, however, did Protestant internationalism become truly intercontinental, and not predominantly trans-atlantic in character, as the different histories of the International Fellowship of Evangelical Students (1947), the World Council of Churches (1948), the World Evangelical Fellowship (1951) and the Lausanne Committee for World Evangelization (1974) all testify.

The globalization of the English language and anglophone education

There is a second and related reason for the inclusion in this book of wider geographical and cultural perspectives. The twentieth century saw a remark-able territorial expansion in the use of the English language. The enormous extension of British territorial control in the half-century from 1880 to 1930 brought much of sub-Saharan Africa, many of the Pacific islands, the Malayan peninsula, Sarawak, Brunei, Iraq, Trans-Jordan, Palestine and much of the Arabian Gulf region within the orbit of direct British cultural influence, along-side the older imperial territories of Canada, Australia and New Zealand, the British West Indies, the Indian subcontinent and Hong Kong. Within the greatly expanded British Empire of the first half of the twentieth century, English was not merely the language of colonial administration and justice; it was frequently also the language in which indigenous politicians from varied ethnic and linguistic backgrounds communicated with each other and articu-lated new concepts of 'national' identity. It was, moreover, most crucially, the

---

[9] See Frykenberg, *Christianity in India*, 213.

language of almost all education from secondary level upwards. A command of English became the coveted passport to employment in government service, the professions and commerce. The imperial historian Andrew Porter has described the British Empire as 'the world's greatest-ever educational enterprise'.[10] After 1945 the British embarked on a major programme of university expansion in the colonies, and encouraged many colonial students to study in British universities: by the academic year 1959–60 there were some twenty-nine thousand of them. The largest contingents were from the West Indies, Nigeria and Ghana,[11] a substantial proportion of whom must already have been Christian on arrival in Britain or at least have been deeply influenced by their education in mission schools. Others may have become Christians as a result of the development of evangelistic ministry among overseas students in Britain; this was a sphere in which the initiatives of F. H. Crittenden, who had taught at the elite Alliance High School in Kenya and at the School of Oriental and African Studies in London before joining the staff of the Inter-Varsity Fellowship (IVF), were crucial.[12] At secondary-school level, pupils in the colonies studied English-language textbooks published in Britain and sat public examinations set by the examination boards of British universities, notably the University of Cambridge Local Examinations Syndicate. The worldwide role of the Syndicate (now known as Cambridge Assessment) survived decolonization, and by the opening of the twenty-first century the organization examined some 8 million candidates a year in 150 different countries.[13]

Under British colonial rule, facility in spoken and written English was also increasingly necessary for those who aspired to positions of pastoral leadership in the churches, particularly in the Anglican communion, whose spread corresponded almost exactly with the widening boundaries of the empire; almost all theological colleges and higher-level Bible schools in British colonies or former British colonies have taught their students in English. Some of the brightest candidates for African or Asian church leadership were brought to Britain for undergraduate- or postgraduate-level theological education. In

[10] Andrew Porter, 'Empires in the Mind', in P. J. Marshall (ed.), *The Cambridge Illustrated History of the British Empire* (Cambridge: Cambridge University Press, 1996), 194.

[11] A. J. Stockwell, 'Leaders, Dissidents and the Disappointed: Colonial Students in Britain as Empire Ended', *Journal of Imperial and Commonwealth History* 36 (2008), 491.

[12] Douglas Johnson, *Contending for the Faith: A History of the Evangelical Movement in the Universities and Colleges* (Leicester: Inter-Varsity Press, 1979), 304–313.

[13] See Sandra Raban, *Examining the World: A History of the University of Cambridge Local Examinations Syndicate* (Cambridge: Cambridge University Press, 2008).

Britain London Bible College (now the London School of Theology) numbered among its students in the 1960s or 1970s Byang Kato (1936–75) from Nigeria, who became the first African general secretary of the Association of Evangelicals of Africa and Madagascar; the Ghanaian Presbyterian Kwame Bediako (1945–2008), who subsequently achieved international renown as an African theologian; and Chua Wee Hian from Singapore, the second general secretary of the International Fellowship of Evangelical Students (IFES).[14] In 1965–6, and again from 1968 to 1971, Tyndale Hall in Bristol trained David Gitari, archbishop of Kenya from 1996 to 2002 and a fearless public critic of corruption in the Kenyan government of Daniel arap Moi;[15] while the Ugandan John Sentamu, consecrated archbishop of York in 2005, was a theological student at Selwyn College and Ridley Hall, Cambridge, from 1974 to 1979. Sentamu has to date exercised his entire pastoral ministry in the Church of England rather than the Church of Uganda. His example, like that of Bediako, illustrates the fact that these educational connections did not simply export British evangelical influence to the majority world; they also introduced Christians in the northern hemisphere to African or Asian approaches to evangelical discipleship.

In these multiple ways Britain and her colonies or former colonies were, and generally still are, intimately linked by cultural and educational ties. Similar but rather more diverse connections were forged by the admission of African, Asian and Latin American students to leading North American evangelical institutions such as Fuller Theological Seminary, Trinity Evangelical Divinity School, Illinois, Wheaton College, or Regent College, Vancouver; Southern Baptist seminaries also played a very important role in this respect within their respective global communions. The greater availability of funding in North American institutions meant that by the 1990s their role in providing theological training for evangelical leaders from the majority world had eclipsed that of their British counterparts. American televangelists, such as Jimmy Swaggart, and pastors of American megachurches, such as Rick Warren, have also had a significant impact on parts of the majority world through their publications and speaking tours. The significance of these linkages for world Christian history is a topic that still awaits the attention of historians.

Although the duration of British colonial rule was comparatively short for most African and some other territories, the legacy of British patterns of

---

[14] Ian M. Randall, *Educating Evangelicalism: The Origins, Development and Impact of London Bible College* (Carlisle: Paternoster Press, 2000), 157, 161, 168, 179.

[15] Tyndale Hall merged in January 1972 with Clifton College and Dalton House to become Trinity College, Bristol.

education and the hegemony of the English language has proved an enduring one. While the British Empire began to shrink again following Indian
independence in 1947, and was rapidly dismantled during the 1960s, the global
supremacy of English has continued apace, reinforced by the increasing predominance of American cultural and economic influence in many parts of the
world: it is the language of science and technology, of international diplomacy,
air traffic control, the World Wide Web and academic conferences. India is
now the second largest English-speaking and English-reading country in the
world (after the United States); English is the only language spoken in every
part of the subcontinent, and is the official language of government and
business.[16] It is hardly surprising, therefore, that English was adopted as the
almost universal mode of discourse in major world Protestant assemblies in
the twentieth century, both in the World Council of Churches and its affili-
ates, and in evangelical bodies such as the Lausanne movement or the World
Evangelical Fellowship. It has become quite rare in such gatherings for speakers to address meetings in languages other than English. When they have done
so, as happened when the Ecuadorian René Padilla, who had a PhD in New
Testament from the University of Manchester under the supervision of F. F.
Bruce, chose to address the Lausanne Congress in 1974 in his native Spanish,
one suspects a political point was being made: Padilla's address was severely
critical of American forms of mere 'culture Christianity'.[17] The English language, therefore, was overwhelmingly the medium in which evangelical theology during the second half of the twentieth century was debated and defined,
just as Greek functioned as the language of Christian theology in the apostolic
age, or Latin within medieval Christendom. It is only a modest exaggeration to
claim that evangelicalism in this period operated within 'an English-speaking
world'.

Evangelical influences from the majority world

There is a third important reason why this book aims to set the story of
English-speaking evangelicalism in a wider global context. Some of the most
determinative trends in modern evangelical history in the western world can
be traced to a greater or lesser extent to Christian experience outside Europe.
The ecumenical movement itself, a development that evoked very mixed or
even hostile responses among conservative evangelicals, derived much of its

---

[16] Frykenberg, *Christianity in India*, 341.

[17] See chapter 6 below, 165–166.

early momentum from the experience of Christians in India and China who found western denominational distinctions an evangelistic hindrance and embarrassment in contexts where Christians were a small and often harassed minority of the population. Possibly the most influential school of thinking in modern evangelical missiology, the body of theory and practical wisdom known as 'church growth theory', was first developed during the 1950s by the American Donald McGavran (1897–1990) on the basis of his experience, as a Disciples of Christ missionary in India, of people movements of conversion, where the rigidity of caste divisions made the conversion of isolated individuals very hard to achieve. The consequent foundational principle of church growth theory, namely that people find it easiest to turn to Christ when they can do so without having to cross a major cultural barrier, has shaped a whole family of approaches to evangelistic strategy, both in the western and non-western worlds, even though many evangelical theologians have expressed unease at an approach that has appeared to minimize the importance of transcending ethnic and cultural divisions within the body of Christ. Present-day 'seeker services' (an approach pioneered by the Willow Creek Community Church near Chicago in the 1980s) and all evangelistic strategies that pay particular attention to the need to express the gospel in terms of the prevalent cultural assumptions of the hearers can trace their origins to lessons learned outside Europe, usually through the medium of church growth theory. More reflective and intellectually penetrating missiological approaches to contemporary western culture were first developed by Lesslie Newbigin (1909–98) on his return to Britain in 1974 from India, where he had served as one of the founding bishops of the Church of South India (1947), and, earlier, as a missionary of the Church of Scotland.[18] Newbigin had been forcibly impressed, or rather depressed, by the extent of secularity he encountered in modern Britain and the degree of resistance to any attempt to proclaim the gospel as a form of 'public truth', relevant to all areas of human thought and activity. The resulting 'Gospel and Our Culture' movement remains a significant force in both the United States and Britain, with some equivalents elsewhere, notably in New Zealand, where the DeepSight Trust owes its perspectives both to Newbigin and to another former Presbyterian missionary (this time with West African experience), Harold W. Turner (1911–2002).[19]

---

[18] For an excellent introduction to Newbigin's life and writings see Paul Weston, *Lesslie Newbigin Missionary Theologian: A Reader* (London: SPCK, 2006).

[19] On Turner see his Festschrift, edited by Andrew F. Walls and Wilbert R. Shenk, *Exploring New Religious Movements: Essays in Honour of Harold W. Turner* (Elkhart, Ind.: Mission Focus, 1990).

Subsequent chapters in this book will expound the theme of non-western influences on western evangelicalism at greater length. Chapter 3 will consider the international impact of the East African or *balokole* Revival. Chapter 5 will include a more detailed consideration of the significance for conservative Christian apologetics of Lesslie Newbigin. Chapter 6 will analyse the profound impact made by African and especially Latin American evangelicals at the Lausanne Congress in 1974, where the distinctive emphases of representatives of a younger generation of Spanish-speaking evangelicals became the main talking point of the assembly. Chapter 7 will note the phenomenon of global Pentecostalism, a movement that, as most scholars now agree, cannot be adequately understood merely as a diffusion of an American style of popular religion to the rest of the globe. Although the charismatic renewal that surfaced within the historic denominations on both sides of the Atlantic in the 1960s initially displayed less obvious connections with spiritual movements in the majority world, attention will be paid to some leading figures in the charismatic renewal whose ministry was, or had been, set in a non-western context: such as the former Bolivian missionary and church growth theorist C. Peter Wagner (1930–), whose ideas were seminal for John Wimber (1934–97), the initiator of the 'Signs and Wonders' movement in the 1980s and primary architect of the Vineyard network of churches; and Bishop Chiu Ban It, the first indigenous Anglican bishop of Singapore and Malaya from 1966 to 1982, whose entry into charismatic experience while attending the World Council of Churches conference on 'Salvation Today' at Bangkok in 1972 was a turning point for his diocese.[20] The discussion in chapter 8 of the growing awareness by evangelicals in that period of hermeneutical issues and arguments will include some consideration of the perspectives of those from the majority world. In the Anglican communion the modern campaign for the ordination of women to the priesthood can be traced to events in the diocese of Hong Kong in the 1940s, although many, though not all, non-western evangelicals have taken a conservative line on whether Scripture permits women to exercise an ordained ministry. On the other major contentious hermeneutical issue that became increasingly prominent in debates among Christians towards the end of the twentieth century – that of homosexuality – southern (and especially African) evangelicals have taken the lead in resisting what they see as a theologically flawed and strategically disastrous concession to western secular moral standards by much liberal Christian opinion in the North.

---

[20] Michael Green, *Asian Tigers for Christ* (London: SPCK, 2001), 7; *CEN*, 8 Aug. 1975, 7. See chapter 7 below, 201.

During the half-century from 1945 to 2000 the history of evangelical Christianity in 'the English-speaking world' (the professed subject of this five-volume series) thus became increasingly intertwined with the history of world Christianity. This book, while it does not pretend to be a history of world Christianity in the late twentieth century, nor even a global history of evangelical styles of Christianity during that period, tells the story of how a religious movement whose genesis is rooted in the cultural and political environment of eighteenth-century Europe and North America has become one of the most powerful religious forces on the globe, and of how, in the process, it has itself undergone some far-reaching changes.

2. 'EVANGELICALS', 'CONSERVATIVE EVANGELICALS' AND 'FUNDAMENTALISTS'

This book, like its four predecessors in the series, is concerned with the evangelical tradition of Christianity. As was emphasized in the introductory chapter, this period is marked by a growing diversification of the evangelical tradition as a result of its increasing cultural and geographical diffusion, as well as of divergent strategic responses by evangelicals to the inroads made by secularism into the intellectual, moral and social fabric of Western Christendom. It would be far too simple, however, to present the narrative of evangelical history from 1945 as a straightforward regression (or progression, depending on one's theological perspective) from a situation of theological unanimity and clarity in 1945 to one of theological breadth and a lack of sharp identity in 2000. Throughout this period debates over the meaning and parameters of evangelical identity were common, and terminological usage varied according to geographical, cultural and denominational context, but particularly between American and British evangelicals.

The contours of evangelical identity have been to a greater or lesser extent fluid throughout the history of the movement. There have been periods of comparative stability, such as the years from the 1780s to the 1820s, and equally decades in which boundaries shifted markedly, such as in the period from the 1890s to the 1930s. Broadly speaking, the story of English-speaking evangelicalism from 1945 may be divided into three sections. First is an initial phase from the mid-1940s in which leaders of the middle ground of the movement sought greater clarity of identity by differentiating their goals and ethos from separatist fundamentalists on the one hand, and, on the other, both doctrinally imprecise 'liberal evangelicals' and the advocates of neo-orthodoxy. Second is an intermediate phase, whose beginning and terminal dates varied according to geographical and denominational context, but which most commonly coincided with what have been termed the 'long 1960s' (spanning approximately the years from 1958 to 1974).[1] During this phase the resulting consensus – self-described in the United States as 'evangelical' or 'new evangelical', and more often in Britain, Canada and Australasia as 'conservative evangelical' – held relatively firm and wielded growing influence. The third and final phase, extending from these intermediate years to the present, has witnessed continued numerical growth in evangelical styles of Christianity, but the trajectories of growth have been increasingly divergent. As chapter 9 will explore, this made it once again problematic by the opening decade of the twenty-first century to determine precisely who was, and was not, 'evangelical'.

The primary focus of this chapter will be on the first two of these three phases, covering the years from 1945 to approximately 1974, the year of the Lausanne Congress on World Evangelization. Reference will be made to the fact that in a variety of contexts by the late 1960s there were already signs that the evangelical united front forged over the preceding twenty years was not as united as had at first sight appeared. Chapters 3 to 8 will analyse the continuing advances made by evangelical Christianity in the 1970s, 1980s and 1990s, but also investigate particular aspects of these underlying tensions that from the early 1970s broke surface and threatened to become open divisions. Chapter 9 will attempt an overall interpretative survey of the third phase, and offer some concluding reflections on the story of evangelicalism during the second half of the twentieth century. That story, contrary to most popular representations of evangelical Christianity in the media to this day, is one of a steadily widening divergence between 'fundamentalism' and 'evangelicalism'. Broadly speaking, until the mid-1970s that process of divergence assisted in clarifying the question of what it meant to be evangelical; since the mid-1970s it can be argued that the continuance of the same process has actually made it more difficult to answer the same question.

---

[1] The 'long 1960s' is a term coined by Arthur Marwick, *The Sixties: Cultural Revolution in Britain, France, Italy and the United States, c. 1958–1974* (Oxford: Oxford University Press, 1998), 7, and employed by Hugh McLeod, *The Religious Crisis of the 1960s* (Oxford: Oxford University Press, 2007), 1.

The United States: the slow differentiation of evangelicals from fundamentalists, 1942–57

In North America, and particularly in the United States, the legacy of the bitter conflicts fought by fundamentalists and modernists during the inter-war period, frequently resulting in the formation of separate fundamentalist denominations or theological institutions, polarized ecclesiastical loyalties and vocabulary to a greater extent than elsewhere. In the 1940s those who repudiated the attempts of modernism to accommodate Christianity to modern approaches to religious truth, the authority of science, and biblical criticism were generally quite happy to accept the label of 'fundamentalist'. The term 'evangelical' had been used comparatively rarely in the United States in the 1930s,[2] and only gradually re-emerged during the 1940s as a self-descriptor that carried alternative overtones to those associated with the term 'fundamentalist'. One of the milestones historians identify as marking the emergence of the 'new evangelicalism' in the 1940s was the publication in 1947 by Carl F. H. Henry (1913–2003), then a younger member of the faculty at Northern Baptist Seminary in Chicago, of a short book entitled *The Uneasy Conscience of Modern Fundamentalism*. Chapter 6 will note the significance of this work as one of the earliest signs of the growing social awareness of American evangelicals, but it should be observed at this point that Henry used the terms 'fundamentalism' and 'evangelicalism' interchangeably throughout the book.[3] The foreword, written by Henry's friend and colleague, the pastor at Park Street Congregational Church in Boston, Harold J. Ockenga (1905–85), called for 'a progressive fundamentalism' that engaged with social issues in the way Henry was advocating.[4] Although those in the liberal mainstream of denominational Christianity in 1947 would have regarded the idea of a 'progressive fundamentalism' as an absurd contradiction in terms, neither Ockenga nor Henry did so at that stage: only gradually did they reach the conclusion that what was needed was not merely a revamped fundamental-ism but rather a form of classical biblical orthodoxy that clearly distanced

---

[2] George M. Marsden, *Understanding Fundamentalism and Evangelicalism* (Grand Rapids: Eerdmans, 1981), 66; David W. Bebbington, 'British and American Evangelicalism Since 1940', in Mark A. Noll, David W. Bebbington and George A. Rawlyk (eds.), *Evangelicalism: Comparative Studies of Popular Protestantism in North America, the British Isles, and Beyond 1700–1990* (New York: Oxford University Press, 1994), 367.

[3] Carl F. H. Henry, *The Uneasy Conscience of Modern Fundamentalism* [1947], new ed. (Grand Rapids: Eerdmans, 2003), 1–3, 39–40.

[4] Ibid. xx.

itself from the unsophisticated theological pugilism beloved of many fundamentalists.

Harold Ockenga was the founding president of a body formed in St. Louis in April 1942, and formally inaugurated at a convention in Chicago in May 1943, which called itself the 'National Association of Evangelicals' (NAE). The NAE was intended to provide a platform for united evangelical witness to the nation and the US government; it was to offer a clear alternative to the predominantly liberal Federal Council of Churches, yet at the same time it was to be more broad-based than the American Council of Christian Churches, formed in 1941 by the 'Bible Presbyterian' Carl McIntire (1906–2002), which claimed to speak for all fundamentalists or evangelicals, but in practice represented only those who belonged to church groupings other than the historic Protestant denominations. The NAE, on the other hand, wished to include such separatists in its united front, thus embodying an ecumenism of all those who stood for the fundamentals of the faith: its monthly journal was entitled *United Evangelical Action*. However, it had only limited success in persuading their leaders to come on board, even including some, like V. Raymond Edman (1900–67), president of Wheaton College from 1940 to 1965, whose fundamentalism placed relatively little emphasis on the need for ecclesiastical separation. The abstention of many separatist fundamentalists from the new NAE pointed towards what would by the late 1950s become almost axiomatic, namely that evangelicals regarded themselves as plainly distinguishable from fundamentalists, not so much by doctrinal content as by their more moderate temper and the extent of their willingness and deter-mination to organize themselves to promote orthodoxy within the historic denominations. In 1947, however, no such clear distinction in vocabulary had emerged in the United States.[5] Nevertheless, by that date the NAE was well established, even though its 1.3 million members came mostly from some thirty smaller American denominations, rather than the mainline denomin-ations that the NAE sought to capture for the evangelical cause. The most notable absentee among predominantly conservative church groupings was the Southern Baptist Convention, which, on account of its de facto majority (even quasi-established) ecclesiastical status in much of the southern states,

---

[5] The foregoing analysis is indebted to Joel Carpenter, *Revive Us Again: The Reawakening of American Fundamentalism* (New York: Oxford University Press, 1997), 84, 144–160; see also George M. Marsden, *Reforming Fundamentalism: Fuller Seminary and the New Evangelicalism* (Grand Rapids: Eerdmans, 1987), 10–11; Robert Wuthnow, *The Restructuring of American Religion: Society and Faith Since World War II* (Princeton: Princeton University Press, 1988), 173–181.

saw little need for the broader basis of evangelical fellowship represented by the NAE.[6] Nevertheless, the NAE provided the first indispensable ingredient of the recipe for the 'new evangelicalism', a term popularized by Ockenga from 1957 – namely a national framework for organization and collective action.

The year 1947 was a key date for the emergence in the United States of a second key constituent of the new evangelicalism. In the September 1947 issue of *United Evangelical Action* there appeared an advertisement soliciting applications to study at 'a center of evangelical scholarship' opening in Pasadena, California, to be named Fuller Theological Seminary, after the founder and chairman of the Board of Trustees, Dr Charles E. Fuller (1887–1968), a former student of Reuben A. Torrey at the Bible Institute of Los Angeles, and widely known for his popular radio programme, 'The Old Fashioned Revival Hour'. Although the advertisement was seeking applications for entry in September 1948, there were already thirty-nine students registered for the 1947 intake.[7] The president of the new seminary was Harold Ockenga, though he chose to remain in his Boston pastorate (a decision that trans-American air travel made possible). Carl Henry was brought across from Chicago to teach theology; his friend Harold Lindsell (1913–98), a young New York Baptist with a PhD in American history, was appointed registrar; Wilbur Moorehead Smith (1894–1976), a Presbyterian on the faculty of Moody Bible Institute in Chicago with an honorary doctorate from Dallas Theological Seminary, came to teach apologetics; and Everett F. Harrison was hired from the faculty of the Dallas Seminary to be the professor of New Testament. The seminary's fundamentalist credentials were transparent: Fuller was perhaps the nation's best-known revivalist broadcaster and saw his new institution primarily as a training school for world missions; Smith, a voracious reader and avid collector of books, was a regular contributor to leading fundamentalist newspapers, such as the *Sunday School Times* and the dispensationalist organ *Our Hope* – he believed that the reference in 2 Peter 3 to the elements being 'dissolved with fervent heat' was an explicit prediction of an atomic holocaust; Ockenga and Harrison were former pupils of J. Gresham Machen, the champion of Presbyterian fundamentalist orthodoxy; and Lindsell and Henry had impeccably conservative credentials.[8]

Nevertheless, in retrospect it is clear that the foundation of Fuller Seminary

[6] Marsden, *Understanding Fundamentalism and Evangelicalism*, 70.

[7] Marsden, *Reforming Fundamentalism*, 54–55.

[8] For two much fuller accounts see ibid., chs. 1, 2 and 4; and Carpenter, *Revive Us Again*, 190–204.

was a turning point, a first step towards the parting of the ways between fundamentalism and evangelicalism. If Fuller emphatically, and Smith in a more qualified sense, represented an older populist style of fundamentalism, Henry and Ockenga stood for the new. Henry was less interested in hunting for references to the atom bomb in the pages of the New Testament than in challenging the humanist presuppositions that underlay Western civilization. His first book, published in 1946, was entitled *Remaking the Modern Mind*, and drew inspiration from three champions of Reformed philosophical theology: Gordon H. Clark, William H. Jellema and Cornelius Van Til.[9] Henry was seeking to articulate a distinctively evangelical world view, and that implied, as his second book, *The Uneasy Conscience of Modern Fundamentalism*, made clear, thinking evangelically about the problems of society and not merely about the salvation of the individual soul.[10] Ockenga was less of an intellectual than Henry, but was a strategist who similarly saw no hope for the future of Western culture other than through a revival of biblical orthodoxy; such a revival would require an 'ecclesiastically positive' church policy rather than a continuance of fundamentalism further down a separatist path. What would by the late 1950s become known as the 'new evangelicalism' was distinguished above all by its sense of a mission to change the prevailing cultural and theological agenda, which meant not the maintenance of scrupulous isolation from all who were in theological error but rather the single-minded pursuit of influence.[11] Chapters 4 and 5 will return to this theme, and suggest that the quest for the formation of an evangelical mind that would be capable of reshaping a culture was bound in the long run to erode many of the attitudes characteristic of the older fundamentalism. Nevertheless, the foundation of one new seminary, however influential it was to become, was too narrow a platform on which to build a new evangelical culture. If 'progressive fundamentalism' were to fulfil the mission Henry and Ockenga had outlined for it, two further elements were required: a public figurehead and a regular published organ of opinion. The former was provided by Billy Graham and the latter by *Christianity Today*.

Until Billy Graham first hit the headlines in the American press as a brash young Southern Baptist evangelist conducting his 'Christ for Greater Los Angeles' campaign in 1949, there was little to distinguish him from innumerable other revival preachers in the fundamentalist tradition. But major press

---

[9] Carl F. H. Henry, *Remaking the Modern Mind* (Grand Rapids: Eerdmans, 1946). See chapter 5, 131, below.

[10] Marsden, *Reforming Fundamentalism*, 75–82.

[11] Ibid. 60–68.

coverage of the Los Angeles crusade through the nation-wide chain of news-papers owned by William Randolph Hearst, and the conversion of some local celebrities – notably the broadcaster and racehorse owner Stuart Hamblen, the former Olympic athlete Louis Zamperini and a notorious gangster, Jim Vaus – propelled Graham on to a wider stage.[12] Ockenga invited him to conduct a crusade in Boston over the New Year in 1950, which was again a resounding success, despite the marked lack of evangelical influence in this strongly Irish Catholic city.[13] In September that year Graham, until late 1948 an employee of the Youth for Christ movement, set up his own Billy Graham Evangelistic Association, of which Ockenga became a director. Later, in 1957, Graham was appointed a trustee of Fuller Theological Seminary. Graham's theology and style were still characteristic of American fundamentalism, and when his crusades reached London in March 1954, the initial response of British church leaders and much of the press was dismissive of his fundamen-talism as unworthy of serious attention or respect.[14] In the event, however, the Greater London Crusade at Harringay attracted support from a wide theo-logical spectrum of British church leaders, setting a precedent Graham was willing to follow in other crusades, notably in accepting an invitation in 1955 from the broad-based Protestant Council of the City of New York to conduct a campaign at Madison Square Garden in the summer of 1957. Such a broad platform meant that in principle Graham was prepared to send the names of converts and enquirers to any participating church, whatever its theological affiliation might be.[15]

Interpretations of this crucial watershed in evangelical history vary. George Marsden's scholarly account of Fuller Seminary confines itself to analysis of the emergence of the new evangelicalism and offers no explicit theological judgment on Graham's increasingly flexible stance, though one suspects he approves of it. Some of Graham's biographers entirely miss the significance of the extending range of Graham's contacts between 1954 and 1957; only William Martin's massive biography correctly identifies the New York crusade of 1957 as a watershed differentiating evangelicalism from fundamental-ism.[16] Iain Murray, writing from a decidedly Reformed perspective, deplores

[12] *SST*, 17 Dec. 1949, (3) 1127–(4) 1128.

[13] Marsden, *Reforming Fundamentalism*, 92; Carpenter, *Revive Us Again*, 224–229.

[14] The Greater London Crusade of 1954 marked Graham's emergence as a religious celebrity in Britain, but it was not his first campaign there: he conducted Youth for Christ campaigns in the British Isles in 1946–7.

[15] Marsden, *Reforming Fundamentalism*, 159, 162.

[16] William Martin, *A Prophet with Honor: The Billy Graham Story* (New York: William

Graham's new policy as a fatal capitulation to multiple pressures to adopt a stance of wider Christian cooperation, with the inevitable theological compromises that resulted. Murray plausibly suggests three sources of such pressure: the personal influence of Graham's father-in-law, L. Nelson Bell, a retired China missionary and a ruling elder in the Southern Presbyterian Church; the financial allure of Graham's most wealthy backer, J. Howard Pew, owner of the Sun Oil Corporation, who was a member (albeit a very conservative one) of another mainline denomination, the Presbyterian Church of the USA; and the undoubted attraction of being assiduously courted by mainstream church leaders, who hoped to use Graham's crusades to boost their flagging membership rolls, leaving local clergy subsequently to wean the converts off their unhealthy diet of fundamentalist fast food.[17] What Murray condemns as shameless pragmatism, Graham himself regarded as a natural application of his commission to be an evangelist, in which his passion to bring others to Christ overrode all party loyalties and criticism from whatever quarter: he believed that God had called him to join in the work of proclaiming the gospel with anyone who was willing to work with him.[18] Graham's ecumenical sympathies broadened during the mid-1950s in response to a variety of stimuli, and were not simply the result of his experiences in Harringay in the spring of 1954: as early as February that year, when invited to address the students and faculty of Union Theological Seminary, New York, the most prestigious of the mainline Protestant seminaries, Graham spoke in terms that convinced one initially unsympathetic member of the Union faculty that 'his whole strategy as an evangelist is now ecumenical'.[19]

The fourth crucial component in the framing of the identity of the 'new evangelicalism' was the foundation of *Christianity Today* in 1956. As early as 1951 Wilbur Smith had shared with Graham his dream of a periodical 'so important that it would be absolutely indispensable for every serious-minded Christian minister in America'. On Christmas Day 1954 Graham and Nelson Bell took up the challenge and laid plans for a new journal that would form

---

Morrow, 1991), 222–224. Marshall Frady, *Billy Graham: A Parable of American Righteousness* (Boston, Mass.: Little Brown, 1979); and John Pollock, *Billy Graham: The Authorized Biography* (New York: McGraw-Hill, 1965), offer no comment on this point.

[17] Iain H. Murray, *Evangelicalism Divided: A Record of Crucial Change in the Years 1950 to 2000* (Edinburgh: Banner of Truth Trust, 2000), 28–30, 33, 55, 58.

[18] Billy Graham, *Just as I Am: The Autobiography of Billy Graham* (London: Harper Collins, 1997), 303–304.

[19] John C. Bennett, 'Billy Graham at Union', *USQR* 9 (1954), 13. Bennett was Professor of Christian Theology and Ethics at Union Theological Seminary.

an evangelical rival to the mainline *Christian Century*. Soon after they offered the post of editor to Smith, but on reflection he declined. Harold Lindsell then suggested Carl Henry in his stead. Graham hesitated, fearing that Henry might be too fundamentalistic for a periodical that, he hoped, would 'plant the evangelical flag in the middle of the road, taking a conservative theological position but a definite liberal approach to social problems', combining 'the best in fundamentalism with the best in liberalism without compromising theologically'.[20] Nevertheless, in 1955 an approach to Henry was made. Henry had his own doubts, fearing both that his theological approach might be too uncompromisingly conservative for a journal along the lines Graham envisaged and that his political views might at the same time be too progressive for the comfort of J. Howard Pew, who was willing to bankroll the new journal. In the end Henry was appointed editor, and on his own terms, having threatened resignation in response to an attempt by Pew to insist on prior vetting of all copy. Harold Ockenga assumed the chairmanship of the editorial board.[21]

The first biweekly issue of *Christianity Today* appeared on 15 October 1956. Henry's opening editorial made the purpose of the journal clear. Evangelical Christianity had been for too long 'neglected, slighted, misrepresented'; it needed 'a clear voice, to speak with conviction and love, and to state its true position and its relevance to the world crisis'. Henry laid particular emphasis on three objectives. First, *Christianity Today* was to be a vehicle for 'an increasing group of evangelical scholars throughout the world' to expound and defend the faith in terms that were relevant to the present generation: it was to be a journal for thinking men and women. Secondly, it would be uncompromising in its stance for the 'complete reliability . . . authority . . . and plenary inspiration' of the Bible as 'the written Word of God'; this was to be no middle-of-the-road periodical. Thirdly, the aim was to penetrate the corridors of power and not simply the seminary lecture room: 'CHRISTIANITY TODAY will apply the biblical revelation to the contemporary social crisis, by presenting the implications of the total Gospel message for every area of life', something that fundamentalism 'has often failed to do'. The location of the *Christianity Today* office in Washington symbolized Henry's ambitious goals: from their tenth-floor suite the editors could 'daily look down Pennsylvania Avenue and glimpse the White House, Blair House, and other strategic centers of national life. Thus CHRISTIANITY TODAY is a symbol of the

---

[20] Graham to Lindsell, 25 Jan. 1955, cited in Marsden, *Reforming Fundamentalism*, 158.

[21] Ibid. 157–161; Carl F. H. Henry, *Confessions of a Theologian: An Autobiography* (Waco: Word Books, 1986), 144–163.

place of the evangelical witness in the life of a republic.'[22] The term 'fundamentalism' appeared only once in the editorial, and that was in the context just
cited, lamenting its failure to address the gospel to social issues; conversely,
the terms 'evangelical' and 'historic evangelical' recurred frequently in Henry's
prose. *Christianity Today* was to be the voice of the 'new evangelicalism',
uncompromisingly orthodox in theology, yet scholarly in intellectual foundations, irenic in tone, and all-embracing in its purview.

The fragility of the 'new evangelical' consensus, 1958–74

The term 'new evangelicalism' invited misunderstanding, as Edward J. Carnell
(1919–67), Ockenga's successor as president of Fuller Theological Seminary
from late 1954 onwards, soon discovered. By December 1958 Carnell was
having to instruct his faculty not to use the term as a descriptor of the
seminary's theological position: he recommended that they speak instead
of 'historic Christianity', a term that never caught on. Increasingly, those in
the United States who wished to align themselves with the theological ethos
represented by Fuller Seminary, the NAE, Billy Graham and *Christianity
Today* found it wise simply to refer to themselves as 'evangelicals', thus
deflecting the attacks of fundamentalists who alleged that the 'new' or (as
they preferred to label them) 'neo-evangelicals' represented no less serious
a departure from the old-time gospel than did 'neo-orthodoxy'. By July
1960 *Christianity Today* could publish an article entitled 'Is There Room for
Fundamentalists?', which asserted that 'fundamentalist' was a term used
'to designate something or someone offensive': although the question was
answered in the affirmative, the implicit assumption was that no readers of
the journal would now wish to apply the label to themselves; it was a term
of abuse that was part of the cost borne by those who sought faithfully to
'stand in the biblical and theological traditions of the churches to which they
belong'.[23]

The linguistic and conceptual separation of American evangelicalism from
fundamentalism was given a decisive push in 1959–60, when Carnell published a book entitled *The Case for Orthodox Theology*, followed by two articles
in *Christian Century*, provocatively entitled 'Post-Fundamentalist Faith' and
'Orthodoxy: Cultic vs. Classical'. Although the book was ostensibly a defence

---

[22] *CT*, 15 Oct. 1956, 20–21. Blair House is the official residence for guests of the
American President.

[23] Ibid., 18 July 1960, 6–7.

of evangelicalism against theological liberalism, it directed its gunfire as much against fundamentalism, which Carnell accused of 'intellectual dishonesty' and 'ethical hypocrisy'. He wrote in scathing terms of dispensationalism and the intolerance of separatism, daring even to censure J. Gresham Machen for his rigidity on the latter issue.[24] Fundamentalist leaders, on the one hand, and Reformed supporters of Machen, on the other, reacted with equal consternation, and Harold Lindsell found himself having to defend his president, claiming that Carnell had attacked only fundamentalism of the wrong sort. But Lindsell was in the minority in trying to bridge the widening gap between evangelicalism and fundamentalism. Carnell himself paid a high personal price for his boldness. Finding the physical and emotional strain of controversy, combined with the responsibility for keeping Fuller's finances healthy, too great, he resigned as president of Fuller in May 1959, though he remained a member of the faculty.[25]

The architects of the new American evangelicalism knew with some precision what style of orthodoxy they wanted, and they were confident God wanted it too, but they were already finding that the tightrope they had suspended between liberalism and fundamentalism was a difficult and demanding one to walk. As the 1960s unfolded, the ambiguities inherent in the position of the 'new evangelicals' gradually became more apparent. In public contexts such as the World Congress of Evangelism convened by the Billy Graham Evangelistic Association in Berlin in 1966, the evangelical united front still held firm. But beneath the surface tensions were mounting. Chapter 4 will analyse the central problem the new evangelicals faced of how to find a stable equilibrium between a conservative doctrine of biblical inspiration and a genuine commitment to scholarship: Fuller Theological Seminary was to be the site of the most public arguments over these issues in the 1960s and 1970s; from 1979 the focus of controversy shifted to a very large constituency in American Christianity that had hitherto played little part in the history of the new evangelicalism: the Southern Baptist Convention. In the *Christianity Today* office Carl Henry found his editorial chair an increasingly uncomfortable one in the 1960s. Theologically, he continued to align the journal with an uncompromisingly conservative position, but in political and ecclesiological terms

---

[24] Edward J. Carnell, *The Case for Orthodox Theology* (Philadelphia: Westminster Press, 1959); Murray, *Evangelicalism Divided*, 188–189. Carnell's first *Christian Century* article appeared in the summer of 1959 and the second in March 1960.

[25] On these episodes in Carnell's life see Marsden, *Reforming Fundamentalism*, 141–196; Rudolph Nelson, *The Making and Unmaking of an Evangelical Mind: The Case of Edward Carnell* (Cambridge: Cambridge University Press, 1987), 106–112.

his editorial policy became too broad-minded for the tastes of J. Howard Pew, who wished to see a harder line being taken against the ecumenical movement and its increasingly radical concerns. In 1968 Henry was levered out of office and his place as editor taken by Harold Lindsell, whose conservativism, unlike Henry's, extended to the realms of politics and society, and not merely to theology.[26] From 1968 to 1978, when Lindsell retired, the chief organ of the new evangelicalism spoke with a voice that was no longer so clearly differentiated from older, more fundamentalist, strains of the evangelical movement. Hence the shock to the American evangelical nervous system caused in 1974 by the emergence onto the international stage at the Lausanne Congress of another and even more radical 'new evangelicalism', emanating from the southern hemisphere, was still a considerable one. From 1979 the growing influence on American conservative Protestantism of the New Christian Right associated with names such as Pat Robertson, Jerry Falwell and James Dobson further narrowed the distance between evangelicals and fundamentalists. Although only a minority of American evangelicals identified themselves with Falwell's Moral Majority movement, the broader political campaigns of the New Christian Right, dedicated to the goal of restoring the United States to its supposed historic status as a nation founded on distinctively biblical principles, succeeded in gaining the support of many evangelicals.[27]

The Church of England: the slow convergence of 'evangelicalism' and 'conservative evangelicalism', 1945–67

In Britain, in contrast to the United States, very few evangelicals in the middle of the twentieth century referred to themselves as fundamentalists. For most British evangelicals, in contrast to their counterparts across the Atlantic, the term 'fundamentalist' had always been little more than a smear-word applied to them by their opponents. Although Britain had experienced fundamentalist controversies in the 1920s, they were neither on the same scale nor as disruptive in their ecclesiastical consequences as those in the United States. British patterns of denominational affiliation were much less fragmentary, with the result that the great majority of evangelicals still retained their membership within the historic denominations.[28] Evangelical separatists in Britain were far

---

[26] Marsden, *Reforming Fundamentalism*, 260; Henry, *Confessions of a Theologian*, 264–301.

[27] Mark A. Noll, *American Evangelical Christianity: An Introduction* (Oxford: Blackwell, 2001), 188–191; Wuthnow, *Restructuring of American Religion*, 205–207.

[28] On these contrasts see David Bebbington, 'Evangelicalism in Its Settings: The British

fewer in number than their counterparts in the United States, with the consequence that non-separatist evangelicals needed to pay less attention to differentiating themselves from fundamentalists. Whereas in the United States the task
of defining evangelical identity in the post-war era was shaped by the imperative of differentiating evangelicals from separatist fundamentalists, in Britain
the dominating agenda at the start of our period was precisely where the line
should be drawn between evangelicals and those of more liberal persuasion.

In Britain, both within the national churches of England and Scotland,
and in the English Free Churches, the term 'evangelical' was employed in
the immediate post-war years with a looseness which contradicts any assertion that there were no problems in defining evangelical identity before the
1970s. When the annual Islington clerical conference of Anglican evangelicals
resumed after the war in January 1947, the vicar of Islington, Hugh Gough,
chose as the conference theme 'Evangelical essentials' in an attempt to delin-
eate more clearly what the various sections of Anglican evangelicalism held
in common. He reported with alarm a case of a clergyman who confessed to
having no personal experience of salvation who had been elected to membership of the committee of a Diocesan Evangelical Fellowship. Yet Gough
(who, with Harold Earnshaw-Smith, had been one of the first two IVF travelling secretaries in the 1930s)[29] called for the abandonment of the labels of
'liberal' and 'conservative', asserting that it was time 'to stop being "hyphenated" Evangelicals and to be once again "Evangelicals", pure and simple'.[30]
He then outlined the five spheres in which evangelical distinctiveness should
be manifest, each of which was the subject of a conference paper: authority,
worship, preaching, the church and the individual. The five addresses that followed illustrated just how difficult it was for evangelical Anglicans to agree on
a definition of their identity. J. R. S. Taylor, bishop of Sodor and Man, began
his address on 'essentials in authority' by relating the theme not to the Bible
but to the Thirty-Nine Articles. When he did get round to discussing biblical
authority, he cited, somewhat selectively and inaccurately, T. M. Lindsay's
History of the Reformation: 'The authority and infallibility attach primarily to the
Word of God, secondarily to the Scriptures. . . . No authority nor infallibility

---

and American Movements Since 1940', in Noll, Bebbington and Rawlyk, *Evangelicalism*,
365–388.

[29] Oliver Barclay, *Evangelicalism in Britain 1935–1995: A Personal Sketch* (Leicester: Inter-
Varsity Press, 1997), 28.

[30] *Evangelical Essentials: Report of the 113th Islington Clerical Conference, Held in the Church House,
Westminster, January 14th, 1947, Under the Chairmanship of the Rev. HUGH R. GOUGH,
O.B.E., M.A.* (London: Church Book Room Press, n.d. [1947]), 13–14.

attach to the Scriptures, which are not otherwise apprehended than by faith.' Taylor identified the Word of God primarily with Christ rather than with the Bible, and went on to define evangelicals in narrowly clerical terms as 'men of the Evangel, servants of the Word, clergy who put the Gospel in the forefront of our Ministry'.[31] It was left to A. T. Houghton, general secretary of the Bible Churchmen's Missionary Society (BCMS; now known as Crosslinks), to expound a distinctively conservative view of biblical inspiration when including devotion to the Word of God in his list of 'essentials in the individual'.[32]

The relative paucity of reference to the authority of Scripture in the 1947 Islington conference addresses highlights the wide divergence between British and American evangelicalism at this juncture. It is explicable by reference to the fact that it was precisely the question of whether an evangelical stance could properly be combined with acceptance of modern biblical criticism that, ever since the schism within the Church Missionary Society (CMS; now known as the Church Mission Society) leading to the formation of the BCMS in 1922, had been the principal fault-line separating conservative from more liberal evangelicals in the Church of England. The most obvious commonality shared by all across the evangelical theological spectrum was simply the priority of evangelism. A very similar conclusion is suggested by the report of the gathering of evangelical Anglicans convened by Max Warren (1904–77), general secretary of the CMS, on the eve of the 1948 Lambeth Conference of Anglican bishops. The meeting submitted an address to the bishops about to assemble in Lambeth which made nine affirmations that defined not *evangelical* identity but what was 'fundamental to any evangelism that is true to the New Testament'. Only the last of these concerned Scripture, and it was phrased in loose terms acceptable to liberal or 'centrist' evangelicals: 'We affirm that the Church stands under the Word of God as revealed in Holy Scripture, and that its faith and order, its worship and its way of life, must be judged in accordance therewith.'[33] As at Islington in the previous year, a more conservative viewpoint was expressed, in this case by Harold Earnshaw-Smith, rector of

---

[31] Ibid. 18–21; Taylor was loosely quoting T. M. Lindsay, *History of the Reformation*, 2 vols. (Edinburgh: T. & T. Clark, 1906–7), I, 464.

[32] *Evangelical Essentials*, 71.

[33] *Evangelicals Affirm in the Year of the Lambeth Conference: The Proceedings of the Congress Held in London, April 13th–14th, 1948* (London: Church Book Room Press, 1948), xii. For an argument that 'centrist evangelicals' should be distinguished from 'liberal evangelicals' in post-war Britain see David W. Bebbington, *Evangelicalism in Modern Britain: A History from the 1730s to the 1980s* (London: Unwin Hyman, 1989), 251–253.

All Souls, Langham Place, in central London, who warned that the words 'evangelical' and 'evangelistic' were not in fact interchangeable, and called for a return to a 'Bible ministry' as the only sure foundation for the recovery of effective evangelism.[34]

Just how broad the Anglican evangelical family was in these years is revealed by reference to the Anglican Evangelical Group Movement and the Evangelical Fellowship for Theological Literature. The former body, constituted in 1923, was explicitly associated with an extremely liberal version of evangelicalism and in the course of the 1950s became virtually indistinguishable from a broad middle-of-the-road Anglicanism.[35] The latter, formed in 1942 on the initiative chiefly of Max Warren, the new general secretary of the CMS, was intended to promote the growth of evangelical theological scholarship, and reflected Warren's conviction that evangelicalism should not be hyphenated by the addition of the epithets 'liberal' or 'conservative'. Initially the Fellowship embraced a wide spectrum of theological opinion, from conservatives such as the Irish principal of Moore College in Sydney, T. C. Hammond (1877–1961), to those who were moving in a decidedly liberal direction, such as Maurice Wiles (1923–2005). Wiles was a former member of the Cambridge Inter-Collegiate Christian Union (CICCU) and chaplain of Ridley Hall, Cambridge, from 1952 to 1955, and in 1970 became Regius Professor of Divinity at Oxford. By 1977 he would be ranked among the contributors to the radical collection of essays *The Myth of God Incarnate*, and was in no sense to be counted any longer as an evangelical. Although extremely distinguished in terms of the academic standing of its membership, the Fellowship became less and less distinctive in its evangelicalism as the years went by, and was disbanded in 1972 on the grounds that, in Warren's words, 'its job really was done'.[36]

In the immediate post-war years, therefore, evangelicalism in the Church of England struggled to achieve any clear doctrinal consensus. During the 1950s the task of achieving such a consensus became noticeably easier for two reasons. The first was the very process of liberalization on the left wing of the movement, whose adherents became progressively disinclined to claim the label of 'evangelical' for themselves and hence gradually disappeared from

---

[34] *Evangelicals Affirm*, 47, 52.

[35] Bebbington, *Evangelicalism in Modern Britain*, 201–202, 252–253.

[36] F. W. Dillistone, *Into All the World: A Biography of Max Warren* (London: Hodder & Stoughton, 1980), 60; see also Michael Hennell, 'An Episode in Twentieth Century Church History', *Theology* 76 (1973), 480–483; Leonard Hickin, 'The Revival of Evangelical Scholarship', *Chm* 92 (1978), 125–133.

the spectrum. The second reason, which in itself may have been an underlying cause of the first, was the impact of the early Graham crusades in England and Scotland, which gave ample opportunity for theological opponents to dismiss evangelicals as fundamentalists who had sacrificed intellectual integrity for the allure of tub-thumping American populism. Hence Graham, at the same time as he was being attacked by American fundamentalists for the expanding range of his Christian connections, was initially interpreted by sections of the press in Britain and, over a longer period, by some mainstream church leaders as being the quintessential American fundamentalist. From 15 to 27 August 1955 there was a protracted exchange of correspondence in *The Times* on the subject of fundamentalism, provoked by Graham's mission to the University of Cambridge.[37] In early 1956 Michael Ramsey, then bishop of Durham and about to become archbishop of York, published an article in his diocesan magazine entitled 'The Menace of Fundamentalism', accusing Graham of being both sectarian and heretical.[38] The heat of public controversy engendered by the Graham crusades compelled those who wished to align themselves with Graham to make clear what they did, and did not, stand for.

John Stott, who had succeeded Earnshaw-Smith in June 1950 as rector of All Souls, Langham Place, joined the fray, publishing two articles in *Crusade* magazine in November 1955 and May 1956, endorsing that form of fundamentalism which held on to the fundamentals of the faith and defending Graham's practice of calling for a decisive commitment to Christ. Nevertheless, Stott distanced himself from the 'extravagances' of fundamentalism, particularly in the United States. The articles were republished in a brief pamphlet, *Fundamentalism and Evangelism*.[39] In retrospect the pamphlet can be viewed as the first clear indication that Stott, by his lucid writings as much as by his strategic preaching ministry in central London, was to become the most influential architect of the British version of the 'new evangelicalism'; like his American counterparts, Stott's governing passion was to promote the influence of evangelical Christianity in the higher echelons of church and society.[40] A more substantial statement of the same case was issued in March 1958 by J. I. Packer, an enthusiast for Puritan theology and member of staff of Tyndale Hall in Bristol, primarily in response to a book by the Anglo-Catholic

---

[37] *The Times*, 15, 17, 18, 19, 20, 22, 23, 24, 25, 26, 27 Aug. 1955.

[38] Owen Chadwick, *Michael Ramsey: A Life* (Oxford: Clarendon Press, 1990), 92.

[39] Alister Chapman, *Godly Ambition: John Stott and the Evangelical Movement* (New York: Oxford University Press, 2012), 47, 177; John R. W. Stott, *Fundamentalism and Evangelism* (London: Crusade Booklets, 1956).

[40] Chapman, *Godly Ambition, passim.*

A. G. Hebert, *Fundamentalism and the Church of God*.[41] Packer's IVF pocketbook *'Fundamentalism' and the Word of God* sold twenty-thousand copies in a year and became a standard defence of evangelicalism in student circles, especially in Britain and Australia (where Hebert lived). The quotation marks were significant: it was Packer's case that the evangelical doctrine of Scripture, rather than being, as Hebert and other critics alleged, 'new, eccentric and in reality untenable', had a respectable historical pedigree, stretching back through the nineteenth-century Princeton theologians Charles Hodge and B. B. Warfield to the sixteenth-century Protestant reformers. '"Fundamentalism"', insisted Packer, 'is just a twentieth-century name for historic Evangelicalism, though not, in our judgment, a very good or useful name.'[42] Packer was in fact defending 'historic Evangelicalism', not the 'fundamentalism' of anti-evangelical polemic.

A further important milestone in the consolidation of Anglican evangelical identity was the purchase in 1959 by two conservative evangelical laymen of the *Church of England Newspaper* (*CEN*), and subsequent appointment as editor of John King, in place of Arthur Dowle, a liberal evangelical who, in addition to his successive roles as assistant editor, associate editor and editor of the *CEN*, had also from 1954 been secretary of the modernist body the Modern Churchmen's Union.[43] From about 1959 evangelicalism in the Church of England displayed a sharper, theologically more conservative and yet intellectually more sophisticated image. A younger generation of evangelical clergy was emerging who combined firmly orthodox theology with a repudiation of sectarian attitudes. They were beginning to organize themselves for fellowship and coordinated action. In 1955 Stott had refounded the Eclectic Society (the original Eclectic Society flourished at the end of the eighteenth century) as a discussion forum in London for evangelical clergy under the age of 40. Like its eighteenth-century predecessor, the Eclectic Society was intended to reshape the Church of England from within.[44] A year later

---

[41] Gabriel Hebert, *Fundamentalism and the Church of God* (London: SCM Press, 1957).

[42] J. I. Packer, *'Fundamentalism' and the Word of God: Some Evangelical Principles* (London: Inter-Varsity Fellowship, 1958), 11, 19, and *passim*; for a full account of the genesis and impact of the book see Alister McGrath, *To Know and Serve God: A Biography of James I. Packer* (London: Hodder & Stoughton, 1997), 80–88.

[43] *CEN*, 29 Jan. 1960, 3; Bebbington, *Evangelicalism in Modern Britain*, 252–253; Kenneth Hylson-Smith, *Evangelicals in the Church of England 1734–1984* (Edinburgh: T. & T. Clark, 1988), 288–289. The two new owners were John Cordle, a Conservative M. P., and Alfred G. B. Owen, a leading industrialist.

[44] Chapman, *Godly Ambition*, 81–82.

Raymond Turvey, vicar of St George's, Leeds, assembled a group of scattered evangelical clergy from the north of England in response to their sense of isolation. By 1960 their meetings had developed into the first Northern Evangelical Conference, held in York, which attracted 250 clergy from all over the northern province. A laymen's conference followed in Leeds in 1964, and the second Northern Conference in York in 1965.[45] From these roots sprang the first National Evangelical Anglican Congress (NEAC) held at Keele University in April 1967, when a thousand delegates, nearly half of them lay people, gathered to discuss what it might mean to be 'deeply committed' as conservative evangelicals to 'the present and future of the Church of England'.[46] NEAC was evidence of a decisive mood-shift among younger evangelicals in the Church of England towards an unprecedented degree of commitment to full participation in a theologically plural church.[47] Conservative evangelicals had emerged from the fundamentalist ghetto and were about to enter an era of predominant influence unparalleled in Anglican history.

The English Free Churches: the continuance of broader expressions of evangelicalism, 1945 – c. 1971

In the English Free Churches also, a broad range of theological opinion continued after the Second World War to lay claim to the label 'evangelical', but for a longer period than in the Church of England, extending as far as the early 1970s. Many English Nonconformist scholars and ministers in the later Victorian period had accepted the new higher criticism of the Bible while retaining a broadly evangelical approach to theology, and the legacy of this synthesis remained apparent into the 1950s and even 1960s.[48] A further influence orienting Free Church evangelicalism in an ecumenical and sometimes liberal direction was the close connection that existed between many Free Church leaders and the Student Christian Movement

---

[45] Philip Crowe (ed.), *Keele '67: The National Evangelical Anglican Congress Statement* (London: Falcon Books, 1967), 7.

[46] Ibid. 38.

[47] Andrew Atherstone, 'The Keele Congress of 1967: A Paradigm Shift in Anglican Evangelical Attitudes', *Journal of Anglican Studies* 9 (2011), 175–197.

[48] Willis B. Glover, *Evangelical Nonconformists and Higher Criticism in the Nineteenth Century* (London: Independent Press, 1954); 'The Old Evangelicalism and the New', *Religion in Life* 23 (1954), 286–296.

(SCM), where students from the historic Free Churches often felt more at home than they did in the IVF, which tended to be dominated by Anglicans, with a considerable infusion of Christian Brethren.[49] The most influential Methodist biblical scholar, C. K. Barrett (1917–2011), professor in the University of Durham, was orthodox and Pauline in his theology but not markedly conservative in his view of Scripture. Of the Methodist theological colleges, only Cliff College in Derbyshire, which specialized in the training of lay evangelists rather than circuit ministers, was clearly conservative in its evangelical commitment. There were, however, forces in Methodism that kept evangelical spirituality alive at congregational level. Pre-eminent among them was the enduring popularity of Charles Wesley's hymns. At Westminster Central Hall in London from 1939 to 1954, the direct and passionately evangelistic preaching of Dr W. E. Sangster (1900–60) exercised a wide influence.[50] Methodists were also prominent in evangelistic efforts, from the 'Commando Campaigns' that targeted particular British towns between 1942 and 1947 to the Nationwide Initiative in Evangelism, launched in 1979 by Donald English, president of the Methodist Conference for that year.[51]

Congregationalism was the most theologically liberal of the English Free Churches. Its scholars were, nevertheless, significantly influenced in the 1940s and 1950s by the theology of Karl Barth and by a 'Genevan school', led by Nathaniel Micklem of Mansfield College, Oxford (1888–1976), which sought to promote orthodoxy, reverence and liturgical order in worship. Conservative evangelicals in the denomination were, however, few in number and lacked influence.

Among the historic English Free Churches conservative evangelicalism retained its strongest base in the Baptist Union, where the legacy of C. H. Spurgeon continued to shape the character of many congregations, particularly in London and the south-east of England. However, conservative theology was not widely reflected in the higher echelons of the denomination until the appointment in 1991 of a conservative evangelical, David Coffey, as general

---

[49] For the close Baptist connections with the SCM in this period see Ian M. Randall, *The English Baptists of the Twentieth Century* (Didcot: Baptist Historical Society, 2005), 219–221, 260–261, 304.

[50] On Sangster see *BDE*, 578–580; Paul Sangster, *Doctor Sangster* (London: Epworth Press, 1962).

[51] David W. Bebbington, 'Evangelism and Spirituality', in Alan P. F. Sell and Anthony R. Cross (eds.), *Protestant Nonconformity in the Twentieth Century* (Carlisle: Paternoster Press, 2003), 201, 207.

secretary of the Union. Many of the leading English Baptist scholars, notably those at Bristol Baptist College or at Regent's Park College in Oxford, regarded themselves as evangelical while accepting more or less advanced critical views of the Bible. Ernest A. Payne (1902–80), general secretary of the Baptist Union from 1951 to 1967, was a leading figure in the World Council of Churches who had few contacts with conservative evangelicals. Even the faculty of Spurgeon's College, always the most conservative of the English Baptist colleges, displayed through the 1950s and 1960s a style of evangelicalism that was not predictably or even consistently conservative.[52] As long as a distinctively Free Church identity remained a more potent force than pan-evangelical sentiment among Nonconformist ministers, the historic English Free Churches were limited in their capacity to shape the destiny of post-war evangelicalism in Britain.

The Church of Scotland: Barthian theology and evangelical cooperation

In the Church of Scotland there were fewer evangelicals at either end of the conservative–liberal spectrum than in the Church of England, and a correspondingly higher concentration in the centre ground. The historic Reformed nature of the Church of Scotland and the status of the Westminster Confession of Faith (1647) as the principal subordinate standard of faith were partly responsible for this. Also relevant was the much greater influence of the neo-orthodox theology of Karl Barth (1886–1968), whose advocates included G. T. Thomson (1887–1958), professor of Christian dogmatics at the University of Edinburgh from 1936 to 1952, and his successor in the chair, Thomas F. Torrance (1913–2007). Torrance, the son of China Inland Mission missionaries, had for a time led the work of the IVF among theological students, but had become dissatisfied with what seemed to him the unduly mechanistic approaches to biblical authority in conservative evan-

---

[52] Eric Worstead, principal of Spurgeon's from 1955 to 1957, was a supporter of Moral Re-Armament. George Beasley-Murray, principal from 1957 to 1973, though an undoubted conservative evangelical in his central emphases, published an influential commentary on Mark 13 which suggested that Jesus had been wrong in his expectation of the timing of the parousia. See Ian M. Randall, *A School of the Prophets: 150 Years of Spurgeon's College* (London: Spurgeon's College, 2005), 116–117. Rex A. Mason, tutor in Old Testament from 1965 to 1975, could be described as more of a 'centrist' than a conservative evangelical.

gelical circles.[53] With Geoffrey W. Bromiley (1915–2009), an Anglican who left New College, Edinburgh, in 1958 to join the faculty of Fuller Theological Seminary, Torrance supervised the translation into English of the thirteen bulky volumes of Barth's *Church Dogmatics*, an immense task that Thomson had begun as the translator of volume I:1. There was also a more broad-based commitment to the priority of evangelism in the national church of Scotland than in the Church of England. From 1947 through to the late 1950s the Church of Scotland, together with other churches, promoted a nationwide programme of lay evangelism known latterly as 'Tell Scotland'. The chairman of the executive committee of Tell Scotland in 1957 was Robert Mackie (1899–1984), former general secretary, first of the SCM and then of the World Student Christian Federation. Yet the campaign also drew personnel from the IVF as well as the SCM, and one of its leaders, Tom Allan, was a strong supporter of Billy Graham.[54] In the Scottish universities, and especially at Edinburgh, where the divinity students of New College provided much of the leadership of both the IVF and the SCM, and where the Christian Union enjoyed the support of senior members of the university faculty of divinity, such as Tom Torrance and the well-known preacher James S. Stewart (1896–1990),[55] the two traditions of Christian student work were closer in spirit in the early 1950s than at any English university. From the autumn of 1951 the IVF-affiliated Christian Union at Edinburgh held a joint weekly prayer meeting and engaged in some acts of joint Christian witness with the SCM group, a policy that eventually led the IVF in London to disaffiliate the Edinburgh University Christian Union in September 1953.[56] It was a symbolic moment, marking the apparent impossibility of retaining conservative evangelicals as simply one element in Scotland within a cooperative 'centrist' evangelicalism. Although some 'centrist' Scottish evangelicals such as Torrance continued to refer to

---

[53] Alister E. McGrath, *Thomas F. Torrance: An Intellectual Biography* (Edinburgh: T. &. T. Clark, 1999), 25–26; Barclay, *Evangelicalism in Britain*, 54. Torrance's first publication was a pamphlet, *The Modern Theological Debate: Notes of Three Addresses Delivered at the T.S.P.U. Conference, Bewdley, Dec. 30–Jan. 2, 1941* (1941), published by the Theological Students' Prayer Union of the IVF.

[54] Bebbington, *Evangelicalism in Modern Britain*, 253; Robin Boyd, *The Witness of the Student Christian Movement: 'Church Ahead of the Church'* (London: SPCK, 2007), 59, 118; Frank Colquhoun, *Harringay Story: The Official Record of the Billy Graham Greater London Crusade 1954* (London: Hodder & Stoughton, 1955), 199–200.

[55] On Stewart see *BDE* and Myles S. Krueger, *James S. Stewart* (Cambridge: James Clarke, 2009).

[56] For a full account from the SCM viewpoint see Boyd, *Witness*, 86–89.

themselves as evangelicals with less hesitation than was true of their English equivalents,[57] the Edinburgh controversy contributed to a process of linguistic transmutation that paralleled the one more strikingly evident south of the border: in Scotland also the term 'evangelical' was gradually becoming the distinctive property of conservative evangelicals, whose most influential leader was William Still, minister of Gilcomston South Parish Church in Aberdeen from 1945 to 1997.

The emergence and erosion of a conservative evangelical consensus in Britain

The 1960s were years of profound religious crisis through much of Western Christendom, in which church membership declined steeply, doctrinal orthodoxies came under increasing question even from within the churches, and the legal foundations underpinning public Christian morality were steadily undermined.[58] As this critical decade unfolded, both the Church of Scotland and the English Free Churches found themselves confronted with much the same choice as Anglican evangelicals had first encountered in the later 1950s: as the scope for maintaining centrist or liberal versions of evangelicalism progressively narrowed, the British churches were left with two principal options: either to merge their residual evangelicalism with the prevailing liberal and increasingly secular mood, or to cultivate an expanding and newly confident conservative evangelicalism that had by now divested itself of most of the attitudes and shibboleths of the pre-war era. The SCM which had nurtured the older generation of denominational leaders capitulated in this decade to a form of quasi-Marxist political activism that relegated prayer and Bible study to the margins, and had no place for mission in any traditional form.[59] Liberal forms of evangelicalism which had hitherto retained more or less of their original commitment to proclaiming the gospel were largely absorbed in the 1960s by the fashion for avowedly secular and political theologies that was sweeping through ecumenical Protestantism on both sides of the Atlantic.

As SCM groups in the universities dwindled to insignificance, the IVF, which changed its name in 1975 to the Universities and Colleges Christian

---

[57] McGrath, *Torrance*, 26.

[58] See McLeod, *Religious Crisis of the 1960s*.

[59] Boyd, *Witness*, 112–116; Risto Lehtonen, *Story of a Storm: The Ecumenical Student Movement in the Turmoil of Revolution, 1968–1973* (Grand Rapids: Eerdmans; Helsinki: Finnish Society of Church History, 1998), 122.

Fellowship (UCCF), reaped a harvest from the enormous expansion of British higher education. During the 1960s twenty-one new universities were founded in the United Kingdom, in addition to polytechnics and other colleges of higher and further education. Although the ethos of the new universities and polytechnics was predominantly secular, varieties of Christianity that stood most clearly apart from a secular agenda appealed more strongly to undergraduates than those that sought to accommodate it.[60] Aggregate national membership of IVF groups rose from about two thousand in 1949 to six thousand in 1959, and to fourteen thousand in UCCF groups by 1977–8.[61] Those who came to faith as students through the witness of the Christian Unions looked for conservative evangelical churches to join on leaving university; the electoral rolls of the leading conservative evangelical Anglican churches in London grew steadily from the late 1950s to the early 1970s, while liberal or Anglo-Catholic churches tended to decline.[62] Significant numbers of evangelical students went on to train for pastoral ministry or other forms of Christian service. Some of the most intellectually able studied theology. Those who did so at postgraduate level often joined the Tyndale Fellowship (established by the IVF in 1945),[63] some of whose members obtained posts in theological colleges and university departments in the 1970s and 1980s.

The guiding spirit and inspiration of the conservative evangelical renaissance in Britain from the 1940s to the mid-1960s was the Welsh physician-turned-pastor Martyn Lloyd-Jones (1899–1981). As the senior pastor of London's Westminster Chapel from 1943 to 1968, 'the Doctor', as he was widely known, exercised a remarkable ministry of expository preaching, writing and speaking that fed the minds and quickened the spirits of his large congregation and of innumerable others, both in Britain and internationally. As a Calvinistic Methodist, Lloyd-Jones was strongly Reformed in doctrine. But, equally, as someone whose early years were shaped by the living memory of the Welsh Revival of 1904–5, he had a vibrant concern that Christians should experience the power of the Holy Spirit, and in later life proved open to the genuineness of the charismatic renewal, though he repudiated the charismatic emphasis on speaking in tongues as the normal

---

[60] McLeod, *Religious Crisis of the 1960s*, 209, notes the symbiotic relationship between the growth of secularism and of religious conservatism.

[61] Pete Lowman, *The Day of His Power: A History of the International Fellowship of Evangelical Students* (Leicester: Inter-Varsity Press, 1983), 96, 99; McLeod, *Religious Crisis of the 1960s*, 211, gives a much lower figure for IVF membership of 'about 3,000' in 1960.

[62] Chapman, *Godly Ambition*, 61–62.

[63] For a fuller account see chapter 4 below.

evidence of baptism in the Spirit. He was fully prepared to share fellowship with Arminians if they were soundly evangelical. He was the chief promoter of the revival in the 1950s and 1960s of Puritan theology, which he advanced through a variety of means: support for the Evangelical Library that opened in London in 1945; hosting the annual Puritan (later 'Westminster') conferences from 1950; the founding of a magazine, *The Banner of Truth*, in 1955 and a publishing house of the same name two years later; and his encouragement of the Evangelical Movement of Wales, formally established in 1955.[64]

In terms of theological content there was little to distinguish Lloyd-Jones from pre-war conservatives. He had received no formal theological training, though he was widely read. He also became increasingly separatist in his ecclesiology, owing to his conviction that Christian identity was defined essentially by belief in a corpus of propositional scriptural truth; those who did not give their assent to this minimum of Christian doctrine could not, he argued, be regarded as Christians; hence he found it hard to understand why fellow-evangelicals in the 'mixed' denominations who shared his concern for evangelical orthodoxy continued to act as if their liberal denominational colleagues were fellow-Christians. This conviction of the Doctor's famously became controversial in October 1966 at the second National Assembly of Evangelicals held at Westminster Central Hall, when Lloyd-Jones, delivering the opening address, appealed for evangelicals to 'come together, not occasionally, but *always*' and expressed a wish for God to speed the day when all evangelicals would be brought within 'a fellowship or an association of evangelical churches'. The chairman of the meeting, John Stott, not unnaturally took this to be a call for secession from the historic denominations such as the Church of England, and in closing the meeting observed that in his view both Scripture and history were against the position advocated by Lloyd-Jones. This episode is much argued over in the literature, and cannot be analysed fully here.[65] Two comments may, however, be made.

---

[64] *BDE*, 370–374; Bebbington, *Evangelicalism in Modern Britain*, 262. The fullest sources on Lloyd-Jones are Andrew Atherstone and David Ceri Jones (eds.), *Engaging with Martyn Lloyd-Jones: The Life and Legacy of 'the Doctor'* (Nottingham: Apollos, 2011); John Brencher, *Martyn Lloyd-Jones and Twentieth-Century Evangelicalism, 1899–1981* (Carlisle: Paternoster, 2002); Iain H. Murray, *David Martyn Lloyd-Jones: The Fight of Faith 1939–1981* (Edinburgh: Banner of Truth Trust, 1990).

[65] Compare Murray, *Fight of Faith*, 522–528; Brencher, *Martyn Lloyd-Jones*, 92–106; Chapman, *Godly Ambition*, 93–95; Timothy Dudley-Smith, *John Stott: A Global Ministry* (Leicester: Inter-Varsity Press, 2001), 65–71. The most recent and fullest discussion is by Andrew Atherstone, 'Lloyd-Jones and the Anglican Secession Crisis', in Atherstone and Ceri Jones, *Engaging with Martyn Lloyd-Jones*, 261–292.

The first is to point out that Lloyd-Jones himself was never averse to dialogue, nor even in his earlier years to common witness, with those who were not evangelical in faith. Iain Murray's biography of Lloyd-Jones describes a joint mission to the University of Edinburgh in November 1948 organized by James Barr, a member of the Edinburgh University Christian Union who subsequently moved away from conservative evangelicalism and mounted a trenchant attack on its doctrine of Scripture in his 1977 book, *Fundamentalism.*[66] The two missioners were to be Lloyd-Jones and Dr Alec Vidler, a liberal Anglo-Catholic who later became Dean of King's College, Cambridge. In the event, Lloyd-Jones had to withdraw on account of illness, being replaced by another member of the IVF national advisory committee, Tom Torrance.[67] Lloyd-Jones also shared an Evangelical Alliance platform in 1948 with the Dean of St Paul's, W. R. Matthews, whose evangelical credentials were decidedly suspect.[68] Thus in 1948 at least, Lloyd-Jones was not a thoroughgoing separatist. He later persisted in attending the full series of private meetings that the British Council of Churches convened between 1957 and 1961 in an ultimately fruitless attempt to see if any common ground could be found for evangelistic cooperation between conservative evangelicals and other Christians, in the light of the experience of the Graham crusades.[69]

The second comment is to suggest that the famous episode in October 1966 was one of the first signs of the fissures that were beginning to appear in the conservative evangelical consensus in Britain. Lloyd-Jones had been very deeply involved in the most significant pan-evangelical institutions of the 1940s and 1950s. He was president of the IVF on five occasions between 1939 and 1964, and exercised an unrivalled influence on its counsels.[70] He was chairman of the International Fellowship of Evangelical Students (IFES) from its inception in 1947 until 1959, and president from 1959 to 1967. He was a prominent supporter of London Bible College in its early years, and was involved in the establishment of Tyndale House. Yet from the early 1960s

---

[66] On Barr (1924–2006), who became a leading biblical scholar and held a series of prestigious academic posts at Edinburgh, Manchester, Oxford and in the USA, see his *Fundamentalism* (London: SCM, 1977) and *Escaping from Fundamentalism* (London: SCM, 1984).

[67] Murray, *Fight of Faith*, 189–190.

[68] Ian Randall, 'Schism and Unity: 1905–1966', in Steve Brady and Harold Rowdon (eds.), *For Such a Time as This: Perspectives on Evangelicalism, Past, Present and Future* (London: Evangelical Alliance; Milton Keynes: Scripture Union, 1996), 170.

[69] Murray, *Fight of Faith*, 314–320.

[70] Brencher, *Martyn Lloyd-Jones*, 216.

his support for the IVF cooled – though his involvement in IFES continued – as it became increasingly moulded by Anglican influence.[71] He distanced himself from the London Bible College even earlier, in protest against its pursuit of secular academic accreditation and the recognition of its graduates by the Baptist Union.[72] Lloyd-Jones's stance towards the ecumenical movement and 'mixed' denominations hardened in the course of the 1960s, and he took Westminster Chapel out of the Congregational Union (on the eve of its transition into the Congregational Church in England and Wales) in January 1966.[73] His appeal at the Westminster Central Hall meeting was only part of a process of disengagement whereby Lloyd-Jones attempted to distance himself from the broad coalition that conservative evangelicalism had now become. That 'the Doctor' should be interpreted as calling for evangelicals to leave mixed denominations was a logical and plausible inference from his remarks, especially in view of the fact that since 1964 there had been several high-profile secessions to Nonconformity of Anglican evangelical clergy dismayed by theological trends within the Church of England.[74] Nonetheless, the clear majority of British evangelical opinion was against Lloyd-Jones. After October 1966, commented J. Alec Motyer, an Anglican evangelical whose own theology was markedly Reformed, 'it was never possible to look at him as a leader and a wise man in quite the same way'.[75] The majority of the conservative evangelical movement in England was positioning itself to follow a course that would leave the Doctor and his disciples marooned on the margins. In Wales the story was different; here the Evangelical Movement of Wales did much to perpetuate Lloyd-Jones's influence.[76]

The contribution of the Christian Brethren to the shaping of conservative evangelicalism in Britain and beyond

The Christian Brethren must be ranked with the Pentecostals and the Salvation Army as one of the few groups in the British Free Churches to

[71] Ibid. 220–221.

[72] Ibid. 199; Ian M. Randall, *Educating Evangelicalism: The Origins, Development and Impact of London Bible College* (Carlisle: Paternoster, 2000), 106.

[73] Brencher, *Martyn Lloyd-Jones*, 119–120.

[74] Atherstone, 'Lloyd-Jones', 262–269.

[75] Cited in Brencher, *Martyn Lloyd-Jones*, 226.

[76] See Noel Gibbard, *The First Fifty Years: The History of the Evangelical Movement of Wales, 1948–98* (Bridgend: Bryntirion Press, 2002).

remain consistently conservative evangelical in the post-war period. Whereas the 'exclusive' or 'connexional' branches of the Brethren movement pursued an isolationism that precluded wider influence on other evangelicals, the 'open' or 'independent' Brethren began from the late 1940s to exercise a significant influence on conservative evangelicalism, both in Britain and more widely.[77] Prominent businessmen from the independent Brethren, such as the construction magnate John Laing (1879–1978), and John Henderson (1888–1975), a Scottish Conservative MP and chairman of a firm of produce importers, were keen supporters of Graham's Greater London Crusade in 1954. It was claimed that as many as 28% of the counsellors at Harringay were from Brethren backgrounds, and the proportion may have been as high or even higher in the Australian crusades in 1959.[78] Laing's wealth also proved strategic for the renaissance of conservative evangelical biblical scholarship in this period, thanks in part to the influence of W. J. Martin, a friend of Laing's who lectured in Hebrew and Semitic studies at the University of Liverpool.[79] Laing money extensively funded both London Bible College (1943) and Tyndale House (1945), the Cambridge centre for biblical research. These institutions, as chapter 4 will explore at greater length, had an impact far beyond the shores of Britain.

Even though the Brethren suffered the transdenominational seepage in this period of some who found their assemblies too constricted an environment for the fulfilment of their sense of vocation, men and women from an originally Brethren background contributed a great deal to the articulation of a sharper and more intellectually confident conservative evangelical identity in post-war Britain.[80] A telling example is Douglas Johnson (1904–91), the medical doctor who was general secretary of the IVF from 1928 until 1964.[81] More generally, both the Church of England and the Baptist denomination, particularly

---

[77] For a justification of the terminology of 'connexional' and 'independent' Brethren, as opposed to the more conventional usage of 'exclusive' and 'open', see Roger Shuff, *Searching for the True Church: Brethren and Evangelicals in Mid-Twentieth-Century England* (Milton Keynes: Paternoster Press, 2005).

[78] Ibid. 151–153; see Stuart Piggin, *Evangelical Christianity in Australia: Spirit, Word and World* (Melbourne: Oxford University Press, 1996), 166, 182.

[79] Shuff, *Searching for the True Church*, 77.

[80] David Bebbington, 'The Place of the Brethren Movement in International Evangelicalism', in Neil T. R. Dickson and Tim Grass (eds.), *The Growth of the Brethren Movement: National and International Experiences: Essays in Honour of Harold Rowdon* (Milton Keynes: Paternoster Press, 2006), 258–260.

[81] *BDE*, 333–334.

in Scotland, benefited from the transferred allegiance of gifted young people from a Brethren background. Those who remained within the Brethren fold also exercised an influence out of all proportion to the size of the Brethren movement, probably for the very reason that the Brethren ideal of true Christian fellowship was essentially a pan-evangelical and non-denominational one. Another doctor, of lifelong Brethren allegiance, the Scotsman John M. Laird (1905–88), returned to Britain at the end of 1945 from an extremely fruitful period of leadership in the Children's Special Service Mission (CSSM) and Crusaders movement in New Zealand, to take up the London-based post of joint, and subsequently sole, general secretary of the international CSSM movement and its partner organization, Scripture Union. In 1947 Laird set in motion procedures for 'decolonization' whereby the various Scripture Union bodies throughout the British Empire could grow towards 'commonwealth status' and autonomy of London, thus initiating a process of internationalization that would ultimately prove to be of great significance, especially in West Africa.[82] Laird was also a great spotter of up-and-coming evangelical talent well beyond the confines of Brethrenism. Following a practice borrowed from the Australian medical missionary in Tanganyika Paul White (author of the immensely popular *Jungle Doctor* children's books), Laird would make a list of 'BWW' – 'Blokes Worth Watching' – and make them the object of his prayers and encouragement. Names on his list in the late 1940s included John Stott, Frederick Catherwood, later a leading Christian businessman and politician (and son-in-law of Martyn Lloyd-Jones), and Michael C. Griffiths, who was to become general director of the Overseas Missionary Fellowship and principal of London Bible College from 1980 to 1989.[83]

The Brethren also supplied the most prominent conservative evangelical biblical scholar of the post-war era, F. F. Bruce (1910–90), who was professor of biblical history and literature at Sheffield University from 1955 to 1959 and from 1959 to 1978 Rylands professor of biblical criticism and exegesis at the University of Manchester.[84] Bruce's role as a conservative New Testament

---

[82] John Laird, *No Mere Chance* (London: Hodder & Stoughton and Scripture Union, 1981); Nigel Sylvester, *God's World in a Young World: The Story of Scripture Union* (London: Scripture Union, 1984), 117–118, 155–160, 246–247. Peter J. Lineham, *No Ordinary Union: The Story of Scripture Union Children's Special Service Mission and Crusader Movement of New Zealand, 1880–1980* (Wellington: Scripture Union in New Zealand, 1980). For more details of the decentralization of Scripture Union in the 1950s and 1960s see chapter 3 below.

[83] Laird, *No Mere Chance*, 120–121.

[84] See T. Grass, *F. F. Bruce: A Life* (Milton Keynes: Authentic Media, 2011).

scholar was paralleled in Old Testament and Semitic scholarship by several other Brethren academics, notably W. J. Martin and his successor, A. R. Millard, at Liverpool University, Donald J. Wiseman, professor of Assyriology at London University from 1961 to 1982, and H. L. Ellison, who taught at London Bible College from 1949 to 1955.[85] In 1966 F. F. Bruce and one of his Brethren research students in Manchester, W. Ward Gasque, were instrumental in the birth of an institution that was to become one of the premier academic institutions of global evangelicalism. Regent College, Vancouver, was the product of a collaboration Bruce and Gasque helped to forge between a number of Brethren in the Vancouver district and another Brethren scholar, James M. Houston, an Oxford geographer who had been thinking for some years about founding a Christian institute of graduate studies on the campus of a major university. His ideas meshed with the concerns of the Vancouver Brethren to provide advanced theological training for the leaders of their assemblies. Houston was appointed the first principal of Regent College, which admitted its first intake of full-time students in 1970.[86] Perhaps surprisingly, the new-found intellectual confidence that conservative evangelicalism gained in the 1960s and 1970s owed a great deal to a group once regarded as thoroughly fundamentalist in outlook: the Christian Brethren.

Australia, New Zealand, Canada: different styles of fundamentalism and evangelicalism

In Canada, as also in Australia and New Zealand, the earlier post-war history of evangelical Christianity was connected more closely to Britain than to the United States. The Inter-Varsity movement, which had taken institutional form in Britain in 1928 with the formation of the IVF, was shaped almost from the beginning by imperial rather then narrowly national horizons. The formation of the Canadian Inter-Varsity Christian Fellowship in September 1929 was the result, first, of a deputation visit to Canada by Norman Grubb of the Worldwide Evangelization Crusade in 1927–8, and then of the consequent tour of Canadian universities by Howard Guinness (1903–79) of the British IVF. The cultural and personal linkages of most Canadian evangelical leaders were not with the United States but rather transoceanic ones with Britain (among Presbyterians or Baptists they were particularly with

[85] Shuff, *Searching for the True Church*, 82–87.
[86] John G. Stackhouse, Jr., *Canadian Evangelicalism in the Twentieth Century: An Introduction to Its Character* (Toronto: University of Toronto Press, 1993), 154–158.

Scotland and Ulster), or increasingly in this period with Australia.[87] Hence
in the English-speaking cities of Toronto, Hamilton and Vancouver, fundamentalism in the 1930s and 1940s was characterized less by American-style
combative defences of Christian civilization against the perils of modernism,
evolutionism and communism than by a traditional Scottish or Northern
Irish brand of anti-Catholicism coupled to a single-minded preoccupation
with missions, whether at home or overseas. The Canadian contribution
to international and interdenominational 'faith missions' such as the China
Inland Mission or the Sudan Interior Mission, both of which had their North
American genesis in Toronto, was out of all proportion to the size of the
national population.[88] Even in cities, such as Winnipeg, that had closer ties to
American fundamentalists the links were more to the Wheaton College tradition of world missions and holiness theology than to separatist fundamentalism.[89] Although there were Canadian supporters of Carl McIntire's brand
of militantly separatist fundamentalism, notably the Toronto Baptist pastor
T. T. Shields (1873–1955), who penned the doctrinal statement for McIntire's
International Council of Christian Churches (established in conscious rivalry
to the World Council of Churches in 1948), Shields and his disciples represented a dwindling minority of Canadian evangelicals in the post-war
years.[90] The non-fundamentalist conservative evangelicalism that emerged
in post-war Canada owed a great deal to the foundations laid before the war
through the work among university students, first of Howard Guinness, and
from 1934 of the Australian C. Stacey Woods (1909–83). Guinness was an
Anglican by upbringing and Woods became one in 1933–4, and hence had
little sympathy for separatist forms of fundamentalism.[91] The secretary of the

---

[87] On the multiple connections between Canadian and Australian evangelicalism in the
twentieth century see Mark Hutchinson, '"Up from Downunder": An Australian
View of Canadian Evangelicalism', in George A. Rawlyk (ed.), *Aspects of the Canadian
Evangelical Experience* (Montreal: McGill-Queen's University Press, 1997),
21–37.

[88] Ian S. Rennie, 'Fundamentalism and the Varieties of North Atlantic Evangelicalism',
in Noll, Bebbington and Rawlyk, *Evangelicalism*, 342–345; Mark A. Noll, 'Canadian
Evangelicalism: A View from the United States', in Rawlyk, *Aspects*, 14, 18.

[89] Bruce Hindmarsh, 'The Winnipeg Fundamentalist Network, 1910–1940: The Roots
of Transdenominational Evangelicalism in Manitoba and Saskatchewan', in Rawlyk,
Aspects, 303–319.

[90] Stackhouse, *Canadian Evangelicalism*, 32–34.

[91] See *BDE*, 272–274, 749–751. Woods was brought up in the Australian Brethren
movement but became an Anglican while a student at Wheaton College.

Canadian Inter-Varsity Christian Fellowship from 1948, Wilber Sutherland, was even more strongly opposed to any style of evangelicalism that majored on separation from the world, and in his later years aroused controversy by his attempts to combine the movement's traditional focus on evangelism with an emphasis on the promotion of Christian values in the artistic, cultural and intellectual life of the universities. Though he presided over a period of remarkable growth in the Inter-Varsity movement, Sutherland's vision was too broad for some members of his constituency, and he resigned in 1969.[92] His successor (from 1972) was a Peruvian Baptist, Samuel Escobar, whose style of conservative evangelicalism was different again but emphatically not fundamentalist, as we shall see in chapter 6. In Canada, as elsewhere by the early 1970s, the unity of the 'new evangelicalism' was showing signs of strain.

Howard Guinness had left Canada in 1930 for Australia and New Zealand, where he was instrumental in establishing southern-hemisphere variants of the British Crusaders Union and Children's Special Service Mission (CSSM), as well as the Australian and New Zealand branches of the IVF in 1936.[93] In both countries there was an existing network of SCM groups, which became less recognizably evangelical in character after the war and declined steadily. By the late 1970s the SCM could count only a hundred members in the whole of Australia.[94] The term 'evangelical' in Australia became increasingly linked with the IVF tradition and its closely associated Anglican embodiment, especially in the diocese of Sydney under the long episcopate from 1933 to his death in 1958 of Howard Mowll, a Cambridge graduate who represented the CICCU tradition at its best.[95] The diocese of Melbourne, and specifically its Ridley College, developed a conservative evangelical reputation of a rather different kind; the college contributed greatly to the revival of conservative biblical scholarship through figures such as Leon Morris (1914–2006),

[92] Stackhouse, *Canadian Evangelicalism*, 98–108.

[93] For fuller accounts see Geoffrey R. Treloar, *The Disruption of Evangelicalism: The Age of Mott, Machen and McPherson* (Leicester: Inter-Varsity Press, forthcoming); also Stackhouse, *Canadian Evangelicalism*, 89–94; Lineham, *No Ordinary Union*; Pete Lowman, *The Day of His Power: A History of the International Fellowship of Evangelical Students* (Leicester: Inter-Varsity Press, 1983), 54–65.

[94] Piggin, *Evangelical Christianity in Australia*, 188.

[95] Mowll was president of CICCU in 1911–12 and Anglican primate of Australia from 1947 onwards. On Mowll see *BDE*, 455–456; Ian Breward, *A History of the Churches in Australasia* (Oxford: Oxford University Press, 2001), 304–306; Piggin, *Evangelical Christianity in Australia*, 128–133.

vice-principal from 1945 to 1959, and principal from 1964 to 1979, and the Old Testament scholar Francis I. Andersen.[96]

Nevertheless, the conservative evangelical tradition in Australia retained rather more of a fundamentalist flavour than was the case in post-war Britain. There were four reasons for this. First was the absence from Australian universities until the 1960s of departments of theology, a policy dictated by a secularist principle that had the effect of isolating theological scholarship from wider currents of intellectual life. Hence until this date there were no Australian equivalents to the English model of theological colleges that were appendages of university departments of theology, or to the Church of Scotland model of training its ministers through the universities.[97] In Australia, as in the United States, independent Bible colleges such as the Melbourne Bible Institute (founded in 1920) had originally set the tone of conservative evangelical life. Even the Anglican evangelical Moore College in Sydney and Ridley College in Melbourne retained a much sharper conservative edge through the 1950s and 1960s than did their counterparts in Oxford or Cambridge. A second reason was that the revival in the English-speaking world from the 1940s of Reformed theology was more pronounced and pervasive in Australia than in Britain. A growing number of Australian evangelicals began to describe themselves as Reformed. A Melbourne Presbyterian, Robert Swanton, founded the *Reformed Review* in 1942, which became an important organ of Reformed opinion.[98] The Anglican diocese of Sydney, through the influence of Moore College and a succession of strongly conservative archbishops, has become an increasingly influential expression of a strongly Reformed Anglican evangelicalism, which, though not styling itself as fundamentalist, is quite widely regarded by others as being implicitly such.[99] A third reason for the more strident tone of Australian evangelicalism in the 1940s and 1950s was ethnic and political. Australian governments until 1972 maintained a 'White Australia' policy, which imposed strict limits on Asian immigration. Leading evangelicals, notably T. C. Hammond and even Archbishop Mowll, were strong supporters of the policy, believing that it was essential to the preservation of the 'whole character of our people' and to Australia's Christian 'witness in the Pacific'.[100] As in South Africa and Rhodesia

---

[96] Piggin, *Evangelical Christianity in Australia*, 139; *BDE*, 448–449.

[97] For the introduction of university-taught or university-validated courses in theology from the 1960s see Piggin, *Evangelical Christianity in Australia*, 177–180.

[98] Ibid. 134–135.

[99] Ibid. 184–188.

[100] T. C. Hammond, 1940, cited in Breward, *History of the Churches*, 321–322. Hammond's

(Zimbabwe) during the final decades of white minority rule, misguided concerns for the integrity of Christian civilization, and an enduring belief in the
providential destiny of Britain's empire, led some Australian evangelicals from
the 1940s to the 1960s to adopt stances that were implicitly racist and akin
to the political preoccupations of American fundamentalists. A final factor
that imparted a fundamentalist and anti-Catholic colour to some strands of
post-war evangelicalism in Australia was the presence of significant numbers
of Irish Protestants, including Anglican clergy such as Hammond, who was
an office-holder in the Orange lodges of New South Wales and Australasia.[101]

Evangelicalism in New Zealand was less influenced by the Anglican tradition than was its Australian counterpart. With the exception of the diocese
of Nelson, Anglicanism in New Zealand has been more High Church in
character. Presbyterianism, particularly strong in the South Island, linked
New Zealand to Scotland rather than England, and, as in Scotland, encompassed a broadening theological range in this period. The principal of Knox
College in Dunedin caused a stir in 1966 when he wrote an article questioning whether the resurrection of Jesus could be described as a historical event
in the ordinary sense.[102] Conversely, New Zealand shared in the revival of
Reformed theology in the post-war era: a group of Presbyterians established
the Westminster Fellowship in 1950 to promote Puritan theology.[103] A group
influenced by Reformed perspectives, 'Presbyterian AFFIRM', formed in
1993, has sought to unite all conservative evangelicals in the Presbyterian
Church of Aotearoa New Zealand in promoting the renewal of biblical orthodoxy within the denomination.[104] Christian Brethren, who probably constitute
a higher percentage of the population than in any other country, have also
wielded a consistently strong influence on evangelical life and mission initiatives in New Zealand, especially through the closely related CSSM-Scripture

---

words were then reproduced almost exactly by Mowll in the Sydney Diocesan
Year Book in 1941; see Brian Fletcher, 'The Diocese of Sydney and the Shaping of
Australian Anglicanism 1940–62', in Geoffrey R. Treloar and Robert D. Linder (eds.),
*Making History for God: Essays on Evangelicalism, Revival and Mission in Honour of Stuart
Piggin* (Sydney: Robert Menzies College, 2004), 116.

[101] Fletcher, 'Diocese of Sydney', 112; *BDE*, 287.

[102] Allan K. Davidson and Peter J. Lineham (eds.), *Transplanted Christianity: Documents
Illustrating Aspects of New Zealand Church History* (Auckland: College Communications,
1987), 338–343.

[103] Breward, *History of the Churches*, 319.

[104] See http://www.presaffirm.org.nz (accessed 5 May 2012).

Union-Crusader and Inter-Varsity movements.[105] In the extent of Presbyterian and Brethren influence on the evangelical movement, and in the exceptionally important role played by interdenominational youth movements in defining evangelical identity, the evangelical trajectory in New Zealand since 1945 shows most similarities to that in Scotland.

Mark Hutchinson points out the irony that in the 1950s, while the Australian Stacey Woods was directing the Inter-Varsity movement in both Canada and the United States, two Americans – Charles H. Troutman and Warner Hutchinson – brought to Australia by the Second World War, were running Inter-Varsity in Australia and New Zealand.[106] Woods and Troutman went on in association with the Latin America Mission to work in Latin American universities, with ultimately far-reaching consequences, which chapter 6 will explore. The Inter-Varsity network disseminated a non-polemical and essentially rather British, even Anglican, style of conservative evangelicalism that transcended continental and imperial boundaries. The imperial chapter of British history drew to a close during the 1960s, but the Inter-Varsity movement, which had been diffused through the arteries of empire, continued to nourish the growth of international conservative evangelicalism into the post-colonial age.

---

[105] Peter J. Lineham, *There We Found Brethren: A History of Assemblies of Brethren in New Zealand* (Palmerston North: G. P. H. Society, 1977), 11, 159. In New Zealand CSSM, Scripture Union and Crusaders formed a single movement operating under different names.

[106] *BDE*, 750.

3. MISSION, EVANGELISM AND REVIVAL: THE GLOBALIZATION OF EVANGELICAL NETWORKS

From its beginnings in the 1730s the evangelical movement has transcended the boundaries of geography, language and politics. In the eighteenth and nineteenth centuries, however, the international character of evangelical linkages was apparent primarily in terms of the mutual exchange of spiritual and cultural influences across the North Atlantic between North America and Europe, particularly the British Isles. Asia, Australasia, Africa and (on a much lesser scale) Latin America were the objects of evangelical missionary activity, but only to a very limited extent were their Christian converts incorporated in the formal and informal networks that linked evangelicals of differing nationalities. In the twentieth century, and especially after 1945, the nature of evangelical internationalism extended and diversified, progressively incorporating all continents in its reach, and in some measure channelling spiritual influences from East to West and from South to North as well as in the reverse direction. The increasingly multidirectional nature of evangelical internationalism is most evident in the spheres of world mission, evangelism and the promotion of spiritual renewal or revival. This chapter will consider some of the most important expressions of this globalization of evangelical networks in relation to these three overlapping realms of activity. Chapter 7 will return at greater length to the subject of spiritual renewal with particular relation to the global charismatic and Pentecostal movements. It will be helpful first to place developments in evangelical internationalism in this period in a secular political context.

The Cold War and new dimensions of Christian internationalism

International relations in the years after 1945 were dominated by the 'Cold War', in which the two post-war superpowers of the United States and the Soviet Union competed for global predominance in both the military and ideological spheres. The starkly ideological character of the Cold War derived from the obvious fact that the Soviet Union was not simply communist in its economic system but aggressively atheistic in its religious stance. For many evangelicals in the United States, and to a lesser extent elsewhere, the defence of the gospel and the defence of the 'Free World' in the West now became closely associated causes. Harold Ockenga returned from a government-sponsored tour of newly liberated Europe in 1947 convinced that the future of western Christian civilization depended on an evangelical renewal of Christian life and national culture, first in the United States itself, and then, through the agency of American evangelical missions, in spiritually impoverished Europe. He saw Germany's devastated post-war condition as sadly symbolic of the spiritual degeneration of the nation where the Protestant Reformation had begun.[1] The allied zones of occupation – which would soon become 'West Germany' – rapidly became a significant mission field for North American fundamentalists owing to their strategic priority in the battle against the advance of atheistic communism. The Youth for Christ movement, whose bright and breezy evangelistic rallies for young people had become a feature of Chicago and a number of other American cities during the early 1940s, developed an international ministry after 1945 through campaigns linked to American military bases and chaplains in Europe, as also in parts of Asia and Latin America. In particular, Youth for Christ pioneered American evangel-istic activity in West Germany and soon extended its range from American servicemen to German youth.[2] New mission agencies, which aimed to reach Europe on both sides of the new Iron Curtain between 'Free' and communist Europe, were also formed, such as Greater Europe Mission (1949) and Trans-World Radio (1954).[3]

---

[1] George M. Marsden, *Reforming Fundamentalism: Fuller Seminary and the New Evangelicalism* (Grand Rapids: Eerdmans, 1987), 61–63; see also Joel Carpenter, *Revive Us Again: The Reawakening of American Fundamentalism* (New York: Oxford University Press, 1997), 149.

[2] Marsden, *Reforming Fundamentalism*, 51; Carpenter, *Revive Us Again*, 164–165, 178–179, 182; James Enns, 'Saving Germany – North American Protestants and Christian Mission to West Germany, 1945–1974' (University of Cambridge PhD thesis, 2012), 150–166.

[3] Carpenter, *Revive Us Again*, 182.

While the Second World War stirred American evangelicals to renewed and more geographically extensive efforts for world evangelization, the plight of the seven million displaced persons in Europe in 1945 prompted Christians in the mainline denominations in both North America and Britain to mount large-scale relief efforts. The agencies they established to accomplish this European relief work would in due course become the instruments of a wider form of Christian internationalism committed to the economic 'development' of poor nations outside Europe. For example, Lutheran World Relief began as a mechanism to enable American and Canadian Lutherans to support Lutheran refugees in Germany and Scandinavia, while in Britain what is now Christian Aid originated as 'Christian Reconstruction in Europe' and later became the Department of Interchurch Aid and Refugee Service of the British Council of Churches.[4] The origins of TEAR Fund (the Evangelical Alliance Relief Fund formed in 1968) similarly lie in a fund created by the Evangelical Alliance in 1959 (World Refugee Year) to provide relief for refugees: the original name of the fund was the Evangelical Alliance Refugee Fund ('EAR Fund').[5] Many evangelicals supported such relief efforts, and it would therefore be quite false to imply that evangelicals as a whole were indifferent to the crises of human displacement that became so marked a feature of the post-war world. In 1950 Bob Pierce, an intensely energetic Youth for Christ evangelist, founded World Vision in response to the plight of orphans he had encountered while conducting his campaigns in Korea during the Korean War: 'Let my heart be broken with the things that break the heart of God' was his motto. World Vision was to grow into one of the largest relief agencies in the world.[6] Nevertheless, in general terms a widening bifurcation of Christian internationalism is discernible in the post-war period. The mainline Protestant denominational missions that before the war had continued to promote evangelism in Asia and Africa, albeit as part of a broader package of 'civilization' and service, were profoundly unsettled by the accusations of imperialism levelled at missionaries by nationalist opinion in India and China, especially by the Chinese Communist Party, and the enforced missionary exodus from China that followed between 1949 and

---

[4] For the origins of Lutheran World Relief see Enns, 'Saving Germany', 57, 296.

[5] Timothy Chester, *Awakening to a World of Need: The Recovery of Evangelical Social Concern* (Leicester: Inter-Varsity Press, 1993), 13–14, 41. The name was changed in 1966 to the Evangelical Alliance Relief Fund, which in turn provided the basis for the creation of TEAR Fund in 1968.

[6] Carpenter, *Revive Us Again*, 182; Tim Stafford, 'The Colossus of Care' and 'Imperfect Instrument', *CT*, March 2005, 51–56.

1952.[7] Increasingly they left evangelistic initiatives to the emerging national churches, and concentrated their efforts on medical and educational work. As traditional missionary work lost its allure, the international conscience of liberal Protestants switched its focus to the new relief and development agencies, leaving the hitherto almost universally shared goal of world evangelization largely to fundamentalists and evangelicals.

In the United States the historic American sense of a God-given national destiny in the world, once firmly yoked to Christian ideas of redemption, was in the post-war period expressed in more secular terms, while still making use of the residual magnetism of Christian patterns of discourse. Thus President Harry S. Truman's inaugural address of 20 January 1949 outlining US policy for post-war reconstruction included 'a bold new program for making the benefits of our scientific advances and industrial progress available for the improvement and growth of underdeveloped areas'.[8] The structure of Truman's manifesto on behalf of 'underdeveloped areas' showed signs of his Baptist background: like an American evangelist's presentation of the old-time gospel it moved from a graphic description of the desperate state of the human condition to the declaration that 'for the first time in history', through American technological and economic capacity, the means of achieving lasting happiness and transformation existed, and culminated in an appeal to his hearers to take the necessary action that would ensure temporal salvation for the poor of the earth as well as continuing prosperity for the United States itself. Truman had set 'development' on its way to becoming a new global faith, no less powerful than the nineteenth-century creed of civilization.[9]

At first the target of economic development was as much war-torn Europe, through the Marshall Plan, as it was Africa or Asia. But from the later 1950s, in view of the German *Wirtschaftswunder* (miraculous economic recovery), the new international agenda of development could be directed exclusively to the 'Third World' (*Tiers Monde*), a term coined in 1952 by the French writer Alfred Sauvy to describe the tropical colonies or former colonies, and which came into widespread currency in the 1960s. Before long, 'development' itself

---

[7] Brian Stanley, *The Bible and the Flag: Protestant Missions and British Imperialism in the Nineteenth and Twentieth Centuries* (Leicester: Apollos, 1990), 14–16.

[8] *Public Papers of the Presidents of the United States, Harry S. Truman*, Year 1949, 5 (Washington, D.C.: United States Government Printing Office, 1964), 114–115.

[9] Gilbert Rist, *The History of Development: From Western Origins to Global Faith* (London: Zed Books, 1997), 70–80. Rist's exposition of Truman's address, while very insightful, is shaped by an anti-capitalist perspective that suspects the philosophy of 'development' as simply another strategy for perpetuating the economic hegemony of the West.

came under attack from theorists on the Left who, with some justice, saw it as a self-interested programme for the extension of capitalism. Nevertheless, as we shall see in chapter 6, evangelicals found themselves confronted with a choice between an approach to world mission that continued to give absolute priority to eternal salvation and one that reached some form of accommodation with the new emphasis on global humanitarianism and economic development. It is against this background that the international ministry of Billy Graham needs to be set.

The globalization of American evangelism: Billy Graham's international ministry

Billy Graham (1918–) was the only evangelical Christian in the second half of the twentieth century to attain what might be called global celebrity status. Indeed, no other evangelical in history has achieved such comprehensive and sustained world renown as Graham. The level of international public recognition he attained was dependent on the new visual medium of television, in which Graham and his advisory team became increasingly adept after their first television broadcast of *The Hour of Decision* in mid-1951 (his radio broadcasts under the same name had commenced in November 1950).[10] Where Graham led, others, such as Oral Roberts, Jerry Falwell, Jim Bakker and Pat Robertson, soon followed. However, none of the often crude and controversial 'televangelists' who came to national prominence in Graham's wake had the benefit of his unrivalled personal friendships with a series of American presidents, from Dwight L. Eisenhower to George W. Bush, though there were times when his close access to the White House threatened to impair his reputation, notably during the Watergate scandal that afflicted Richard Nixon's presidency in 1972–4.[11]

Even more than these factors, Graham's high public profile was a reflection of the unprecedented geographical reach of his ministry, which far surpassed even that of his predecessor, D. L. Moody (1837–99), whose campaigns outside the United States were restricted to four visits to the British Isles and occasional forays into Canada and Mexico.[12] Graham's style of mass evangelism

---

[10] William Martin, *A Prophet with Honor: The Billy Graham Story* (New York: William Morrow, 1991), 136–137.

[11] On Graham's relationship with Nixon during Watergate see ibid. 424–435.

[12] *BDE*; David W. Bebbington, *The Dominance of Evangelicalism: The Age of Spurgeon and Moody* (Leicester: Inter-Varsity Press, 2005), 42–43.

stood clearly enough in the American revivalist tradition of Charles G. Finney, Moody and Billy Sunday, and remained essentially consistent throughout his career, irrespective of the geographical and cultural context of his crusades. Almost equally consistent was the team at the heart of his campaigns, which remained substantially intact even from before the incorporation of the Billy Graham Evangelistic Association (BGEA) in 1950 right through to the close of the 1980s: George Wilson as business manager ruled the organization and its finances with an iron hand; Walter Smyth was head of team operations, latterly with special responsibility for Graham's international ministry; Grady Wilson was associate evangelist (though troubled by ill health from the late 1970s to his death in 1987); his elder brother, T. W. Wilson, was Graham's personal aide and travelling companion; Cliff Barrows led the singing of the classic crusade hymns, such as 'Blessed Assurance'; Tedd Smith played the piano; and George Beverley Shea sang the gospel solos in his rich bass-baritone voice.[13]

Gilbert Kirby, the British evangelical leader, aptly described Graham's team as analogous to the apostle Paul and his companions, who took the gospel to the strategic cities of Asia Minor in the first century.[14] Graham's international ministry began as early as 1946, when, as part of a Youth for Christ evangelistic team, he left Chicago on the first ever passenger flight to London to conduct a forty-six-day tour of Britain and Europe.[15] A further six-month tour of Britain followed in the autumn and winter of 1946, a campaign of continuous evangelism often forgotten owing to the much greater publicity that surrounded the Greater London Crusade at Harringay in 1954.[16] The first major European tour, covering Scandinavia, Germany and the Netherlands, was in 1955. Graham visited Japan and Korea as early as 1952, preaching mainly to American servicemen; his first public rallies in Asia were conducted in 1956, when he visited India, Formosa, Hawaii, Hong Kong, Japan, Korea and the Philippines. The year 1958 saw crusades in the Caribbean, Mexico and Guatemala. His first visit to Australia and New Zealand took place in 1959. A three-month tour of Africa and the first crusade in Brazil (Rio de Janeiro) followed in 1960. Graham maintained his punishing global itinerary of evangelism through the 1960s, 1970s and 1980s, and only began to scale down his overseas travel in the 1990s.[17]

---

[13] Martin, *Prophet with Honor*, 136, 559–573.

[14] Ibid. 573.

[15] Ibid. 95.

[16] Graham also visited Britain in 1948; on these early British campaigns see Ian Randall, 'Conservative Constructionist: The Early Influence of Billy Graham in England', *EvQ* 95 (1995), 312–318.

[17] See the chronology of events in the life of Billy Graham and of the history of the

The fact that Graham's international ministry spanned such a vast geographical range without any obvious cultural disasters is remarkable, given the fact that the style of his crusades was generally uniform in all contexts. Nevertheless, he was naturally most at home when ministering among white Americans or in cultures with some affinity to the United States. He was not afraid to take risks. His first German crusade in 1954 was held in the Berlin stadium where the 1936 Olympic Games had taken place under Hitler's patronage, and his second visit to Germany in 1955 included a crusade situated at the Zeppelin airfield in Nürnberg, where Hitler had once roused the Nazi crowds to frenzy. Some letters to the West German press took delight in drawing the unkind comparison, accusing Graham of manipulating the crowds, but these events were an undoubted success.[18] In other contexts there were harder lessons to learn.

In the United States itself the question of racially segregated seating was a keenly sensitive issue. Graham was criticized for having segregated seating in his southern crusades, where local custom appeared to demand it, and for accepting hospitality from prominent segregationists. Nevertheless, Graham first spoke out cautiously against segregation in 1952 in Jackson, Mississippi, and in the following year at a crusade in Chattanooga, Tennessee, he 'personally removed the rope separating the black and white sections of the audience. A photograph of the Chattanooga crusade, later used in a Graham promotional booklet, showed white and black audience members sitting together.'[19] This was a year before the American Supreme Court ruled that racial segregation in schools was unconstitutional. Thereafter, Graham insisted on integrated seating, yet relatively few African-Americans came to hear him, perhaps in protest against Graham's very hesitant attitude to the civil rights movement.[20]

For many years Graham refused to conduct campaigns in South Africa in protest against the racial segregation that would have been imposed by law on his meetings. He lifted his boycott only in 1973 when he agreed to preach at rallies in Durban and Johannesburg on condition they were multiracial in character: they were the first major multiracial public gatherings in South African history; Graham's public profile was such that the South African government

Billy Graham Evangelistic Association at http://www.wheaton.edu/bgc/archives/bgeachro/bgeachrono2.htm. (accessed 27 Apr. 2012).

[18] I owe these references to my former PhD student, James Enns.

[19] Steven P. Miller, 'Billy Graham, Civil Rights, and the Changing Postwar South', in Glenn Feldman (ed.), *Politics and Religion in the White South* (Lexington: University Press of Kentucky, 2005), 160–161.

[20] Martin, *Prophet with Honor*, 168–172, 409, 413–414.

had no option but to condone the rallies.[21] Outside South Africa and Rhodesia (Zimbabwe), where his audiences in February 1960 were mainly white, Graham found the African continent the least congenial of all the settings for his crusades. With the exception of Lagos, attendances at his meetings were modest, and he struggled to come to terms with African cultural perspectives, rehearsing the conventional missionary dictum that coming to Christ must entail a complete repudiation of 'tribal religion'. In 1960 Graham, along with almost all missionary and indeed scholarly opinion, showed no awareness of the fact that those who belonged to a 'primal' religious background were about to participate in perhaps the greatest movement of Christian conversion in church history.[22] With the exception of his visit to South Africa in 1973, Graham never again conducted a major campaign in Africa.

Graham's international ministry covered the globe, but its significance for the history of evangelicalism is not simply a matter of geographical diffusion. The BGEA spun a web of offices around the globe, encompassing key cities such as London, Berlin, Paris, Hong Kong, Tokyo, Sydney and Buenos Aires. Although Graham began to dismantle this international structure of offices after 1986,[23] the Association had by then played its part in making evangelicalism arguably as comprehensive in its global networks as was the official ecumenical movement represented by the World Council of Churches. The Christians of diverse nationalities who chose to associate themselves openly with the Graham crusades were selecting a certain family allegiance, positioning themselves on a particular section of the map of world Christianity. In Germany such supporters, who were mainly, though not entirely, from the Free Churches, began by the mid-1960s to describe themselves as those who were *evangelikal*, in distinction from those in the state Lutheran church who, ever since the Reformation, had been simply *evangelisch* (meaning 'Protestant').[24] Vocabulary had to change to reflect what was, for Germans, a new and specifically global style of Protestant identity.

---

[21] Ibid. 410–413; Michael Green, *Adventure of Faith: Reflections on Fifty Years of Christian Service* (Harrow: Zondervan, 2001), 213.

[22] See Kwame Bediako, *Christianity in Africa: The Renewal of a Non-Western Religion* (Edinburgh: T. & T. Clark, 1995).

[23] Martin, *Prophet with Honor*, 341, 519, 608.

[24] Erich Geldbach, "'Evangelisch", "Evangelical", and Pietism: Some Remarks on Early Evangelicalism and Globalization from a German Perspective', in M. Hutchinson and O. Kalu (eds.), *A Global Faith: Essays on Evangelicalism and Globalization* (Sydney: Centre for the Study of Australian Christianity, 1998), 157; Enns, 'Saving Germany', 188–189, 200–201, 230–231.

Globalization inevitably implied a measure of indigenization, though the BGEA appears to have made use of indigenous evangelists from India and Latin America only. The most distinguished of these was Dr Akbar Abdul-Haqq, a young Methodist scholar on the staff of the Henry Martyn Institute for Islamic Studies (then located in Lahore), who had been recruited, somewhat reluctantly, to translate for Graham at his rallies in New Delhi in February 1956. Graham was much impressed with Abdul-Haqq, believing him to be 'God's chosen vessel for this type of evangelism in the Orient'.[25] He invited him to the United States, where at Graham's crusade in Louisville in October Abdul-Haqq discovered 'a new fire' and his own calling to be an evangelist. By March 1957 Abdul-Haqq was conducting an evangelistic campaign of his own in Kanpur, which attracted crowds of up to 2,500. In 1960 he became an associate evangelist of the BGEA, and in that capacity exercised a highly influential evangelistic ministry in India and throughout the globe, which continued till his retirement in about 1998. As a regular evangelistic speaker on North American university and seminary campuses in the 1960s and 1970s Abdul-Haqq became a notable early example of what has come to be known as 'reverse mission'.[26] The BGEA also began in the 1960s to recruit Latin Americans to its staff, such as Fernando Vangiona from Buenos Aires.[27] In the 1990s many of the BGEA crusades in Latin America were led by Paul Finkenbinder, who was widely known as Hermano Pablo (Brother Paul), a leading Spanish-speaking evangelist born of missionary parents in Puerto Rico.[28]

At the end of October 1966 Graham convened the World Congress on Evangelism in Berlin as a celebration of the tenth birthday of *Christianity Today*. The representation granted to non-western Christians among a total delegate body of 1,262 was, in the eyes of some majority world delegates, too modest, but others present, such as Carl Henry, were favourably impressed by

---

[25] Robert J. McMahon, *To God Be the Glory: An Account of the Evangelical Fellowship of India's First Twenty Years, 1951–1971* (New Delhi: Christian Literature Institute, 1970), 28.

[26] Martin, *A Prophet with Honor*, 198, 404–405; McMahon, *To God Be the Glory*, 28–30. Al-Haqq's campaigns, like those of all the BGEA evangelists, can be traced via the chronology at http://www.wheaton.edu/bgc/archives/bgeachro/bgeachro02.htm (accessed 6 May 2012).

[27] Carl F. H. Henry and W. Stanley Mooneyham (eds.), *One Race, One Gospel, One Task: World Congress on Evangelism Berlin 1966: Official Reference Volumes: Papers and Reports*, 2 vols. (Minneapolis: World Wide Publications, 1967), I, 142.

[28] See http://www.wheaton.edu/bgc/archives/bgeachro/bgeachro02.htm (accessed 6 May 2012).

the presence of numerous national Christians involved in evangelism in their own countries. Two of the now converted Waodani (Auca) Indians who had murdered Nate Saint and four other American missionaries in the Ecuadorian jungle in 1956 were in attendance.[29] Stanley Mooneyham of the BGEA pulled off a major coup by securing Emperor Haile Selassie, 'born-again ruler' (as Carl Henry's autobiography assures us) of the ancient Christian state of Ethiopia, to address the gathering. Selassie, speaking in Amharic, urged that the present age was one above all others 'when it should be our prime duty to preach the Gospel of grace to all our fellow men and women'.[30] Although the six position papers presented at the congress were all delivered by Europeans or North Americans, 7 of the 24 main addresses or Bible studies were delivered by non-western Christians, of whom one was Abdul-Haqq, and, in all, 57 of the 200 speakers at the congress hailed from the majority world.[31] The Berlin congress thus made visible for the first time the fact that conservative evangelicalism could no longer be dismissed as a peculiarity of Anglo-American culture, but was now a vigorous religious force in all continents.[32] In terms of content of the addresses there was little dissent from the party line, imposed by J. Howard Pew, conservative heir of the Sun Oil fortune and the principal benefactor of the event, that too much emphasis on social action would constitute a dangerous diversion from the centrality of evangelism, which was, after all, the subject of the congress.[33] Eight years later, at the Lausanne Congress in Switzerland in 1974, as we shall see in chapter 6, the representation from the majority world was too large, and the independence of mind of some of its spokesmen too great, to permit this consensus to remain unchallenged.

The durability of the conversions registered during Graham's campaigns continues to be a matter of debate. At the crusades at Harringay in 1954 and Glasgow in 1955 the proportion of Graham's hearers who registered a decision to follow Christ was as low as 2.1%.[34] At Madison Square Garden,

---

[29] *MM*, Nov. 1966, 4; Martin, *Prophet with Honor*, 328; Carl F. H. Henry, *Confessions of a Theologian: An Autobiography* (Waco: Word Books, 1986), 259.

[30] *CT*, 11 Nov. 1966, 49; Henry, *Confessions of a Theologian*, 257.

[31] Henry and Mooneyham, *One Race, One Gospel*, table of contents in vols. I and II. Some of the 57 (a figure that excludes Dr Ishaya Audu from Nigeria, who was unable to present his address in person) spoke more than once.

[32] Henry, *Confessions of a Theologian*, 261.

[33] Martin, *Prophet with Honor*, 328–330.

[34] Callum G. Brown, *Religion and Society in Twentieth-Century Britain* (Harlow: Pearson Longman, 2006), 195. In Glasgow the figure was 2.2%.

New York, in 1957 the percentage was a little higher at 2.75%.[35] Evidence suggests that, at least in the western world, many of those who responded to the appeal to 'come forward', which invariably concluded Graham's meetings, were middle class and already on the fringes of church life; it also seems likely that a considerable proportion failed to sustain their Christian commitment in the long term.[36] Nevertheless, it remains undeniable that through Graham's long ministry countless numbers in many nations have found Christ. At the closing service of the Seoul crusade on 3 June 1973 Graham addressed what is probably the largest Christian gathering ever in history – a crowd estimated at 1.12 million people.[37] Over the course of the crusade 72,365 people registered decisions to follow Christ, and some churches grew significantly as a result: the Seoul Baptist church whose pastor, Billy Kim, was Graham's translator, grew by 30% almost immediately. But once again the apparently large number of recorded decisions for Christ represents only 2.25% of total aggregate attendance.[38] However spectacular the size of the crowds who thronged to hear Graham in South Korea, this extraordinary campaign must be judged to be more an indicator than a cause of the explosive growth the nation's Protestant churches experienced in the 1970s and 1980s. As a global religious phenomenon the Graham crusades were a striking measure of the increased salience of evangelical Christianity, but not one of its more important causes. In Britain perhaps the most significant result of the crusades in 1954–5 was the undoubted boost they gave to levels of evangelical recruitment to the ordained ministry, particularly in the Church of England, thus contributing substantially to the marked growth of evangelical influence in the British churches in the 1960s and 1970s.[39] There is no doubt that Billy Graham did more than anyone else to raise the public profile of evangelical Christianity throughout the globe. Equally, the organization he established has played an important part in the construction of a pan-evangelicalism that, for all its divisions, remains one of the most powerful forces in world Christianity.

---

[35] Martin, *Prophet with Honor*, 236.

[36] Randall, 'Conservative Constructionist', 331; Alister Chapman, 'Anglican Evangelicals and Revival 1945–59', in Kate Cooper and Jeremy Gregory (eds.), *Revival and Resurgence in Christian History*, SCH 44 (Woodbridge: Boydell & Brewer for the Ecclesiastical History Society, 2008), 313–314.

[37] Martin, *Prophet with Honor*, 418.

[38] Ibid. 419; aggregate attendance at the Seoul crusade was estimated at 3.21 million; http://www.wheaton.edu/bgc/archives/bgeachro/bgeachro02.htm (accessed 27 Apr. 2012).

[39] Randall, 'Conservative Constructionist', 330–331; Green, *Adventure of Faith*, 250.

Seeking a global evangelical identity: the World Evangelical Fellowship

The resurgence of internationalism stimulated by the end of the Second World War took the form of attempts to create a new and more stable world order in the spheres of economics and politics, through the World Bank and International Monetary Fund, established in 1944–5, and the United Nations, whose Charter was signed on 26 June 1945. This secular internationalism had its Christian parallels in the creation of the World Council of Churches (1948) and the World Evangelical Fellowship (WEF, 1951), which in their differing ways sought to create a new spiritual order of global Christian fellowship. The origins of the WEF can be traced to the vision of the founders of the National Association of Evangelicals (NAE) for the renewal and better coordination of distinctively evangelical witness throughout the globe.[40] The NAE, formally organized in Chicago in May 1943, almost from the outset adopted horizons that were broader than the United States alone. In 1946 Dr J. Elwin Wright, its first executive secretary, toured Europe, consulting evangelical leaders in England, France, Belgium, the Netherlands, Germany and Switzerland. As a result of these initial contacts a meeting was held in Clarens, Switzerland, in 1948, to which the NAE invited leaders from the various European branches of the Evangelical Alliance, including the veteran general secretary of the Evangelical Alliance in Britain, H. Martyn Gooch. The British Evangelical Alliance still bore the grandiose title of the 'World's Evangelical Alliance (British Organization)' but in reality was at a low ebb in its history and had not summoned an international conference since 1907.[41] The Clarens meeting discussed the possibility of convening a world conference of evangelicals, but deemed it inadvisable or impractical at this stage. However, two years later, on 7–10 March 1950, an international delegate conference was held at Hildenborough Hall, a residential conference centre in Kent established in 1945 by the British evangelist Tom Rees.[42] Delegates

---

[40] On the origins of the WEF see David M. Howard, *The Dream That Would Not Die: The Birth and Growth of the World Evangelical Fellowship 1846–1986* (Exeter: Paternoster Press, 1986), 25–32.

[41] Ibid. 26; J. B. A. Kessler, Jr., *A Study of the Evangelical Alliance in Great Britain* (Goes, Netherlands: Oosterbaan & Le Cointre, 1968), 79–88; Ian Randall, 'Schism and Unity: 1905–1966', in Steve Brady and Harold Rowdon (eds.), *For Such a Time as This: Perspectives on Evangelicalism, Past, Present and Future* (London: Evangelical Alliance; Milton Keynes: Scripture Union, 1996), 163–170.

[42] On Rees (1912–70) see Jean Rees, *His Name Was Tom: The Biography of Tom Rees* (London: Hodder & Stoughton, 1971).

from twelve European countries, including Britain, attended, alongside representatives of the NAE. An international committee was set up under the chairmanship of Lieutenant-General Sir Arthur Smith, a British army officer who had recently retired after a distinguished career culminating in India, where he was the officer-in-command of British forces at the time of independence in 1947.[43] A similar American conference followed from 4 to 8 September at Gordon Divinity School (now Gordon-Conwell Seminary), in Boston. This recommended the formation of an International Association of Evangelicals with the threefold purpose of witnessing to 'evangelical and historic Christianity', encouraging and promoting fellowship among evangelicals, and stimulating evangelism and promoting united evangelical action.[44]

As a result of the two meetings held in 1950 at Hildenborough Hall and Gordon Seminary, J. Elwin Wright and Clyde W. Taylor of the NAE embarked on a world tour to lay the foundations for the projected new instrument of global evangelical cooperation. Between 12 October 1950 and 28 January 1951 they visited Tokyo, Manila, Hong Kong, Bangkok, Calcutta, Nagpur, Akola, Bombay, Fatehpur, Allahabad, New Delhi, Beirut, Damascus, Amman, Jericho and Jerusalem, as well as a number of European cities.[45] It should be noted that they did not visit Australasia, Latin America or Africa. In response to their findings, the international committee formed at Hildenborough Hall summoned an International Convention of Evangelicals to meet at Woudschoten in the Netherlands on 5–11 August 1951. At the Woudschoten meeting, attended by ninety-one delegates from twenty-one countries, the World Evangelical Fellowship was formed. A general committee was established under the presidency of Lieutenant-General Sir Arthur Smith, and two co-secretaries were appointed: J. Elwin Wright from the NAE and Roy Cattell, who had worked both for Tom Rees and the IVF and had succeeded Gooch as general secretary of the British Evangelical Alliance in 1949. The purpose of the new body was defined in similar terms to those used by the Boston meeting, but using language based on the first chapter of Paul's letter to the Philippians, which John Stott had suggested to A. Jack Dain, present in his capacity as overseas secretary of the British Evangelical Alliance:

---

[43] On Smith (1890–1977) see *Who Was Who, 1971–1980*, 2nd ed. (London: A. & C. Black, 1989), 736. Smith was for twenty-three years president of the highly influential Crusaders Union youth movement in Britain; see Jack D. Watford, *Yesterday and Today: A History of Crusaders* (n.p. [Crusaders Union], 1995), 106–107.

[44] Howard, *Dream That Would Not Die*, 28.

[45] Ibid. 29.

to promote the furtherance of the gospel, the defence and confirmation of the gospel, and fellowship in the gospel.[46]

From 30 October to 9 December 1951 Sir Arthur Smith and Dr Oswald J. Smith, pastor of the Peoples Church in Toronto, held a series of mass meetings across the United States to introduce the WEF to the evangelical public. At the end of that year J. Elwin Wright and the NAE president, Dr Paul S. Rees, embarked on a world tour that spanned 31,000 miles and twenty-four countries.[47] On the face of it, the prospects appeared bright for international evangelical cooperation in mission on a scale hitherto unknown. The new organization was not lacking in ambition. In 1956 it even contemplated making an application to the United Nations Organization for recognition as a corresponding member, though after a visit by Clyde Taylor to the UN headquarters in New York, and on further reflection, it was decided not to pursue such an exalted goal.[48] The effectiveness of the WEF as an expression of global evangelical identity was, however, hampered by three closely related restrictions.

The first problem was the lack of congruence between the theological and ecclesiastical perspectives of many, though not all, of the Fellowship's American supporters, who were unsympathetic to evangelicals holding membership in historic and theologically 'mixed' denominations, and the reality that a large segment of the world evangelical constituency belonged to such denominations. A number of continental European delegations at the Woudschoten conference had objected to the use in the new organization's basis of faith of the world 'infallible' with reference to Scripture; in consequence, a European Evangelical Alliance was formed independently of the WEF, and did not affiliate until 1968.[49] The lack of congruence was, however, most marked and serious in relation to the continent of Africa. The WEF opened an Africa office in Nairobi in 1962 under the leadership of Kenneth Downing of the Africa Inland Mission (AIM). This led in 1968 to the formation of the Association of Evangelicals of Africa and Madagascar (AEAM). The AEAM tended to reflect the perspectives of members of the 'separatist' denominations founded by non-denominational American missions, such as the African Inland Church established by the AIM in Kenya. However, the majority of evangelical Christians in Africa in this period belonged to historic

---

[46] Ibid. 31–32.

[47] Ibid. 33.

[48] Ibid. 47.

[49] Ibid. 30, 34. The objection was presumably that 'infallible' could be taken to imply a rigid doctrine of inerrancy.

churches, many of which owed their origin to British missions, particularly Anglican and Presbyterian ones. This was notably the case in Kenya where the National Council of Churches was so overwhelmingly evangelical in membership that the case for the creation of a separate national evangelical fellowship was far from clear. As a result, there were tensions in the WEF in the late 1960s between British spokesmen, such as A. Morgan Derham of the Evangelical Alliance, and leaders of American missions belonging to the Interdenominational Foreign Missions Association (IFMA) or the NAE-related Evangelical Foreign Missions Association (EFMA).[50]

Secondly, the resourcing of the WEF has been a perpetual problem. The Fellowship's income has been very largely dependent on funds contributed in the United States: in November 1976 it was reported that 98.5% of income of the WEF international office for the past year had been supplied from the United States, and that membership fees from other WEF national bodies made up less than 0.5% of total income.[51] Until 1975 the WEF had to function without any full-time salaried staff: the first full-time executive officer, Waldron Scott, an American who had served with the Navigators in the Middle East, made valiant efforts to expand the support base and internationalize the leadership of the WEF, but resigned in December 1980, having concluded that 'unity and cooperation are close to the very bottom of the priority lists of most evangelical leaders' in the western nations, and in the United States in particular.[52]

Thirdly, as a body brought into existence largely through the initiative of the NAE and being heavily funded, and to a lesser extent staffed, from American sources, the Fellowship struggled to divest itself of the image of being an extension into the global arena of a distinctively American and strongly conservative brand of evangelicalism. This problem became most acute after the Lausanne Congress of 1974 had uncovered the extent to which evangelicalism was becoming dissociated from its historic North Atlantic centre of gravity, as we shall see in chapter 6. Hence, when in March 1980 the WEF assembly, meeting at High Leigh conference centre in England, invited

---

[50] Ibid. 67–77. The IFMA was founded in 1917 as an association of interdenominational missions; see Edwin L. Frizen, Jr., *Seventy-Five Years of IFMA, 1917–1992: The Nondenominational Missions Movement* (Pasadena: William Carey Library, 1992). The EFMA originated in 1946 as the missionary arm of the NAE. It changed its name in 2007 to Mission Exchange.

[51] Howard, *Dream That Would Not Die*, 117.

[52] Ibid. 124–126, 140. Scott's successor, David Howard, faced similar difficulties; see ibid. 150–155.

the Lausanne Committee for World Evangelization to constitute itself as the evangelistic task force of WEF, the response from the Lausanne body was distinctly unenthusiastic.[53] During the 1980s the gap between the two bodies narrowed considerably, in part because the Lausanne movement appeared to step back a little from the evangelical radicalism it had demonstrated in 1974,[54] but mainly because the WEF, through its Theological Commission under the creative leadership of a New Zealander, Bruce Nicholls, undertook some serious theological thinking on the subject of holistic mission.[55] Nevertheless, to this day, the WEF and the Lausanne Committee remain as distinct but overlapping expressions of global evangelical identity.

An inclusive and revival-focused evangelicalism: the Evangelical Fellowship of India

In the course of their Asian tour in 1950–1 J. Elwin Wright and Clyde Taylor participated in the inaugural meeting of one of the first national constituent bodies of the WEF – the Evangelical Fellowship of India. The EFI was constituted at a meeting at Yeotmal Bible School in Pune from 16 to 18 January 1951, attended by sixty-three people, of whom only about six were Indians. One of those present, A. Jack Dain, general secretary of the Bible and Medical Missionary Fellowship (now Interserve) as well as overseas secretary of the British Evangelical Alliance, was appointed chairman. Dain had been converted in India, had served there as a missionary, and during the war had been an officer in the Royal Indian Navy, being liaison officer at the India Office in London at the time of the transfer of power in 1947.[56]

When the constitution was debated at the Pune meeting, there was a move to exclude from membership any missions or churches connected to the National Christian Council of India or other ecumenical bodies. Dain was unsympathetic to this extreme separatist view, but sought to be an impartial chairman. One American missionary, Everett Cattell, and one British, Canon Sam Burgoyne, both pleaded for the EFI to be kept open to all convinced

---

[53] Ibid. 133. The actual phrase used by the WEF assembly was 'Evangelical Task Force', but presumably 'evangelistic' was meant.

[54] See chapter 6 below, 177–178.

[55] See the papers of the Commission's consultation at Wheaton College in 1983 on 'The Nature and Mission of the Church', published as Bruce Nicholls (ed.), *The Church: God's Agent for Change* (Exeter: Paternoster Press for the World Evangelical Fellowship, 1986).

[56] McMahon, *To God Be the Glory*, 6, and photograph facing p. 8.

evangelicals, irrespective of their church affiliation. By a substantial majority their arguments prevailed. The constitution included the clause 'It is understood that membership shall not adversely affect other affiliations which members may have.'[57] Cattell was elected as both chairman and executive secretary of the EFI. A member of the American Friends (Quaker) mission, he was subsequently co-opted to the executive committee of the National Christian Council [of India], and found this to be 'a very rich experience of being liaison between the evangelicals and the N.C.C., interpreting each to the other'.[58] Yet his conservative evangelical credentials were such that he later became president of the WEF executive committee.[59] One of the first and most important member bodies of the WEF had set its own course in a direction appropriate to the Indian church context and that contrasted with the more exclusive stance later adopted by the AEAM. As the principal of the Yeotmal Bible School, Dr Frank Kline, put it in an address to the Pune meeting, 'we are not interested in wasting time, energy or money in hunting and denouncing heresies . . . nor are we desirous of duplicating functions well performed by the National Christian Council'. Rather, the EFI was interested in 'emphasizing Biblical revelation-truth in the most positive manner we know, in the assurance that this is the best way to overcome heresy'.[60] With backing from the EFI, the Yeotmal Bible School was reconstituted in September 1953 as the Union Biblical Seminary, a degree-level institution that has since established its reputation as the leading evangelical theological college in the subcontinent.

The EFI instituted the Evangelical Literature Fellowship of India in 1954, and later set up its own programmes of Christian education and radio ministry.[61] One of those converted under Billy Graham's ministry in India in 1956 (a tour made at the invitation of the EFI) was Thomas Samuel, originally from Kerala, and at that time working in Delhi. Samuel became involved in the Evangelical Literature Fellowship and spent a period studying at the new Union Biblical Seminary in Pune. In 1963 he heard about the campaigns in Europe for the large-scale distribution of evangelistic literature that a graduate of Moody Bible Institute, George Verwer, had organized for young people in the previous summer under the name 'Operation Mobilisation' (OM), and was planning to repeat in 1963. Samuel raised the funds to travel to France to

---

[57] Ibid. 7–8.

[58] Ibid. 11.

[59] Howard, *Dream That Would Not Die*, 74.

[60] McMahon, *To God Be the Glory*, 9.

[61] Ibid. 32–35.

attend the conference that launched the 1963 campaign. There he sowed in Verwer's mind the idea of undertaking similar literature evangelism in India. Samuel wrote an article describing the work of OM, 'Miracles in Europe', for the information bulletin of the Evangelical Literature Fellowship of India.[62] On New Year's Day 1964 the first OM evangelistic team crossed the West Pakistan border into India and headed for Delhi.[63] The connection Samuel had forged became the basis for an Indian mission venture that indigenized rapidly, principally through contacts with the Brethren-style congregations connected to the Indian evangelist Bakht Singh.[64] The work of OM in India experienced remarkable growth. Within three years OM was operating in most of the states of India, and under the leadership of Indian nationals. By the 1990s India had become the largest national provider of mission personnel for a mission agency whose work involved some 2,500 staff and spanned 90 countries.[65]

The EFI aimed to be inclusive of all conservative evangelical opinion in India, but it was no less strongly committed to seeking 'revival' in India's Christian community. At one of Wright and Taylor's first meetings on their tour, at Allahabad in December 1950, Wright gave an account of recent 'revivals' in America, including mention of a young evangelist called Billy Graham. He remarked that 'revival could sweep India in the same way, but not until the Christians here paid the same price in prayer and fasting that was being paid in the United States today'.[66] Initially, therefore, the expectation of revival adhered to an American model and assumed American leadership. With time, however, perspectives began to change. One of the participants in the second EFI conference at Akola in January 1952 was Norman Burns of the Dohnavur Fellowship in Tamil Nadu.[67] In 1949 he had visited East Africa

---

[62] Ian M. Randall, *Spiritual Revolution: The Story of OM* (Milton Keynes: Authentic Media, 2008), 45–46, 235.

[63] Ibid. 48. From independence in 1947 until 1971 Pakistan comprised two territories – West Pakistan, comprising what is now Pakistan, and East Pakistan, which seceded in 1971 to form Bangladesh.

[64] On Bakht Singh see J. Edwin Orr, *Evangelical Awakenings in Southern Asia* (Minneapolis: Bethany Fellowship, 1975), 167–169, 178–179; Norman P. Grubb, *Once Caught, No Escape: My Life Story* (London: Lutterworth Press, 1969), 149–152.

[65] In 1994 India supplied 437 out of 2,450 personnel. By 2000 OM had 2,800 personnel. Randall, *Spiritual Revolution*, 63–64, 155, 197.

[66] McMahon, *To God Be the Glory*, 5–6.

[67] For a brief introduction to the Dohnavur Fellowship, founded by the Ulster Presbyterian Amy Carmichael (1867–1951), see the *BDE* entry on Carmichael. The Fellowship was influenced by the Keswick holiness tradition, and worked especially

and been deeply affected by the East African Revival which had first surfaced in the Keswick-oriented Ruanda Mission in Rwanda and Uganda in the early 1930s.[68] He felt led by the Spirit to travel the 1,200 miles to Akola, and shared a train compartment with a fellow-missionary who urged him to speak of his African experiences at the conference. This he did, referring to the African emphasis on the necessity of openness before God and one another, 'keeping short accounts' with God, and being continually cleansed by the blood of Jesus.[69] The main speaker, Paul S. Rees, acknowledged that 'many of us in America feel that we must readjust the two concepts of revival and evangelism. We have had a deal of confusion regarding those two terms and the ideas they represent.' Rees described Billy Graham's mission to his own home city of Minneapolis in January 1951 as evangelism, and not revival, even though it was 'the most powerful single challenge that it had for a generation'. In response to the ministry of Burns and Rees, spiritual need was openly confessed, mutual apologies were offered, reconciliation effected, and 'a general melting' took place.[70]

The ripples of the East African Revival had reached the shores of India. The Akola conference issued an invitation to the Revival's chief promoter, the Anglican medical missionary J. E. ('Joe') Church (1899–1989), to send a team to India in the coming summer. A letter from Sam Burgoyne of the EFI assured Joe Church that 'the flame has leapt the seas' and that the time was ripe for spreading the revival message in India. Church and his leading Ugandan associate, William Nagenda (1912–73), arrived in Madras in May 1952, and conducted revival meetings at Madras, Kotagiri and Coonoor in South India, and at Calcutta, Darjeeling and Landour in the north.[71] In East Africa the Revival message that all, whether black or white, needed openly

with children, and young women rescued from temple prostitution.

[68] There is now a large literature on the East African Revival; for surveys see Brian Stanley, 'The East African Revival: African Initiative Within a European Tradition', *Chm* 92 (1978), 6–22; Kevin Ward, 'The East African Revival of the Twentieth Century: The Search for an Evangelical African Christianity', in Cooper and Gregory, *Revival and Resurgence*, 365–387; Kevin Ward and Emma Wild-Wood (eds.), *The East African Revival: History and Legacies* (Farnham: Ashgate, 2012).

[69] McMahon, *To God Be the Glory*, 13–14.

[70] Ibid. 15–16.

[71] Ibid. 17; J. E. Church, *Quest for the Highest: An Autobiographical Account of the East African Revival* (Exeter: Paternoster Press, 1981), 239–240. Nagenda's father was a leading Bagandan chief who acted as one of the regents of the kingdom of Buganda when the British deported the Kabaka (ruler) in 1955.

to confess their sin and 'walk in the light' proved a searching challenge to missionary paternalism. It may not be wholly coincidental that at the next EFI annual conference in 1953 an approach was made to Imchaba Bendang Wati, a young Baptist Bible college teacher from Nagaland, a predominantly Christian state in north-east India, with a view to his becoming the 'national secretary' of EFI, to serve under Cattell as executive secretary. Wati eventually agreed, and served as national secretary till 1957, when he succeeded Cattell as executive secretary.[72] In 1968 Wati became the first non-Westerner to be elected president of the WEF.[73] Although the proportion of Indian nationals attending EFI conferences rose steadily through the 1950s, in 1961 Wati was still the only Indian among the ten full-time secretaries on the EFI staff.[74] But the foreign missionary era in India was rapidly approaching its end. The last year in which a western missionary chaired the EFI conference was 1964, and in 1965 the EFI established its own Indian Evangelical Mission under the leadership of a South Indian Methodist, Dr Theodore Williams.[75] This has grown into one of the largest indigenous Indian mission agencies, with some 580 missionaries working throughout India and abroad by 2010.[76]

The pursuit of 'revival' remained a prominent feature of EFI conferences through the 1950s and early 1960s. The 1954 conference at Deolali in Maharashtra was attended by two well-known apostles of revival – Norman Grubb, of the Worldwide Evangelization Crusade, and J. Edwin Orr, an Ulsterman based in southern California who had researched the 1858–60 evangelical awakening in Britain for his doctorate at Oxford.[77] The conference was marked by spontaneous outbursts of confession, testimony and praise. It was also distinguished by the fervent singing by a Naga Baptist choir of a new arrangement of 'How Great Thou Art', originally a Swedish hymn that

---

[72] McMahon, *To God Be the Glory*, 17–31. For the remarkable growth of Baptist churches in Nagaland see Frederick S. Downs, *The Mighty Works of God: A Brief History of the Council of Baptist Churches in North East India: The Mission Period, 1836–1950* (Gauhati: Christian Literature Society, 1971).

[73] Howard, *Dream That Would Not Die*, 89–90.

[74] McMahon, *To God Be the Glory*, 40–41.

[75] Ibid. 45–47.

[76] See http://www.iemoutreach.org (accessed 20 Apr. 2012).

[77] On Grubb (1895–1993) and his links with the East African Revival, see his *Once Caught, No Escape*, 153–158; and Church, *Quest for the Highest*, 236, 244. On Orr (1912–87) see A. J. Appasamy, *Write the Vision! Edwin Orr's Thirty Years of Adventurous Service* (London: Marshall, Morgan & Scott, 1965), and http://www.jedwinorr.com/bio.htm (accessed 20 Apr. 2012).

had been translated, first into Russian, and from that into English by Stuart Hine in 1927. The hymn, introduced to India in about 1952, so impressed Edwin Orr that he popularized it among the Christian public on his return to the United States. A music publisher took it up, using the harmonization first used at Deolali. With the aid of George Beverley Shea's solos it soon became a favourite at the Billy Graham crusades and one of the most widely sung hymns in evangelical churches on both sides of the Atlantic.[78]

By the 1960s Indian evangelical Christians were taking note of spiritual renewal of a more distinctly Pentecostal variety. Pentecostalism in South India dates from the 1920s, but only from the late 1940s did the movement begin to spread from its original base in Kerala to Tamil Nadu and Andhra Pradesh. By the 1960s South Indian Pentecostalism was developing into a vigorous indigenous movement.[79] The first signs of charismatic renewal in the United States were also reported in the EFI magazine *Evangelical Fellowship*, and the EFI conference at Lucknow in 1963 was devoted to the topic of the Holy Spirit. However, the EFI later became more cautious about the growing Pentecostal and charismatic movements in India itself. In so far as the Fellowship's early expectations of 'revival' in India have been fulfilled, the fulfilment has taken a more overtly Pentecostal form than many of the EFI pioneers anticipated.[80] Whether through its own rapidly expanding body of national missionaries, or through the impact made on Westerners by encounters with the vibrant spirituality of Christians from the north-eastern states, or through the extending influence of Indian Pentecostalism, evangelical Christianity in India was now making its own distinctive contributions to world evangelicalism.

Walking the Calvary road: the East African Revival and its message

India was not alone in being touched by the influence of the East African Revival. From 1944 through to the late 1970s a series of international tours

---

[78] McMahon, *To God Be the Glory*, 19; Orr, *Evangelical Awakenings in Southern Asia*, 180. McMahon and Orr both imply that Orr was the first to introduce the hymn to the US, but http://christianmusic.suite101.com/article.cfm/stuart_hine_how_great_thou_art (accessed 20 Apr. 2012) suggests that it was first sung in the US at the Stoney Brook Bible Conference in Long Island in 1951. In 1967 Elvis Presley recorded his own version of the hymn in his gospel album *How Great Thou Art*.

[79] Michael Bergunder, *The South Indian Pentecostal Movement in the Twentieth Century* (Grand Rapids: Eerdmans, 2008), 34–85, 92–106.

[80] McMahon, *To God Be the Glory*, 43–44.

by both missionary and African leaders of the Revival disseminated its characteristic emphases beyond East Africa and eventually to all corners of the globe, from Brazil in the west to the Far East. The sequence began with a series of meetings in Cape Town in October–November 1944 conducted by Joe Church and two missionary colleagues, Lawrence Barham and Godfrey Hindley: the South African authorities refused entry to the originally projected multiracial team.[81] The first tour outside Africa was to England, France, Germany and Switzerland in the summer of 1947. Church, Barham, William Nagenda and Yosiya Kinuka (Church's senior hospital assistant at Gahini in Rwanda) made up the team. Their ministry in England began with an end-of-term garden party for the CICCU at Tyndale House in Cambridge, and included a visit to the Keswick Convention, where Nagenda spoke.[82] Two more Europe tours followed in 1948 and 1949. During the 1948 tour Church established close links both with Martyn Lloyd-Jones's Westminster Chapel and with All Souls, Langham Place, whose rector, Harold Earnshaw-Smith, was chairman of the Ruanda Mission Council.[83] In November 1951 Church took a team to Nyasaland (Malawi) for a month-long tour sponsored by the Church of Scotland Mission, the Dutch Reformed Church and two interdenominational missions, the Zambezi Mission and the South Africa General Mission.[84] A series of meetings in Angola in March 1952 was followed almost immediately by the tour of India in May.[85]

The tours made by Church, Nagenda and their associates were not the only channel by which the Revival message spread beyond Africa. Also crucial was the influence of two short books – Roy and Revel Hession's *The Calvary Road* (1950) and Norman P. Grubb's *Continuous Revival* (1952).[86] At Easter 1947 Lawrence Barham and two other Rwanda missionaries, Bill Butler and Peter Guillebaud, testified at a young people's conference at Matlock in Derbyshire, England, to the spiritual transformation they had experienced through encoun-

---

[81]   Church, *Quest for the Highest*, 209–210; Richard K. MacMaster with Donald R. Jacobs, *A Gentle Wind of God: The Influence of the East Africa Revival* (Scottdale, Pa.: Herald Press, 2006), 83–84. Church's papers, which are housed in the Henry Martyn Centre in Cambridge, are a rich resource for students of the Revival and its international diffusion.

[82]   Church, *Quest for the Highest*, 227.

[83]   Ibid. 229.

[84]   Ibid. 237.

[85]   Ibid. 238–244.

[86]   Roy and Revel Hession, *The Calvary Road* (London: Christian Literature Crusade, 1950); Norman P. Grubb, *Continuous Revival* (London: Christian Literature Crusade, 1952).

ter with the Revival. The invitation to the Ruanda Mission to supply three speakers had come from Roy Hession (1908–92), an evangelist with the National Young Life Campaign. To his dismay, Hession realized at Matlock that the spiritual reality of which they were speaking was unknown in his own experience. After much heart-searching, Hession found his own way to the repentance and in-filling of the Spirit described by Barham, Butler and Guillebaud. The conference proved a watershed in the lives of Hession and his wife, Revel. They began a small monthly paper, *Challenge*, designed to call Christians to a deeper experience of Christ. The demand proved such that in 1950 they incorporated a series of articles from *Challenge* in a book, *The Calvary Road*, published by Christian Literature Crusade in both London and Fort Washington, Pennsylvania. Within two years the American edition had been reprinted five times.[87]

The Hessions' book, which has remained in print to this day, did more than any other publication to popularize the crucicentric spirituality of the East African Revival throughout the English-speaking world. It did much to shape the distinctive brand of passionate Christian discipleship that George Verwer nurtured among the thousands of young people who served in OM, with its emphasis on continual repentance and complete surrender to Christ.[88] In Australia it had a profound impact on Geoffrey Bingham, incumbent of Holy Trinity Church, Millers Point, in Sydney, from 1953, who began holding revival meetings on the East African pattern, and saw hundreds flocking to his services.[89] Although the excitement at Miller's Point proved short-lived, Australia's connections with the Revival became very close. In 1959 the Australian Church Missionary Society brought two East Africans to the country – Yohana Omari, assistant bishop of the diocese of central Tanganyika, and a little-known Ugandan teacher at the Alliance High School in Dodoma named Festo Kivengere. Kivengere's month-long ministry among aboriginal people in the Northern Territory had a lasting impact, stimulating not simply revival phenomena but also the inculturation of the faith into aboriginal forms. Years later, in 1970 and 1978, Kivengere returned to Australia, on the second occasion on behalf of the BGEA in order to prepare the way for the 1979 Graham crusades in Sydney and Melbourne. One result of his 1978 visit was a trip to Tanzania by three aboriginal Christian leaders, which gave them renewed confidence to express their faith in ways that departed

---

[87] MacMaster with Jacobs, *Gentle Wind of God*, 120–122; Roy Hession, *My Calvary Road: One Man's Pilgrimage* (Fearn: Christian Focus, 1996), 94–106.

[88] Randall, *Spiritual Revolution*, 43, 105, 107.

[89] Colin Reed, *Walking in the Light: Reflections on the East African Revival and Its Link to Australia* (Brunswick East, Victoria: Acorn Press, 2007), 153–155.

from European patterns. Aboriginal Christian communities in the Northern Territory experienced a revival in 1979 that owed an obvious debt to East African influences.[90]

The British tour that Church, Nagenda, Kinuka and Barham undertook in 1947 was funded by the Worldwide Evangelization Crusade (WEC). Through his extensive contacts with the East African team, Norman Grubb, executive secretary of WEC, became an enthusiast for the Revival. Grubb's booklet *Continuous Revival* achieved a very wide international circulation.[91] The rapid American sales of both *The Calvary Road* and *Continuous Revival*, coupled with an offer of sponsorship from Grubb and WEC, encouraged Church, Nagenda, Roy and Revel Hession to embark on a six-month tour of North America at the end of May 1953. They spoke in Pennsylvania, New York and Washington, at Harold Ockenga's Park Street Church in Boston, Oswald Smith's Peoples Church in Toronto, in Detroit, Chicago (at Moody Bible Institute and A. W. Tozer's Southside Christian and Missionary Alliance church), and at Paul Rees's First Covenant Church in Minneapolis.[92]

In Pennsylvania the ministry of Church and his team was focused on the Mennonite community. The American Mennonite mission in Tanganyika (modern Tanzania) on the eastern shores of Lake Victoria had been caught up in the Revival from August 1942.[93] As missionaries returned to the Mennonite heartland in eastern Pennsylvania after the end of the World War, they perceived the Revival message as heaven-sent medicine for a community that was being torn by the threat of nascent theological liberalism, suffering from legalistic attempts to preserve traditional Mennonite standards of simplicity, and conflicted over lapses from its historical pacifism during the Second World War. The East African team's visit to Pennsylvania in 1953 forged a relationship that proved of lasting significance both for the American Mennonite community and for the Revival movement in East Africa. When Donald and Anna Ruth Jacobs, a young Mennonite missionary couple, arrived in Tanganyika in 1954, at a time when the anti-colonial Mau Mau crisis in neighbouring Kenya posed great challenges to Christian faithfulness, they were immediately struck by the resonance between the fearless discipleship of the Revival brethren and their own Anabaptist tradition: 'I have met the

---

[90] Ibid. 201–205, 226–230; Anne Coomes, *Festo Kivengere: A Biography* (Eastbourne: Monarch, 1990), 185–190, 273, 386.

[91] Church, *Quest for the Highest*, 236; MacMaster with Jacobs, *Gentle Wind of God*, 119–120.

[92] Church, *Quest for the Highest*, 244–245; MacMaster with Jacobs, *Gentle Wind of God*, 140–141.

[93] MacMaster with Jacobs, *Gentle Wind of God*, 67–117.

Anabaptists and they are Africans,' exclaimed Donald in a letter to John Howard Yoder, the Mennonite theologian.[94] Jacobs and his wife were radically transformed by the encounter. Don Jacobs later became a close associate of Festo Kivengere, who, as bishop of Kigezi from 1972 almost to his death from leukaemia in 1988, was the best-known international spokesman for the Revival in the 1970s and 1980s. Jacobs gave one of two orations at Kivengere's funeral in Kabale Anglican cathedral, a service that attracted a crowd of twenty thousand.[95] Events in East Africa may have been an important factor pushing American Mennonites towards closer association with evangelicals in North America.

After Kivengere's death, Jacobs served as chairman of the board of African Enterprise, an organization founded in South Africa in 1961 by the South African Anglican Michael Cassidy, and extended to East Africa under Kivengere's leadership in 1970–1. African Enterprise fused the emphasis of the Revival on the interracial and interdenominational unity of all the saved in Christ with a holistic approach to mission that appealed to Jacobs's Anabaptist loyalties.[96] Through the ministry of African Enterprise, and in other ways as well, the Revival, in the hands of some of its second generation of leaders, showed itself capable of transmutation from a narrowly pietistic expression of evangelicalism to one that could display great courage in challenging political injustice.[97] Evangelicalism has always placed the cross of Christ at the centre of its theology of atonement and salvation. The East African Revival was no exception, but it also extended this emphasis to the spheres of Christian discipleship and fellowship. Those evangelicals in the twenty-first century who place particular stress on the need for the Christian life of both the individual and the church to be characterized by continual repentance in the light of the cross are, often unconsciously, reflecting something of the influence of this remarkable movement.

---

[94] Ibid. 165; Donald R. Jacobs, 'My Pilgrimage in Mission', *International Bulletin of Missionary Research* 42 (Oct. 1992), 146–149.

[95] MacMaster with Jacobs, *Gentle Wind of God*, 272–273; Coomes, *Festo Kivengere*, 465–466.

[96] MacMaster with Jacobs, *Gentle Wind of God*, 260–269; see Anne Coomes, *African Harvest: The Captivating Story of Michael Cassidy and African Enterprise* (London: Monarch, 2002), 490–491.

[97] Kevin Ward, *A History of Global Anglicanism* (Cambridge: Cambridge University Press, 2006), 184. However, it must be stated that in Rwanda some Hutu Anglican leaders influenced by the Revival failed to maintain an unambiguous Christian witness in the face of the horrendous genocide (mainly of Tutsis) in 1994. On this see Roger Bowen, 'Rwanda: Missionary Reflections on a Catastrophe', *Anvil* 13 (1996), 33–44.

The evangelical commonwealth: the Scripture Union movement and evangelical growth in Ghana and Nigeria

Until 1947 all Scripture Union (SU) work throughout the world (with the exception of Switzerland and France) was answerable to the CSSM Council in London. As mentioned in the last chapter, when John Laird returned to Britain from New Zealand at the end of 1945 to become joint, and in due course sole, general secretary of CSSM-Scripture Union, one of his first policy initiatives in 1947 was to amend the movement's 'imperial' structure. His goal was to enable the various national Scripture Union bodies to grow towards autonomy within a spiritual 'commonwealth' of shared family loyalties. The London Council agreed to alter its legal articles and delegate its power, and two categories of national movements were recognized. Those that were financially independent of London (New Zealand, New South Wales, Queensland and Victoria) were granted full autonomy. This enabled the New Zealand movement, which had hitherto operated under the three different names of Crusaders (in the schools), CSSM (the beach missions) and Scripture Union (the Bible reading notes) to unify its activities under the single name of Scripture Union. Those movements still financially dependent on London (Canada, South Africa, East Africa, South Australia and the two non-anglophone movements in France and Peru) agreed not to incur debt or appoint staff without London's approval, but were given their own advisory councils and encouraged to become self-supporting and self-governing as soon as possible. By 1960 Canada, France, South Africa and South Australia had become autonomous, while several new Scripture Union movements (e.g. India and Singapore-Malaya) were constituted in the second category and given their own advisory councils. Laird also encouraged the different SU bodies in the various Australian states to move towards the goal of a single national movement.[98]

In Africa SU literature had been widely circulated by missionaries for many years, but there was no specific SU youth work except among white children in South Africa, and occasional missions led in East Africa by Fred Crittenden and John Duncan. However, the expanding economy of the British colonies in the early 1950s led to a proliferation of opportunities for Britons to take up teaching or other government posts. Some of these were evangelical Christians with a background in such movements as Scripture Union or IVF. The first SU camp in West Africa was held in the Gold Coast

---

[98] Nigel Sylvester, *God's Word in a Young World: The Story of Scripture Union* (London: Scripture Union, 1984), 117–121.

(Ghana) in January 1953, led by Jim Findlay, who had helped with SU camps in Scotland. Only thirteen boys came, but the next year the numbers grew to sixty-five in a camp led by an Oxford graduate, Tony Wilmot. A girls' camp was also instituted in 1954. One of those converted then, through a talk by Wilmot, was Florence Yeboah, who joined the SU staff in 1962, and exercised a very fruitful ministry. Another early convert was Gottfried Osei-Mensah, who would later became widely known as pastor of Nairobi Baptist Church and through his role in the Lausanne movement. In view of the expanding opportunities, Wilmot requested the London office to appoint a staff worker for West Africa. Nigel Sylvester, a young Cambridge graduate and Anglican minister, arrived in the Gold Coast in November 1955. Under his leadership the Ghanaian movement expanded rapidly.[99]

In 1957 a national SU committee was opened in Nigeria under the chairmanship of Dr Ishaya Audu, who later became the Nigerian minister of foreign affairs.[100] The first staff worker in Nigeria, John Dean, was appointed in 1958. Like Sylvester, Dean had been converted as a student at Cambridge, and was an agricultural missionary with the Sudan United Mission, which seconded him to the SU. From his base at Ibadan Dean was very active over a period of twenty years, travelling many thousands of miles. By 1960 he was able to report the existence of twenty-two SU groups in the west of the country, eleven in the east and thirty-eight in the north.[101]

In May 1960 Laird's programme of 'decolonization' was taken a decisive stage further when he convened an international conference of SU leaders at Old Jordans in Buckinghamshire. The meeting, in Laird's words, 'proved to be a watershed in the history of our movement'.[102] The challenge the

---

[99] Ibid. 150–152; John Laird, *No Mere Chance* (London: Hodder & Stoughton and Scripture Union, 1981), 172–173. Sylvester was converted at Cambridge during the CICCU mission of 1949 led by the Philadelphia fundamentalist preacher Donald Grey Barnhouse (1895–1960). On Barnhouse's two Cambridge University missions of 1946 and 1949 see Oliver R. Barclay and Robert M. Horn, *From Cambridge to the World: 125 Years of Student Witness* (Leicester: Inter-Varsity Press, 2002), 136–138; and David Goodhew, 'The Rise of the Cambridge Inter-Collegiate Christian Union, 1910–1971', *JEH* 54 (2003), 75–77.

[100] Audu was invited to present a paper at the Berlin Congress on Evangelism in 1966, but was unable to come at the last moment; see n. 31 above.

[101] Sylvester, *God's Word*, 152–153; Dean's conversion through the CICCU 'freshers' (new students') sermon in 1950 is recorded by Barclay and Horn, *From Cambridge to the World*, 143.

[102] Laird, *No Mere Chance*, 157.

conference faced was how to preserve the principle, established in 1947, of autonomy for national SU bodies while devising a structure that would keep the proliferating international movement from total disintegration into its component parts. It was decided to follow the pattern set by Australasia, which had set up an ANZEA regional council for Australia, New Zealand and the newly developing work in Singapore, Malaya and Japan. The regional councils were to give national movements their autonomy but promote collaboration and encouraged the initiation of SU work in new countries within the region. An international committee was established, Armin Hoppler from Switzerland was appointed to the new post of international secretary, policy and doctrinal guidelines for all national movements were drawn up, and it was agreed that the name Scripture Union (or its vernacular equivalents) should be employed by all movements. During the 1960s regional councils were created for the Americas, South Asia, Africa and Madagascar, and Europe. The number of autonomous national councils grew from seven in 1960 to twenty-four in 1984.[103]

The most dramatic growth during the 1960s and 1970s was in Africa, where by 1982 there were ninety-one staff working in twenty-five nations. Progress was most rapid where SU was able to create a honeycombed network of secondary-school groups, such as Sylvester and Dean had created in Ghana and Nigeria. SU appointed its first African travelling secretaries in 1962–3: Florence Yeboah in Ghana (1962), Philip Mpunzwana in Rhodesia (1962) and Reuben Ariko with the Fellowship of Christian Students in northern Nigeria in 1963. In South Africa the first black member of staff, Nat Nkosi, was appointed in 1970. Ghana (an independent nation from 1957) gained its autonomous status in 1965, followed in 1966 by Nigeria (which had gained national independence in 1960). When Sylvester visited Nigeria in 1983, he was told that no one knew how many school SU groups there were in the country, but he estimated that there were at least a thousand, with another thousand operating in the north under the auspices of the Fellowship of Christian Students.[104]

The remarkable growth of SU in Africa owed something to the immense appetite for literature that was a feature of many emerging nations at the time, but perhaps more crucial was the example SU staff often gave of egalitarian personal relationships between Africans and whites. As was the case with the SU and Crusader movements in Britain, the role of camps in the school holidays was strategic. Folu Soyannwo, one of the first Nigerian staff workers, was

---

[103] Sylvester, *God's Word*, 155–160.

[104] Ibid. 208–209, 218, 220–221.

converted at a camp at which he was staggered by the sight of white leaders doing the washing up for black students. He became in due course general secretary of SU in Nigeria, and, after his ordination, an active member of the SU Council in Nigeria. Similarly, Phineas Dube, a schoolboy attending the first interracial SU camp held in Rhodesia shortly before Ian Smith's unilateral declaration of independence from Britain in 1965, was so impressed by a white leader who gave up his blankets for some black boys who had arrived with too few, that he too was converted. He became Field Director of SU in Zimbabwe in 1981. In contrast to the practice of too many conventional missionary societies at this time, the SU was willing to entrust young Africans with responsibility, including the care of finances: John Dean's motto was to 'train and trust'.[105] Many of those trained through SU went on to full-time Christian service. When Nigel Sylvester visited Ghana in 1972, he was told by the principal of the largest theological college, Trinity College, Legon, that 60% of his students had an SU background. The head of the Methodist Church in Sierra Leone informed Sylvester on the same trip that all of his candidates for Methodist ministry and all new lay preachers over the previous three years had come from an SU background.[106]

The movement in West Africa had acquired its own momentum, and in Nigeria especially was soon beyond the capacity of European staff to control. Here the ministry of Scripture Union rapidly became at least as significant among young adults as among school children, owing to the institution in 1967 of 'Pilgrims Groups' for school-leavers, and the establishment of SU groups in some Nigerian universities, such as the new University of Nigeria at Nsukka in northern Igboland, where a group was started in the early 1960s.[107] Chapter 7 will expound the independent initiatives taken by young adults (particularly Igbos) in the Nigerian SU movement in the aftermath of the Biafran war of 1967 to 1970 in shaping and disseminating explicitly Pentecostal varieties of evangelicalism. These initiatives had immense repercussions for the future of Christianity in West Africa, leading eventually to the formation of many of the 'new Pentecostal' churches that are now so marked a feature of

---

[105] Ibid. 209–210, 223–225.

[106] Ibid. 222. Trinity College (now Trinity Seminary) was founded in 1942 as an ecumenical venture in ministerial training by the Methodist Church, Presbyterian Church of Ghana, and the Evangelical Presbyterian Church. In 1967 the Joint Anglican Diocesan Council in Ghana joined, followed shortly thereafter by the African Methodist Episcopal Zion Church.

[107] Richard Burgess, *Nigeria's Christian Revolution: The Civil War Revival and Its Pentecostal Progeny (1967–2006)* (Carlisle: Paternoster Press, 2008), 56, 92.

West African Christianity. By the time of his death in 1988 John Laird had lived to see the international Scripture Union movement, of which he was the principal architect, give birth to a large family of Christian churches whose ethos and spirituality were very far removed from the restrained biblical pietism of the Brethren movement to which he belonged.[108]

Conclusion: new patterns of mission and discipleship

By the 1990s the networks of evangelical international missionary endeavour were infinitely more diverse and complex in structure than they had been in 1945. By the close of the century the numbers of foreign missionaries from Asia (especially South Korea, India and the Philippines), Africa (mainly Ghana and Nigeria) and Latin America (notably Brazil), were rapidly catching up with those sent from Europe and North America.[109] Movements of human population, which had prompted many of the new initiatives in Christian internationalism in the post-war years, were by the 1990s of a more diverse character. While the predicament of refugees, especially those who were fleeing from famine, flood or civil war in parts of Africa, continued to arouse Christian sympathies, the larger flows of human migration were now those that were themselves carriers of mission.[110] Economic migrants moved in increasing numbers from South to North and from East to West, bringing the distinctive styles of African, Asian and Hispanic Christianity into the cities of Europe and North America. Over 13 million migrants arrived in the United States during the 1990s. By 2000, 35 million Americans were of Hispanic ancestry, and almost 12 million more were of Asian descent. About 20% of

---

[108] This paragraph is indebted to Sylvester, *God's Word*, 219–220; Ogbu Kalu, 'Passive Revolution and Its Saboteurs: African Christian Initiative in the Era of Decolonization, 1955–1975', in Brian Stanley (ed.), *Missions, Nationalism, and the End of Empire* (Grand Rapids: Eerdmans, 2003), 250–277; and Ogbu Kalu, *African Pentecostalism: An Introduction* (Oxford: Oxford University Press, 2008), 88–94. For a fuller discussion of the origins of Nigerian Pentecostalism see chapter 7, 203–204.

[109] Towards the end of the first decade of the twenty-first century, estimated numbers of foreign missionaries sent from Asia, Africa and Latin America totalled 126,200, compared with 135,000 from North America and 132,800 from Europe; see Todd M. Johnson and Kenneth R. Ross (eds.), *Atlas of Global Christianity* (Edinburgh: Edinburgh University Press, 2009), 261.

[110] On this theme see Jehu Hanciles, *Beyond Christendom: Globalization, African Migration, and the Transformation of the West* (Maryknoll: Orbis Books, 2008).

these Hispanics were evangelical Protestants, while among the American Korean community, Christians (the majority of them evangelical Protestants) outnumbered Buddhists by at least ten to one.[111] Institutional mission agencies continued to play their part in the story of Christian world mission, but most of the denominational missionary societies from the northern hemisphere that had still dominated the picture in 1945 were by 2000 of marginal significance. New and energetic non-denominational and international missions, such as OM or Youth With a Mission (YWAM – founded by the Californian Loren Cunningham in 1960), were more adept at capturing the enthusiasm of young evangelicals in the northern hemisphere. In Asia, Africa and Latin America also, the key actors in mission were frequently young people or women.[112] Like the young Igbo evangelicals who seized the initiative in the Nigerian Scripture Union movement in the 1970s, these evangelists, often anonymous to our view, have transformed existing mission structures, invented new ones or operated with very little structure at all. Many of them, as we shall consider more fully in chapter 7, adhered to an understanding of the Christian faith that Westerners label as 'Pentecostal' and that diverged quite markedly from some of the features that have been characteristic of evangelicalism in the North Atlantic world since its genesis in the age of the Enlightenment.

---

[111] Philip Jenkins, *The Next Christendom: The Coming of Global Christianity*, 3rd ed. (New York: Oxford University Press, 2002), 100–103. In the third edition of his book, published in 2011, Jenkins estimated the Hispanic population of the United States as 50 million (126), and raised his estimate of the proportion of Christians to Buddhists among Korean Americans from ten to one to 'from ten or twenty to one' (131).

[112] See Dana Robert, 'World Christianity as a Women's Movement', *International Bulletin of Missionary Research* 30:4 (Oct. 2006), 180–188.

4. SCHOLARSHIP, THE BIBLE AND PREACHING

Researching the Bible

The pursuit of evangelical biblical scholarship

Conservative evangelicalism in the late 1930s and 1940s was at a low ebb in terms of its intellectual standing and scholarly productivity. While the battles over evolution and biblical criticism in North America had nurtured an aggressive form of fundamentalism that stifled genuine intellectual endeavour, in Britain, and to an extent in Australasia, theological conservatism tended to adopt a less militant stance, but one no less suspicious of scholarship as a supposed enemy of the spiritual keenness that evangelicals so prized. The most obvious exception in the anglophone world was Scotland, where the combined influence of a dominant Reformed tradition and an unrivalled system of public education ensured that evangelical faith and theological learning were not widely assumed to be sworn enemies. It is worthy of note that the origins of the Tyndale Fellowship for Biblical Research are to be found in a meeting convened by senior members and friends of the IVF in the vicarage of St Luke's Church, Hampstead, in London in 1938 to discuss 'how best the reproach of obscurantism and anti-intellectual prejudice might be removed from Evangelical Christianity in *England*'.[1] That meeting eventually

---

[1] F. F. Bruce, 'The Tyndale Fellowship for Biblical Research', *EvQ* 19 (1947), 52
   (my italics); Douglas Johnson, *Contending for the Faith: A History of the Evangelical*

gave rise to the Biblical Research Committee of the IVF, which in 1942 instituted annual Tyndale Lectures in Old and New Testament Studies, and in September 1944, aided by the generosity of the Brethren building magnate John Laing, purchased a property at 16 Selwyn Gardens in Cambridge; this became known as Tyndale House. In its turn the infant library and research centre of Tyndale House gave birth in April 1945 to the Tyndale Fellowship for Biblical Research.[2] The fellowship of biblical scholars it nurtured was to play an unparalleled role in the intellectual rejuvenation of conservative evangelicalism. This was true not simply in England or the British Isles but also in the United States (through the many American evangelicals who resided at Tyndale House, or who studied for their PhDs in different British universities under the supervision of members of the Fellowship) and indeed scattered throughout the world. Professor Don Carson of Trinity Evangelical Divinity School, Illinois, has aptly said of Tyndale House, 'I know of no other Christian institution with comparable global influence for such comparatively little investment.'[3]

One of the first articles introducing the Tyndale Fellowship to the wider evangelical constituency was written for the *Evangelical Quarterly* in 1947 by its Scottish assistant editor, Frederick Fyvie Bruce (1910–90).[4] Bruce, a lifelong member of the Christian Brethren, was then a lecturer in classical Greek at Leeds University, and, though at that stage primarily a classicist rather than a biblical scholar, was used by the IVF's Biblical Research Committee at its summer schools as its New Testament specialist. The corresponding Old Testament specialist was W. J. Martin of the University of Liverpool, to whom, along with a young Australian Anglican, David Broughton Knox, belongs the credit for the idea of Tyndale House.[5] Martin also was a member of the Brethren, and, like Bruce, was not a theologian or biblical scholar, but a lecturer in Semitic languages. Bruce comments in his autobiography that for a

---

Movement in the Universities and Colleges (Leicester: Inter-Varsity Press, 1979), 209–210.

[2] Bruce, 'Tyndale Fellowship', 54–55; T. A. Noble, *Tyndale House and Fellowship: The First Sixty Years* (Leicester: Inter-Varsity Press, 2006), 48–57.

[3] Cited in Noble, *Tyndale House and Fellowship*, 264.

[4] On Bruce see Tim Grass, *F. F. Bruce: A Life* (Milton Keynes: Authentic Media, 2011).

[5] Noble, *Tyndale House and Fellowship*, 36–38, 43–45; Grass, *F. F. Bruce*, 44. Martin's original vision was for a research institute. The idea of a biblical studies library was inspired by Knox as a result of a summer vacation in 1940 spent studying in Gladstone's Library at St Deiniol's, Hawarden, in Cheshire. Knox was a friend of the New Zealander Stuart Barton Babbage, secretary of the Biblical Research Committee from 1942 until he was appointed Dean of Sydney in 1947.

predominantly Anglican committee to have had recourse for its chief sources of biblical expertise to two members of the Brethren, neither of whom was a member of a theology department, is indicative of the state of biblical scholarship in the IVF at the time.[6] In fact a recurring theme throughout the history of the Tyndale Fellowship has been its relative weakness in theology as opposed to biblical studies, and the somewhat intermittent history of its various study groups in theological subjects in comparison with those in Old and New Testament Studies.[7]

Bruce's article for the *Evangelical Quarterly* expressed the hope that the new Tyndale Fellowship would play an important apologetic role in the revival of what he termed 'the full-orbed historic Evangelical Faith'.[8] It also made plain his belief that for the Fellowship to play this role its research must 'necessarily be unfettered'; he explained that members of the Fellowship were entirely free to adopt whatever conclusions they believed the evidence warranted on such matters as the composition of the Pentateuch or the book of Isaiah, the date of Daniel, the sources of the Gospels or the authenticity of the Pastoral Epistles – precisely the points on which most conservative evangelicals in the past had thought it necessary to resist the higher critics. Throughout his career in biblical scholarship Bruce never saw any inconsistency between such academic freedom and subscription to the IVF doctrinal basis, with its ascription of infallibility to Holy Scripture as originally given. In accordance with the official explanation in the first edition of the IVF's pamphlet *Evangelical Belief* that this statement meant that Scripture should be taken as 'in itself a true and sufficient guide, which may be trusted implicitly', Bruce interpreted this clause as meaning that Scripture would 'never lead astray the soul who is sincerely seeking truth'. 'Evangelical Christians', his article concluded, 'must, once and for all, give the lie to the common idea that they are afraid of scientific research'.[9]

The emerging 'new' or 'neo-' evangelicals in the United States[10] were also concerned at this time to remove the stigma of intellectual obscurantism from conservative Protestantism. One consequence was the formation of the

---

[6] F. F. Bruce, *In Retrospect: Remembrance of Things Past* (Glasgow: Pickering & Inglis, 1980), 110–111.

[7] See Noble, *Tyndale House and Fellowship*, 147–150, 152, 162–163, 174, 183, 195, 252–253.

[8] Bruce, 'Tyndale Fellowship', 61.

[9] Ibid. 57–59; cf. Inter-Varsity Fellowship, *Evangelical Belief* (London: Inter-Varsity Fellowship, 1935), 11. For a full discussion of Bruce's doctrine of Scripture see Grass, *F. F. Bruce*, 144–159.

[10] See chapter 2 above, 29–38.

Evangelical Theological Society (ETS) in 1949, with the stated purpose 'To foster conservative Biblical scholarship by providing a medium for the oral exchange and written expression of thought and research in the general field of the theological disciplines as centered in the Scriptures.' However, unlike the Tyndale Fellowship, which has always shared the doctrinal basis of the IVF/ UCCF, the ETS has its own brief doctrinal basis, which commits its members to two axioms only: trinitarian belief and an explicit doctrine of inerrancy: 'The Bible alone, and the Bible in its entirety, is the Word of God written and is therefore inerrant in the autographs.'[11] Probably for this reason, a smaller body limited in membership to professional scholars and with an ethos and doctrinal basis more closely akin to that of the Tyndale Fellowship was established in 1973 by the Southern Baptist New Testament scholar E. Earle Ellis (1926–2010): the Institute for Biblical Research (IBR) had reached 150 full members by 1985, and 311 by 1994. It holds its main meetings in association with the annual meetings of the Society for Biblical Literature, the premier scholarly association for biblical studies in North America.[12] While the ETS has generally stood for what Mark Noll has termed 'critical anti-criticism' (using scholarly methods to attempt to rebut a corpus of received critical opinions viewed as incompatible with orthodoxy), the IBR, like the Tyndale Fellowship in Britain, has followed F. F. Bruce's principle of 'believing criticism' – holding that trust in Scripture's revelatory truthfulness may be combined with a variety of critical positions on matters such as date, authorship or composition.[13]

Throughout the English-speaking world the revival of conservative biblical scholarship has been more evident in New Testament studies than in Old Testament studies. In the former, scholars such as the Americans George Eldon Ladd, E. Earle Ellis and Bruce Metzger, the Britons F. F. Bruce, I. Howard Marshall and N. T. Wright, the Australian Leon Morris and the New Zealander Graham N. Stanton have attained renown far beyond the confines of evangelicalism. In the study of the Old Testament, by comparison, few evangelical scholars have attained global pre-eminence. Two of the most notable exceptions have, once again, been members of the Christian Brethren movement in England: Donald J. Wiseman (1918–2010) of the University of London, as mentioned in chapter 2; and Hugh G. M. Williamson, Regius Professor of Hebrew at the University of Oxford since 1992. Mention should

---

[11] See http://www.etsjets.org/about/constitution (accessed 27 Apr. 2012).
[12] Mark A. Noll, *Between Faith and Criticism: Evangelicals, Scholarship, and the Bible*, 2nd ed. (Leicester: Apollos, 1991), 105; http://www.ibr-bbr.org/brief-history-ibr (accessed 27 Apr. 2012).
[13] Ibid. 156–158.

also be made of Francis I. Andersen (1925–), an Australian Anglican who has made seminal contributions to the study of both Hebrew syntax and the minor prophets. Despite these exceptions, the conclusions of modern biblical criticism have generally proved easier for conservatives to accept in New Testament than in Old Testament studies. In North America especially, evangelicals have struggled to reconcile the developmental assumptions of modern historical criticism (notably of the Pentateuch) with their traditional use of the Old Testament as a source of predictive prophecy and a quarry for the fashioning of arguments for creation over against evolution.[14]

The most striking difference between the growth of conservative biblical scholarship on the two sides of the Atlantic since the 1950s is that in the United Kingdom scholars of evangelical commitment have substantially infiltrated departments of theology or biblical studies in the major research universities, while in North America the impact of the revival of conservative scholarship has remained mostly limited to evangelical seminaries, whose academic stand-ards have risen markedly as a result.[15] One reason for this contrast is that while several of the leading British universities have retained departments whose primary – though, in most cases, no longer exclusive[16] – emphasis remains the study of Christian theology, in many American and Canadian universities biblical studies and even Christian theology became progressively marginal-ized from the 1960s as a result of the growing dominance of social scientific or phenomenological approaches to the study of religion. The trend was most marked after the formation of the American Academy of Religion in 1964.[17] Another reason may be that whereas in Britain the Church of England gave evangelicals ready access to the intellectual and social elites formed in the ancient universities of Oxford and Cambridge, in the United States, they have found it much harder to establish themselves in the Ivy League universities, and hence to penetrate the American intellectual establishment: at Harvard, for example, the Inter-Varsity group in 1953 had only five members.[18]

---

[14] Ibid. 188–189.

[15] Ibid. 97–98, 138–139.

[16] The University of St Andrews is probably the sole remaining exception in almost entirely resisting the trend towards a plural approach to religious studies, though it does teach Jewish studies.

[17] D. G. Hart, 'Evangelicals, Biblical Scholarship and the Politics of the Modern American Academy', in David N. Livingstone, D. G. Hart and Mark A. Noll (eds.), *Evangelicals and Science in Historical Perspective* (New York: Oxford University Press, 1999), 306–326.

[18] Timothy Dudley-Smith, *John Stott: The Making of a Leader* (Leicester: Inter-Varsity Press, 1979), 392.

One consequence of the continued weakness of evangelical biblical scholarship in American university departments is that most American evangelicals
wishing to pursue doctoral research in biblical studies have chosen to do
so under the guidance of sympathetic supervisors (often members of the
Tyndale Fellowship) in the older British universities, whose departments of
theology have become significantly dependent on the American evangelical
market for postgraduate recruitment, and hence for financial survival. It was
estimated in the mid-1980s that up to half of evangelical scholars working on
any particular biblical project in North America had been trained in Britain.[19]
By such means the commitment of British evangelical scholars such as F. F.
Bruce or Howard Marshall to 'believing criticism' was transmitted to intellectual leaders of the evangelical constituency in America and elsewhere. Bruce's
doctoral students came not from the United States alone but from all over the
world – they included René Padilla from Ecuador, Ronald Fung from Hong
Kong and Murray Harris from New Zealand; his recent biographer notes that
the region of North America in which his influence was most apparent was
British Columbia.[20]

Mediating evangelical scholarship to the churches: The New Bible Commentary and its two successors

Post-war evangelical leaders were concerned not just to influence the world of
academic biblical scholarship but even more to encourage the systematic and
reverent use of the Bible in the churches, both in and out of the pulpit. To that
end there was an obvious need to make resources available that would provide
sound but up-to-date biblical scholarship in a form accessible to ministers and
lay leaders, especially those involved in teaching the Bible to young people. A
first step in this direction was the publication by the IVF in 1947 of *The New
Bible Handbook*.[21] This was followed in 1953 by a much larger work of 1,199
pages, *The New Bible Commentary*. Of the thirty thousand copies of the first
print run, twenty-two thousand were ordered and partly paid for in advance
by Eerdmans and the IVCF in the USA.[22] The editor was Francis Davidson,
principal of the Bible Training Institute in Glasgow, assisted by Alan Stibbs,

---

[19] Noll, *Between Faith and Criticism*, 138.

[20] Peter Oakes, 'F. F. Bruce and the Development of Evangelical Biblical Scholarship',
      BJRL 86 (2004), 99–124, lists some of Bruce's students on p. 120; Grass, *F. F. Bruce*,
      215.

[21] G. T. Manley, G. R. Robinson and A. M. Stibbs (eds.), *The New Bible Handbook*
      (London: Inter-Varsity Fellowship, 1947).

[22] Noll, *Between Faith and Criticism*, 103.

vice-principal of the Anglican Oak Hill College, and Ernest Kevan, the first full-time principal of the London Bible College (now the London School of Theology), whose foundation in 1943 was another sign of the serious-ness of evangelical aspirations to raise the level of scholarship within the constituency.[23] Of the fifty (all male) contributors, only twelve had research doctorates,[24] and only six occupied, or had previously occupied, university teaching posts. The writing team was predominantly British and relied heavily on Scottish or Ulster Presbyterians, most of whom were in pastorates, though some had teaching posts. There were only five contributors from North America.

The New Bible Commentary was prefaced by two general theological articles on the Bible. The first, on 'the authority of Scripture', was written by a young Anglican evangelical, Geoffrey W. Bromiley, then rector of St Thomas's English (now Scottish) Episcopal Church, Edinburgh. Bromiley was to become, from 1958 to 1987, one of Fuller Theological Seminary's most dis-tinguished members of faculty, and a leading evangelical commentator on, and translator of, Karl Barth's writings.[25] His article was virtually identical to an article he wrote for the *Evangelical Quarterly* in 1947.[26] The second of the two articles, on 'revelation and inspiration', was a posthumous publication by Daniel Lamont (1869–1950), formerly professor of Christian ethics and practical theology in the University of Edinburgh. Lamont was one of the few senior friends of the IVF to hold a university post in the 1940s, and served as president of the IVF from 1945 to 1946.[27]

Both articles sought to defend a conservative evangelical understanding of Scripture as being essentially continuous with that of the sixteenth-century Reformers, and both gave primary emphasis to the Reformers' teaching on the necessity of the internal witness of the Holy Spirit to the authority of Scripture. Neither article made any explicit reference to either the infallibility or the inerrancy of Scripture. However, the two authors adopted divergent approaches to the nature of biblical inspiration. Bromiley, with an eye to

---

[23] F. Davidson, A. M. Stibbs and E. F. Kevan (eds.), *The New Bible Commentary* (London: Inter-Varsity Fellowship, 1953).

[24] Noll, *Between Faith and Criticism*, 123.

[25] G. W. Bromiley, 'The Authority of Scripture', *New Bible Commentary*, 15–23.

[26] G. W. Bromiley, 'The Authority of the Bible: The Attitude of Modern Theologians', *EvQ* 19 (1947), 127–136.

[27] Daniel Lamont, 'Revelation and Inspiration', *New Bible Commentary*, 24–30; on Lamont see George R. Logan, 'A Memoir of Dr Lamont's Life', in Daniel Lamont, *Studies in the Johannine Writings* (London: James Clarke, 1956), 7–62.

correcting Barthian perspectives, insisted that the Reformers did not term the Spirit's illumination of the believer 'inspiration', and followed the *New Bible Handbook* article on 'inspiration and authority' in drawing a clear distinction between objective inspiration and subjective illumination.[28] Lamont's article, in contrast, moved from 'the Spirit-filled apostles' to 'the inspired Bible' to 'the inspired readers', affirming that 'He who inspired the biblical writers can alone inspire the readers of the Bible to recognize in Jesus the divine Lord and Saviour of all who will receive Him.' Lamont located the inspiration of Scripture primarily in the indwelling of the apostles by the Spirit rather than in the text itself:

> It is well to remember that the written witness *followed* the primary and central inspiration. The gospel was in existence in all its fullness and was preached in the power of the Spirit *before* any part of the New Testament was written.[29]

Lamont's experiential (some would say loose) understanding of inspiration confirms the accuracy of David F. Wright's interpretation of the doctrine of Scripture among British evangelicals in the first half of the twentieth century: the concept of biblical inspiration, Wright notes, was understood in 'a surprisingly wide variety of ways'.[30] Even Bromiley, whose article propounded a tighter view of the distinctive inspiration of the biblical text, stopped short of any mention of biblical infallibility. The *Commentary*, a great publishing success, with a second edition appearing in 1954, displayed some characteristic features of an earlier generation of evangelical views of Scripture. Its judgments on major points of historical criticism were conservative, but not uniformly so. Whereas Alan Stibbs's article on the Pastoral Epistles affirmed roundly that to deny the Pauline authorship of the letters was to impugn their canonical status, the article on the historical literature of the Old Testament by the Dutch scholar G. C. Aalders tentatively suggested that the Pentateuch was compiled during the early monarchy while incorporating Mosaic and pre-Mosaic material.[31] The commentary on the book of Isaiah by William Fitch, a

---

[28] Bromiley, 'Authority of Scripture', *New Bible Commentary*, 21–22; cf. Manley, Robinson and Stibbs, *New Bible Handbook*, 10–11.

[29] Lamont, 'Revelation and Inspiration', 29 (his italics).

[30] David F. Wright, 'Soundings in the Doctrine of Scripture in British Evangelicalism in the First Half of the Twentieth Century', *TynB* 31 (1980), 87–106, quotation at 103.

[31] A. M. Stibbs, 'Introduction to the Epistles to Timothy and Titus'; and G. C. Aalders, 'The Historical Literature of the Old Testament', *New Bible Commentary*, 1063 and 34.

Church of Scotland minister, affirmed the unity of the book, but only after an extensive and even-handed survey of the arguments on both sides.[32]

Encouraged by the success of the one-volume commentary, the IVF Literature Committee began publication of the Tyndale New Testament commentary series in 1956, with the Old Testament series following from 1964. The commentaries were published in Britain by the IVF (later IVP) under its academic imprint of the Tyndale Press, and in the United States by Eerdmans. *The New Bible Dictionary* followed in 1962. In 1970 Inter-Varsity Press published *The New Bible Commentary Revised*, edited by Donald Guthrie, lecturer in New Testament at London Bible College, and Alec Motyer, then vicar of St Luke's Church, Hampstead.[33] Of the fifty-one contributors, a higher proportion had research doctorates than in the first edition (nineteen as opposed to twelve), but the number occupying university teaching posts had increased by only one to seven. The most striking differences from 1953 in the range of contributors were the increase from five to twelve in the number of those teaching or ministering in the United States or Canada, and the marked diminution in the Scottish and Irish Presbyterian presence – down from twenty-two to five. There was one female contributor: Joyce G. Baldwin, later principal of Trinity College, Bristol.

Bromiley's opening article, 'The Authority of Scripture', was retained from 1953 with very little updating. The only significant amendments were in the section formerly entitled 'The Theology of Crisis', which now became 'Neo-Orthodoxy'. Whereas in the first edition Bromiley's verdict on the emerging Barthian movement had been necessarily provisional, but quite critical of Barth himself, by 1970 Bromiley was at pains to distinguish the mature Barth, whose doctrine of Scripture he commended as 'very close to biblical and Reformed teaching', from wider neo-orthodoxy.[34]

Unsurprisingly, Lamont's article on revelation and inspiration was replaced by one by J. I. Packer, then principal of Tyndale Hall in Bristol.[35] Packer retained nine lines on the testimony of the Spirit (which he termed the

---

[32] W. Fitch, 'Introduction to the Book of Isaiah', section on 'Authorship: The Special Problem of Chapters XL to LXVI', *New Bible Commentary*, 558–562; Fitch's assistant in his parish at Springburn Hill, Glasgow, for a year (1944–5) was the young William Still.

[33] D. Guthrie and J. A. Motyer (eds.), *The New Bible Commentary Revised* (London: Inter-Varsity Press, 1970).

[34] Compare Bromiley, 'Authority of Scripture', *New Bible Commentary*, 21–22, with the corresponding section of the revised article in *New Bible Commentary Revised*, 10–11.

[35] J. I. Packer, 'Revelation and Inspiration', *New Bible Commentary Revised*, 12–18.

'internal proof' of the authority of Scripture), but this was preceded by a much longer section on the 'external proof' of the testimony of Christ to the divine authority of the Old Testament and his teaching of the apostles to adopt a Christological reading of the Old Testament, which then shaped their claims for the equivalent authority of their own writings.[36] In contrast to Lamont, Packer stressed the verbal inspiration of the text rather than the personal inspiration of the apostles, and argued that this necessarily implied inerrancy:

> Since truth is communicated through words, and verbal inaccuracy misrepresents meaning, inspiration must be verbal in the nature of the case. And if the words of Scripture are 'God-breathed', it is almost blasphemy to deny that it is free from error in that which it is intended to teach and infallible in the guidance it gives.[37]

On critical issues the *New Bible Commentary Revised* was, on the whole, more conservative than its predecessor on the Old Testament, but marginally less so on the New. John Wenham's article on the Pentateuch declared the books of Genesis to Numbers to be the virtually unedited work of Moses, and suggested that Deuteronomy was compiled, using Mosaic discourses, during the time of Joshua.[38] Less space was given than in 1953 to putting the case for more than one Isaiah.[39] The authorship of the Fourth Gospel by John the apostle, on the other hand, which had been decisively asserted in the original commentary, was, though still affirmed, regarded as more of an open question.[40] The Pauline authorship of the Pastorals was similarly still defended, though now as highly probable rather than as a question on which the canonicity of the letters depended.[41]

In 1994 IVP, this time in association with IVP-USA, published a third version of the commentary, entitled the *New Bible Commentary 21st Century Edition*. Alec Motyer remained from the 1970 editorial team. He was joined by three others: the Canadian Reformed Baptist Don Carson, of Trinity Evangelical Divinity School, Illinois; the principal of Wycliffe Hall, Oxford, Dick France; and the English Pentateuchal scholar Gordon Wenham. The preface explained that nothing remained from the 1953 edition, and little from

---

[36] Packer, 'Revelation and Inspiration', 16–17.

[37] Ibid. 17.

[38] John W. Wenham, 'Moses and the Pentateuch', *New Bible Commentary Revised*, 43.

[39] Derek Kidner, 'Introduction to Isaiah', *New Bible Commentary Revised*, 589–591.

[40] Donald Guthrie, 'Introduction to John', *New Bible Commentary Revised*, 926–927.

[41] A. M. Stibbs, 'The Pastoral Epistles', *New Bible Commentary Revised*, 1166–1167.

the 1970 one.[42] In fact there was a solitary survivor from the 1953 edition, the English Baptist New Testament scholar George R. Beasley-Murray, who wrote on the book of Revelation in all three editions. Joyce Baldwin was again the only female contributor, and there was still no one from the majority world, other than Moisés Silva, then Professor of New Testament at Westminster Theological Seminary, who was Cuban-born, but had lived in the USA since 1960. Silva had been a PhD student of F. F. Bruce at Manchester. Thirty-four of the forty-six contributors had earned doctorates, yet only six held or had held university teaching posts, no more than in 1953. The great majority were employed by conservative theological institutions in North America, Britain or Australasia (where there were seven, as opposed to four in 1970 and two in 1953; four of the seven were on the staff of Moore Theological College in Sydney). The Tyndale Fellowship had by 1994 achieved a considerable measure of success in penetrating British university departments, but few of its most academically distinguished members chose to, or perhaps were invited to, contribute to the *Commentary*, which was particularly intended to serve the needs of the University Christian Unions. In the Theological Students' Fellowship (later Religious and Theological Students Fellowship) there had been periodic questions raised about the compatibility of writings by some members of the Tyndale Fellowship with the doctrinal basis of the IVF/UCCF.[43] In the United States conservative biblical scholarship was by 1994 immeasurably stronger than it had been in 1953, but its exponents had mostly progressed from doctoral studies in British universities to posts in evangelical seminaries in the USA: the major American research universities remained largely impervious to evangelical influence.[44]

The only introductory article on biblical authority in the 1994 edition was by Don Carson on 'Approaching the Bible'. Like Packer in 1970, Carson emphasized verbal revelation, but with less explicit reference to inerrancy. Unlike Lamont in 1953, Carson located inspiration primarily in the biblical

---

[42] D. A. Carson, R. T. France, Alec Motyer and Gordon J. Wenham (eds.), *New Bible Commentary 21st Century Edition* (Leicester: Inter-Varsity Press; Downers Grove: InterVarsity Press, 1994), vii.

[43] Noble, *Tyndale House and Fellowship*, 163–165, 222–223; Grass, *F. F. Bruce*, 146. For an implicit endorsement of these questions see John W. Wenham, *Facing Hell: An Autobiography 1913–1996* (Carlisle: Paternoster Press, 1998), 196, which traces the 'liberalizing' of the Tyndale Fellowship to F. F. Bruce's lack of a clear doctrine of Scripture. The Theological Students' Fellowship was formed in 1933, and changed its name to the Religious and Theological Studies Fellowship in the 1980s.

[44] See Noll, *Between Faith and Criticism*, 137–139.

text, rather than in Spirit-filled authors. In contrast to 1953 and 1970 there was a major emphasis, as the title of the article implies, on hermeneutics, a subject that since the 1970s had forced itself to the fore of debates in biblical studies.[45] On the Pentateuch Gordon Wenham's article was a little closer to the mainstream of contemporary critical orthodoxy than his father's article in 1970: it claimed that Mosaic authorship was too simple; and argued for a revision of Genesis in the monarchy period, though for an early, if post-Mosaic, date for Deuteronomy.[46] On other points of major critical argument, however, there was little change from 1970: Derek Kidner's commentary on Isaiah, as also the late Donald Guthrie's on the fourth Gospel, was retained with very little amendment from the previous edition.[47] By 1994 conservative evangelical biblical scholarship was far more extensive and intellectually substantial than it had been in 1953, but how far this scholarship was accessible or acceptable to lay evangelicals must remain doubtful.

Arguing over the Bible

British arguments over the nature of inspiration
Commitment to the supreme authority of Scripture is one of the distinguishing marks of all Christians who own the name 'evangelical', yet it proved no easier in the second half of the twentieth century to secure general agreement among evangelicals on the boundaries distinguishing permissible from illegitimate opinion on critical matters than it had been during the heyday of the fundamentalist–modernist debates earlier in the century. Indeed, in Britain in the 1950s, to a greater extent than in North America, evangelicals of impeccably conservative credentials could disagree on a question as fundamental as the nature of inspiration itself.

Daniel Lamont's contribution to the *New Bible Commentary* could have provoked widespread dissent, but it did not, apparently, attract notice. However, in 1954, the year following the publication of the *Commentary*, an article appeared in the *Evangelical Quarterly* expounding essentially the same view of inspiration as Lamont, but with markedly different consequences. The author was H. L. Ellison, a Messianic Jew who taught Old Testament at London Bible College.

---

[45] D. A. Carson, 'Approaching the Bible', *New Bible Commentary 21st Century Edition*, 1–19.

[46] G. J. Wenham, 'The Pentateuch', *New Bible Commentary 21st Century Edition*, 47–53.

[47] Derek Kidner, 'Introduction to Isaiah', and Donald Guthrie 'Introduction to John', *New Bible Commentary 21st Century Edition*, 630–632 and 1021–1022 respectively. Guthrie died in 1992.

Ellison pointed out that the Scriptures never apply the term 'the Word of God' to themselves, and suggested that a satisfactory formula would be to say that 'the Scriptures contain, are, and become the Word of God'. 'The writing of the Scriptures', he maintained, was only a 'half-way house in the process of inspiration': the 'inbreathing of the Holy Spirit into the reader' was 'as essential for the right understanding of the Scriptures as it was in the original writers for their right production of them'.[48] Although Ellison added a footnote claiming that his view of inspiration was identical to that expounded in *The New Bible Handbook*,[49] a furore ensued, in which he was accused of Barthianism. The editor of the *Quarterly*, which at that time was both owned and published by the IVF, was F. F. Bruce, who sympathized with much of Barth's theology. Bruce found himself in a difficult position, as he agreed with Ellison, who was a fellow-member of the Christian Brethren and a friend. The painful upshot was Ellison's enforced resignation from the college staff.[50]

American arguments over inerrancy

In the post-war United States, where conservative evangelicals were generally slower to espouse modern critical methods, controversies on biblical authority and interpretation came rather later than in Britain. They were less concerned with the doctrine of inspiration than with issues of biblical criticism and interpretation, especially when these appeared to touch on the biblical witness to the person of Christ or to challenge the affirmation that the Bible was without error. From the early 1960s through to the late 1980s a series of these public controversies afflicted different sections of American evangelicalism; all ultimately focused on whether the adoption by evangelical scholars of modern critical approaches to biblical studies could be reconciled

---

[48] H. L. Ellison, 'Some Thoughts on Inspiration', *EvQ* 26 (1954), 212, 214.

[49] The *Handbook* article, while distinguishing inspiration from illumination, stressed the necessity of the inward witness of the Spirit, and conceded that 'whilst we affirm that the Bible is itself the inspired Word of God, yet in another sense, its messages become the present Word of the living God to the individual when received by faith, and applied by the work of the Spirit' (11). The articles were not attributed, but the author was not Lamont, who did not contribute to the book.

[50] Bruce, *In Retrospect*, 187–188; Grass, *F. F. Bruce*, 88–91; Ian M. Randall, *Educating Evangelicalism: The Origins, Development and Impact of London Bible College* (Carlisle: Paternoster Press, 2000), 85–87; Roger Shuff, *Searching for the True Church: Brethren and Evangelicals in Mid-Twentieth-Century England* (Milton Keynes: Paternoster, 2005), 90–93; see the allusions in H. L. Ellison, *From Tragedy to Triumph: The Message of the Book of Job* (London: Paternoster Press, 1958), preface and p. 61.

with traditional views of the authority of Scripture. Evangelical seminaries and their faculties thus found themselves at the centre of the storm.

The earliest and one of the most protracted of these controversies concerned Fuller Theological Seminary. As discussed in chapter 2, the publication in 1959 of Edward Carnell's *The Case for Orthodox Theology* was a key marker signalling the desire of some of the Fuller faculty to distance themselves from fundamentalism. Some of Carnell's colleagues went further than he did in adopting the view that any claim for the inerrancy of the Bible on matters of history or science was intellectually untenable. One such from December 1962 was the new dean, Daniel Fuller, son of the founder, Charles Fuller, and a former PhD student of Karl Barth's in Basel. The shift in Fuller's theological position seemed to be confirmed by the election as president in January 1963 of David A. Hubbard, a Fuller alumnus and member of faculty at Westmont College in California, an institution established in 1940 with a strong constitutional commitment to biblical inerrancy.[51] At Westmont Hubbard had been jointly responsible for a new Old Testament syllabus that adopted moderate positions on various critical issues. Public pronouncements by Daniel Fuller, Hubbard and other members of the Fuller faculty in the course of the 1960s and early 1970s raised increasing questions in the supporting constituency about the wholeheartedness of their subscription to the seminary's basis of faith, which affirmed the inerrancy of the original scriptural autographs in their entirety. In February 1964 the most conservative members of faculty resigned, among them the vice-president, Harold Lindsell. In 1972 the seminary adopted a new statement of faith which affirmed the trustworthiness of the Old and New Testaments as 'the only infallible rule of faith and practice' – a phrase taken from the Westminster Confession of Faith: to conservatives, this signalled Fuller's abandonment of a commitment to full biblical inerrancy.[52]

In 1976 Lindsell, who had succeeded Carl Henry as editor of *Christianity Today* in 1968, published *The Battle for the Bible*. The foundational premise of the book was the assertion that 'orthodoxy and the historical-critical method are deadly enemies that are antithetical and cannot be reconciled without the destruction of the one or the other'.[53] Lindsell accordingly mounted a

---

[51] George M. Marsden, *Reforming Fundamentalism: Fuller Seminary and the New Evangelicalism* (Grand Rapids: Eerdmans, 1987), 209.

[52] Harold Lindsell, *The Battle for the Bible* (Grand Rapids: Zondervan, 1976), 116. For a full and authoritative account of Fuller Seminary during this period see Marsden, *Reforming Fundamentalism*.

[53] Lindsell, *Battle for the Bible*, 82.

full-blooded attack on evangelical theological institutions that had adopted the historical-critical method; he devoted a whole chapter to Fuller Seminary. He also attempted to provide solutions to some of the most obvious difficulties confronting a strict inerrantist view of Scripture: in an ingenious but self-defeating attempt to harmonize the various synoptic accounts of Peter's denial of Christ, he concluded that Peter must have denied Jesus six times, rather than the three times the gospel writers recorded.[54] Lindsell renewed the onslaught on his former institution in 1979 with a sequel, *The Bible in the Balance*, in which he proclaimed that he now preferred to repudiate the label 'evangelical' in favour of 'fundamentalist', as only the latter term now indicated unambiguously that one stood for a Bible wholly without error.[55]

Few conservative evangelicals followed Lindsell in being prepared to abandon the term 'evangelical' and return to a fundamentalist self-designation. But his insistence that inerrancy was *the* watershed issue defining evangelical identity attracted widespread American support. With the evangelical philosopher Francis Schaeffer and the Anglican theologian J. I. Packer he was a prime mover in 1977 in forming the International Council on Biblical Inerrancy (ICBI).[56] In its origins the ICBI was 'International' only as a result of Packer's participation: he was the sole non-American member.[57] In 1978 the Council issued 'The Chicago Statement on Biblical Inerrancy', which affirmed the inerrancy of the autographs in relation to all areas of knowledge, including science. Drafted mainly by Packer, it has been compared with *The Fundamentals* of the early twentieth century, though not all the authors of *The Fundamentals* were inerrantists.[58] Certainly, the tone of many ICBI publications has been reminiscent of American fundamentalism, and has caused embarrassment to more scholarly conservatives, such as Don Carson, who have sought to retain the concept of inerrancy but to define it in ways that

---

[54] Ibid. 174–176.

[55] Harold Lindsell, *The Bible in the Balance* (Grand Rapids: Zondervan, 1979), 319, 322; see Marsden, *Reforming Fundamentalism*, 287.

[56] On Schaeffer see chapter 5 below, 133–139.

[57] Alister E. McGrath, *To Know and Serve God: A Biography of James I. Packer* (London: Hodder & Stoughton, 1997), 198–199.

[58] Ibid. 199; J. W. Wenham, *Facing Hell*, 193; Robert M. Price, 'Inerrant the Wind: The Troubled House of North American Evangelicals', *EvQ* 55 (1983), 129–144; Stanley J. Grenz, 'Nurturing the Soul, Informing the Mind. The Genesis of the Evangelical Scripture Principle', in Vincent Bacote, Laura C. Miguélez and Dennis L. Okholm (eds.), *Evangelicals and Scripture: Tradition, Authority and Hermeneutics* (Downers Grove: InterVarsity Press, 2004), 32.

give more room for intellectual manoeuvre than some ICBI authors would allow.[59]

Others who were unhappy with the new Fuller position that scriptural infallibility could not be extended to the spheres of history and science felt obliged to limit the notion slightly differently, by invoking the principle that Scripture was infallible only in relation to its divinely intended purpose. This was essentially the stance taken by both F. F. Bruce and Howard Marshall in Britain, and even by D. Broughton Knox in Australia, who as principal of Moore College from 1959 to 1985 exercised a strongly conservative influence on Anglicanism in the Sydney diocese.[60] In North America it is significant that perhaps the most influential exponent of this view has been a former PhD student of Bruce's at Manchester: the Canadian Baptist, Clark Pinnock. Pinnock had given the Tyndale Lecture in Biblical Theology in Cambridge in 1966 under the title *A Defense of Biblical Infallibility*, in which he defended strict inerrancy, a principle he derived from B. B. Warfield and Francis Schaeffer. By 1984, however, he was arguing in *The Scripture Principle* that while the concept of inerrancy should be retained as a way of expressing the Church's proper confidence in the revelatory capacity and entire trustworthiness of Scripture, recognition of the humanity of the biblical authors made a strict notion of inerrancy untenable. It was a shift that he himself described in terms of a move from Schaeffer's militant rationalism to Bruce's irenic inductive scholarship.[61]

By the 1980s the spotlight of controversy over inerrancy was moving from Fuller Seminary to other institutions, and indeed, as will be indicated shortly, to an entire American denomination. In 1983 J. Ramsey Michaels, for twenty-five years a faculty member at Gordon-Conwell Seminary in Massachusetts,

---

[59] D. A. Carson, 'Recent Developments in the Doctrine of Scripture', in D. A. Carson and J. D. Woodbridge (eds.), *Hermeneutics, Authority and Canon* (Leicester: Inter-Varsity Press, 1986), 7 and 364, n. 9.

[60] For Bruce's view of biblical inspiration see Oakes, 'F. F. Bruce', 110–113; for Marshall's see his *Biblical Inspiration* (London: Hodder & Stoughton, 1982); for Knox's see Robert J. Banks, 'The Theology of D. B. Knox – a Preliminary Estimate', in Peter T. O'Brien and David G. Peterson (eds.), *God Who Is Rich in Mercy: Essays Presented to Dr. D. B. Knox* (Homebush West, NSW: Lancer Books, 1986), 380–381.

[61] Clark H. Pinnock, *A Defense of Biblical Infallibility* (Nutley, N.J.: P. & R. Publishing, 1967); *The Scripture Principle* (San Francisco: Harper & Row, 1984); Barry L. Callen, 'Clark H. Pinnock, His Life and Work', in Stanley E. Porter and Anthony R. Cross (eds.), *Semper Reformandum: Studies in Honour of Clark H. Pinnock* (Carlisle: Paternoster Press, 2003), 2, 5. Pinnock also moved from a Reformed position to one of Arminianism and 'open theism'.

was forced to resign from the faculty following the publication two years previously of his *Servant and Son: Jesus in Parable and Gospel*.[62] Michaels's book aimed, in a way that was unprecedented in the evangelical community, to explore the human consciousness and experience of Jesus as one who himself learned from, and was subject to influence by, other humans, notably John the Baptist. Michaels no doubt believed he was simply taking the human nature of Jesus seriously, and his book received a favourable review from Howard Marshall in the *Evangelical Quarterly*.[63] For many evangelicals, however, statements such as his suggestion that Jesus' hard line on divorce might have been shaped by John the Baptist's stance towards Herod's marital life seemed to strike at the heart of the traditional understanding of the unique authority of Jesus as the Son of God.[64]

In the year following the appearance of Michaels's book, Robert H. Gundry, another former PhD student of F. F. Bruce and a member of faculty at Westmont College, published a commentary on Matthew's Gospel that questioned how far the Gospel could be called 'historical in a modern sense'. According to Gundry, Matthew's redaction (editorial reworking) of the traditions about Jesus that he had received went 'beyond the bounds we nowadays want a historian to respect': 'We are not dealing with a few scattered difficulties', concluded Gundry; 'We are dealing with a vast network of tendentious changes.'[65] Gundry was well aware of the likely reaction of many of his fellow-evangelicals, and therefore added a long theological postscript seeking to justify his interpretation; it called for conservatives to retain their confidence that the Bible could be equated with the Word of God but to abandon 'the straining to resolve all historical difficulties'.[66] The Evangelical Theological Society, of which Gundry was a member, was not persuaded by Gundry's pleas, and at its 1983 annual meeting in Dallas voted by 199 to 36 to go on record as 'rejecting any position that states that Matthew or any other biblical writer materially altered and embellished historical tradition or departed from the actuality of events'. It then voted by 116 to 41 to request Gundry's resignation as a member.[67]

---

[62] Noll, *Between Faith and Criticism*, 171–173.

[63] *EvQ* 56 (1984), 50.

[64] J. Ramsey Michaels, *Servant and Son: Jesus in Parable and Gospel* (Atlanta: John Knox Press, 1981), 22.

[65] Robert H. Gundry, *Matthew: A Commentary on His Literary and Theological Art* (Grand Rapids: Eerdmans, 1982), 623, 625.

[66] Ibid. 623–640 (quotation at 627).

[67] Noll, *Between Faith and Criticism*, 169.

One of the founding members of the ICBI in 1977 was W. A. Criswell (1909–2002), pastor since 1944 of First Baptist Church, Dallas, probably the largest and most influential congregation in the Southern Baptist Convention, the dominant form of Protestantism in most of the southern states. During the 1960s and 1970s, as Southern Baptist scholars endeavoured to reconnect their large but insular denomination with the mainstream of American Protestant culture, periodic controversy arose over publications written by some faculty members in Southern Baptist seminaries, or by more liberal British Baptist scholars recruited to write for the Convention, which appeared to contradict the Convention's inerrantist statement of faith. The most notable furore was in 1970–1 over a commentary on Genesis written by G. Henton Davies, the Welsh principal of Regent's Park College, Oxford, for the new Broadman series of commentaries issued by the Convention's Sunday School Board, which was eventually compelled to withdraw it from the series. Conservatives such as Criswell became increasingly suspicious of the leading Southern Baptist seminaries, and in 1971 he established his own Criswell Center for Biblical Studies in Dallas. A new and explicitly inerrantist seminary, Mid-America Baptist Seminary, was founded in 1972 in Little Rock, Arkansas, though it soon moved to Memphis, Tennessee.[68]

By the end of the 1970s, conservatives in the Convention were beginning to organize a systematic campaign to limit the exposure of Southern Baptists to what the president of the Criswell Center for Biblical Studies, Paige Patterson, graphically described as 'harmful theological radiation'.[69] They saw the truth of the Bible as the essential issue at stake, and vested in trusted senior pastors such as Criswell the power to determine where the boundaries of legitimate biblical interpretation lay – a subordination of biblical to ecclesiastical authority that resembled Catholic more than Protestant principles.[70] In his address to the Southern Baptist Pastors Conference in Dallas in 1985 Criswell outlined a grim 'pattern of death for a denomination' by referring to British Baptists in the aftermath of the Downgrade controversy of the 1880s. Criswell believed that the numerical and spiritual decline of British Baptists had begun with the Baptist Union's repudiation of Spurgeon's allegations. He also alluded to the

---

[68] See Nancy Tatom Ammermann, *Baptist Battles: Social Change and Religious Conflict in the Southern Baptist Convention* (New Brunswick, N.J.: Rutgers University Press, 1990), 63–70.

[69] *MM*, Sept. 1979, 126.

[70] Joe E. Barnhart, 'What's All the Fighting About? Southern Baptists and the Bible?', in Nancy Tatom Ammerman (ed.), *Southern Baptists Observed: Multiple Perspectives on a Changing Denomination* (Knoxville: University of Tennessee Press, 1993), 132–134.

Northern Baptists' Divinity School in Chicago as proof of the 'rot' caused by higher criticism.[71]

The breakthrough for the conservatives came in June 1985, when some forty-five thousand delegates gathered in Dallas for the annual Convention, at which a conservative coalition led by Paige Patterson and Paul Pressler, a Houston judge, consolidated their control of the appointment process for the nomination of trustees, and hence of the whole Southern Baptist machinery. A systematic purge of non-inerrantists – including many who were by no means liberal – from the faculties of the leading Southern Baptist seminaries followed.[72] At Southeastern seminary in Wake Forest one-third of the faculty and one-half of the administration had gone by the end of the 1988–9 academic year. There was a drastic fall in both student enrolment and alumni contributions.[73] More serious still, the Southern Baptist Convention itself began to fragment. Some of the individual state Baptist conventions effectively declared independence, and two new moderate groupings emerged in protest against the fundamentalist takeover: the Cooperative Baptist Fellowship, formalized in 1991, and the smaller and more liberal Alliance of Baptists, formed in 1987.[74] As in the 1930s, battles over the nature of biblical authority proved capable of splitting denominations whose roots and predominant ethos were essentially evangelical.

Preaching the Bible

The revival of expository preaching
The renaissance of conservative biblical scholarship was undoubtedly one of the most striking developments in the history of evangelical attitudes to the Bible in the second half of the twentieth century, but its significance is rivalled by the revival in many parts of the English-speaking world of a tradition of expository preaching. Early twentieth-century evangelical preaching had not generally been marked by the systematic weekly exposition of the message of different biblical books, with some exceptions, most notably the two ministries of George Campbell Morgan (1863–1945) at Westminster

---

[71] Ammermann, *Baptist Battles*, 80–81.

[72] Ibid. 3–12.

[73] Ibid. 249–250.

[74] For the founding document of the Cooperative Baptist Fellowship see http://thefellow ship.info/cbf/files/29/2982b463-235d-43ad-9173-917ee67d6b8b.pdf (accessed 27 Apr. 2012). For the Alliance of Baptists see http://www.allianceofbaptists.org (accessed 27 Apr. 2012).

Chapel in London from 1904 to 1917 and 1933 to 1943.[75] More characteristic of the evangelical tradition in the mid-twentieth century was the celebrated Scottish preacher James S. Stewart (1896–1990), who usually preached on a single verse as a text, and for whom the tradition of expounding whole sections of Scripture was 'alien'.[76] Nevertheless, Campbell Morgan's successor at Westminster Chapel, D. Martyn Lloyd-Jones, testified that he had encountered many ministers, both Free Church and Anglican, who claimed to derive their method of preaching from Campbell Morgan's example.[77] Lloyd-Jones himself was, of course, to take this method of preaching to a new level, and give it a specifically Reformed theological imprint, which Morgan lacked.[78] During his own long and influential ministry at the Chapel from 1943 to 1968, Lloyd-Jones became renowned for his mammoth weekly series on books of the Bible, with pride of place going to Romans, which took thirteen years to complete, and Ephesians, which took eight.[79] The attraction of Lloyd-Jones's lengthy sermons (which usually lasted for 50–60 minutes) lay in their unusual combination of clinical Reformed logic and a spiritual passion shaped by the heritage of the Welsh Revival: he defined preaching as 'Logic on fire! Eloquent reason!'[80]

The influence of Martyn Lloyd-Jones extended far beyond the 1,500 to 2,000 who came regularly to hear him on a Sunday. His style of expository preaching was followed, though rarely with such brilliance, by many Free Church pastors of Reformed inclination in England and Wales, and had imitators in North America. A trip to North America in 1947 undertaken on behalf of the International Fellowship of Evangelical Students (IFES), of which he was chairman for thirteen years, made a great impact on those who heard him, not least on C. Stacey Woods, the Australian-born first general secretary of the InterVarsity Christian Fellowship; Woods became convinced that the shallowness of much contemporary evangelicalism was due to the neglect of expository preaching.[81]

---

[75] Jill Morgan, *A Man of the Word: Life of G. Campbell Morgan* (London: Pickering & Inglis, 1951), 158.

[76] Robin Barbour, *J. S. Stewart in a Nutshell* (n.p.: Handsel Press, 2000), 15.

[77] Morgan, *Man of the Word*, 330.

[78] John Brencher, *Martyn Lloyd-Jones (1899–1981) and Twentieth-Century Evangelicalism* (Carlisle: Paternoster Press, 2006), 19.

[79] Ibid. 28.

[80] Ibid. 31.

[81] A. Donald MacLeod, *C. Stacey Woods and the Evangelical Rediscovery of the University* (Downers Grove: IVP Academic, 2007), 102–103.

The closest equivalents to Lloyd-Jones in the United States were probably Donald Grey Barnhouse (1895–1960) and James Montgomery Boice (1938–2000), both senior ministers of Tenth Presbyterian Church, Philadelphia. Barnhouse, pastor from 1927 to 1960, began his own series of expository sermons on Romans in 1949, which were broadcast weekly on his Bible Study Hour programme on NBC radio. The series continued for nearly twelve years until his death, and was published in ten volumes. For over thirty years he conducted a weekly Bible study class in New York City, which drew an attendance of more than five hundred. Barnhouse combined Reformed theology with an old-style fundamentalism and a premillennial dispensational view of prophecy.[82] Boice, pastor from 1968 to 2000, shared Lloyd-Jones's passion for systematic expository preaching, his love for Reformed theology and his unshakeable conviction in biblical inspiration. Boice was chairman of the ICBI from 1977 to 1988, and the founder in 1994 of the Reformed coalition, the Alliance of Confessing Evangelicals.[83]

The Church of Scotland also witnessed a significant revival of expository preaching during this period, although it appears to have been more of a parallel development to that led by Lloyd-Jones in England and Wales than a direct consequence of it. The pioneer of the expository revival in Scotland was Willie Still (1911–97), minister of Gilcomston South Church in Aberdeen from 1945 to shortly before his death. Although Still was present at the first service Lloyd-Jones took as senior pastor of Westminster Chapel, he claimed that in late 1946 he 'stumbled' on the method of systematic expository preaching 'almost by accident', but 'surely by divine providence', rather than borrowing it from Lloyd-Jones.[84] Still was no less committed than Lloyd-Jones to Reformed theology, though the range of his evangelical sympathies was broader. Unlike Lloyd-Jones he was an unequivocal supporter of the Billy Graham crusades, and was a more regular speaker at university Christian Unions. A close friend and regular attendee at Sunday evening services and midweek Bible studies was Howard Marshall, the leading New Testament

---

[82] *American National Biography*, II, 207–209; C. Allyn Russell, 'Donald Grey Barnhouse: Fundamentalist Who Changed', *Journal of Presbyterian History* 59 (1981), 33–57; http://www.alliancenet.org/partner/Article_Display_Page/0,,PTID307086_CHID581348_CIID1907714,00.html (accessed 27 Apr. 2012).

[83] See Philip G. Ryken, Derek W. H. Thomas and J. Ligon Duncan III, *Give Praise to God: A Vision for Reforming Worship: Celebrating the Legacy of James Montgomery Boice* (Phillipsburg: P. & R. Publishing, 2003); http://www.alliancenet.org/CC_Content_Page/0,,PTID307086_CHID798774_CIID,00.html (accessed 27 Apr. 2012).

[84] William Still, *Dying to Live* (Fearn: Christian Focus Publications, 1991), 119–120, 128.

scholar, who as a Methodist was Arminian in theology.[85] Particularly through a gathering of invited ministers known as the Crieff Brotherhood, established in 1970, Still's influence extended to a whole school of evangelical ministers in the Church of Scotland.

Lloyd-Jones's ministry was reaching the peak of its influence when in June 1950 John R. W. Stott (1921–2011) was appointed as rector of All Souls, Langham Place, the church where he had been reared as a youngster and which he had served as assistant curate since 1945. Like Lloyd-Jones, Boice and Still, Stott's preaching ministry was to be centred on a single pastoral charge extending over several decades: although he was succeeded as rector in 1970 by Michael Baughen, Stott continued as rector emeritus to preach regularly at All Souls well into the 1990s. While Stott's theology stood squarely in the tradition of the English Reformers, it was softer in its Calvinistic emphases than was Lloyd-Jones's. Similarly, while Stott also favoured systematic Bible exposition, his preaching series were markedly shorter, more varied in subject matter and more consistently evangelistic or apologetic in intent than were his London neighbour's. His model for an expository ministry was not any of the Puritans who so inspired Lloyd-Jones, but the evangelical Anglican clergyman E. J. H. Nash ('Bash'), who as an evangelist with the Scripture Union working with public schoolboys had first led Stott to Christ at Rugby School in 1938.[86]

Perhaps the greatest contrast between the two British evangelical leaders lies in the means whereby their influence was exercised. Though prominent in IVF circles in the 1940s and 1950s, from the mid-1960s Lloyd-Jones distanced himself from evangelical student work in Britain, fearing that the doctrinal purity of the IVF was being compromised by Anglican influence.[87] Despite his senior role in IFES, he travelled little beyond the British Isles. Although he wrote some thirty-nine books, none was a best-seller. In contrast, the formative role John Stott played in the shaping of modern evangelicalism was exercised not so much through his preaching ministry in the West End of London, strategic though that undoubtedly was, but through a combination of regular participation in Christian unions and missions in universities in Britain and overseas, international speaking tours and writing many extremely

---

[85] I. Howard Marshall, 'Church and Ministry in I Timothy', in Nigel M. de S. Cameron and Sinclair B. Ferguson (eds.), *Pulpit and People: Essays in Honour of William Still on his 75th Birthday* (Edinburgh: Rutherford House Books, 1986), 51.

[86] Dudley-Smith, *Making of a Leader*, 91–96, 232; Alister Chapman, *Godly Ambition: John Stott and the Evangelical Movement* (New York: Oxford University Press, 2012), 13–18, 63–64, 79, 115, 131.

[87] Brencher, *Martyn Lloyd-Jones*, 220–221.

successful books. His evangelistic addresses delivered in various universities in Britain, Canada, the United States, Australia and South Africa during the early 1950s became the source of his most widely read book, *Basic Christianity*, first published in 1958. Sales had reached over 1.3 million copies by 1988, and by 1997 the book had been translated into over fifty languages.[88] The book he judged to be his best and that most fully expounded his foundational convictions about the atonement – *The Cross of Christ* (1986) – was translated into twenty languages.[89] As a result of this global ministry, Stott became the dominant intellectual influence and role model for a whole generation or more of those who assumed positions of leadership in evangelical churches and parachurch organizations in many parts of the world. Always one with a keen eye for training future evangelical leaders, Stott established the Langham Trust in 1969 to assist emerging scholars from the Majority World to study theology in Britain. The Langham Partnership International Scholars' Scheme, as it subsequently became, and its sister body in the United States, John Stott Ministries, have proved extraordinarily strategic ever since in providing high-level training for evangelical theological educators and church leaders from beyond the West.[90] Stott was also passionately concerned to encourage evangelicals to apply the principles of biblical Christianity to all areas of society, a broad vision that led him to institute the London Lectures in Contemporary Christianity in 1974, which led in turn to the establishment of the London Institute for Contemporary Christianity in 1982.[91]

Nowhere outside Britain was Stott's influence more evident than in Australia, which he visited in 1958, 1965, 1971, 1979, 1981 and 1986.[92] Although his six visits to the country are clearly not the only source of the current strength of Australian evangelical Anglicanism, which has a much longer history, they have contributed to it. It has been suggested that Stott's example is largely responsible for the popularity of expository preaching in the Sydney diocese.[93] That outcome, however, may owe even more to the long principalships at Moore

---

[88] Dudley-Smith, *Making of a Leader*, 456.

[89] 'John Stott: Preacher and writer who exerted a colossal influence on evangelical Christianity', obituary in *The Independent*, 29 July 2011.

[90] Timothy Dudley-Smith, *John Stott: A Global Ministry* (Leicester: Inter-Varsity Press, 2001), 141–142; http://www.langhampartnership.org/about-us/history (accessed 27 Apr. 2012).

[91] Chapman, *Godly Ambition*, 128.

[92] Dudley-Smith, *Global Ministry*, 533–534.

[93] See http://en.wikipedia.org/wiki/Anglican_Diocese_of_Sydney (accessed 27 Apr. 2012).

College of T. C. Hammond (1935–53) and David Broughton Knox (1959–85), which secured a stream of Anglican clergy committed to the centrality of biblical exposition and to Knox's uncompromising view that all divine revelation was propositional in character, an emphasis continued after 1985 by his successor, Peter Jensen.[94] Sydney Anglicanism has acquired a pronounced Reformed edge, which it is hard to attribute to the influence of John Stott, whose defence of biblical truth exhibited a rather softer tone.

A contrasting style of evangelical preaching

Systematic expository preaching as modelled by Lloyd-Jones, Barnhouse, Boice, Still and Stott is the style of preaching that most observers associate with the evangelical tradition in the late twentieth century. It was not, however, the only style practised by those who may be denominated as evangelical. A very different, more populist, style of biblical preaching was evident in the African-American churches of the United States, with close parallels in Afro-Caribbean churches in Britain and elsewhere. One outstanding example of the genre must suffice to illustrate the point.

Gardner Calvin Taylor (1918–) was for forty-two years, from 1948 to 1990, pastor of Concord Baptist Church of Christ in Brooklyn, New York. During his ministry the membership grew from five thousand to fourteen thousand, making the church the largest congregation in New York City. Taylor was a keen supporter of the civil rights movement, and a close associate of Martin Luther King. Yet he was never an advocate of the 'social gospel' alone: 'Taylor never understood his mission as bringing the kingdom of God on earth, the utopian goal of nineteenth-century liberalism, but rather the prophetic task of "making straight in the desert a highway for our God".'[95] Taylor was a master of oratory in the African-American style, with an extraordinary vocal range and ability to convey the drama of biblical narrative. His method of preaching was to select 'a great preaching text of the Bible' and then 'proceed to "seek my footing in the Word of God"', incisively applying the text to the social context of his congregation.[96] A Baylor University survey published in

---

[94] Stuart Piggin, *Evangelical Christianity in Australia: Spirit, Word, and World* (Melbourne: Oxford University Press, 1996), 185–186; see also O'Brien and Peterson, *God Who Is Rich*.

[95] Timothy George, James Earl Massey and Robert Smith, Jr. (eds.), *Our Sufficiency Is of God: Essays on Preaching in Honor of Gardner C. Taylor* (Macon, Ga.: Mercer University Press, 2010), xv.

[96] Richard Lischer, 'Taylor, Gardner C.', in William H. Willimon and Richard Lischer (eds.), *Concise Encyclopedia of Preaching* (Louisville, Ky.: John Knox Press, 1995), 466; see

Newsweek in 1997 named him as one of the twelve greatest preachers in the English-speaking world.[97] In 1995 *Christianity Today* featured Taylor in an article entitled 'The Pulpit King', which noted that he combined passionate preaching for social justice with an explicitly evangelical understanding of the atonement. It also reported Taylor's own judgment that he was an evangelical 'in the European sense', in that he shared European evangelicalism's 'commitment to the gospel in its outreach toward human beings and the sufficient work of Jesus Christ', but without 'a rigid kind of doctrinaire position', which he associated with many evangelicals in America. In spite of his undoubted stature, he remains a largely unknown name among white evangelicals, even in his own country.[98]

Reading and hearing the Bible

The Bible in modern African Christianity

Taylor's example is a reminder that there are large sections of the global evangelical constituency for whom the authority of Scripture is not so much a theoretical axiom to be defended, defined and argued over, as an unquestioned basis for a living and prophetic Christian faith. In concluding this chapter it is therefore appropriate to make some reference to evangelicals from the continent of Africa whose way of using the Bible reflects a cultural context far removed from that of the post-Enlightenment West. African Christians have been very little concerned with the questions of historicity, textual criticism or the credibility of biblical accounts of miracles that have been so central in European or North American debates between liberals and conservatives over Scripture. The worlds of the Old and New Testaments (particularly the former) have often appeared remarkably close to the cultural experience of modern African Christians for whom drought and famine, war and exile, landlessness and poverty, epidemic disease and untimely death are as tragically familiar as they were for many characters in biblical narrative. African approaches to the Bible are often labelled in the North as being 'fundamentalist', but their concerns are strikingly different from those that characterized northern conservatives during the fundamentalist debates. As one leader of an African independent church has expressed it:

---

also Martha Simmons and Frank A. Thomas (eds.), *Preaching with Sacred Fire: An Anthology of African American Sermons, 1750 to the Present* (New York: W. W. Norton, 2010), 829–831.

[97]   George, Massey and Smith, *Our Sufficiency Is of God*, xxi.

[98]   Edward Gilbreath, 'The Pulpit King', *CT*, 11 Dec. 1995, 25–28 (quotation at 28).

We read the Bible as a book that comes from God and we take every word in the Bible seriously. Some people will say that we are therefore fundamentalists. We do not know whether this word applies to us or not but we are not interested in any interpretation of the Bible that softens or waters down the message. We do not have the same problems about the Bible as white people have with their scientific mentality.[99]

This is not to say that there have been no battles to fight over the authority and interpretation of the Bible in an African context. There have been African evangelical leaders who have been particularly concerned at the apparent threat to scriptural authority posed by liberal approaches to inculturation and the theological status of traditional religious beliefs and practices. Chief among these was the Nigerian Byang H. Kato, the first African general secretary of the Association of Evangelicals of Africa and Madagascar until his untimely death in a swimming accident. Kato, who had studied at London Bible College and the dispensationalist Dallas Theological Seminary, voiced his profound anxiety at apparently syncretistic tendencies in African theology in his book *Theological Pitfalls in Africa* (1975). Kato was insistent that the gospel as good *news* stands in radical discontinuity from traditional African beliefs. His legacy has shaped the more conservative sections of African evangelicalism through such institutions as the Nairobi Evangelical Graduate School of Theology, established in 1983 (now part of Africa International University), whose chapel bears his name.[100]

An altogether different style of African evangelicalism was represented by the Ghanaian Presbyterian minister and theologian Kwame Bediako. Bediako was a brilliant intellectual who was converted from atheism to Christ while studying French and African Francophone literature at the University of Bordeaux. After theological studies at London Bible College, Bediako studied for his (second) doctorate at Aberdeen for a thesis, subsequently published,[101] which compared the theological issues raised for the church in the second century by the Greco-Roman religious and philosophical heritage with those raised for modern African Christianity by the African religious past. His supervisor was the leading missiologist and scholar of world Christianity

---

[99] Cited in Philip Jenkins, *The New Faces of Christianity: Believing the Bible in the Global South* (New York: Oxford University Press, 2006), 11.

[100] On Kato see Keith Ferdinando, 'The Legacy of Byang Kato', *International Bulletin of Missionary Research* 28 (2004), 169–174.

[101] Kwame Bediako, *Theology and Identity: The Impact of Culture upon Christian Thought in the Second Century and Modern Africa* (Oxford: Regnum Books, 1992).

Andrew F. Walls, who had started his academic career as a patristic scholar and as such had served as librarian of Tyndale House from 1952 to 1957. While Kato's contribution has been to warn African Christians not to forget the liberating novelty of the gospel, Bediako's has been to help them to hear the message of the Bible and the gospel 'as *our story*, not as some alien story',[102] and hence to find ways of expressing their faith that do not sever them from their cultural backgrounds. Through his numerous publications, his active involvement in the Lausanne movement, the International Fellowship of Evangelical Mission Theologians and the Oxford Centre for Mission Studies, and his role from 1985 as the founding director of Ghana's Akrofi-Christaller Institute of Theology, Mission, and Culture, Bediako charted a pathway for African Christianity that combined scholarly excellence, fidelity to the Bible and cultural authenticity.[103]

By the final years of the twentieth century, as the extraordinary scale of African adhesion to Christianity became plain, it was clear that the key theological issues for African Christians were not so much the authority of the Bible in principle – which almost all accepted – as the nature of its interpretation, particularly in the area of salvation. For African believers, as for many others in the non-western world, the new life Christ came to bring is emphatically a present and tangible reality in this world, and not simply for the life to come. This emphasis has provided a needed corrective to elements of northern-hemisphere evangelical tradition, but it has also opened the door to readings of the Bible among sections of the neo-Pentecostal movement that virtually reduce the biblical concept of salvation to this-worldly prosperity. The Second Pan-African Christian Leadership Assembly meeting in Nairobi in September 1994 accordingly voiced a concern – one that is widely repeated by African church leaders and not merely by expatriate missionaries – that 'the church in Africa was a mile long in terms of quantity, but only an inch-deep in terms of quality'.[104] This concern gave rise in January 2001 to a meeting at the

---

102 Kwame Bediako, 'Jesus in African Culture: A Ghanaian Perspective', in William A. Dyrness (ed.), *Emerging Voices in Global Christian Theology* (Grand Rapids: Zondervan, 1994), 100–101 (his italics).

103 See Andrew F. Walls, 'Kwame Bediako and Christian Scholarship in Africa', *International Bulletin of Missionary Research* 32 (2008), 188–193; Cephas Omenyo, 'In Remembrance of the Late Professor Dr. Kwame Bediako', *Exchange* 37 (2008), 387–389; J. K. Asamoah-Gyadu, 'Bediako of Africa: A Late 20th Century Outstanding Theologian and Teacher', *Mission Studies* 26 (2009), 5–16.

104 Tokunboh Adeyemo (ed.), *Africa Bible Commentary* (Nairobi: WordAlive Publishers, 2006), viii.

Nairobi Evangelical Graduate School of Theology that agreed to commission a one-volume Bible commentary, written by African evangelical scholars for Africans. *The Africa Bible Commentary* was eventually published in 2006, with a team of seventy African contributors that included Kwame Bediako as well as others who stood in the tradition of Byang Kato. The pursuit of a distinctively evangelical but scholarly approach to the Bible, an endeavour initiated by the Biblical Research Committee of the IVF in Britain in the 1940s, remains a priority in the twenty-first century, but one now increasingly set within a global and multicultural framework and that hence finds itself addressing a new and broader set of theological questions.

5. DEFENDING THE FAITH IN A CHANGING CULTURAL CLIMATE

Evangelical apologetics and the legacy of the Enlightenment

Evangelicalism, although it draws deeply from the wells of Reformation and Puritan theology, was born in the Enlightenment era. It is not surprising, therefore, that for much of its history it has been shaped by characteristically 'modern' assumptions, especially in the field of epistemology (the philosophy of knowledge). This chapter will explore the changing patterns of apologetic by which evangelicals in the second half of the twentieth century sought to defend and commend their understanding of the Christian faith in a period when Enlightenment assumptions were increasingly eroded by the fundamental shifts in cultural and philosophical understanding that now carry the label of 'postmodernity' or 'postmodernism'. To a greater extent than any other chapter in this book, this chapter will be Anglo-American in its focus. Defending the faith was a necessary preoccupation of evangelicals in the post-Enlightenment Western context. Evangelicals in the non-Western world saw no great need to defend the faith against rationalist attack: in contexts where the main antagonists of Christianity were militant forms of Islam or Hinduism they tended to take the view that attack was the best form of defence, and concentrated their energies on the propagation of the Christian faith.

One of the ironies of the story, at least in the immediate post-war years when evangelicalism in America was still emerging from its fundamentalist chrysalis, is the extent to which evangelicals, who perceived the impact of

Enlightenment rationalism on biblical truth to be nothing short of disastrous, relied on rational, sometimes even rationalistic, arguments in their
endeavours to defend the authority of Scripture and traditional theism. As
a result, they often found themselves disagreeing with one another about
the limits of the capacity of reason or logic to commend divine revelation
to fallen human minds. Protestants have tended to be less enthusiastic than
Catholics about natural theology – which has traditionally been understood
as the attempt to draw theistic inferences or proofs from the observable structure and beauty of the natural world.[1] Nevertheless, one of the
consequences of the disruptive Enlightenment impact on theology was to
render Protestants more sympathetic to the quest to turn the armoury of
rational argument from being an opponent into being an ally of the historic
Christian faith. Evangelicals, especially those who stood within the tradition
of John Calvin, were thus more inclined in their apologetics than were liberal
Protestants to quarry those intellectual resources in the Reformation tradition that stressed the continuing imprint of the *imago Dei* (image of God) on
the consciousness even of sinful men and women. The legacy of Calvin was,
however, ambiguous: British evangelicals tended to rely more heavily than
their American counterparts on Calvin's emphatic insistence in the *Institutes of
the Christian Religion* that only 'the inward testimony of the Spirit', rather than
rational demonstration, would convince men and women of the truth of the
Scriptures.[2]

The chapter begins with a survey of four apologists (Cornelius Van Til,
Edward J. Carnell, Carl F. H. Henry and Francis A. Schaeffer), all of whom
stood unambiguously in the conservative evangelical camp. So, of course, did
John Stott, whose extraordinarily successful work of evangelistic apologetics,
Basic Christianity, mentioned in the previous chapter, had by 2010 sold over 2.5
million copies worldwide since its first appearance in 1958.[3] It is characteristic
of British evangelicalism that its most successful work of apologetics was
evangelistic in intent, Christocentric in focus and from the pen of an exposi-

---

[1] See Alister E. McGrath, *The Open Secret: A New Vision for Natural Theology* (Malden,
    Mass.: Blackwell, 2009), for a convincing exposition of the view that natural theology,
    properly understood, is not in fact an attempt to 'prove' the existence of God from
    the natural world, but rather a *reinforcement of* an existing belief in God through the
    consonance or fit between faith and observation. Natural theology also enables those
    who have faith to gain an enhanced aesthetic appreciation of nature: it is about the
    appreciation of beauty as well as the determination of truth.

[2] John Calvin, *Institutes of the Christian Religion*, bk. 1, ch. 7.

[3] See chapter 4 above, 115.

tory preacher rather than an academic theologian. In Britain evangelicals looked primarily to preachers and secondarily to conservative biblical scholars as the necessary channels for 'the inward testimony of the Spirit' to be heard. In the United States, perhaps because of the legacy of the fundamentalist debates of the inter-war years, there was a greater investment in attempts to construct systematic and philosophical defences of conservative Christianity: Van Til, Carnell, Henry and Schaeffer were the most notable examples of this endeavour. The contrast is observable even at the more popular level of apologetics. The best-known American evangelical apologist, Josh McDowell (1939–), was even more of an evangelist than was John Stott – he was a student evangelist with Campus Crusade for Christ – but his apologetic approach was more appropriate for the courtroom than the pulpit. His best-selling *Evidence That Demands a Verdict*, first published by Campus Crusade in 1972, was identified by *Christianity Today* in 2006 as number thirteen in its list of the top fifty books that have shaped evangelicals.[4] McDowell's book has strengthened the confidence in the Bible of millions, both in North America and in other parts of the English-speaking world, but has limited scholarly credentials.

This chapter will also introduce a Protestant intellectual who has been uniquely influential in defending the right of Christian theism to occupy a place within the hostile environment of the contemporary secular academy. The American Reformed philosopher Alvin Plantinga, although an uncompromising champion of the deployment of logic in the defence of orthodox Christian faith, has devoted his academic career to the achievement of a goal much more limited in scope than that pursued by most evangelical apologists, namely to persuading others of the case that faith in God, whether or not it can be shown to be true, is at least reasonable. While undoubtedly evangelical in his foundational theological affirmations, Plantinga has charted his course quite independently of the mainstream of evangelical theology, and, as a result, has attracted only selective attention in broader evangelical circles.

The penultimate section of the chapter will note how, in the last two decades of the twentieth century, the Christian thinker who, perhaps more than any other, gave inspiration and confidence to evangelicals in the defence of their faith was Bishop Lesslie Newbigin, who had not generally been reckoned hitherto as a member of the conservative evangelical family, and was never an enthusiastic advocate of the deployment of Enlightenment methodologies in support of Christianity. It is significant that Newbigin, as someone who spent much of his life as a missionary in South India commending the

---

[4] *CT*, Oct. 2006, 51–55.

Christian faith in a Hindu environment, latterly adopted a perspective on how to counter the challenges of western modernity that differed markedly from the first three names mentioned, though it bore some intriguing similarities to the positions held by Schaeffer and Plantinga.

While evangelical theologians for the greater part of this period devoted a great deal of energy to the construction of a rational apologetic for biblical Christianity, it is striking that the evangelical reading public, especially in North America, consistently expressed a preference for the writings of a Christian apologist who was neither an evangelical nor a disciple of the clinical rationality of modernity: C. S. Lewis, the Ulster-born scholar of medieval literature and popular author of Christian apologetics, science fiction and children's literature will therefore receive some attention in the final section of this chapter.

It has not been possible to give adequate attention in this chapter to one specific and extremely important dimension of evangelical apologetics, namely that devoted to a defence of the compatibility between evangelical faith and modern science. Through organizations such as the American Scientific Affiliation (founded in 1941) and the Research Scientists' Christian Fellowship (which originated in Britain in 1944) professional scientists who were evangelicals have sought to demonstrate that there is no necessary conflict between modern scientific methodology and biblical Christianity. While such a case has undoubtedly been necessary in view of the volubility of certain public voices attacking Christianity in the name of science, the proportion of Christians among professional scientists in the late twentieth century was in fact consistently higher than that among academics in the humanities, perhaps precisely because conservative Christian apologetics tended to rely so widely on modern rather than postmodern approaches to factuality and truth.[5] A small number of Christian professional scientists have made the challenging methodological transition from scientific work to theological apologetics. Two British scientists did so with such intellectual distinction that they have gained renown as theologians: the theoretical physicist Sir John Polkinghorne (1930–) and the molecular biophysicist and subsequent historical theologian Alister McGrath (1953–). Polkinghorne to a certain extent, and McGrath unambiguously, have been associated with the evangelical movement.

---

[5] The same may be said about the Inter-Varsity movement, which has always been much stronger among students in the physical sciences than among those in the humanities and social sciences.

Cornelius Van Til – rational defender of Calvinism

Cornelius Van Til (1895–1987) was one of the first and most distinguished representatives of a stream of thinkers nurtured in the Christian Reformed Church, a denomination established by Dutch immigrants to the United States that has made an enormous contribution to evangelical scholarship. This has been expressed both through individual scholars such as Van Til and, more broadly, through its associated publishing houses, such as Eerdmans and Zondervan, which have been based in the Dutch American city of Grand Rapids, Michigan.[6] Cornelius Van Til was born in Grootegast in the Netherlands in 1895, and moved with his family to Indiana at the age of 10. He studied in the Christian Reformed Church's Calvin College and for one year at the associated Calvin Theological Seminary, before transferring to Princeton Theological Seminary for doctoral work. At Calvin College his teachers included the influential philosopher William Harry Jellema, and, in the Seminary, Louis Berkhof, the celebrated Reformed systematic theologian. His thought was also shaped by the Dutch theorists Abraham Kuyper and Herman Bavinck, notable advocates of the application of a Christian world view to all spheres of human knowledge and activity. Another of Van Til's mentors (though not his formal teacher) was J. Gresham Machen, the doughty opponent of theological liberalism, and in 1929 he joined the faculty of Machen's newly opened Westminster Theological Seminary, formed as a fundamentalist reaction to the Presbyterian Church–USA's determination to broaden the theological stance of Princeton Seminary. Van Til continued to teach at Westminster, latterly as professor of apologetics, until his retirement in 1972. In sympathy with Machen, Van Til transferred his membership in 1936 from the Christian Reformed Church to the overtly fundamentalist Presbyterian Church of America (later known as the Orthodox Presbyterian Church), where he retained his membership for the rest of his life.[7]

As John Frame notes, 'Van Til was not, like C. S. Lewis, a defender of "mere Christianity". He intended to defend the entire Reformed faith down to the smallest detail.'[8] For him there was no such thing as 'mere Christianity', no

---

[6] See Mark A. Noll, *The Scandal of the Evangelical Mind* (Grand Rapids: Eerdmans; Leicester: Inter-Varsity Press, 1994), 225–227; and, more fully, James D. Bratt, *Dutch Calvinism in Modern America: A History of a Conservative Subculture* (Grand Rapids: Eerdmans, 1984).

[7] For Van Til's life and thought see John M. Frame, *Cornelius Van Til: An Analysis of His Thought* (Phillipsburg: P. & R. Publishing, 1995).

[8] Ibid. 36.

halfway house between full-blown Calvinistic orthodoxy of the most unbend-
ing kind and a pernicious liberalism. Theological approaches other than classic
Reformed orthodoxy were to be confronted, not engaged in irenic dialogue.[9]
The title of his first major work, *The New Modernism: An Appraisal of the Theology
of Barth and Brunner* (1946), made explicit his dismissive verdict on neo-
orthodoxy. Bernard Ramm commented in 1983 that 'for many evangelicals
this book became the official evangelical interpretation of neoorthodoxy, and
for many it remains so even now'.[10] Van Til returned to the onslaught against
Barth in a number of later publications, notably *Christianity and Barthianism*
(1964), whose title was a deliberate echo of Machen's *Christianity and Liberalism*.

Van Til's apologetic approach is often described as 'presuppositionalist'.
He insisted that 'a consistently Christian method of apologetic argument, in
agreement with its own basic conception of the starting point, must be by
presupposition'.[11] The truth of Christianity and the falsity of other systems
simply had to be presupposed: 'The Reformed apologist will frankly admit
that his own methodology presupposes the truth of Christian theism.'[12] In
support of this apparently circular argument Van Til argued that there was,
and could be, no neutral starting point: all methodologies presupposed either
the truth or falsity of Christian theism; the only true methodology must be the
one that leads to the truth of Christian theism. Whereas a Roman Catholic or
an Arminian may appeal to rational perception of the autonomous facts of the
natural order in an endeavour to persuade an interlocutor that the Christian
presupposition was the correct one, that option, according to Van Til, is not
open to the Reformed apologist who knows that, as a result of total deprav-
ity, humans inevitably suppress that knowledge of the truth afforded by the
creation.[13] Nevertheless, Van Til maintained that Christian theism was the
unacknowledged presupposition on which scientists depended in order to do
their work, since nothing else could account for the uniformity of nature and
coherence of all things. 'Thus', concluded Van Til with considerable audacity,
'there is absolutely certain proof for the existence of God and the truth of
Christian theism.'[14]

---

[9] Ibid. 34–35.

[10] Bernard L. Ramm, *After Fundamentalism: The Future of Evangelical Theology* (San Francisco:
     Harper & Row, 1983), 23.

[11] Cornelius Van Til, *The Defense of the Faith*, 3rd ed. (Philadelphia: P. & R. Publishing,
     1967), 99.

[12] Ibid. 99–100.

[13] Ibid. 98–99, 101.

[14] Ibid. 103.

Hence Van Til may appear to demolish natural theology with the one hand, but to reconstruct it with the other. Evaluations of his position can thus vary widely, even from within the family of Reformed theology: while he is represented by most commentators as a fideist, insisting on the a priori character of the Christian revelation, other writers have been able to claim that he was not in fact as dismissive of the value of 'Christian evidences' as may appear at first sight.[15] Despite this ambiguity, his significance for later exponents of Reformed apologetics is undoubted. He was an early (though not a continuing) influence on Edward J. Carnell and a primary source of inspiration for Carl Henry. His thought has been seminal for American Christian reconstructionists (or theonomists) such as R. J. Rushdoony (1916–2001) and Gary North (1942–) who have argued for the duty of Christians to impose the dominion of biblical (including Mosaic) law on secular society, and in that respect Van Til may be identified as one of the philosophical architects of the extreme Christian right in the United States.[16] He was also a primary source of intellectual inspiration for Francis Schaeffer.

Edward J. Carnell – advocate of orthodox theology

Edward John Carnell may be less widely read today than Van Til, but he deserves to be remembered as one of the ablest evangelical apologists of post-war America. Son of a Baptist minister of fundamentalist persuasion, Carnell entered Wheaton College in 1937, where he fell under the spell of Gordon H. Clark (1902–85), an outstanding teacher of Reformed philosophy.[17] Clark, who, no less than Van Til, was a disciple of J. Gresham Machen and opponent of Karl Barth, believed that the task of Christian apologetics was to expose the rational inconsistencies of all systems other than biblical trinitarian Christianity. This was to be achieved not by the application of any distinctively biblical insight but rather through the application of the philosophical

---

[15] E.g. Greg Bahnsen, 'Pressing Toward the Mark: Machen, Van Til, and the Apologetical Tradition of the OPC' (1986), at http://www.cmfnow.com/articles/PA064.htm (accessed 20 Apr. 2012).

[16] Noll, *Scandal of the Evangelical Mind*, 224; see Chip Berlet and Matthew N. Lyons, *Right-Wing Populism in America: Too Close for Comfort* (London: Guilford Press, 2000), 212–213.

[17] For an enthusiastic appraisal of Clark see John W. Robbins, 'An Introduction to Gordon H. Clark', *Trinity Review* (July–Aug. 1993), 1–10; online at http://www.trinityfoundation.org/PDF/101a-AnIntroductiontoGordonHClark.pdf (accessed 20 Apr. 2012).

law of contradiction (sometimes termed the law of non-contradiction), as expounded by Aristotle in Book 4 of his *Metaphysics*, namely that 'The most certain of all basic principles is that contradictory propositions are not true simultaneously.'[18] Clark believed that 'every word of the Bible . . . exemplifies the law of contradiction' and that the task of hermeneutics was to make logical deductions from the propositional statements found in Scripture.[19] Although his period at Wheaton College was limited to the years from 1936 to 1943, Clark made a profound and lasting impact on a number of Wheaton students who later became distinguished proponents or evangelists of the Christian message, among them Carnell, Carl Henry, Edmund P. Clowney, Paul King Jewett, Harold Lindsell and Billy Graham.[20] Carnell left Wheaton in 1941 for Westminster Theological Seminary, where he studied under Van Til, before proceeding to do two simultaneous doctorates (on Reinhold Niebuhr and Søren Kierkegaard respectively) at Harvard and Boston Universities.

Although Van Til had regarded him as a brilliant student and as a personal friend while at Westminster, Carnell's intellectual pathway soon began to diverge from his professor's teaching. He followed Clark in endorsing the law of contradiction as the foundation of apologetics, and felt that Van Til 'did not do justice to Aristotle's fourth book of the *Metaphysics*' and that his apparent endorsement of 'blind faith' left no possible basis for rational appeal to the unbeliever.[21] In his first book, *An Introduction to Christian Apologetics*, published in 1948, Carnell called the law of contradiction 'the most perfect philosophical argument ever devised', and put it to use to mount a conventional Protestant attack on Roman Catholic soteriology:

> The Reformers, one and all, saw that the Bible teaches we are saved *solely* by grace through faith, while the Romish Church says we are saved by grace *plus* the merit which accrues by our own good works. In a rational universe these two propositions cannot simultaneously be true.[22]

---

[18] Aristotle, *Metaphysics*, 1011b13–14.

[19] Robbins, 'Introduction to Gordon H. Clark', 5.

[20] George M. Marsden, *Reforming Fundamentalism: Fuller Seminary and the New Evangelicalism* (Grand Rapids: Eerdmans, 1987), 45; for Clark's influence on Henry and Schaeffer respectively see pp. 132, 136–137 below.

[21] Rudolph Nelson, *The Making and Unmaking of an Evangelical Mind: The Case of Edward Carnell* (Cambridge: Cambridge University Press, 1987), 44–45, 64, 129–130.

[22] Edward J. Carnell, *An Introduction to Christian Apologetics: A Philosophic Defense of the Trinitarian-Theistic Faith* (Grand Rapids: Eerdmans, 1948), 73, cited in Nelson, *Making and Unmaking*, 130–131; see also 152. Carnell repeated this description of the law of

The book won first prize in an Evangelical Book Award competition mounted by the Reformed publisher Eerdmans, and was probably the clinching factor in leading Harold J. Ockenga to endorse his application to the new Fuller Theological Seminary for a faculty appointment in systematic theology.[23] Carnell was to spend the rest of his life on the Fuller faculty, serving as president from September 1954 to May 1959. He is remembered as a 'master teacher' who, in the memory of David Hubbard, meant the difference for many students 'between believing and not believing'.[24] His *Introduction to Christian Apologetics* stood in the tradition of Charles Hodge and B. B. Warfield in its unequivocal commitment to the plenary inspiration and inerrancy of the Bible,[25] and at this stage he was still happy to own the label 'fundamentalist': his letter of application to Ockenga (who was his pastor at Park Street Congregational Church in Boston) for the post at Fuller in September 1947 indicated his approval of Ockenga's 'happy appreciation of Reformation Christianity with a love for the Fundamentalists of our present day'.[26]

However, Carnell's thought was already developing in a direction that diverged not simply from Van Til's presuppositionalism but even from Clark's more 'rational' and highly propositional view of the nature of biblical authority. In private correspondence with Clark during January–February 1953 Carnell asserted that his confidence in the Bible was not simply based on a rational assurance that it was infallibly true; it was also 'a spiritual response based upon a source of life'. He challenged Clark's apparent conviction that

[i]f science could develop an electron machine capable of employing the law of contradiction perfectly, it could see the truth of the Bible. On my view only a man of humble and contrite heart can see it. Biblical propositions are truth only (so far as the *receiver* is concerned; I do not refer to the objective state of the text) when they transform.[27]

There were at least echoes here of the neo-orthodox theology of Karl Barth. Although Carnell never turned his back completely on biblical inerrancy, in the course of the 1950s he moved away from a fundamentalist approach

contradiction in his *Christian Commitment: An Apologetic* (New York: Macmillan, 1957), 40.

[23] Nelson, *Making and Unmaking*, 70–71.

[24] Ibid. 78–79.

[25] Marsden, *Reforming Fundamentalism*, 113.

[26] Nelson, *Making and Unmaking*, 70.

[27] Cited in ibid. 153.

that grounded biblical authority in a logical sequence of rational propositions to one that viewed Scripture as God's infallible means for instructing and transforming the Christian believer. His next venture in Christian apologetics, *Christian Commitment* (1957), was aimed at a secular audience and published by a major secular publisher, but was a failure as a work of apologetics, selling poorly.[28] Carnell had hoped that it would change the direction of Christian apologetics, moving from rational arguments for the existence of God towards a more inward or spiritual perspective. It represented a further step along the road taking him further away from the rigorous Reformed logic of his mentors Clark and Van Til. His biographer notes that it was a watershed publication for Carnell, but in the wrong sense.[29]

Carnell's growing distance from fundamentalism became more apparent with the publication in 1959 of *The Case for Orthodox Theology*, which, as noted in chapter 2, was scathing in its treatment of dispensational theology and a separatist mentality.[30] In spite of its dismissive references to fundamentalism as 'orthodoxy gone cultic', the book relied heavily on authorities from a bygone era for its defence of Christian orthodoxy. Carnell included repeated citations from authors such as Matthew Henry, William Paley, Horatius Bonar and Charles Hodge. His most recent authorities, such as B. B. Warfield, James Orr and Abraham Kuyper, had all been born more than a century before.[31] Carnell was too academic an author to appeal to the evangelical public and too backward-looking to secure a ready audience among non-evangelical theologians. Nevertheless, in 1962 he was chosen as the evangelical participant in a public dialogue with Karl Barth organized by the University of Chicago Divinity School. In challenging Barth to explain how he harmonized his appeal to Scripture as the objective Word of God with his admission that the Bible was 'sullied with errors, theological as well as historical or factual', Carnell added, 'This is a problem for me, I cheerfully confess.' Gordon Clark, who was covering the debate for *Christianity Today*, expressed his dismay in private at Carnell's apparent admission of errors in Scripture and made his disappointment with his former pupil clear in his article on the debate.[32] It was thus ironic and arguably misleading that *The Battle for the Bible*, published by his former Fuller colleague Harold Lindsell in 1976 with a later and less conservative generation of Fuller faculty members as its primary targets, should

---

[28] Carnell, *Christian Commitment*; see Nelson, *Making and Unmaking*, 103.

[29] Nelson, *Making and Unmaking*, 161.

[30] See chapter 2 above, 36–37.

[31] Nelson, *Making and Unmaking*, 108, 137.

[32] Marsden, *Reforming Fundamentalism*, 194–195; Nelson, *Making and Unmaking*, 186–188.

have been dedicated to Carnell (alongside Gleason L. Archer, Carl Henry and Wilbur M. Smith) as one of the colleagues who had 'stood or stand steadfastly for biblical inerrancy'.[33] Carnell's career had been going steadily downhill since the late 1950s. His personal problems of depression and insomnia intensified, and he died in April 1967 in tragic circumstances from an overdose of barbiturates.[34]

Carl F. H. Henry – apologist for revelation

Carl F. H. Henry, like Edward Carnell, was a student of philosophy at Wheaton College in the late 1930s under Gordon Clark, and his theological perspective was similarly shaped by Clark's emphasis on the rationality of theism and the propositional nature of biblical truth. Like Cornelius van Til he was influenced by W. Harry Jellema, under whom he studied at Indiana University in the summer of 1944.[35] Henry's first theological book, *Remaking the Modern Mind*, was published by Eerdmans in 1946 and was dedicated to Clark, Jellema and Van Til, as 'Three "men of Athens" who have sharpened my convictions by action and reaction, in delightful philosophical interchange.'[36] As a doctoral student at Boston University in the later 1940s he had the same PhD supervisor as Carnell (Edgar S. Brightman) for a thesis on the Baptist systematic theologian Augustus H. Strong. Originally a journalist by profession, Henry served the National Association of Evangelicals from its formation in 1942 as publicity officer for its conventions and literary editor of its monthly newsletter, *United Evangelical Action*. With Clark, Van Til and a number of other evangelical scholars he also played an important role in forming the Evangelical Theological Society in December 1949. Henry was a founding member of faculty at Fuller Theological Seminary alongside Carnell, until 1956, when he left to become the first editor of *Christianity Today*. He had to resign as editor in 1968 after pressure from its financial backer, the Presbyterian oil magnate J. Howard Pew, who regarded Henry as being insufficiently aggressive in his criticism of mainline churches for their commitment to a social gospel. He

---

[33] Harold Lindsell, *The Battle for the Bible* (Grand Rapids: Zondervan, 1976); see chapter 4 above and the discussion in Nelson, *Making and Unmaking*, 179–190.

[34] Although the possibility of suicide was quite widely mooted, Carnell's biographer thinks it unlikely; see Nelson, *Making and Unmaking*, 201–215.

[35] Carl F. H. Henry, *Confessions of a Theologian: An Autobiography* (Waco: Word Books, 1986), 109.

[36] Ibid. 111.

returned to theological teaching, at Eastern Baptist Seminary, and to writing. His magnum opus *God, Revelation, and Authority*, published by Word Books in six fat volumes between 1976 and 1983, represents the most substantial work of theological scholarship produced by any conservative evangelical in the twentieth century.

In the preface to volume I of *God, Revelation, and Authority* Henry singled out Gordon Clark as the teacher to whom he owed a more profound debt than any other, describing him as 'the peer of evangelical philosophers in identifying the logical inconsistencies that beset nonevangelical alternatives and in exhibiting the intellectual superiority of Christian theism'; he also noted that Clark had offered helpful comments on many of the draft chapters.[37] The essential argument of Henry's great work was that theology should begin with the presumption that in Scripture God had revealed himself to humanity in rational, verbal and propositional form, that the fact of this self-revelation stood up to the scrutiny of human reason better than any other presupposition, and that all systems of thought other than evangelical Christianity could be proved to be false by the application of the law of contradiction.[38] Divine revelation was the source of all truth; reason was the divinely instilled capacity whereby human beings could recognize that revelation; Scripture was both the 'verifying principle' and the conduit of revealed truth; while the axiom of logical consistency (non-contradiction) could be applied as a negative test to disqualify all competing claims to truth. The task of Christian theology was to exhibit the content of biblical revelation as an orderly, systematic and self-consistent whole.[39]

Henry expanded his view of the Bible as a repository of propositional revelation in volume III of *God, Revelation, and Authority*. Propositions were verbal statements that were either true or false, to be believed, doubted or denied. He cited with approval Gordon Clark's remarkable statement that 'aside from imperative statements and a few exclamations in the Psalms, the Bible is composed of propositions' that give information about God and his dealings with humanity.[40] Henry responded to the growing number of theologians, including evangelical ones, such as Fuller Theological Seminary's leading New Testament scholar, George Eldon Ladd, who maintained that divine revelation was personal as well as propositional. While conceding that God was,

---

[37] Carl F. H. Henry, *God, Revelation and Authority*. Vol. I: *God Who Speaks and Shows: Preliminary Considerations* (Waco: Word Books, 1976), 10.

[38] Bob E. Patterson, *Carl F. H. Henry* (Waco: Word Books, 1983), 63.

[39] Ibid. 64; Henry, *God, Revelation and Authority*, I, 215.

[40] Henry, *God, Revelation and Authority*, III, 456; citing Gordon H. Clark, *Karl Barth's Theological Method* (Nutley, N.J.: P. & R. Publishing, 1963), 150.

obviously, 'more than a set of propositions', Henry held his ground in denying that God made himself known in any other way than by 'rational disclosure and intelligible truths' that could be apprehended cognitively.[41] 'Evangelicals', he affirmed, 'need not tremble and take to the hills whenever others charge us with rationalism.'[42]

The strength of Henry's evangelical apologetic lay in its robust insistence that theological truths about God cannot be divorced from rationally testable claims about what God has done in the sphere of space and time. No appeal to mystery or paradox can circumvent the fact that Christianity is a religion of history that willingly lays itself open to the rational scrutiny of its factual claims. The weaknesses of Henry's approach lay in his apparent reduction of the encounter between God and humans to a process of ratiocination, his narrowing of the rich variety of Scripture to a compendium of propositions, and the lack of emphasis he gave to the role of the Spirit in both enlightening unbelievers and transforming believers. In the very different cultural climate of a postmodern age, and from the perspective of evangelicals living in a non-western context, his theological system is likely to appear spiritually arid and unduly cerebral. Nevertheless, he retains some influential admirers, such as Donald A. Carson of Trinity Evangelical Divinity School.[43] Henry's enduring significance in the history of evangelicalism lies less in the character of his apologetic than in the decisive steer he gave to the American evangelical tradition, helping to turn it from a primarily negative relationship to culture, politics and society, to a force with the potential to infuse biblical values into the public sphere. I shall suggest in chapter 6 that in that respect his small book *The Uneasy Conscience of Modern Fundamentalism* (1948) may prove to have exerted greater lasting influence than the six weighty volumes of *God, Revelation, and Authority*.

Francis A. Schaeffer – evangelical interrogator of secular culture

Cornelius Van Til, Edward Carnell and Carl Henry were all evangelical scholars whose often demanding writings were read mainly within the

---

[41] Henry, *God, Revelation and Authority*, III, 457–462.

[42] Ibid. 480, cited in Stanley J. Grenz, *Renewing the Center: Evangelical Theology in a Post-Theological Era* (Grand Rapids: Baker Academic, 2000), 93. Grenz's evaluation of Henry on pp. 86–102 of his book is penetrating but not unsympathetic.

[43] See D. A. Carson and J. D. Woodbridge (eds.), *God and Culture: Essays in Honor of Carl F. H. Henry* (Grand Rapids: Eerdmans, 1993), viii; D. A. Carson, *The Gagging of God: Christianity Confronts Pluralism* (Grand Rapids: Zondervan, 1996), 187.

walls of seminaries and Christian colleges, though to some extent also within the pastor's study. For Van Til and Carnell, certainly, and, to a lesser extent, for Henry, the task of apologetics was more about giving evangelical leaders the intellectual weapons they needed to defend biblical orthodoxy (especially against liberal or neo-orthodox competitors) than about direct engagement with the philosophical assumptions of twentieth-century secular culture. The evangelical who did more than any other in the 1960s and 1970s to promote and facilitate such engagement was Francis A. Schaeffer (1912–84).

Francis Schaeffer's early theological formation shows some similarities with that of Edward Carnell, though his denominational affiliation was Presbyterian rather than Baptist. He entered Westminster Theological Seminary in 1935, where he too sat under the feet of Cornelius Van Til. After two years at Westminster, however, Schaeffer's Christian pathway diverged from that of Carnell, and in a direction that at first sight did not look promising for any future contribution to evangelical apologetics. Schaeffer followed a number of the most conservative members of faculty and students at Westminster in seceding from the seminary and starting a new institution, Faith Seminary, in Wilmington, Delaware. The leaders of the secession included Carl McIntire (1906–2002), who would soon become known as the architect in 1941 of the militantly fundamentalist and separatist American Council of Christian Churches. The grounds of the separation were a strange mixture of theological and behavioural issues: the secessionists deemed Westminster to be too high in its Calvinism, too lax in its toleration of alcohol and insufficiently rigorous in its commitment to separatism from the doctrinally mixed Presbyterian Church–USA.[44] Schaeffer's early experience in Christian ministry, in Pennsylvania and St. Louis, Missouri, was in McIntire's small separatist denomination, the Bible Presbyterian Church. It is noteworthy that when the National Association of Evangelicals was formed in St. Louis in 1942, Schaeffer declined to get involved, viewing the NAE as fatally compromised by its refusal to endorse a policy of total separation from all mainline denominations.[45] When Francis and Edith Schaeffer first left for Europe in the summer of 1947, they did so (initially on a temporary basis) as missionaries sent by the Independent Board for Foreign Missions, the body set up by Gresham Machen in 1933 but by this time controlled by McIntire and the Bible Presbyterian Church. The Schaeffers were two of the fundamen-

---

[44] Barry Hankins, *Francis Schaeffer and the Shaping of Evangelical America* (Grand Rapids: Eerdmans, 2008), 13–15.

[45] Ibid. 25.

talist representatives of the wider movement in American Protestantism in the aftermath of the Second World War that aimed to reclaim a godless Europe for Christ and Christian civilization.

From 1948 the Schaeffers' missionary posting to western Europe was made permanent, and they settled in Switzerland. Francis's particular mission was to persuade conservative churches to join McIntire's International Council of Christian Churches (ICCC), which was formed in Amsterdam in August that year. He also began to write and speak on contemporary theological issues, particularly the challenges raised by the theology of Karl Barth. At the second plenary congress of the ICCC, held in Geneva in the summer of 1950, Schaeffer gave an address on 'The New Modernism', in which he attacked Barthians for intellectual dishonesty, because they were trying to say that something could be theologically true even though historically false. Schaeffer had in fact met Barth shortly beforehand and had given him a copy of his paper, which was subsequently published by the Independent Board for Foreign Missions. Although it is not clear that Schaeffer had actually read Van Til's *The New Modernism*, the debt to Van Til is evident. Less conclusive and probably less direct is the apparent dependence on Gordon Clark's appeal to the law of contradiction: no proposition could be both true and false at the same time.[46] Schaeffer's knowledge of Barth's work was superficial at best, and he was something of an intellectual magpie, picking up snippets of other thinkers' writings without necessarily engaging with them in depth. Nevertheless, in the very different theological and ecclesiastical climate of western Europe, Schaeffer found the rigid separatism of Carl McIntire increasingly unacceptable, and in June 1955 the Schaeffers severed their connection with the Independent Board. What was even more significant, however, was that by 1955 the Schaeffers were developing a ministry of a quite different kind from their Swiss Alpine base of 'L'Abri' (the shelter). Their chalet home became a haven and a seminar base for a growing number of young people, especially university students, who were engaged in a sometimes anguished personal quest for spiritual meaning and intellectual truth. By 1960 this developing ministry had attracted the notice of *Time* magazine, which devoted a brief article to Schaeffer's mission to intellectuals.[47] Schaeffer's thesis was that modern western thought since Kant and Hegel, as a result of its repudiation of the authority of biblical revelation, as enshrined in the teaching of the Protestant Reformation, had descended into

---

[46] Ibid. 38–40, 243 n. 23. Hankins's biography makes no mention of Clark's possible influence on Schaeffer.

[47] 'Mission to Intellectuals', *Time*, 11 Jan. 1960, cited in Hankins, *Francis Schaeffer*, 74.

an abyss of relativism in which there was no stable foundation for morality or the meaning of human life. Hegel in particular was the villain of the piece because his synthetic philosophy of history had undermined the essential incompatibility between truth and untruth. The only apparent (but ultimately illusory) escape from the resulting despair was for humans to immerse themselves in the pleasures of individual experience, reinforced by the unbridled pursuit of capital accumulation. These ideas Schaeffer expounded in a trilogy of highly successful paperbacks published between 1968 and 1972, *The God Who Is There*, *Escape from Reason* and *He Is There and Is Not Silent*.

In his trilogy Schaeffer followed in the footsteps of Van Til in insisting on the absolute priority of God's self-revelation – the simple fact that God really was *there* – as the only coherent starting point for all knowledge and construction of meaning to life. He departed from Van Til in his much greater confidence that human rationality could provide a bridge for meaningful discourse between Christians and non-Christians, and here he made repeated use, in the propositional tradition of Gordon Clark, of the law of contradiction: Christian apologetics could appeal to the God-given rational capacity of human beings to perceive which propositions did or did not make sense.[48] Schaeffer's central contention was that ultimately only the Christian theistic propositions revealed in Scripture did make sense of life, and that the task of apologetics was to help non-Christians to perceive that.

As a historian of western thought, Schaeffer's analysis is idiosyncratic and frequently wide of the mark. It makes little historical sense to castigate, as he did, the Renaissance as a godless assertion of human autonomy yet to idealize the Reformation, and he failed to see the extent to which the Reformation through its challenge to the Catholic monopoly of religious knowledge anticipated the Enlightenment's more secular erosions of the authority of revelation over reason. As a theologian he is susceptible to the charge that Bernard Ramm has levelled at him, alongside Van Til, Clark and Henry, namely that in their various attacks on Barth's reformulation of evangelical theology they took insufficient account of the radicality of the Enlightenment's attack on the historical reliability of the Bible and hence on the entire framework of Christian theology.[49] He depended quite heavily on Carl Henry (and hence, indirectly on Gordon Clark) for his insistence that the Bible was a storehouse of 'propositional facts', and that the Reformation enshrined the principle of 'verbal, propositional revelation' in which there was no sign of the dichotomy

---

[48] Hankins, *Francis Schaeffer*, 91–92.

[49] Ramm, *After Fundamentalism*, 26.

between nature and grace that Schaeffer lamented in modern post-Enlightenment culture.[50]

Although Schaeffer's historical analysis of western thought has not commanded wide assent, even among evangelical writers, his enduring significance for the history of evangelicalism lies in the way in which he opened up whole areas of cultural analysis to evangelicals who had hitherto regarded such engagement as alien or even forbidden territory. For evangelical students in humanities departments in North American and British universities in the 1970s, Schaeffer provided an all-too-rare Christian perspective on the spiritually barren fields of intellectual inquiry that were their daily concern. He was one of the first evangelicals to develop a theological response to the environmental crisis, publishing a booklet in 1970 on *Pollution and the Death of Man*. A larger book, *How Should We Then Live?* (1976), called evangelicals to adopt a simpler lifestyle, and critiqued American evangelicalism in particular for its failure to apply Christian principles to questions of race and the distribution of wealth.

Perhaps most significant of all, Schaeffer's interest in modern popular culture took him into the realms of film, music and the visual arts. In Amsterdam in 1948 he had been introduced to a Dutch doctoral student in art history, Hans R. Rookmaaker (1922–77), whose fiancée, Anky, then worked as a secretary in the office for the founding assembly of the ICCC. The Schaeffers and the Rookmaakers soon became firm friends. Influenced particularly by the Dutch Reformed thinker Groen van Prinsterer, Rookmaaker applied a presuppositional approach to the history of art in a way that resonated with Schaeffer's own presuppositionalism. In 1965 he was appointed Professor of the History of Art at the Free University of Amsterdam. His book *Modern Art and the Death of a Culture*, published by Inter-Varsity Press in 1970, applied to western art the thesis that modern western culture was in a process of decay as a result of its fatal separation between nature and grace, faith and reason. The book so impressed the British journalist Malcolm Muggeridge (1903–90), a recent convert to Christianity, that he selected it as his *Observer* book of the year in 1971.[51] In Britain Rookmaaker spoke at a conference for art students

[50] Hankins, *Francis Schaeffer*, 94–95, citing Francis A. Schaeffer, *He is There and Is Not Silent*, in *The Complete Works of Francis A. Schaeffer*, vol. I, bk. 3 (Wheaton: Crossway Books, 1982), 302–303, 323.

[51] Linette Martin, *Hans Rookmaaker: A Biography* (London: Hodder & Stoughton, 1979), 152; Jeremy Begbie, *Voicing Creation's Praise: Toward a Theology of the Arts* (Edinburgh: T. & T. Clark, 1991), 127. Muggeridge associated himself quite closely with evangelicals in the early 1970s (speaking at the Lausanne Congress in 1974) but became a Catholic in 1982.

organized by the IVF in September 1967, which was influential in leading the IVF to develop its embryonic work among colleges of art.[52] One of its first travelling secretaries in the art colleges, Tim Dean, later became editor of *Third Way*, a fortnightly (later monthly) magazine founded in 1977 that endeavoured to apply evangelical perspectives to a wide range of issues in culture and politics.[53] Dean was succeeded in his travelling secretary role in 1976 by Paul Clowney, one of Rookmaaker's students and the second son of Edmund P. Clowney, first president of Westminster Theological Seminary from 1966 to 1984.[54] Rookmaaker also exercised a formative influence on a British actor, Nigel Goodwin, who in 1971 founded the Arts Centre Group in London, probably the first centre in the world catering for Christians who were professionally involved in the arts.[55] Evangelical apologetics were by the 1970s broadening their scope from a defence of propositional revelation to a dialogical engagement with the arts and other aspects of contemporary culture.

In his later years, spent largely in the United States, Schaeffer's original fundamentalist militancy reasserted itself. As seen in chapter 4, he was a stalwart supporter of unlimited biblical inerrancy, and he came close to endorsing the cause of creation science, though without adopting a 'young earth' position.[56] He associated himself increasingly with the Christian Right in the United States, and as a result lost much of the appeal he had in the later 1960s and early 1970s for evangelicals concerned to enter into critical dialogue with contemporary culture. His *A Christian Manifesto* (1981) was influenced by the ideas of the conservative lawyer and Christian thinker John W. Whitehead, founder in 1982 of the Rutherford Institute. The *Manifesto* advanced the historically dubious and implicitly sectarian claim that the founding fathers of the United States had sought to construct the nation and its laws on biblical principles, which had subsequently been eroded by mass immigration of Catholics. As such, the book did little to advance his reputation among evangelical schol-

---

[52] The IVF had appointed its first travelling secretary for the art colleges, Mavis Edwards, in 1964. Douglas Johnson, *Contending for the Faith: A History of the Evangelical Movement in the Universities and Colleges* (Leicester: Inter-Varsity Press, 1979), 248–249, 354. The IVF became the Universities and Colleges Christian Fellowship (UCCF) in 1975.

[53] *Third Way* still exists, but with more tenuous links to evangelicalism. Dean was editor from 1982 to 1989.

[54] Johnson, *Contending for the Faith*, 353.

[55] See http://www.yuricareport.com/Dominionism/HansRookmaakerAndSchaefferIn Art.html (accessed 20 Apr. 2012); http://www.artscentregroup.org.uk/about_history. php (accessed 20 Apr. 2012).

[56] Hankins, *Francis Schaeffer*, 150–151.

ars.[57] Furthermore, by the end of his life Schaeffer's pronounced emphasis on rational argument as a way to faith was losing its appeal to young people whose cultural assumptions had moved beyond the Enlightenment framework on which his apologetic was predicated.

Alvin Plantinga – evangelical philosopher

Schaeffer's apologetic, though he rarely described it in these terms, was in effect devoted to exploring the implications of the legacy of the European Enlightenment, whose casting off of the authority of ecclesiastical tradition left reason as the unchallenged arbiter of human belief. The same essential preoccupation underlies the very different career of the American Reformed philosopher who, perhaps more than any other evangelical, has achieved an international academic reputation in circles that extend well beyond the evangelical constituency. Alvin Plantinga (1932–) has earned widespread respect for the cogency of his response to the question raised by such seminal modern thinkers as Nietzsche, Marx and Freud, namely 'Is Christian theistic belief intellectually acceptable for educated, intelligent people living now?' Plantinga's answer has been that it is indeed acceptable, because belief in God is properly 'basic', that is, rationally warranted quite independently of evidence that may be afforded by any other propositions.[58] The effect of Plantinga's arguments on academic philosophy, a field in which the supremacy of logical positivism had left virtually no space for religious assertions, has been remarkable. As early as the spring of 1980 *Time* magazine reported that in

> a quiet revolution in thought and arguments that hardly anyone could have foreseen only two decades ago, God is making a comeback. Most intriguingly, this is happening not among theologians or ordinary believers . . . but in the crisp, intellectual circles of academic philosophers, where the consensus had long banished the Almighty from fruitful discourse.

The article identified Plantinga as the central figure in this quiet revolution, and labelled him 'the world's leading Protestant philosopher of God'.[59]

---

57 See ibid. 192–227.

58 Deane-Peter Baker, *Tayloring Reformed Epistemology: Charles Taylor, Alvin Plantinga and the de jure Challenge to Christian Belief* (London: SCM Press, 2007), 63.

59 Cited in Deane-Peter Baker (ed.), *Alvin Plantinga* (Cambridge: Cambridge University Press, 2007), 1.

Alvin Plantinga's grandparents on both sides came from the Gereformeerde Kerken in the Netherlands, the product of the evangelical *Afscheiding* (secession from the state church) of the 1830s, and the community that established the Free University of Amsterdam under the leadership of Abraham Kuyper. His grandfather, Andrew Plantinga, emigrated from Friesland to Michigan in 1913.[60] Like Cornelius Van Til, Plantinga was reared within the Christian Reformed Church, and he too studied under W. H. Jellema at Calvin College. Plantinga recalls Jellema as the most gifted teacher of philosophy he had ever encountered, and acknowledges his continuing debt to the founding principle of Calvin College, namely that Christian truth is relevant to all areas of intellectual life.[61] In 1963 Plantinga moved back to Calvin College from his first teaching post at Wayne State University to succeed Jellema and to join his former undergraduate friend Nicholas Wolterstorff in teaching philosophy. He was to remain at Calvin for nineteen years, pursuing an agenda in philosophy of religion that was unashamedly apologetic in intent. In 1982 he moved to the University of Notre Dame, a leading Catholic institution that has proved a congenial environment for a succession of leading evangelical scholars, such as Nathan Hatch, George Marsden and Mark Noll.

Plantinga's first book, *God and Other Minds* (1967), addressed the evidentialist objection that theistic belief was irrational because there was no, or very little, evidence for it by arguing that belief in God and belief in the existence of minds other than our own are in the same epistemological boat, and are equally rational.[62] He then moved on in the 1970s to wrestling with the problem of evil and the nature of human free will,[63] while also pursuing further the question of what rationality means, and in exactly what sense it is rational to believe in God. This latter quest led to a number of publications, culminating in his magnum opus *Warranted Christian Belief* (2000), a book that one authority describes as having established him as 'without doubt the preeminent figure in contemporary philosophy of religion'.[64] In contrast to Schaeffer, Plantinga's goal is not to convince the unbeliever of the truth of

---

[60] Alvin Plantinga, 'Self-Profile', in James E. Tomberlin and Peter Van Inwagen (eds.), *Alvin Plantinga* (Dordrecht: D. Reidel Publishing, 1985), 4.

[61] Ibid. 9, 13.

[62] Alvin Plantinga, *God and Other Minds: A Study of the Rational Justification of Belief in God* (Ithaca, N.Y.: Cornell University Press, 1967); Plantinga, 'Self-Profile', 55.

[63] Alvin Plantinga, *God, Freedom and Evil*, 2nd ed. (Grand Rapids: Eerdmans, 1977); *The Nature of Necessity* (Oxford: Clarendon Press, 1974).

[64] Alvin Plantinga, *Warranted Christian Belief* (Oxford: Oxford University Press, 2000); Baker, *Alvin Plantinga*, 2.

Christian claims, but simply to defend the much more limited assertion that orthodox Christian belief is justified, rational and warranted, even if none of the theistic arguments works, and even if there is no non-circular evidence for it.[65] He thus avoided both the fideism of Van Til and the different Reformed variants of natural theology represented by Clark, Carnell, Henry or Schaeffer, with their varying degrees of dependence on propositional argument from evidence. Belief in God, Plantinga insists, is 'basic'; it can be accepted as properly rational without the need to rely on the evidence of other propositions one believes.

Plantinga kept well clear of the fundamentalist circles from which Schaeffer originated, though he occasionally wrote for *Christianity Today* and spoke at a major consultation of Christian scholars convened by the magazine in the early 1970s.[66] It is noteworthy that nowhere in the ninety-two pages of his intellectual autobiography, published as part of a wider study of his work in 1985, does the word 'evangelical' even appear.[67] Plantinga has preferred to characterize his scholarly vocation as the defence of orthodox Christian theism against the multiple attacks modernity has launched against it. Nevertheless, one commentator on his *Warranted Christian Belief* observes that those unfamiliar with his thought may be taken aback by its unashamed conservatism of theology, accepting the inspiration of Scripture, the divine instigation of faith, and the noetic effects of sin, and 'other theological concepts that many academics have relegated to a bygone era'.[68] He deserves a prominent place in any survey of evangelical apologetics in the late twentieth century.

Lesslie Newbigin – missionary to Western culture

A good deal of conservative evangelical scholarly apologetic in the post-war decades had sought to justify and explain the gospel in terms that yielded implicit authority to 'modern' scientific criteria of rationality. American evangelicals in particular had responded to liberal or secularist critiques of orthodox doctrinal tenets by arguing for the reasonableness of accepting the truth claims contained in the Bible, and insisting that they were empirically valid propositions no less worthy of acceptance than the testable propositions

---

[65] Baker, *Tayloring Reformed Epistemology*, 11.

[66] Henry, *Confessions of a Theologian*, 226, 272.

[67] Plantinga, 'Self-Profile', 3–95.

[68] James Beilby, 'Plantinga's Model of Warranted Christian Belief', in Baker, *Alvin Plantinga*, 125.

made by modern knowledge in the field of the natural or social sciences. While this enterprise was to a degree necessary, the problem intrinsic to such an approach, as Plantinga correctly diagnosed, was its implicit acceptance of the right of the contemporary secular world view to define the linguistic and epistemological field of the debate. Plantinga's contribution, though invaluable, was mainly within the walls of the academy. Schaeffer, though enormously influential in encouraging a generation of evangelicals to engage critically with contemporary intellectual culture, never really questioned the methodological adequacy of the propositionalism he had inherited from Van Til and Clark. From the mid-1980s, however, English-speaking evangelicals, especially in Britain, became increasingly aware of a conservative Protestant thinker who insisted that the first priority in contemporary Christian apologetics was to start at the other end from Van Til, Carnell or Henry, namely to explain and indeed challenge the modern scientific world view from the point of view of the gospel.[69]

J. E. Lesslie Newbigin (1909–98) was an English Presbyterian from Newcastle upon Tyne who had spent much of his life in South India, first as a missionary of the Church of Scotland (from 1936 to 1947) and then as one of the founding bishops of the united Church of South India, formed in September 1947. From 1959 to 1965 he was seconded from his diocese of Madras to play a leading role in the ecumenical movement, initially as general secretary of the International Missionary Council (IMC) and then after the merger of the IMC with the World Council of Churches in 1961 as the first general secretary of the WCC's Division of World Mission and Evangelism. Newbigin went back to India in 1965, where he remained until his retirement in 1974. It was his return to a secularized Britain after so many years in India that prompted Newbigin to reflect deeply on a question he first heard posed by a retired Indonesian general, T. B. Simatupang, at the Bangkok conference of the WCC in 1973 on 'Salvation Today': 'Can the West be converted?'[70]

For most of his career Lesslie Newbigin did not move in conservative evangelical circles. As a student in Cambridge in the late 1920s and early 1930s, he had identified himself with the SCM rather than the CICCU, and his prominence in the ecumenical movement at a time of its increasing radicalization in the early 1960s did not endear him to evangelicals. Indeed, his theological emphasis from the 1950s through to 1968 was partially sympathetic to

[69] Geoffrey Wainwright, *Lesslie Newbigin: A Theological Life* (New York: Oxford University Press, 1976), 357.

[70] Ibid. 336; Paul Weston (comp.), *Lesslie Newbigin, Missionary Theologian: A Reader* (London: SPCK, 2006), 207–208.

the overtly secular theologies of that period, as revealed by his Firth Lectures given at the University of Nottingham in 1964 and published in 1966 as *Honest Religion for Secular Man*, a title that evoked John A. T. Robinson's highly controversial paperback *Honest to God* (1963).[71] Newbigin's concern was, however, always a missionary one, and he deplored Robinson's depersonalizing of God. His experience of the Uppsala assembly of the WCC in 1968 convinced him that secular theologies of mission that stressed humanization at the expense of reconciliation with God were leading the church up a blind alley, and his essential Reformed orthodoxy thenceforward became more pronounced.

Newbigin's apologetic for a genuinely missionary engagement with western culture was first sketched out in a brief pamphlet written for a British Council of Churches study project, *The Other Side of 1984*.[72] It was then more fully articulated in his Warfield lectures at Princeton Theological Seminary in March 1984, published under the title *Foolishness to the Greeks*.[73] Newbigin himself traced the genesis of this critique of patterns of western thought that he had previously taken for granted to a period he spent reading at St Deiniol's (now Gladstone's) Library at Hawarden in North Wales. He read W. E. Gladstone's first book, *The State in Its Relations to the Church* (1838), and was impressed by its exposition 'so foreign to present ways of thinking', of 'the Church as the great, solid enduring reality in comparison with which the state is a fragile and ephemeral affair'. His eyes also lit upon Paul Hazard's *La Crise de la Conscience Européene: 1680–1715* (1935), a book that (in English translation) set him thinking deeply about the impact of the Enlightenment on European culture, a subject, Newbigin admitted, 'about which I had never thought'.[74] The burden of his future writing and public speaking was to be the antithesis between, on the one hand, the one body of Christ spanning all ages and cultures, and, on the other, the ephemeral and ultimately unsustainable edifice of western post-Enlightenment thought, with its absolute divorce between reason and faith, fact and value, 'public' scientific knowledge and supposedly 'private' religious opinion. Such separations, Newbigin argued, removed morality and any sense of human purpose into the subjective realm of personal preference, and hence

---

[71] Lesslie Newbigin, *Honest Religion for Secular Man* (London: SCM Press, 1966).

[72] Lesslie Newbigin, *The Other Side of 1984: Questions for the Churches* (Geneva: World Council of Churches, 1983).

[73] Lesslie Newbigin, *Foolishness to the Greeks: The Gospel and Western Culture* (London: SPCK, 1986).

[74] Lesslie Newbigin, *Unfinished Agenda: An Updated Autobiography* (Edinburgh: St Andrew Press, 1993), 251. Hazard's book in English translation was entitled *The European Mind, 1680–1715*.

left modern western society in an abyss of relativism and despair – the similarity to Schaeffer's diagnosis, though far from total, is striking.

The only answer to such relativism, Newbigin argued in typically Reformed vein, lay in the claim of the Christian gospel to be 'public truth', truth that was for all people and for all areas of human activity. In marked contrast to Schaeffer and his American mentors, however, Newbigin located the verification of this claim to public truth not in any appeal to the law of contradiction as destructive of all contrary propositions, but rather in the embodiment of the gospel in the Christian community that takes the Word of God as its 'plausibility structure' (a term borrowed from the Christian sociologist Peter L. Berger):

> Although it may be very shocking to a certain kind of post-Enlightenment Protestant conscience, it is not the Bible by itself but the church confessing the mystery of the faith that is spoken of as the pillar and bulwark of the truth (1 Tim. 3:15–16.).[75]

The church herself, as the body of Christ, rather than any attempt to construct a logically watertight defence of biblical authority, is the only missiologically effective 'hermeneutic of the gospel', bearing witness with 'proper confidence' (a favourite phrase of Newbigin's) to the revelation she has received, neither claiming the right to rule human society according to Christian norms, nor, on the other hand, meekly accepting the Enlightenment's relegation of religion to the private sphere.[76]

Newbigin's high doctrine of the church as the only agent able to commend the authority of the biblical gospel to a sceptical western world was not phrased in terms best calculated to win the allegiance of the most conservative sections of evangelicalism. Nevertheless, his message was adopted with enthusiasm by growing numbers of evangelicals, first in Britain and then in North America, continental Europe and further afield. From the publication in 1983 of *The Other Side of 1984*, the project that he led, initially under the auspices of the British Council of Churches, was known as 'The Gospel and Our Culture'. Its most high-profile event was an international conference on the theme of 'The Gospel as Public Truth' held at Swanwick in Derbyshire in July 1992, attended by some four hundred delegates, many of them evangelicals. Parallel organizations were formed in North America (the Gospel and our Culture Network, led by George Hunsberger) and New Zealand (the

---

[75] Newbigin, *Foolishness to the Greeks*, 58, cited in Wainwright, *Lesslie Newbigin*, 362.

[76] For Newbigin's fullest exposition of this theme see his *The Gospel in a Pluralist Society* (London: SPCK, 1989), 222–233.

Gospel and Cultures Trust, set up by Harold W. Turner, and later known as the DeepSight Trust). All three organizations continued beyond his death.[77] In spite of failing eyesight during the 1990s, Newbigin found himself in great demand as a speaker at British evangelical theological colleges. More surprisingly, from the summer of 1994 he became a regular and much appreciated lecturer at study courses run by the leading London charismatic Anglican church, Holy Trinity, Brompton. 'HTB', in his view, was 'a gushing oil well which simply needed capping'.[78] By the time of his death in 1998 this former leading light in the WCC had been taken to their hearts by many in the evangelical family.

C. S. Lewis – apostle of the Christian imagination

Clive Staples Lewis (1898–1963) was born in Belfast to pious Church of Ireland parents. His academic career as a scholar of English literature was spent wholly in the two ancient English universities, first in Oxford and then, from 1954, as the first Professor of Medieval and Renaissance English at Cambridge. As an undergraduate at Oxford he had inclined towards atheism, but as a young don in English literature at Magdalen College, Oxford, he had a conversion experience that irreversibly changed the direction of his life and work. His autobiography famously relates how in his college rooms one evening in the summer of 1929 he 'gave in, and admitted that God was God, and knelt and prayed; perhaps, that night, the most dejected and reluctant convert in all England'.[79] Lewis, however, describes his new-found faith as initially no more than 'rational theism', and records that it took another two years for him to accept an orthodox Christian position on the identity of Christ as the Son of God.[80] During this transitional period he read widely from authors in the mystical tradition, most notably the German mystic Jacob Boehme (1575–1624), the Scottish writer of fantasy tales George MacDonald (1824–1905) and the Anglican scholar of mysticism W. R. Inge (1860–1954).[81]

Lewis's scholarly interests in medieval and early modern English literature,

---

[77] For the first two see http://gospel-culture.org.uk and http://www.gocn.org (accessed 20 Apr. 2012).

[78] Wainwright, *Lesslie Newbigin*, 16.

[79] C. S. Lewis, *Surprised by Joy: The Shape of My Early Life* (London: Geoffrey Bles, 1955), 215.

[80] Ibid. 217–224.

[81] A. N. Wilson, *C. S. Lewis: A Biography*, new ed. (London: Harper Collins, 1991), 123.

and the mystical direction of his spiritual pilgrimage, gradually converged. The result from 1933 onwards was a stream of books covering subjects from Arthurian poetry to popular Christian apologetics, and from science fiction to children's literature, though the boundaries between these categories were more porous than has frequently been supposed. As a Christian apologist Lewis is remembered particularly for a series of paperback books such as *The Problem of Pain* (1940), *The Screwtape Letters* (1942), *Miracles* (1947) and *Mere Christianity* (1952). However, his public renown today rests primarily on *The Chronicles of Narnia*, beginning with *The Lion, the Witch and the Wardrobe*, first published in 1950. The seven books in the series had by 2005 amassed estimated aggregate sales of 120 million copies.[82] Immensely popular with children, they are in fact Christian apologetic of a highly allusive and inexplicit kind that relies for its power on symbol and metaphor rather than rational argument. Lewis himself explained that 'the whole Narnian story is about Christ', but it is only recently that the seven stories have been shown to correspond to the symbolical characteristics of the seven medieval planets: they present a seven-fold iconography in which Christ is serially represented as King, Commander, Light, Son, Word, Life and Mystery.[83]

In a survey conducted in 2000 by *Christianity Today* based on a poll of one hundred of its contributors and evangelical church leaders, *Mere Christianity* easily secured the accolade of being the best religious book of the twentieth century. *The Lion, the Witch and the Wardrobe* and *The Screwtape Letters* (which first appeared in an American edition in 1943 that became an instant best-seller) also featured prominently in the returns.[84] The wardrobe from Little Lea, the house in Belfast in which Lewis grew up, and the model for the wardrobe that provides the magical entrance into the kingdom of Narnia in *The Lion, the Witch and the Wardrobe*, sits in iconic splendour in the Marion E. Wade Center at Wheaton College in Illinois.[85] Among North American Protestant churchgoers, perhaps the majority of whom are evangelicals, Lewis has come to stand in a class of his own as a Christian author who commands a veneration that borders on the hagiographical. Elsewhere in the evangelical world his status is now less elevated, although in the last two decades of his life his

---

[82] See http://www.manhattan-institute.org/html/_chicsuntimes-hollywood.htm (accessed 20 Apr. 2012).

[83] Michael Ward, *Planet Narnia: The Seven Heavens in the Imagination of C. S. Lewis* (New York: Oxford University Press, 2008), 11, 238, and *passim*.

[84] *CT*, 24 Apr. 2000, 1–2.

[85] Wilson, *C. S. Lewis*, xii–xiii.

public influence in Britain as a radio broadcaster and religious writer was very significant.

The extraordinary and enduring popularity of C. S. Lewis in the North American evangelical constituency requires some explanation, particularly in view of the fact that his own theological position was not an evangelical one. His ecclesiastical allegiance was to a markedly sacramental High Church Anglicanism, and his view of the Bible did not conform to evangelical norms. He was quite prepared to categorize parts of the Old Testament, notably the early chapters of Genesis and the book of Job, as myth or legend rather than history. He castigated the imprecatory psalms (such as Psalm 109) as 'terrible', even 'contemptible'. He took pains to distance himself from fundamentalism by insisting that the Bible contained errors and contradictions. He taught that the Bible 'carries' the Word of God rather than being in itself the Word of God.[86] These aspects of Lewis's writings may not be generally known among his evangelical admirers, but they do accentuate the point of the question 'What is it about the defence of Christianity mounted by this down-to-earth, chain-smoking, and hard-drinking British academic that has so appealed to American evangelicals?'

Lewis was no lover of modernist theology, and was quite prepared to poke fun at demythologizing theologians: he liked to call John A. T. Robinson, bishop of Woolwich and author of *Honest to God*, 'the Bishop of Woolworth's'.[87] His writings on the Bible, though dismissive of fundamentalism, were conservative in general intent, above all in his defence of the historicity of biblical stories that contained elements of the miraculous: 'I have never', he asserted, 'found any philosophical grounds for the universal negative proposition that miracles do not happen.'[88] The demythologizers in his view had made the fatal error of trying to strip biblical narratives of their mythological elements, while fundamentalists through their obsession with literalism were falling in reaction for the opposite mistake of denying that these elements were present at all. For Lewis, as a literary scholar, it was precisely the fact that the Bible stories functioned as myths – narratives of intrinsic transcendental and symbolic power – that was the secret of their enduring attraction, even in a post-Enlightenment age. This was an emphasis that he

---

[86] C. S. Lewis, *Reflections on the Psalms*, new ed. (London: Fontana, 1961), 23–24, 92–94; *Screwtape Proposes a Toast* (London: Fontana, 1965), 50.

[87] Humphrey Carpenter, *The Inklings: C. S. Lewis, J. R. R. Tolkien, Charles Williams and Their Friends* (London: George Allen & Unwin, 1978), 176. F. W. Woolworth's was a popular British department store renowned for its cheap or tawdry goods.

[88] Lewis, *Reflections on the Psalms*, 92.

drew particularly from George MacDonald.[89] Lewis discerned within Scripture a gradual convergence between history and myth: in the opening chapters of Genesis, myth and history were far apart, but as the story of Israel proceeded it became more firmly anchored in history. The culmination of this process of convergence was the incarnation, when 'God became Man' and 'Myth became Fact'.[90] Shortly after his conversion, in October 1931, Lewis had written to his friend Arthur Greeves, 'Now the story of Christ is simply a true myth: a myth working on us in the same way as the others, but with this tremendous difference, that it really *happened*.'[91]

The tenor of American conservative Christian apologetic for most of the twentieth century was to attempt to rebut the attacks of scientific reductionism by defending the facticity and historicity of biblical narrative. By reducing biblical narrative to a series of verbal propositions the hope was that biblical claims would be given the respect due to scientific propositions. Lewis, by contrast, cheerfully admitted that 'The picture so often painted of Christians huddling together on an ever narrower strip of beach while the incoming tide of "Science" mounts higher and higher, corresponds to nothing in my own experience.'[92] The closed system of scientific rationalism was precisely what he had abandoned as internally inconsistent on his conversion to theism in 1929, on the grounds that the much-vaunted absolute of Reason was, according to the popular reading of Darwinian science, 'simply the unforeseen and unintended by-product of mindless matter at one stage of its endless and aimless becoming'.[93] The claim of the radical Enlightenment that the Christian story was a myth, and that *therefore* it was illusory, was profoundly mistaken, not because of the claim itself, but because of the invalid inference drawn from that claim. On the contrary, Lewis insisted, the unique mythological power of the story was a signal of its divine transcendence. To appreciate fully that power, what was needed was a blend of logic and imagination. Logic was indeed necessary, because the Bible presented the incarnation as a historical event and therefore it must be subject to the logical scrutiny of the

---

[89] Mark Edwards Freshwater, *C. S. Lewis and the Truth of Myth* (Lanham, Md.: University Press of America, 1988), 16–17, 57, 68, 93–94.

[90] Lewis, *Screwtape Proposes a Toast*, 50–51.

[91] *They Stand Together: The Letters of C. S. Lewis to Arthur Greeves (1914–1963)*, ed. Walter Hooper (New York: Macmillan, 1979), 428, cited in Freshwater, *C. S. Lewis*, 34.

[92] Lewis, *Screwtape Proposes a Toast*, 54. Lewis may be alluding to Matthew Arnold's poem 'On Dover Beach' (1867), which had been widely interpreted as a symbolic description of the erosion of Christian faith by the impact of modern science.

[93] Ibid. 55.

historical method of the Enlightenment. But in itself logic was not enough to draw people to faith. Imagination was equally necessary, because only by the exercise of the imagination could the enquirer after the truth of God enter into the mysterious 'Narnian' world revealed by the biblical narratives, a world in which the creator of the cosmos became human, spoke to fellow-humans, died at their hands and then rose again in victory over evil and death. This, it may be suggested, was exactly the element that had been missing from previous evangelical apologetic, especially in the United States. It was Lewis's consistent appeal to the romantic imagination, united with his resounding defence of the historicity of the central claim of the New Testament, that supplied evangelicals with a highly attractive form of apologetic that none of their own theologians had hitherto been able to articulate.[94]

In their contrasting ways Lesslie Newbigin, a missionary whose perspectives on the modern European world view had been shaped by decades of exposure to Hinduism, and C. S. Lewis, a medievalist who was profoundly out of sympathy with the presuppositions of modern western scientism, supplied evangelical Christians in the late twentieth century with intellectual resources to defend the faith. In the age of 'late modernity', when the philosophical canons of the Enlightenment, though retaining much of their hold on the world of scholarship, were losing their explanatory power in the realm of popular culture, evangelicals found in Newbigin and Lewis an intellectual armoury of a very different kind from that offered by the sterling efforts of conservative theologians. They were given the confidence to enunciate more clearly their latent sense that the authority of the Bible was, perhaps, not best defended by an Enlightenment propositional methodology.

---

[94] This section is dependent on the argument of Freshwater, *C. S. Lewis*. See especially ix–x, 2, 47, 113. Freshwater, however, is concerned merely to explicate the nature of Lewis's understanding of the power of myth, and does not relate his appeal to the nature of existing conservative Protestant apologetic.

6. CHRISTIAN MISSION AND SOCIAL JUSTICE: LAUSANNE 1974 AND THE CHALLENGE FROM THE MAJORITY WORLD

The reawakening of evangelical social concern

Evangelicals in the years immediately after 1945 were not generally distinguished by their commitment to issues of economic or social justice. The phrase 'the social gospel', a movement on both sides of the Atlantic in the late nineteenth and early twentieth centuries that in historical reality had deep roots in evangelical tradition, had become equated in the fundamentalist-evangelical memory with a doctrinally effete liberalism. As a result, attempts in the second half of the twentieth century to rediscover a socially oriented evangelicalism frequently had to contend with accusations that they were opening the door to liberal theology. During the first twenty-five years of this period there were a number of such attempts, emanating chiefly from the stable of the 'new evangelicalism' in the United States or from the parallel Inter-Varsity movement in Britain.

In 1947 Carl Henry wrote a series of articles for a Michigan paper, the *Religious Digest*, lamenting that 'evangelical Christianity has become increasingly inarticulate about the social reference of the Gospel'. The paper declined to publish such combustible material, which appeared instead from the Dutch-American publishing house, Eerdmans, under the title *The Uneasy Conscience of Modern Fundamentalism*, with an introduction by Harold Ockenga which urged that 'the church needs a progressive Fundamentalism with a social message'.[1]

---

[1] Carl F. H. Henry, *The Uneasy Conscience of Modern Fundamentalism* (Grand Rapids:

Joel Carpenter is surely right to observe that Henry, at the same time as finishing his book, was completing his doctoral thesis at Boston University under the supervision of Edgar S. Brightman, a leading proponent of the social gospel who would shortly afterwards supervise the postgraduate studies of a more famous student, Martin Luther King.[2] Twenty years after the publication of Henry's book the editor of the Billy Graham Evangelistic Association's *Decision* magazine, Sherwood Wirt, returned to the theme with a book entitled *The Social Conscience of the Evangelical*. This was the fruit of an informal meeting in Chicago in 1965 of a small group of evangelical leaders (including Ockenga and David Hubbard) which concluded that a study of the subject was long overdue. Wirt's book was surprisingly radical for its day: it suggested that Mary's Magnificat was a song of revolution that may have been 'out of line with her Son's eternal purpose for mankind', roundly condemned racial segregation and devoted a whole chapter to environmental issues.[3] In 1969 a major congress on evangelism held in Minneapolis included in its programme an address by Leighton Ford of the Billy Graham Evangelistic Association on 'The Church and evangelism in a day of revolution'.[4] In the summer of 1971 seven students of Trinity Evangelical Divinity School led by Jim Wallis published a tabloid newspaper, *The Post-American*, which sought to apply the prophetic biblical tradition to issues such as the Vietnam War, white racism and poverty: the newspaper would later (in 1975) be renamed *Sojourners* and become the focus of a radical brand of communal Christian witness that has become renowned well beyond the confines of evangelicalism.[5] In 1972 the evangelical social scientist David O. Moberg published *The Great Reversal*, a book that took up the historian Timothy L. Smith's phrase describing evangelicals' repudiation in the early twentieth century of their nineteenth-century tradition of social engagement.[6] In November 1973 Ronald J. Sider, one of the

Eerdmans, 1947; new ed. 2003), quotations at xx and 13–14; see George M. Marsden, *Reforming Fundamentalism: Fuller Seminary and the New Evangelicalism*, Grand Rapids: Eerdmans, 1987), 79–82; Sherwood E. Wirt, *The Social Conscience of the Evangelical* (New York: Harper & Row; London: Scripture Union, 1968), 47–48.

[2] Joel Carpenter, *Revive Us Again: The Reawakening of American Fundamentalism* (New York: Oxford University Press, 1997), 193; but see Carl F. H. Henry, *Confessions of a Theologian: An Autobiography* (Waco: Word Books, 1986), 111–113, 120–122.

[3] Wirt, *Social Conscience*, 12–13, 80–81, 102–112.

[4] Personal communication from Leighton Ford, 19 Apr. 2011.

[5] See Jim Wallis and Joyce Holladay (eds.), *Cloud of Witnesses* (Maryknoll: Orbis Books; Washington, D.C.: Sojourners, 1991), xiv.

[6] David O. Moberg, *The Great Reversal: Evangelism Versus Social Concern* (Philadelphia:

most prominent of those younger American evangelicals who were inspired by the Anabaptist tradition of radical discipleship, convened a meeting in Chicago of some fifty evangelical leaders to address the subject of social concern. The meeting produced a statement, 'A Declaration of Evangelical Social Concern', which though an inevitable compromise between divergent perspectives, was signed by some mainstream evangelicals, such as Carl Henry, as well by Moberg, Wallis, Sider and others committed to a radical social expression of Christian discipleship. The Declaration became the manifesto of a group, led by Sider, known as 'Evangelicals for Social Action'.[7]

Bob Pierce's experience of the Korean War as a Youth for Christ evangelist led in 1950 to the foundation of World Vision, whose rapid growth was an important indicator of the awakening of the conscience of American evangelicals in the 'new evangelical' tradition to international humanitarian causes, particularly the need to help the innocent victims of war. In Britain a similar development was the establishment by the Evangelical Alliance in 1959 of a fund to relieve the suffering of refugees. This led to the creation of the Evangelical Alliance Relief (TEAR) Fund in 1968, which proved extraordinarily successful in broadening the British evangelical global conscience from purely missionary objectives to encompass humanitarian and developmental concerns.[8] The founding director of TEAR Fund, George Hoffman (1933–92), was an Anglican who had been much influenced by the National Evangelical Anglican Congress (NEAC) at Keele in 1967, which had insisted that 'both evangelism and social action are . . . universal obligations laid upon us by the authority of Christ'.[9] Also important was the foundation in 1969 of the Shaftesbury Project, which applied evangelical perspectives to social questions, with particular reference to the multiplying problems of Britain's inner cities. In 1970 the general secretary of the IVF, Oliver Barclay, published *Whose World?* (although it is significant that he felt he had to do so pseudonymously), which urged evangelicals to develop a Christian mind on a wide range of 'secular' topics.[10]

Among thinking evangelicals on both sides of the Atlantic, therefore,

---

Lippincott; London: Scripture Union, 1972).

[7] 'A Declaration of Evangelical Social Concern', *IRM* 63:249 (July 1974), 274–275; Henry, *Confessions of a Theologian*, 348.

[8] Timothy Chester, *Awakening to a World of Need: The Recovery of Evangelical Social Concern* (Leicester: Inter-Varsity Press, 1993), 13–14, 41–43.

[9] Ibid. 41; *The Nottingham Statement: The Official Statement of the Second Evangelical Anglican Congress Held in April 1977* (London: Church Pastoral Aid Society, 1977), 7.

[10] A. N. Triton, *Whose World?* (London: Inter-Varsity Press, 1970).

there was by the early 1970s a strengthening trend in favour of the application of evangelical thought to contemporary social issues. In the United States some of these evangelicals were members of the African-American community who sympathized with the civil rights movement – men such as the evangelists Tom Skinner and Bill Pannell, or the community developer John Perkins.[11] In many cases, however, it was a question of evangelicals who were themselves white and affluent turning their minds to what their Christian responsibility might be towards those who were less affluent, and often non-white. Such thinking did not always distinguish clearly between the call to renew the tradition of evangelical philanthropy, associated with figures from the past such as Lord Shaftesbury, and the question of whether a more radical commitment to challenge unjust economic structures in the name of the kingdom of God was necessary. Those who issued such a challenge were frequently viewed with suspicion by evangelicals, on the grounds that they appeared to be jeopardizing the divinely sanctioned forces of law and constituted authority. The reactions of some white American evangelicals to the assassination of Martin Luther King in April 1968 made this very clear: while King was to be admired for his vision of racial equality, his encouragement of civil disobedience and apparent inability to curb black power militants who were turning to violent protest attracted general censure. An editorial in *Christianity Today* delivered an ambivalent verdict on King, applauding him as an avowed apostle of non-violence who 'courageously led the struggle against racism', yet going on to criticize him for undermining 'the law of the community' through his support for mass civil disobedience. Readers were reminded that 'Americans are in Asia [Vietnam was meant] presumably to rebuke lawless forces', and hence no American ought to 'minimize the importance of law at home'. The editorial assumed a racist tone in castigating the black population in Washington for reacting to King's murder 'in a way that was primitive, even barbaric'.[12] The assassination of Robert Kennedy later that year prompted a gloomy editorial in *Christianity Today* entitled 'Where Is America Going?', which asked despairingly why if any state or federal law still discriminated against blacks (which it seriously doubted), resort was still being made to militancy and violence rather than to the democratic process.[13] The year in which the civil rights movement in America and radical student protest on both sides of the Atlantic reached unprecedented heights of

---

[11] Personal communication from Leighton Ford, 19 Apr. 2011.

[12] *CT*, 26 Apr. 1968, 24–25. For a rather more balanced assessment in the same issue see *CT*, 26 Apr. 1968, 37–38.

[13] *CT*, 21 June 1968, 23.

militancy, 1968, saw much evangelical opinion reinforced in its innate social conservatism.

Furthermore, the limited re-evaluation of Christian social responsibility that had taken place by the end of the 1960s was normally viewed as an aspect of Christian ethics, and was not always permitted to impact the evangelical understanding of the mission of the church, which still tended to be expressed primarily in terms of saving souls (though this was certainly not true of NEAC in 1967). The World Congress on Evangelism held in Berlin in 1966 reflected the salience of the American civil rights movement in the first part of its motto 'One Race, One Gospel, One Task', yet gave only slight attention to issues of racial or social justice. John Stott's authoritative and scholarly Bible expositions at Berlin on the 'Great Commission' given by Christ to the church still defined the Commission as 'not to reform society, but to preach the Gospel . . . the primary task of the members of Christ's church is to be Gospel heralds, not social reformers'.[14] Although by the early 1970s the voices of radical and socially engaged evangelicals such as Ronald Sider and Jim Wallis were becoming increasingly difficult to ignore, for many evangelicals issues of social and economic justice remained marginal to their understanding of the mission of the church. That situation began to change only once it became clear that evangelicalism was now a multicultural global community that included a large and rapidly growing sector that was neither white nor affluent.

The point at which that realization dawned on some evangelicals in the North can be identified quite precisely: it was at the International Congress on World Evangelization held at Lausanne in July 1974. This event was of such seminal importance for the cultural identity and future missiological orientation of the world evangelical movement that the remainder of this chapter will be devoted to the background to the Congress, the event itself and the Lausanne movement to which it gave birth.

The origins of the Lausanne Congress

The Berlin Congress in 1966 had been conceived as a singular event that would not be repeated, although it gave rise to various regional gatherings of evangelicals, some of which imparted significant impetus to evangelistic efforts in their respective parts of the globe. In January 1970 the Billy Graham Evangelistic Association convened a small international group of advisors in

---

[14] See http://www2.wheaton.edu/bgc/archives/docs/Berlin66/stott3.htm (accessed 30 May 2012).

Washington to consider whether a sequel to Berlin would be desirable; the unanimous view, at least among the overseas members of the group, was that it would not. However, when Graham invited a similar group of sixteen to a meeting at White Sulphur Springs at the end of November 1971 to reconsider the question, he found a much more favourable response. Although there was no desire simply to repeat the Berlin experience, 'a fairly clear consensus of opinion' was now evident that 'we ought to be looking again at the whole mission of the Church, bearing in mind that this involves making disciples, baptising and teaching'.[15] It was agreed to consider planning a second world congress to take place in the summer of 1974 with the aim 'To unite all evangelicals in the common task of total evangelization of the world'. The proposed congress would have a more pronounced emphasis on the church than did Berlin: it would involve 'the entire mission of the church'.[16] Exactly what that phrase meant would turn out to be a central issue at Lausanne.

A major influence on evangelical thinking at the time was the radical turn taken by mainline ecumenism in the wake of the Uppsala Assembly of the World Council of Churches in 1968. The World Council's Programme to Combat Racism, initiated in 1969, which awarded grants to liberation movements in southern Africa and to Black Power organizations in the United States, had attracted considerable attention in the media, caused immense disquiet among Christians of conservative inclination, and, in the view of some American evangelicals, was the principal reason for the steep decline in the number of recruits for missionary service coming forward from the mainline American denominations. The WCC appeared increasingly to be defining the mission of the church in terms of humanization and political liberation; evangelical leaders felt that a restatement of a more orthodox yet properly comprehensive view of the Christian missionary task was imperative. Billy Graham in particular was convinced that 'There is a vacuum developing in the world church. Radical theology has had its heyday.' Graham's vision was for a congress in which 'every participant must be totally and thoroughly evangelical' and at least half should be under the age of 40.[17] Although the final decision to hold the congress was not taken until March 1972, it was clear from

---

[15] Billy Graham, *Just as I Am: The Autobiography of Billy Graham* (London: Harper Collins, 1997), 568; Wheaton College, BGCA, Collection 46, LCWE [hereafter cited as BGCA 46], Box 30/1; A. J. Dain to Charles Troutman, 17 Feb. 1972.

[16] BGCA 46, Box 30/27, minutes, World Evangelization Strategy Consultation, 27 Nov. and 2 Dec. 1971.

[17] Ibid., Box 30/27, International Congress on World Evangelization. Meeting of the consultative conference, Vero Beach, Florida, 23–24 Mar. 1972.

December 1971 onwards that Graham and his organization were committed to bringing this vision to reality.[18]

One participant in the meetings in 1970 and 1971 was A. J. (known as 'Jack') Dain, assistant bishop in Sydney diocese, the stronghold of Australian evangelical Anglicanism. Jack Dain was English, and had served as a lay missionary in north India with the Regions Beyond Missionary Union before becoming general secretary of the Zenana Bible and Medical Mission (later the Bible and Medical Missionary Fellowship, now Interserve); he also acted as the overseas secretary of the British Evangelical Alliance, and in that capacity had come to Graham's notice as the organizer of his tour of India in January 1956. After his training for the Anglican ministry at Ridley Hall and ordination in 1959, he became federal secretary of the Australian CMS until 1965, when he was consecrated as assistant bishop.[19] At the December 1971 meeting Graham asked him to be chairman of a ten-man central steering committee (later known as the planning or executive committee) that would be responsible for planning the congress.[20] Dain then wrote a number of letters to contacts on different continents, inviting nominations of suitable 'younger' national leaders to serve on the planning committee: Graham was emphatic in his view that the committee should not be dominated by Americans, and that 'national representatives of the younger Churches' should share in the planning 'right from the outset'.[21] Although Jack Dain's name is rarely mentioned today, he was to perform a crucial role as planning chairman of the Lausanne Congress, alongside Graham's brother-in-law, Leighton Ford, as programme chair, and Paul Little of the American Inter-Varsity movement, as programme director. Although formally he was co-chairman with Graham of the congress itself, it was Dain who did the crucial spadework of recruiting key evangelical

---

[18] William Martin, *A Prophet with Honor: The Billy Graham Story* (New York: William Morrow, 1991), 441.

[19] Graham, *Just as I Am*, 264; John C. Pollock, *Shadows Fall Apart: The Story of the Zenana Bible and Medical Mission* (London: Hodder & Stoughton, 1958), 186, 200; *Crockford's Clerical Directory*, 1973–4.

[20] BGCA 46, Box 30/27, minutes, World Evangelization Strategy Consultation, 2 Dec. 1971. In addition to Graham and Dain, the members were Leighton Ford, Gilbert Kirby, Robert Evans, Don Hoke, Charles Ward, Akbar Abdul-Haqq, Harold Lindsell and Victor Nelson.

[21] Ibid., Box 30/1, A. J. Dain to Charles Troutman, 17 Feb. 1972; see also Dain to S. H. Iggulden, 23 Feb. 1972; Dain to S. Escobar, 12 Apr. 1972; see also Dain's letters in the same file to David Stewart (New Zealand), Michael Griffiths (Singapore), David McLagan (Scotland) and Ben Wati (India).

leaders and reconciling their often divergent views of the form the congress should take.

The new evangelicals of Latin America, Africa and Asia

One of those to whom Jack Dain wrote seeking nominations for membership of the planning committee was Charles H. Troutman (1914–90), a senior staff member of the Latin America Mission, and a leading figure in the American Inter-Varsity movement. Troutman had served as general secretary or director of both the Australian (1954–61) and American (1961–5) Inter-Varsity organizations.[22] He was also involved in the pioneering transition of the Latin America Mission from being an American-led foreign mission to an indigenous Christian movement led by nationals, under the new Spanish name of the Comunidad Latinoamericana de Ministerios Evangélicos (CLAME). As director of Latin America Mission/CLAME's Ministry to the Student World from 1967, Troutman forged close links with the International Fellowship of Evangelical Students (IFES). In its expanding work among university students in Latin America IFES had encountered the predominant influence of Marxist ideology to a greater extent than in any other continent. David Evans, the British general secretary of the Association Biblia Universitaria Argentina, reported in 1972 that a political atmosphere marked by the cry for armed struggle and the slogan 'Long live Che Guevara' was 'the major conditioning factor' in seeking to present the Christian message to Argentinean students.[23] The emerging leaders of the evangelical student movement in Latin America accordingly articulated a version of evangelicalism that placed a high priority on the construction of a thoughtful biblical response to the Marxist analysis of structural injustice in society. They were also keenly sensitive to the dangers of identifying the evangelical cause in the continent with the influence of the United States, and in consequence emphasized the importance of following 'the missionary principles found in the New Testament . . . the respect for local initiative, the search for local leadership, the decision not to impose prefabricated patterns of action and witness'.[24] A leadership training course run in four Latin American cities in 1966 by Dr Hans Bürki of IFES combined teaching on the Bible and discipleship with an analysis of the social and ecclesiastical situation of the continent. The course proved

---

[22] Troutman's papers are preserved at Wheaton College.

[23] *IFES Journal* 25:2 (1972), 25.

[24] Samuel Escobar, cited in Pete Lowman, *The Day of His Power: A History of the International Fellowship of Evangelical Students* (Leicester: Inter-Varsity Press, 1983), 194.

seminal in shaping the distinctive ethos of IFES in the Latin American context: a new style of being evangelical that was penetrating in its social criticism and unusually conscious of the dangers of religious imperialism.[25]

Troutman's response to Dain urged that the forthcoming congress must take seriously the perspectives of a younger generation of Christian leaders. It must also, he insisted, take a strong stand on the question of race and take full cognisance of 'the environment of the third world', where 'the element of revolution is the natural habitat for the proclamation of the Gospel'. In his reply Dain agreed that such pressing issues could no longer be left to the liberals.[26] Troutman's nominations for membership of the planning committee included the name of a young Peruvian Baptist, Samuel Escobar, as well as those of three of the other leaders of the new Latin American evangelicals: Dr C. René Padilla, an Ecuadorean Baptist now based in Argentina, who was associate general secretary of IFES for Latin America; Orlando Costas (1942–87), a young Puerto Rican Baptist teaching at the Latin American Biblical Seminary in Costa Rica under the auspices of the Latin America Mission, who would soon attract global attention for his 'radical evangelical' brand of missiology; and Sergio García of Mexico, the Latin American Director of Campus Crusade for Christ. Escobar had been a leader of the Peruvian evangelical student movement, the Circulo Biblico Universitario, and first attracted wider attention as a speaker at a seminal IFES Latin America conference held at Cochabamba in Bolivia in 1958, which appointed him as staff worker for Columbia, Ecuador and Peru.[27] He soon became well known as a leader of university missions throughout the continent, and as the author of a study in apologetics written for students, *Dialogo entre Cristo y Marx*. In 1972 he was appointed as general director of Inter-Varsity Christian Fellowship in Canada, a bold appointment that brought one of the leading voices of the new Latin American evangelicalism into an influential position in the North. In 1973 he was the only representative of the southern hemisphere among the published signatories of the Chicago Declaration of Evangelical Social Concern.[28] Escobar readily agreed to serve on the congress planning committee as one of the two Latin American representatives.[29]

---

[25] Ibid. 202–203.

[26] BGCA 46, Box 30/1, Troutman to Dain, 28 Feb. 1972; Dain to Troutman, 7 Mar. 1972.

[27] Lowman, *Day of His Power*, 195–197.

[28] *IRM* 63 (July 1974), 275.

[29] The other was Alcebíades Vasconcelos from the Assemblies of God in Brazil, a church that tended to be towards the right in the spectrum of Brazilian Protestant politics; see R. A. Chestnut, 'The Salvation Army or the Army's Salvation? Pentecostal Politics in

With René Padilla, Escobar would be one of the two speakers at Lausanne who proved most challenging to northern and more conservative ears; he was the only representative of the majority world to be appointed to the subcommittee of five given the task of drafting what became the Lausanne Covenant.

The planning committee also included two Africans: Festo Kivengere, Anglican bishop of Kigezi in Uganda, the best-known international spokesperson of the East African Revival; and Gottfried Osei-Mensah, the Ghanaian Baptist who was pastor of Nairobi Baptist Church. A third African, considered but not selected as a member of the planning committee, was John Gatu, general secretary of the Presbyterian Church of East Africa. Gatu, another product of the East African Revival, would, however, attend the congress and exercise a significant influence on the text of the Lausanne Covenant. Although voices from Latin America and Africa were to sound the clearest notes of a radical alternative evangelicalism at Lausanne, the thirty-one members of the planning committee also included six Asians.

British doubts about the congress

In addition to recruiting suitable members of the planning committee, there was a need to attract broad-based international support for the proposed congress. By mid-July 1972 Billy Graham and Jack Dain had between them sent a total of eighty-five letters to evangelical leaders around the world, inviting them to serve as convenors of the congress. Seventy-two affirmative replies had immediately been received, a total that in time would grow to 150. One of those so invited by Graham was John Stott, but Stott's initial reply to Graham, which he copied to Dain, was disappointingly hesitant. Stott wanted to see the purpose of the congress defined in terms of the formulation of a carefully considered strategy for world evangelization (rather than simply rousing exhortations to finish the task), and expressed grave concern at reports that the congress would have between three thousand and five thousand delegates – a sure recipe for ineffectiveness in his view.[30] Graham's reply assured Stott that his point concerning the size of the congress was 'well taken', but reiterated his vision that it would 'make an impact on the world', a goal that required a larger event than Stott had in mind.[31] Dain also wrote a personal

---

Amazonian Brazil, 1962–1992', *Luso-Brazilian Review* 36 (1999), 33–49.

[30] BGCA 46, Box 29/35, Stott to Graham, 30 May 1972.

[31] Ibid., Box 29/35, Graham to Stott, 28 June 1972.

letter urging Stott to lend his unequivocal backing: he noted that in contrast to the enthusiastic letters that had flooded in from those involved in 'real missionary outreach throughout the world', Europe had been the source of some theological criticism of the idea; he evidently feared that Stott was about to join the ranks of the critics, which would have been fatal to the standing of the congress.[32]

Dain's alarm was increased by the receipt of a long letter from the general secretary of the Evangelical Alliance in Britain, Gordon Landreth, which was 'full of criticisms and misgivings'. He received a similar letter of concern from Dr John Laird, the veteran and much-respected former general secretary of Scripture Union in Britain who served as president of the Evangelical Alliance in Britain from 1970 to 1972. Dain therefore wrote again to Stott, asking for his advice on whether he should make a special visit to London, given that the relationship between the congress and the British EA seemed to be 'running into extremely heavy water'.[33] Stott did not reply immediately to either of Dain's letters, but consulted the EA leadership and telephoned Dain on 23 August. Stott informed Dain in a letter written the next day that he had sufficiently reassured him that the congress was to be a properly prepared study conference, though his anxieties about size remained. Nevertheless, he indicated that he would, contrary to rumour, be willing to join the planning committee;[34] in the event, he was not to do so, though he became the most influential member of the preparatory committee charged with drafting what has become known as the Lausanne Covenant.

The misgivings held by British evangelical leaders about the planned congress were deep-rooted and symptomatic of fundamental differences between British and American evangelical culture. Dain confessed to Stott in September 1972 that as 'one who is still in many ways an Englishman', he found the swelling chorus of British disapproval, viewed against the favourable reactions of the rest of the world, 'particularly distressing'. However, he was able to report to Stott a number of changes to the plans that ought to give British critics some encouragement – all staff members of the Billy Graham Evangelistic Association, except Leighton Ford, had been removed from the planning committee, and seven majority world evangelical leaders

---

[32] Ibid., Box 30/1, Dain to Stott, 18 July 1972.

[33] Ibid., Box 30/1, Dain to Stott, 26 July 1972 and 11 Sept. 1972. Landreth did in fact attend Lausanne and defended the congress in the *CEN* against more strident critics, such as David Winter: *CEN*, 14 June 1974, 9. For Laird see his autobiography, *No Mere Chance* (London: Hodder & Stoughton and Scripture Union, 1981).

[34] BGCA 46, Box 30/1, Stott to Dain, 24 Aug. 1972.

had been added in their place.[35] Nevertheless, British concerns over the coming world congress continued to be voiced openly in the Christian press: it was feared that the congress would be on a grand scale, would prove inappropriately expensive in view of the current scale of global poverty, and that a venue would be chosen in which delegates would be accommodated in plush hotels, thus making attendance impossible for many from the majority world. The Council of the British Evangelical Alliance urged that the event should instead be located in a Pontins-style holiday camp with simple chalet accommodation.[36] Jack Dain shared many of his compatriots' concerns, and would have preferred an event limited to 1,250 participants, but confessed to Gilbert Kirby, principal of London Bible College and a member of the planning committee, that he had been unable to persuade the Americans regarding his case.[37] The latter gave the holiday camp suggestion short shrift. Possible venues considered included Rome (though this was soon discarded 'in view of possible difficulties'),[38] Amsterdam, Brussels, Stockholm and Lausanne, Switzerland. In September 1972 a decision was made to hold the congress at the prestigious Palais de Beaulieu in Lausanne, with delegates accommodated in a variety of hotels according to their various tastes and budgets.[39]

British criticism of the forthcoming congress showed no sign of abating during 1973. The former editor of *Crusade* magazine, David Winter, had a pungent letter published in the *Christian Record* lambasting 'the evangelical jet-set, for ever flying from one "vital, strategic" talking-shop to another, usually at our expense'.[40] Michael Harper of the Fountain Trust, the key spokesman for charismatic evangelicals in Britain, joined the fray with a letter to the *Church Times* attacking Lausanne as both extravagant and exclusive in the narrow theological range of its proponents.[41] In common with numerous other British evangelical leaders, Harper had been 'dismayed' by a campaign run in London by the Billy Graham Evangelistic Association in the summer of 1973 known as SPRE-E '73 (the initials stood for Spiritual Re-Emphasis).

---

[35] Ibid., Box 30/12, Dain to Stott, 11 Sept. 1972. In June 1972 there had been only four members from the majority world out of seventeen on the planning committee: Escobar, Kivengere, Chua Wee Hian and Akira Hatori (ibid., Box 30/3).

[36] Ibid., Box 30/12, G. Landreth to G. Kirby, 7 Sept. 1972.

[37] Ibid., Box 30/12, Dain to Kirby, 7 July 1972.

[38] Ibid., Box 30/28, minutes of planning committee, 24–25 Aug. 1972.

[39] Ibid., Box 30/23, report on congress sites and recommendation concerning congress location.

[40] *Christian Record*, 2 Nov. 1973, cutting in BGCA 46, Box 29/40.

[41] *Church Times*, 16 Nov. 1973, 14.

Harper saw both SPRE-E '73 and Lausanne as 'American dominated and financed endeavours that present an "establishment" image of evangelism that we are all too familiar with'.[42] The *Church of England Newspaper* agreed, dismissing the congress as 'an expensive, imposed, pretentious talk-in'.[43] It may be significant that *Crusade* made no mention of the Lausanne Congress until January 1974, when a brief report noted that increasing costs had forced a 10% reduction in the planned number of delegates from 3,000 to 2,700, and that prices for United Kingdom participants had been 'considerably lowered'.[44] The magazine pointedly made no further reference to the congress until its July 1974 issue.

Global participation

Participation in Lausanne was on an invitation-only basis according to national quotas agreed by the planning committee: each country was allowed seven participants for every one million Protestants in the population, and a further two participants for every ten million unevangelized people in the country. One thousand five hundred scholarships of £208 each were awarded to participants from the majority world.[45] The congress budget of £1.32 million was substantially, but not solely, dependent on American largesse. A letter was sent out over the signatures of Billy Graham and Harold Lindsell seeking financial help for the majority world participants. Nearly half of the total sums contributed in response from Europe and the Far East came in a single donation of 50,000 dollars from a wealthy member of the French Brethren movement, Jean André. Britain, however, had by 11 June contributed not a single cent.[46]

The lukewarm attitude of many British evangelicals towards the congress was reflected in a low level of enrolments from England, notably from the Church of England, and even lower levels from other parts of the United Kingdom; Scotland recorded a particularly low percentage of acceptances to invitations.[47] More generally, it was striking that rates of acceptance from

---

[42] *Crusade*, Apr. 1973, 11; July 1973, 13–16; BGCA 46, Box 29/40, Harper to G. Kirby, 20 Nov. 1973 and to A. J. Dain, 26 Nov. 1973.

[43] *CEN*, 4 Jan. 1974, 5.

[44] *Crusade*, Jan. 1974, 16.

[45] *Crusade*, Sept. 1974, 25. £208 in 1974 equates to about £1,690 or US$2,653 in July 2012.

[46] *CT*, 7 June 1974, 3; *CT*, 16 Aug. 1974, 35; BGCA 46, Box 30/1, Director's monthly report from Donald E. Hoke, 11 June 1974.

[47] BGCA 46, Box 30/1, Director's monthly report from Donald E. Hoke, 26 Feb. 1974.;

Europe as a whole were well below those of other continents, principally owing to the poor response from Britain as well as Germany: with less than three months to go to the opening of the congress, rates of acceptance were as follows:

Africa	86%
Asia	96%
Central America	88%
South America	85%
Oceania	85%
North America	90%
Europe	51%[48]

The final total of official participants was 2,473, from 150 different countries and 135 Protestant denominations. Over a thousand were from the non-Western world, but only three African Independent Churches (all from South Africa) were represented. Women accounted for only 7.1% of all attendees; Billy Graham had modestly hoped for 10%.[49] Fewer than 10% of attendees were lay people, whereas Graham had hoped for one-third: for an evangelical gathering, the preponderance of professional ministers was staggering. More encouraging was the fact that half of all those attending were under the age of 44.[50] Graham's original vision of a congress in which half of the participants would be from the non-Western world and under the age of 40, and one-third would be lay people, was not fulfilled, but the composition of the delegate body at Lausanne came close to meeting two of these three targets.[51]

Voices from Latin America and Africa

The dynamics of an event as large as the Lausanne Congress are bound to be complex, and to concentrate on the impact made by some of the spokes-

---

CEN, 5 Apr. 1974, 12; 24 May 1974, 9; 14 June 1974, 9. There were 94 participants at Lausanne from England, 5 from Wales, 10 from Northern Ireland and 7 from Scotland.

[48] BGCA 46, Box 30/1, Director's monthly report from Donald E. Hoke, 23 Apr. 1974.

[49] Martin, *Prophet with Honor*, 442.

[50] Ibid.; BGCA 46, Box 122/1, minutes of planning committee, 15 July 1974. C. René Padilla (ed.), *The New Face of Evangelicalism: An International Symposium on the Lausanne Covenant* (London: Hodder & Stoughton, 1976), 9.

[51] Martin, *Prophet with Honor*, 442–443.

men for the majority world is to isolate only one dimension of a many-sided event, and hence to risk distortion. It equally deserves to be remembered, for example, as the occasion at which the single-minded emphasis of Donald McGavran and Ralph Winter of Fuller Theological Seminary on the need to remember the 'unreached peoples' of the world first imprinted itself indelibly on the global evangelical conscience. Nonetheless, the question of the relationship of social justice to Christian mission was the dimension that attracted most press comment and provoked the most vigorous debates among participants. I shall select four of the contributions made by majority world participants for particular analysis. Two took the form of plenary congress addresses; one was an 'evangelistic strategy paper and report' submitted to one of the optional study groups; and one was a contribution made behind the scenes, yet with signal effect. Eleven of the plenary papers were pre-circulated to participants, and in these cases a separate address under the same title was given in the congress itself, responding to comments received on the pre-circulated paper.

Probably the most controversial of the eleven pre-circulated papers was by René Padilla on the topic 'Evangelism and the World'. His paper insisted that the gospel has cosmic as well as personal dimensions, and openly attacked American forms of 'culture Christianity', which reduced the Christian message to a form of cheap grace, a marketed product that guaranteed to the consumer 'the highest values – *success* in life and personal *happiness* now and forever'. The paper also criticized the strategists of the church growth movement for treating the task of world evangelization as a mere mathematical calculation of how to 'produce the greatest number of Christians at the least possible cost in the shortest possible time', employing the new technological wizardry of computers to solve the problem.[52] According to John Capon, editor of *Crusade*, Padilla's paper caused 'a minor sensation' and was attacked as a 'caricature'. The address that followed, pointedly delivered in Spanish rather than English (and simultaneously translated), continued on the same theme, and 'really set the congress alight', attracting the warmest applause of any speaker so far.[53] In response to those who had questioned why he had attacked the identification of the gospel with the American way of life but not with other cultures, Padilla replied that because of the predominant role of the United States both in world affairs and in missionary endeavour, 'this particular form of Christianity, as no

---

[52] René Padilla, 'Evangelism and the World', in J. D. Douglas (ed.), *Let the Earth Hear His Voice. International Congress on World Evangelization Lausanne, Switzerland: Official Reference Volume: Papers and Responses* (Minneapolis: World Wide Publications, 1975), 126.

[53] *Crusade*, Sept. 1974, 26; *CEN*, 26 July 1974, 3.

other today, has a powerful influence far beyond the borders of that nation'. Still more fundamentally, Padilla answered the charge that he was confusing evangelism with political action by insisting that 'the imperative of the evangelical ethic forms an indissoluble whole with the indicative of the Gospel'.[54]

The second majority world contribution that attracted particular comment was Samuel Escobar's circulated paper and ensuing address on 'Evangelism and Man's Search for Freedom, Justice and Fulfilment'. Escobar warned against the danger of making Christianity the official ideology of the West in the same way as Communism had become the official ideology of the eastern bloc. Like Padilla, Escobar also identified the temptation currently facing evangelicalism as one of withdrawal from the ethical demands of a discipleship lived out in engagement with a social context in which injustice was rife.[55] In his congress address Escobar boldly took the text dear to liberation theologians, the 'Nazareth manifesto' of Luke 4:18–19, and insisted that it could not be spiritualized in a world where millions were poor, broken-hearted, captive, blind and bruised. While he emphasized that the freedom of which the gospel speaks is not simply freedom from human masters, he went on to argue that 'the heart which has been made free with the freedom of Christ cannot be indifferent to the human longings for deliverance from economic, political, or social oppression'. He pointed out that many of the countries that had succumbed to a violent revolution conducted on Marxist principles were those where Christianity had allowed itself to be identified with the interests of the ruling class.[56] Harold Lindsell, writing in *Christianity Today*, felt it necessary to give considerable space to Escobar's address, interpreting it with obvious disapproval as saying that 'socialism is preferable to capitalism'.[57] John Stott later described it as having 'put the cat among the pigeons'.[58]

The third radical voice from Latin America audible at Lausanne was that of Orlando Costas, then only 32 years of age. Costas wrote two papers for the congress, both on the theme of 'Evangelism-in-Depth', a programme of contextual evangelism developed by the Latin America Mission from 1959 onwards, which was now being adopted in some locations beyond Latin America.[59] His longer paper at Lausanne, entitled 'Depth in Evangelism – an

---

[54] Douglas, *Let the Earth Hear*, 134–136, at 136 and 144.

[55] Ibid. 303–318.

[56] Ibid. 319–326, at 322 and 326.

[57] *CT*, 13 Sept. 1974, 24–25.

[58] John Stott, 'The Significance of Lausanne', *IRM* 64:255 (July 1975), 289.

[59] See Allen Yeh, '*Se hace camino al andar*: Periphery and Center in the Missiology of Orlando Costas' (University of Oxford DPhil thesis, 2008), 42–44.

Interpretation of "In-Depth" Evangelism Around the World', formed one of the main evangelistic strategy papers submitted to the study group on 'Christian Higher Education and World Evangelization'.[60] While the bulk of his paper was devoted to an illustrated exposition of what 'evangelism-in-depth' meant in practice, Costas rendered the message of Padilla and Escobar still more explicit by arguing that the Great Commission had an inescapably structural dimension: to evangelize 'in-depth' meant bringing the gospel to bear not simply on individuals but on the socio-economic structures of the present age. In language whose radical connotations may have escaped many of his readers Costas also borrowed the term, coined by the Brazilian educationalist Paulo Freire in his classic work *Pedagogy of the Oppressed*, to describe the process of *conscientization* that had to take place if ordinary Christian believers were to be mobilized to apply the gospel to all areas of their lives.[61] Not being a platform speaker, Costas was less visible at Lausanne than Padilla or Escobar, yet it is significant that Carl Henry, writing in *Christianity Today*, identified him as the leader of the most radical group among the Latin American evangelicals at the congress, distinguished by his accusation that 'American evangelical missionary support is tainted by links to imperialistic culture and vested economic interests'.[62]

The fourth contribution from a 'Third World' participant was of a quite different kind. One of the official convenors of the congress was John Gatu (1925–), the Kenyan general secretary of the Presbyterian Church of East Africa, who had been converted in 1950 under the influence of the East African Revival. Joe Church's autobiography lists Gatu as one of the Revival's most notable Kenyan supporters, and Gatu's unashamed indebtedness to the Revival's focus on the cross is evident on the cover and title page of his own book, *Joyfully Christian + Truly African*, in which the title and subtitle are connected not by a colon but by the symbol of the cross.[63] At the same time Gatu became a well-known figure in ecumenical circles, especially after his call at the Milwaukee Mission Festival in 1971 for a moratorium on the sending of western missionaries, in order to promote the responsible selfhood of the

---

[60] See also Costas's shorter paper 'In-Depth Evangelism in Latin America', in Douglas, *Let the Earth Hear*, 211–212.

[61] Ibid. 675–694, at 682. Freire's book was published in Portuguese in 1968 and first appeared in English translation in 1970.

[62] *CT*, 13 Sept. 1974, 66.

[63] J. E. Church, *Quest for the Highest: An Autobiographical Account of the East African Revival* (Exeter: Paternoster Press, 1981), 248; John G. Gatu, *Joyfully Christian + Truly African* (Nairobi: Acton Publishers, 2006).

non-western (and particularly African) churches, many of which remained heavily dependent on external aid.[64] Gatu raised the moratorium issue again at the WCC Commission on World Mission and Evangelism conference in Bangkok in December 1972–January 1973, when his call for Africa to 'be sending missionaries out to other continents rather than always receiving them' is said to have 'startled delegates'.[65]

The International Congress on World Evangelization thus gathered with the originator of the call for a missionary moratorium present as one of the official convenors, a paradox that many conservative participants, such as the Tübingen theologian Professor Peter Beyerhaus, regarded as anomalous in the extreme. Gatu accordingly found that his credentials as an evangelical were widely questioned. Billy Graham, in his opening evening address to the congress, received 'roaring' applause when he urged the rejection of limitation of evangelism to near-neighbours on the grounds that this would 'shut out at least a billion from any possibility of knowing the Savior'.[66] Gatu was asked privately what he thought of Graham's remark, and said that he was entitled to his view, but was in danger of speaking on an issue he did not understand. The issue was taken up in a 'spirited debate' among the sixty members of the East Africa strategy group (national or regional strategy groups met for six daily 90-minute sessions). Some leading members, such as Erica Sabiti, former archbishop of Uganda, and Henry Okullu, Anglican bishop of Maseno South, both of whom were also deeply influenced by the East African Revival, took a different view from Gatu. Nevertheless, Festo Kivengere urged that the group needed to say something on the question, 'because of all the bad press and negative understanding attached to the word'. The group's official statement declined to endorse the idea of a general moratorium, but highlighted the issue of unhealthy dependence on foreign resources, and recommended 'the concept behind moratorium' for consideration in specific contexts.[67]

Gatu had enough support from the East Africa strategy group to be given the opportunity to address the full congress on the issue as a spokesman for the group: he told delegates that the African church was overdependent on the West, and that a temporary cessation of western assistance 'would force Africans to assume new responsibilities'.[68] As a result, a significant

---

[64] For Gatu's Milwaukee address see his *Joyfully Christian*, 169–176; Elliott Kendall, *The End of an Era: Africa and the Missionary* (London: SPCK, 1978), 86–107.

[65] Kendall, *End of an Era*, 92; *CC*, 25 Sept. 1974, 871.

[66] *CT*, 13 Sept. 1974, 90; Douglas, *Let the Earth Hear*, 33; *Crusade*, Sept. 1974, 24.

[67] *CT*, 16 Aug. 1974, 36–37.

[68] *Crusade*, Sept. 1974, 30; *CC*, 21–28 Aug. 1974, 790.

insertion was made in the draft text of the section of the Lausanne Covenant dealing with 'the urgency of the evangelistic task':

> A reduction of foreign missionaries and money in an evangelized country may some-times be necessary to facilitate the national church's growth in self-reliance and to release resources for unevangelized areas. Missionaries should flow ever more freely from and to all continents in a spirit of humble service.[69]

John Stott's subsequent exposition and commentary on the Covenant referred to the currency given to the call for a missionary moratorium by the Bangkok conference, though without mentioning Gatu, noted that the call was 'emotive' and 'not altogether understood', and explained that the Covenant had therefore avoided the term 'moratorium' and clarified the concept.[70] Gatu himself felt that, despite the substantial amendment of the original concept of a missionary 'withdrawal' to a mere 'reduction', the fact that the Congress had faced the issue 'showed a promising change in attitude on the part of the evangelicals' that he had not anticipated.[71] Most northern evangelicals of con-servative inclination remained unpersuaded of Gatu's case.[72] Among the 'new evangelicals' who saw Lausanne as an endorsement of their position, Gatu's credentials as an evangelical remained secure. He was selected to present the paper on 'the urgency of the evangelistic task' in a subsequent symposium convened by René Padilla and Samuel Escobar to discuss the fifteen sections of the Covenant, which was published in 1976 as *The New Face of Evangelicalism* with a foreword by John Stott.[73]

The drafting of the Lausanne Covenant

The insertion John Gatu secured in the section of the Covenant dealing with the urgency of the evangelistic task was only one, and not even the most important, of a series of changes made to the Covenant in the course of the

---

[69] Compare para. 8 of what is termed 'the first draft' of the Covenant in BGCA 46, Box 27/4, with para. 9 of the final version in Douglas, *Let the Earth Hear*, 6.

[70] See http://www.lausanne.org/all-documents/lop-3.html#9, section 9D (accessed 30 May 2012).

[71] Padilla, *New Face of Evangelicalism*, 165; also in Gatu, *Joyfully Christian*, 136. This section is indebted to my personal conversation with John Gatu on 22 Apr. 2008.

[72] See, for example, the brief reference to the issue in *MM*, Sept. 1974, 25.

[73] Padilla, *New Face of Evangelicalism*, 163–176.

congress. The Covenant originated in a fifteen-paragraph statement drafted on the basis of the pre-circulated papers in March 1974 by Dr J. D. Douglas from Scotland, former editor of *The Christian* newspaper.[74] Although later described by John Stott as bearing 'no resemblance' to the final Covenant,[75] Douglas's fifteen-point structure appears to have survived substantially intact right through to the final version, apart from some minor surgery and reordering. His statement was submitted to an administrative committee that met in Lausanne at the end of March, was there modified and then considered at the congress itself by a drafting committee comprising Stott as chairman, Hudson Armerding (president of Wheaton College), Samuel Escobar, Jim Douglas, and Leighton Ford of the Billy Graham Evangelistic Association.[76] The drafting committee made further revisions before circulating the third draft of the document (now known as the Covenant) to all participants, with a request that individuals or groups submit proposals for amendment. Several hundred proposals for amendment were submitted. The largest group to do so was the Theology and Radical Discipleship group, whose fringe meetings attracted over five hundred participants, mainly of the younger generation. It represented both the new Latin American evangelicals and some more radical evangelicals in the North, such as the American Mennonite John Howard Yoder, or Jim Punton of the Frontier Youth Trust, an offshoot of the Scripture Union movement in Britain with a radical vision for mission to youth in the inner cities. Before the final version of the Covenant appeared, the group circulated an alternative statement of its own, 'A Response to Lausanne', which affirmed the cosmic scope of redemption and repudiated any attempt 'to drive a wedge between evangelism and social action' as 'demonic'.[77] Although Stott, who had held a series of cordial

---

[74] Accounts of origins of the Covenant vary in the respective roles given to Douglas and Stott. Compare the following: BGCA 46, Box 27/4, minutes of administrative committee, 26 Mar. 1974 (to which is appended what is termed 'the first draft' of the Covenant, but is in fact the third draft submitted to all participants midway through the Congress); Stott's own preface to the Covenant is available at http://www.lausanne. org/all-documents/lop-3.html#P (accessed 30 May 2012); *Crusade*, Sept. 1974, 31; Timothy Dudley-Smith, *John Stott: A Global Ministry* (Leicester: Inter-Varsity Press, 2001), 212–213; Padilla, *New Face of Evangelicalism*, 10.

[75] Dudley-Smith, *Global Ministry*, 212.

[76] BGCA 46, Box 122/1, minutes of planning committee, 19 July 1974. Douglas's fifteen points were reduced to fourteen by the third draft, but the final version reverted to fifteen through the addition of a section on freedom and persecution.

[77] 'A Response to Lausanne', *IRM* 63 (Oct. 1974), 574–576; Dain described the Theology

meetings with the group's leaders, privately regretted the undermining of evangelical unity represented by their unilateral action, he borrowed some key phrases from the Response in the Covenant, notably the emphasis that 'those who proclaim the cross must be continually marked by the cross'. He also took some of the wind out of the radicals' sails by publicly announcing that he would sign the Response statement in addition to the Covenant itself.[78]

The final version of the Covenant was prepared by Stott during two long nights of editorial work. Comparison of the third draft, circulated earlier in the congress, with the final version reveals the skill with which he amended the text in ways calculated to bridge the gap between the more radical evangelicals and conservatives such as Francis Schaeffer and Peter Beyerhaus. Crucially, the section on Christian social responsibility was promoted from paragraph 7 to paragraph 5, and was significantly strengthened in its phrasing.

Paragraph 8 on churches in evangelistic partnership now began with a bold declaration: 'We rejoice that a new missionary era has dawned. The dominant role of western missions is fast disappearing.' Paragraph 9 on the urgency of the evangelistic task gained both the section already discussed on possible national reductions in expatriate missionary numbers and funding, and a hard-hitting conclusion on the duty incumbent on the more affluent to develop a simple lifestyle (which led Ruth Graham to decline to sign the Covenant on the grounds that it was impossible to define what the standard of simplicity should be).[79] In paragraph 10 on evangelism and culture the initial statement that 'missions have *sometimes* exported with the gospel an alien culture' became 'missions have *all too frequently* exported with the gospel an alien culture' (my italics). In paragraph 12 on 'spiritual conflict' an undue preoccupation by the church with statistics or their dishonest use (a point raised by both Padilla and Escobar in their plenary addresses) was now more roundly castigated as an example of worldliness infiltrating the church.[80]

---

and Radical Discipleship group as comprising 'mainly younger men and women' in *CEN*, 9 Aug. 1974, 2.

[78] *Crusade*, Sept. 1974, 29; *CT*, 13 Sept. 1974, 66–67; Dudley-Smith, *Global Ministry*, 215; para. 6 of the Covenant urged that 'a church which preaches the cross must itself be marked by the cross'.

[79] Dudley-Smith, *Global Ministry*, 216.

[80] Compare the third draft in BGCA 46, Box 27/4, with the Covenant in its final form in Douglas, *Let the Earth Hear*, 3–9.

The role of John Stott

On day nine of the congress Stott presented the final text of the Covenant to participants not for official 'adoption' but with the invitation that those who so wished should sign it. Some 2,000 out of the 2,473 participants did so. John Capon commented in *Crusade* that it was Stott's masterly performance in this presentation, even more than his opening address on the biblical basis of evangelism, that clearly established him as 'the key figure in contemporary world evangelicalism', a judgment that arguably undervalued Graham's significance.[81] However, it was Stott, more than any other leading figure at Lausanne, who had taken up the concerns of those who spoke for evangelicals in the majority world, and interpreted them sympathetically to those, in the United States in particular, who were instinctively fearful that the new radical evangelicalism was simply a reincarnation of the old 'social gospel', which they believed had led inexorably to the spiritual bankruptcy of the WCC. There is little doubt that Stott's own capacity to endorse the concerns of the southern evangelicals was enhanced by the fact that the two leading spokesmen – Padilla and Escobar – were trusted leaders in the evangelical student movements so close to his own heart.

Stott also played an important mediatory role in the negotiations over the nature and leadership of the Lausanne Continuation Committee for World Evangelization (LCCWE), later abbreviated to the Lausanne Committee for World Evangelization (LCWE), which was set up towards the close of the congress and of which he was made a member. As at the World Missionary Conference in Edinburgh in 1910,[82] the question of what form a continuation committee should take was one that required sensitive diplomacy, not least in this case because of the prior existence of the World Evangelical Fellowship, as well as the desire of some evangelicals to see a more elaborate global structure created as an alternative to the WCC.

It is significant that neither Padilla nor Escobar was invited to become a member of the continuation committee.[83] At the first meeting of the LCCWE after the congress, held in Mexico City (chosen as the cheapest avail-

---

[81] *Crusade*, Sept. 1974, 31; cited in Dudley-Smith, *John Stott: A Global Ministry*, 215.

[82] See Brian Stanley, *The World Missionary Conference, Edinburgh 1910* (Grand Rapids: Eerdmans, 2009), 277–302.

[83] Alister Chapman, *Godly Ambition: John Stott and the Evangelical Movement* (New York: Oxford University Press, 2012), 142.

able majority world location)[84] in January 1975, Stott felt obliged to oppose Graham's strict interpretation of what its brief should be: while Graham was primarily concerned not to create a structure with a dangerously wide brief, Stott was convinced that a restriction of the Committee's scope to the coordination of evangelistic efforts would have been a betrayal of the commitment made at the congress to a broader concept of mission that included the penetration of society by Christian witness. To the annoyance of the American members he indicated that he would have to resign if the narrower concept prevailed, and Jack Dain did the same. A compromise formula was agreed that defined the aim of the LCCWE as 'to further the total biblical mission of the church, recognizing that in this mission of sacrificial service, evangelism is primary, and that our particular concern must be the evangelization of the 2,700 million unreached peoples [sic] of the world'.[85] It was enough to keep Stott and Dain on board, but Alister Chapman is surely right in his judgment that the Mexico City meeting revealed that Lausanne did not in fact signal an immediate victory for Stott's more holistic concept of mission. Many delegates might have left Lausanne more enthused by the sharply statistical vision of 'unreached people groups' adumbrated by Donald McGavran and Peter Wagner than by the pleas of the radical evangelicals for an integration of ministries of justice, mercy and evangelism. Nevertheless, it is to Stott's eternal credit that he discerned the direction in which the majority of global evangelical thinking was moving. When asked in 1992 why he had been so determined to preserve social action as part of the brief of the LCWE, Stott replied that it 'was because I knew that the framers of the alternative, the Radical statement, were all the younger, rising . . . [e]vangelical leadership, and that if we didn't find room for their concerns, Lausanne was doomed'.[86]

Appraisals of Lausanne in Britain and the United States

Especially in Britain Lausanne tends to be remembered for John Stott's remarkable skills of conciliation and Christian diplomacy, and that reputation is well merited, though he was in no sense the architect of the congress itself. Stott's achievement enabled British evangelicals quietly to forget the suspicion

---

[84] For the reasons for the choice of Mexico City see BGCA 46, Box 29/35, Dain to Stott, 26 Aug. 1974.

[85] Cited in CT, 4 July 1975, 9. The words 'in this mission of sacrificial service, evangelism is primary' were drawn from the Lausanne Covenant, para. 6.

[86] Chapman, Godly Ambition, 141–144, citing Chester, Awakening, 85.

with which so many of them (including, in some measure, Stott himself) had initially viewed the plans for the congress. Anglicans in particular might have been tempted to present the event as a triumph for the Anglican *via media* between the two poles of American fundamentalism and the new evangelical radicalism from the South. Among some of the British evangelicals most intimately involved in the congress, however, it was the role of Jack Dain as chairman that elicited the warmest admiration in the immediate aftermath of the congress. Gilbert Kirby wrote to Dain both immediately before and after the congress expressing his admiration for his 'truly magnificent leadership'.[87] Dain himself remained deeply grateful to Stott for the hours of work he had devoted to the drafting of the Covenant and to consultations with the Radical Discipleship group, which he correctly regarded as 'tremendously important . . . for the whole integrity of the Congress'.[88] He was also encouraged at the overall tone of the reporting of Lausanne in the British Christian press, and observed in a letter to Kirby that 'quite a number of people who went almost cynical realized that their cynicism was not well founded and have been honest enough to admit to a change of mind'.[89] Dain's comment may well have been applicable to the journalist who exercised the greatest influence over evangelical opinion in Britain, John Capon, the editor of *Crusade*, who in the July 1974 edition was still lambasting the event for being 'too big, much too big' and conceited in its sense of self-importance, but whose detailed account of the congress in the September issue was, while not uncritical, broadly sympathetic.[90]

If much British evangelical opinion on the Lausanne Congress moved from initial scepticism to retrospective enthusiasm for the Covenant and all that it stood for, some American evangelicals appear to have moved in the opposite direction, from initial enthusiasm for the congress as a rallying cry for world evangelization to a more guarded attitude towards the broadening of the evangelical concept of mission which the Covenant undoubtedly represented. An alternative American response was to suggest that the radical voices were quite unrepresentative of the views of participants, even of those from the southern hemisphere. *Christianity Today* under Harold Lindsell's editorship took a broadly favourable but not uncritical view of the congress. A report by Edward Plowman in the 16 August issue claimed that Padilla

[87] BGCA 46, Box 30/12, Kirby to Dain, 13 and 30 July 1974.

[88] Ibid., Box 29/35, Dain to Stott, 20 Aug. 1974.

[89] Ibid., Box 30/12, Dain to Kirby, 1 Oct. 1974. For one such change of mind from a British observer see the letter from Malcolm MacRae in *CT*, 25 Oct. 1974, 21.

[90] *Crusade*, July 1974, 7; Sept. 1974, 23–32.

and Escobar had received more support from Anglo-Saxons than they did from their Latin American peers, citing one meeting of Latin American participants at which Escobar had been 'promptly rebuked by a dozen leaders' for supporting the concept of a missionary moratorium. Escobar had a letter published in reply pointing out that no such rebuke had been issued, and that he personally supported not a moratorium but the development of missions 'on a more biblical basis'.[91] Lindsell's first reaction to the congress, published in the 30 August issue of the journal, commented that it was a sign of growing maturity in the worldwide evangelical constituency that 'there was nothing resembling a party-line at the congress except the common allegiance to the Word of God', a comment later echoed by John Stott in an article in the *International Review of Mission*.[92] However, Lindsell criticized both 'the data-oriented church-growth school' and 'the discipleship-demanding compassion and justice group' for insufficient sensitivity to 'the kind of evangelism that permeates society across a broad spectrum embracing the arts and, in fact, all vocational pursuits'.[93] A major appraisal followed in the 13 September 1974 issue that again applauded the congress for 'reaching a new high in evangelical co-operation'. Nevertheless, Lindsell's article placed a distinctively conservative interpretation on the congress: Lausanne had made clear that the ecumenical and evangelical movements preached two wholly antithetical gospels, so that 'whoever accepts one must repudiate the other'; it had defined mission as 'the evangelization of the world'; and it had commendably refused to put social action 'on the same plane with the proclamation of the Gospel'. Lindsell also implicitly criticized Samuel Escobar for his attack on 'American imperialism' and castigated him for omitting from his catalogue of social evils the more traditional evangelical targets of alcohol, tobacco, drugs and pornography; Padilla's similar attack on American 'culture Christianity' was summarized without comment.[94]

Escobar was dismayed at the coverage of the congress in *Christianity Today* and wrote to Dain to express his frustration at what he regarded as the 'totally biased report' in *Christianity Today*. To him it was symptomatic of the fact that

> segments of Evangelicalism that particularly in the USA were not happy with the way God let the Congress go, are unable to dialogue with Evangelicals from a different

---

[91] *CT*, 16 Aug. 1974, 36; 27 Sept. 1974, 21–22.
[92] John Stott, 'The Significance of Lausanne', *IRM* 64 (1975), 288–290.
[93] *CT*, 30 Aug. 1974, 27.
[94] *CT*, 13 Sept. 1974, 21–26.

perspective. The WCC has registered our message; some large denominations are
open to the impact. It would be a pity if the impact of the Congress is manipulated
by the more closed and triumphalistic sectors of Evangelicalism.[95]

On receipt of Escobar's letter Dain promptly wrote a full and sympathetic reply. In his view Escobar's 'was one of the prophetic voices in the
Congress and I think the prophet must always be prepared for a measure of
misunderstanding. The prophet is always a little ahead of the people of God
and I think that this may have well been the case at Lausanne.' He sought to
reassure Escobar by informing him that 'All the reports that I have received
from the English speaking world throughout Great Britain, Canada, and in
certain cases the United States, certainly Australia, New Zealand and South
Africa' were supportive of 'the new emphasis . . . in which you particularly
were involved'.[96]

Dain could not, however, speak for the American evangelical constituency, where the narrower interpretation of Lausanne expounded by Lindsell
in the pages of *Christianity Today* continued to command widespread assent.
The perspective of the Fuller Theological Seminary School of World Mission
was emphatically presented in an article by Peter Wagner, 'Lausanne Twelve
Months Later', published in *Christianity Today* in July 1975. Wagner described
three 'torpedoes' that in his view had been launched in an attempt to divert
the congress from its proper goal of promoting world evangelization. The
first was 'an attempt to confuse evangelism with social action'; the second
'an attempt to confuse evangelism with Christian co-operation'; and the
third an 'attempt to confuse evangelism with Christian nurture'. According
to Wagner, the objective of the Theology and Radical Discipleship group
had been to turn Lausanne into a congress on social concern. He declared
it a fallacy to suggest that Christian unity necessarily promotes evangelism,
and deplored an overemphasis on discipleship as a threat to the priority of 'winning lost men and women to the Christian faith'. The congress
itself had in Wagner's view rejected all three fallacies, but not decisively.
Hence the LCCWE meeting in Mexico City witnessed 'a last-ditch attempt
to reverse the course of events and once again constitute the LCCWE as
an agency designed not just for evangelism but for all aspects of the total
mission of the Church'. The compromise formula reached in Mexico City,
with its insistence that 'our particular concern must be the evangelization of the 2,700 million unreached peoples of the world' was for Wagner

---

[95] BGCA 46, Box 30/5, Escobar to Dain, 10 Oct. 1974.
[96] Ibid., Box 30/5, Dain to Escobar, 17 Oct. 1974.

a welcome sign that, in the end, all three torpedoes had missed their target.[97]

The Lausanne movement after 1974

The Lausanne movement, which has continued into the twenty-first century, has thus had to negotiate a winding path between divergent interpretations of what the true message of the 1974 congress was. There is evidence that Billy Graham lost interest in the Lausanne movement after the Mexico City meeting, feeling that the resources of the Billy Graham Evangelistic Association would be more productively employed in funding conferences specifically for practising evangelists.[98] In contrast, some on the left wing of evangelicalism felt that the movement had failed to maintain the momentum of gospel radicalism generated in 1974. In their view, at the Lausanne consultation held in Pattaya, Thailand, in June 1980 the holistic missionary vision of Lausanne was overwhelmed by a resurgent strategic pragmatism focused on the concept of unreached peoples.[99] In response nearly one-third of the delegates signed a statement of concerns on the future of the LCWE drawn up by Orlando Costas and six others.[100] The statement complained that the LCWE 'does not seem to have been seriously concerned with the social, political and economic issues in many parts of the world that are a great stumbling block to the proclamation of the gospel', and called for the LCWE to convene a world congress on social responsibility and its implications for evangelization. Costas found the response to the statement from the leadership of the LCWE disappointing, feeling that only John Stott took its concerns seriously.[101] No world congress on social responsibility was forthcoming, although LCWE

---

[97] C. Peter Wagner, 'Lausanne Twelve Months Later', *CT*, 4 July 1975, 7–9.

[98] Chapman, *Godly Ambition*, 149.

[99] See Kwame Bediako, 'World Evangelisation, Institutional Evangelicalism and the Future of the Christian World Mission', in Vinay Samuel and Albrecht Hauser (eds.), *Proclaiming Christ in Christ's Way: Studies in Integral Evangelism* (Oxford: Regnum Books, 1989), 57–61.

[100] The others were David Gitari (Kenya), Clarence Hilliard (African American), Andrew Kirk (UK), Peter Kuzmic (Yugoslavia), Vinay Samuel (India) and Ronald Sider (USA).

[101] C. René Padilla and Chris Sugden (eds.), *Texts on Evangelical Social Ethics 1974–1983 (i)*, Grove Booklet on Ethics 58 (Bramcote: Grove, 1985), 22–25; V. Samuel and C. Sugden (eds.), *Sharing Jesus in the Two-Thirds World* (Bangalore: Partnership in Mission-Asia, 1983), 1–6.

was already committed to holding a consultation on evangelism and Christian social responsibility in June 1982. It was at this significant event, held in Grand Rapids, that Stott composed what has since become a well-known definition of the relationship between Christian social action and evangelism as being like 'the two blades of a pair of scissors or the two wings of a bird'.[102] Nonetheless, in response to what they saw as Pattaya's apparent indifference to the concerns of the radical evangelicals, Costas and twenty-four other evangelical theologians from the Latin American Theological Fraternity, Partnership in Mission-Asia, and the Africa Theological Fellowship felt it necessary in March 1982 to set up their own organization, known originally as the International Fellowship of Evangelical Mission Theologians (from the Two-Thirds World) (INFEMIT).[103]

The Lausanne movement's second full congress, held in Manila in 1989, marked something of a resurgence of a holistic emphasis. Its documentation included a powerful paper on 'Reaching the Oppressed' written by Caesar Molebatsi, a black South African who had been prominent in the gathering campaign against the apartheid regime.[104] The Manila Congress produced a series of twenty-one affirmations that built on the statements of the Lausanne Covenant. They included both an explicit commitment to denounce injustice in the name of God's kingdom of justice and peace (no. 9) and an insistence on the urgency of world evangelization and the possibility of reaching unreached peoples (no. 19). The last of the twenty-one affirmed, using the words of the Lausanne Covenant, that 'God is calling the whole church to take the whole gospel to the whole world'.[105] Samuel Escobar has continued to be closely involved in the Lausanne movement and René Padilla's daughter, Ruth Padilla DeBorst, was one of the plenary speakers at the third Lausanne Congress held in Cape Town in October 2010.[106]

---

[102] See http://www.lausanne.org/en/documents/lops/79-lop-21.html (accessed 30 May 2012).

[103] Samuel and Sugden, *Sharing Jesus*, 6. The 'from the Two-Thirds World' was later dropped to permit the inclusion of ethnic minorities from North America and eastern Europe. INFEMIT set up the Oxford Centre for Mission Studies in 1983.

[104] See http://www.lausanne.org/documents/lau2docs/294.pdf (accessed 30 May 2012).

[105] See http://www.lausanne.org/en/documents/manila-manifesto.html (accessed 30 May 2012).

[106] The foregoing paragraph is indebted to Yeh, '*Se hace camino al andar*', 190–194; see also Al Tizon, *Transformation After Lausanne: Radical-Evangelical Mission in Global–Local Perspective* (Oxford: Regnum Books, 2008); and Jacob Thomas, *From Lausanne to Manila: Evangelical Social Thought* (New Delhi: ISPCK, 2003).

The Lausanne Congress did not settle the arguments over identity and missiological emphasis that were emerging in world evangelicalism. Rather, it brought them into the open and raised them to a new level of intensity. As Carl Henry observed, 'the gathering postponed rather than resolved the conflicts and ambiguities in contemporary evangelicalism over the Church's socio-political involvement'.[107] Just as the documents of the Second Vatican Council, which took place a decade earlier, have continued to this day to be the subject of conflicting interpretations between progressive and traditionalist Roman Catholics, so has the Lausanne Covenant been a contested text that has continued to yield diverse interpretations.[108] Nevertheless, just as Vatican II must be judged to have made an irreversible difference to the worship, theology and cultural stance of the Roman Catholic Church, so it can fairly be concluded that after the Lausanne Congress world evangelicalism would never quite be the same again. No longer could evangelicals in the North define what it meant to be evangelical Christians on the basis of unspoken assumptions about their differentiation from the liberal and ecumenical mainstream of the historic European and North American denominations. Nor could it any longer be taken for granted that 'social action' or a gospel whose contours were shaped by the concerns of the poor could be left to the liberals, or that mission and evangelism were essentially synonymous terms. Perhaps most fundamental of all, Lausanne revealed the first clear signs of a radical decentring of the geographical and cultural identity of evangelicalism that has since become unmistakeable: evangelicals on either side of the North Atlantic can no longer assume that they can in isolation either define the content of the gospel or determine appropriate strategies for Christian mission. The third Lausanne congress in Cape Town in October 2010 provided further illustration of this fact.[109]

---

[107] Henry, *Confessions of a Theologian*, 350.

[108] The analogy between Lausanne and Vatican II is drawn by Paul Freston, *Evangelicals and Politics in Asia, Africa and Latin America* (Cambridge: Cambridge University Press, 2001), 36, 150, 242.

[109] See http://www.lausanne.org/en/gatherings/cape-town-2010.html (accessed 30 May 2012).

7. THE FERMENT OF THE SPIRIT: NEW CHARISMATIC AND PENTECOSTAL MOVEMENTS

The Christian history of the second half of the twentieth century witnessed a remarkable global process of 'Pentecostalization' of the Christian faith. In every continent, though most notably in Latin America, rural China and Africa, Pentecostal varieties of Christianity experienced tremendous growth. Although the older Pentecostal bodies established in the early twentieth century participated in this expansion, the two most prominent features of this movement were the emergence of new networks of Pentecostal churches and the penetration of many non-Pentecostal denominations from the mid-1960s onwards by an unprecedented emphasis on the person and gifts of the Holy Spirit. This chapter can make only very limited reference to the proliferation of new Pentecostal churches, a subject on which a substantial literature is now available. Its primary focus will be on the charismatic renewal or 'neo-Pentecostal' movement in the mainstream denominations – a movement that originated beyond the frontiers of mainstream conservative evangelicalism but was destined to transform large sections of the evangelical movement by the end of the century.

Contrasting continental patterns of spiritual renewal

Although influences emanating from historic Pentecostalism can be traced behind many of its early manifestations, the striking feature about the early charismatic movement of the 1960s is its source in sacramental rather than evangelical strands of Christian tradition – particularly among the pre-dominantly Anglo-Catholic Protestant Episcopal Church, but also among American Lutherans, and, from 1967 onwards, some Roman Catholics. In the United States the great majority of conservative evangelicals were at first largely unaffected and suspicious. At the end of 1963, after a period of four years in which the charismatic movement had hit the headlines in the main-stream American religious press with some regularity, the editors of the main evangelical papers in the United States ranked the charismatic revival only as fifth in their list of top stories of the year.[1] In Britain, on the other hand, the charismatic movement made its initial appeal not primarily to Anglo-Catholics but to the increasingly dominant evangelical wings of both the Church of England and the Baptist Union, with the result that renewal has had a much greater impact on evangelicals within the historic denominations.

Other parts of the English-speaking world have seen the movement take different trajectories. In South Africa, as in the United States, the initial impact of the movement was within a section of the Anglican communion that owed allegiance to Anglo-Catholic rather than evangelical traditions, though with time its influence broadened. In New Zealand renewal rapidly established a following among the Christian Brethren, with significant support from Anglicans, Presbyterians and Baptists. In Australia the dominant influence in New South Wales of a strongly Reformed variety of the evangelical Anglican tradition has limited the impact of renewal among Anglicans, though other sections of the evangelical constituency have been more deeply affected. From 1978 onwards sections of the aboriginal population in northern and western Australia experienced a remarkable charismatic revival that began on Elcho Island in Arnhem Land.[2] From the mid-1990s onwards charismatic renewal in Australia has increasingly found its home outside the historic denomin-ations, with some notable independent megachurches emerging in the major cities.

The revival of divine healing

A major source of the multifaceted movement of spiritual renewal in the late twentieth century was the revival of Christian interest in the subject of divine healing, a trend whose roots can be traced to late nineteenth-

---

[1] 'These Were the Big Stories in 1963', *MM*, Jan. 1964, 8–10.

[2] Stuart Piggin, *Evangelical Christianity in Australia: Spirit, Word and World* (Melbourne: Oxford University Press, 1996), 197–202.

century North America.[3] In the Anglican communion this first became discernible in the aftermath of the traumas of the First World War, being particularly associated with the ministry of a lay evangelist, James Moore Hickson, who conducted healing tours in much of the English-speaking world, notably in Australia, between 1919 and 1924.[4] However, interest in the topic remained sporadic until after the Second World War, and, with the obvious exception of Pentecostals, evangelicals were little affected.

After 1945 the topic of divine healing gained new salience on both sides of the Atlantic, owing in part to the writings and ministry of the American Episcopalian Agnes Sanford (1897–1982). Born in China of American Presbyterian parents, Sanford's interest in divine healing stemmed from her own deliverance from depression in response to the laying on of hands.[5] Like many of the American pioneers of charismatic renewal, Sanford's approach to the gifts of the Spirit had an explicitly sacramental dimension: although originally from an evangelical background, she testified that it was her first experience of sacramental confession to a priest that led to her own inner healing and the start of her ministry of healing to others.[6] In her first book, *The Healing Light*, published in the USA in 1947, Sanford expounded a view of divine healing that had little or no relation to any concept of a baptism in the Holy Spirit: healing was understood simply as a manifestation of the power and presence of Christ. However, in about 1953 or 1954 Sanford began speaking in tongues after two friends had laid hands on her, praying that she would receive the baptism in the Spirit. From that point on, her ministry acquired a more pronounced charismatic character. Through Summer Schools of Pastoral Care and their participation in a healing fraternity named the Order of St Luke (incorporated in 1953), Sanford and her husband, Edgar Lewis Sanford (an Episcopal priest in New Jersey), quietly disseminated awareness

---

[3] See James Opp, *The Lord for the Body: Religion, Medicine, and Protestant Faith Healing in Canada, 1880–1930* (Montreal: McGill-Queen's University Press, 2006); Heather D. Curtis, *Faith in the Great Physician: Suffering and Divine Healing in American Culture, 1860–1900* (Baltimore: Johns Hopkins University Press, 2007).

[4] Stuart Mews, 'The Revival of Spiritual Healing in the Church of England 1920–26', in W. J. Sheils (ed.), *The Church and Healing*, SCH 19 (Oxford: Blackwell, 1982), 299–331; Piggin, *Evangelical Christianity in Australia*, 103.

[5] Agnes Sanford, *The Healing Light* (Evesham: Arthur James, 1949), vii; Peter Hocken, *Streams of Renewal: The Origins and Early Development of the Charismatic Movement in Great Britain* (Exeter: Paternoster Press, 1986), 181.

[6] Sanford, *Healing Light*, 133–139.

of the supernatural gifts of the Spirit among American clergy, especially Episcopalians.[7]

One of those who attended the first Order of St Luke conference in Philadelphia in 1956 was Richard Winkler, rector of Trinity Episcopal Church in Wheaton, Illinois, who in April that year entered into an experience of 'baptism in the Spirit' at a meeting addressed by an Assemblies of God evangelist. Winkler then instigated what was probably the first explicitly charismatic prayer meeting in an American Episcopal church.[8] Edgar Sanford died in 1960, but Agnes Sanford's ministry continued, and had an increasing impact on Britain, as well as on the United States. She was a crucial influence on Bill Wood, an Australian Anglo-Catholic priest who was warden of the London Healing Mission from 1949 onwards. Wood visited the USA in 1956 and 1958, meeting Sanford and attending conferences of the Order of St Luke. Sanford then visited Britain in August 1963 and June 1964, on the second visit addressing two clergy retreats at the Anglican retreat centre at Lee Abbey in north Devon. Partly as a result of her visits, outbreaks of glossolalia at Lee Abbey were being reported by the summer of 1964.[9]

Another and more typically evangelical source of teaching on the subject of healing was Kathryn Kuhlman (1907–76). Kuhlman had fulfilled an itinerant evangelistic ministry in various parts of the United States, notably in Denver, since the early 1930s. In 1946 she began a teaching series on the Holy Spirit in Franklin, western Pennsylvania, as a result of which some began to experience miraculous healings.[10] She commenced a radio ministry and became America's best-known female evangelist. She was not, however, widely accepted in Pentecostal circles, partly because she was a divorcee and partly because she did not permit tongues-speaking in her 'miracle' services. Nevertheless, from the mid-1960s she was one of the most influential disseminators in North America not simply of a charismatic understanding of the gift of healing but also of a style of healing in which those whom she prayed for frequently fell to the floor, 'slain in the Spirit', in classical Pentecostal terminology.[11] She was a major posthumous role model for two leading personalities in the Canadian charismatic movement: Benny Hinn, the Israeli-born but Toronto-based evangelist and proponent of the gospel of special 'anointing' by the Spirit, and

[7] Hocken, *Streams of Renewal*, 181.

[8] Ibid. 182.

[9] Ibid. 107, 120.

[10] Benny Hinn, *The Anointing* (Milton Keynes: Word, 1992), 75–85.

[11] Stanley M. Burgess (ed.), *The New International Dictionary of Pentecostal and Charismatic Movements* (Grand Rapids: Zondervan, 2002), 826–827.

John Arnott, pastor of the Toronto Airport Vineyard church at the time of the 'Toronto Blessing' in 1994.[12]

Pentecostal influence and the hunger for revival

A second source of the Spirit movements in this period was the tendency of a growing number of historic Pentecostals to repudiate sectarian isolation and seek a wider sphere of influence among other Christians. That search was not in vain. As those in the historic churches became more conscious of their denominations' numerical decline, some, at least, became more open to looking for revival from quarters they had hitherto regarded with suspicion. Pre-eminent in this respect was the role of David du Plessis (1905–87). Du Plessis was an Afrikaner whose family were drawn into the early Pentecostal movement through the Apostolic Faith Mission, whose first missionaries arrived in South Africa in 1908 from John Alexander Dowie's Christian Catholic Apostolic Church in Zion City, Illinois.[13] The Apostolic Faith Mission soon became the largest Pentecostal church in South Africa, and Du Plessis, entering its service as an evangelist, subsequently became general secretary of the church. In January 1936 the veteran British Pentecostal evangelist Smith Wigglesworth (1859–1947) had prophesied to du Plessis's face that God would use him in a coming worldwide revival of unprecedented proportions.[14] Du Plessis kept this prophecy to himself for twenty-five years. However, in May 1947 a new international sphere of ministry opened up for him following the establishment of the Pentecostal World Conference at Zurich. He moved to the United States, and from 1951 began to forge links with mainstream ecumenical leaders in the National Council of Churches, and internationally through contact with the World Council of Churches as well as the Roman Catholic Church (he was an unofficial observer during the third session of the Second Vatican Council). His role as a roving ambassador for a Pentecostal understanding of Christianity earned him the title of 'Mr Pentecost': no other single figure was as instrumental in bridging the gap between the Pentecostal movement and the historic churches.

---

[12] David Hilborn (ed.), 'Toronto' in Perspective: Papers on the New Charismatic Wave of the Mid-1990s (Carlisle: Paternoster Press, 2001), 131–132.

[13] David J. Maxwell, African Gifts of the Spirit: Pentecostalism & the Rise of a Zimbabwean Transnational Religious Movement (Oxford: J. Currey; Harare: Weaver; Athens, Ohio: Ohio University Press, 2006), 38–40.

[14] Hocken, Streams of Renewal, 19, 206.

Nevertheless, other Pentecostals played important parts in disseminating among non-Pentecostals a hunger for a new outpouring of the Spirit. In North America W. H. Branham (1909–65), T. L. Osborn (1923–) and Oral Roberts (1923–2009) popularized the message of divine healing.[15] The Methodist and holiness traditions proved particularly receptive soil. Whilst Branham's doctrinal eccentricities eventually took him beyond the realm of trinitarian Christianity, Roberts in May 1968 left the Pentecostal Holiness Church for the recently formed United Methodist Church, a rare example of a Pentecostal becoming a 'charismatic' within a historic denomination.[16] The graduate school of theology of Oral Roberts University, which he established in 1976, was from 1982 to 1987 formally recognized by the United Methodist Church as an approved institution for ministerial training. Although Roberts left the Church in 1987, the United Methodist Renewal Services Fellowship, formed in 1977, continued to promote charismatic influence within the United Methodist Church.[17]

From 1948 onwards the Latter Rain movement in North America encouraged a growing sense of dissatisfaction with the organized ethos of the existing Pentecostal denominations, notably the Assemblies of God, and an emphasis on the 'new order' characterized by the divine purpose in the end times to restore an apostolic pattern of ministry to the whole church.[18] In Britain Donald Gee (1891–1966), a leading Assemblies of God pastor, and Cecil Cousen (1913–89), whose background was in the Apostolic Church, exercised similar roles in conveying Pentecostal emphases to evangelicals with a thirst for revival. As a minister in Hamilton, Ontario, from 1949 to 1951, Cousen had come into close contact with the Latter Rain movement, and from 1957 he disseminated some of its teaching by means of the first charismatic magazine in Britain, *The Voice of Faith*, which eventually attained a circu-

---

[15] For a general survey of the growth of healing ministries in North America during this period see D. E. Harrell, *All Things Are Possible: The Healing and Charismatic Revivals in Modern America* (Bloomington: Indiana University Press, 1975).

[16] Allan Anderson, *An Introduction to Pentecostalism* (Cambridge: Cambridge University Press, 2004), 58–59, 150. The United Methodist Church was a Union between the Methodist Church and the Evangelical United Brethren Church.

[17] Michael T. Girolimon, '"The Charismatic Wiggle": United Methodism's Twentieth-Century Neo-Pentecostal Impulses', *Pneuma* 17 (1995), 89–103. Since 1995 the United Methodist Renewal Services Fellowship has been known as Aldersgate Renewal Ministries.

[18] Edith Blumhofer, *Restoring the Faith: The Assemblies of God, Pentecostalism, and American Culture* (Urbana: University of Illinois Press, 1993), 203–219.

lation of eleven thousand copies.[19] In evangelical circles the quest for revival gained added impetus at the end of the 1950s from the centenary of the 1859 Revival movements. As noted in chapter 3, the Ulsterman J. Edwin Orr, who wrote his Oxford DPhil thesis on the 1858–60 evangelical awakening in Britain, was an indefatigable global propagator through pulpit and print of the message of continuing revival. He was a major influence on three of the pioneers of charismatic renewal in the English-speaking world, all of whom came from a Brethren background: the South African Denis Clark, the Scotsman Campbell McAlpine, and the Englishman Arthur Wallis.[20] Reformed evangelicals as much as Arminian ones shared this enthusiasm, thanks in part to the enthusiasm of Martyn Lloyd-Jones for genuine revival. As it happened, although 1959 did indeed mark the opening of a new chapter in the history of renewal movements, the first obvious signs of this breakthrough appeared where evangelicals least expected to find them.

California Episcopalians and Lutherans receive the Spirit

In the spring of 1959 two young California Episcopalians, John and Joan Baker, visited a Pentecostal church and there received the 'baptism in the Holy Spirit' with speaking in tongues.[21] Their experience then spread to other Episcopalians in the parish of The Holy Spirit at Monterey Park, California. The vicar, Frank Maguire, sought advice from a neighbouring priest, Dennis Bennett, rector of St Mark's Episcopal Church in Van Nuys. Bennett (1917–91) was born in Britain, the son of a Congregational minister, though he had lived in the United States from childhood. From 1949 to 1951 he served as a Congregational minister in San Diego, before entering the ministry of the Protestant Episcopal Church. In November 1959 both Maguire and Bennett, together with many of their congregations, entered into charismatic experience. Quite independently, another Episcopal parish, St Luke's, Monrovia, in Los Angeles, experienced similar phenomena. These outbreaks of renewal might have attracted only local notice had it not been for the initiative of Jean Stone, an Anglo-Catholic member of the St Mark's congregation, who contacted *Newsweek* and *Time* magazines. Stone was to

---

[19] Hocken, *Streams of Renewal*, 25–29.

[20] A. J. Appasamy, *Write the Vision! Edwin Orr's Thirty Years of Adventurous Service* (London: Marshall, Morgan & Scott, 1965), 211–212, 240.

[21] On the origins of charismatic renewal in the United States see Burgess, *New International Dictionary*, 369–370, 479–481.

prove one of the most influential publicists of 'charismatic renewal' – with the New York Lutheran Harald Bredesen she coined the term. The result of her initiative was the appearance of two articles, one in *Newsweek* and the other in *Time* magazine, that made the Van Nuys outbreak a topic of national interest.[22]

Following opposition from some of his flock, Bennett resigned from St Mark's in April 1960, and was appointed vicar of St Luke's Episcopal Church in Seattle. Under Bennett's leadership this hitherto declining parish was transformed into perhaps the best-known centre of charismatic renewal in the United States. Bennett published several books that disseminated the message of renewal throughout the United States and internationally, especially in Britain – the most influential being *Nine O'Clock in the Morning* (1970).[23] Another influential propagator of the message of renewal via pulpit and print was Larry Christenson (1928–), a pastor in the American Lutheran Church in San Pedro, California. Christenson was influenced by reading the works of Agnes Sanford, and experienced the 'baptism' in August 1961 at a Foursquare Gospel church. Although many American Lutherans resisted the charismatic claim to have revived the gift of prophecy as a threat to the Lutheran emphasis on the authority of Scripture, Christenson remained a Lutheran pastor and became the chief international apostle of renewal in the Lutheran world.

Renewal crosses the Atlantic

As so often in the history of evangelicalism, a movement of spiritual renewal or revival initiated either in North America or in Britain spread across the Atlantic Ocean by means of the Christian press. In the case of the charismatic movement four such channels of transatlantic print transmission can be identified as having particular importance.

At an early stage of the renewal movement in St Mark's, Van Nuys, in 1960, Jean Stone formed a group in the parish known as the Blessed Trinity Society. In the autumn of the following year the Society began publication of a quarterly magazine, *Trinity*, which Stone mailed to every Episcopal priest in the United States. From March 1962 it was distributed in Britain on a small scale, initially by David du Plessis, a member of the editorial board. *Trinity* magazine was one of the first conduits whereby the California movement began to make an impact on evangelicals in Britain, one of them being Michael

---

22 'Rector and a Rumpus', *Newsweek*, 4 July 1960; 'Speaking in Tongues', *Time*, 15 Aug. 1960.

23 Dennis Bennett, *Nine O'Clock in the Morning* (Plainfield, N.J.: Logos International, 1970).

Harper (1931–2010), curate to John Stott at All Souls, Langham Place, in London.[24]

The second printed medium of eastward transatlantic transmission was the *Church of England Newspaper* (*CEN*). On 28 April 1961 an article, with accompanying editorial comment, in the *CEN* noted the outbreak of tongues in what was described as a suburban Chicago parish – Trinity Church in Wheaton was meant. The article was written by the archdeacon of Chicago, who had been appointed by the bishop of Chicago as chairman of a commission charged with investigating the Pentecostal outbreak.[25] A further article on 4 August 1961 described the phenomena surfacing in various American Episcopal churches in the Catholic tradition, mentioning both Wheaton and Dennis Bennett's former parish in Van Nuys, California. It noted that in most cases there was a close link with the movement for spiritual healing, but also that, since Los Angeles was 'the home of strange cults and movements', 'a certain Pentecostal infiltration' could not be discounted. While the article stressed that these phenomena had not emerged from within the evangelical constituency, it nevertheless commended a response of 'genuine openness and sympathy'.[26] Then on 8 September 1961 the *CEN* published a full article by Dennis Bennett himself, arguing that what had taken place was precisely what was intended by the Anglican rite of confirmation: the full reception of the Spirit. Although Bennett's article was accompanied by an insert noting 'Pentecostal trends in England' (such as the ministry of Richard Bolt, a former Anglican ordinand from All Souls', who had become a Pentecostal pastor), it seems to have had relatively little impact on evangelicals in Britain.[27]

A third and more significant channel of printed transmission was an editorial in the Anglican evangelical journal *The Churchman*, published in September 1962. The editor, Philip Edgcumbe Hughes (1915–90), was a strong Calvinist and accomplished scholar who had been on the staff of Tyndale Hall in Bristol from 1947 to 1953; he was also a friend and confidant of Martyn Lloyd-Jones.[28]

---

[24] Burgess, *New International Dictionary*, 479–480; Hocken, *Streams of Renewal*, 116–117.

[25] *CEN*, 3507 (28 Apr. 1961), 10, 13, 14; see Hocken, *Streams of Renewal*, 115–116.

[26] *CEN*, 3521 (4 Aug. 1961), 7.

[27] *CEN*, 3526 (8 Sept. 1961), 9; see Hocken, *Streams of Renewal*, 116.

[28] Andrew Atherstone, David Ceri Jones and William K. Kay, 'Lloyd-Jones and the Charismatic Controversy', in Andrew Atherstone and David Ceri Jones (eds.), *Engaging with Martyn Lloyd-Jones: The Life and Legacy of 'the Doctor'* (Nottingham: Apollos, 2011), 115. Hughes was born in Australia, but reared as an Anglican in the small and conservative 'Church of England in South Africa'; see his obituary by Roger Beckwith in *Chm* 104 (1990), 351–352.

Earlier in 1962 Hughes had visited the United States. He had heard reports of both clerical and lay Episcopalians in California speaking in tongues, but was initially inclined to attribute such surprising phenomena to 'a flirtation under the hot California sun with the extravagances of pentecostalism'. On arrival in Washington, however, he found awaiting him a letter from Jean Stone, elicited by reading an article Hughes had written, recounting her own recent experience of charismatic renewal, and inviting him to visit California to see for himself. Hughes accepted the invitation, and reproduced Stone's letter at length in his editorial, though he was careful not to disclose the identity, or even the gender, of the author. The letter spoke frankly of how this anonymous Anglo-Catholic had found, to her 'horror', her theology changing in response to her experience of glossolalia, and of how the Book of Common Prayer, which she had formerly 'lamented as terribly "protestant"', now struck her as 'being remarkably sound and filled with the rustlings of the Holy Spirit'. Hughes's editorial went on to give a thoroughly favourable assessment of the movement he had observed with his own eyes: it was 'transforming lives' and 'revitalizing congregations'. His conclusion was that 'Christians should pray earnestly and expectantly that the Acts of the Holy Spirit may be powerfully manifested once again in the Church of our day through the lives of those who profess the name of Christ.'[29]

Such an up-beat assessment of the movement among California Episcopalians, coming from the pen of an impeccably Reformed evangel-ical Anglican, had an extraordinary effect. Hughes's editorial was seminal for some of the evangelical Anglican clergy who became pioneers of renewal in Britain, among them Michael Harper at All Souls, Philip Smith at St John's, Burslem, in the Midlands, and John Collins at St Mark's, Gillingham, in Kent. John Stott showed a copy to Bill Grant, a member of the All Souls' congrega-tion with a keen interest in prayer for world revival. Grant obtained Hughes's permission to reprint his editorial. Some thirty-nine thousand copies of the reprint were distributed through two prayer networks closely associated with All Souls: the interdenominational Nights of Prayer for World-Wide Revival, created by a retired CMS India missionary, George Ingram (d. 1969), and a smaller Anglican network established by Ingram at the end of 1959, Anglican Prayer for Revival.[30]

Printed books formed a fourth and extremely important channel of propagation. Works such as Bennett's *Nine O'Clock in the Morning* or John L. Sherrill's *They Speak with Other Tongues* (1964) popularized charismatic teaching and experience throughout the English-speaking Christian world. Perhaps the

---

[29] *Chm* 76 (1962), 131–135.
[30] Hocken, *Streams of Renewal*, 79, 100, 110, 117–118.

most influential of such books was David Wilkerson's paperback *The Cross and the Switchblade* (1963), which proved a best-seller on both sides of the Atlantic. Wilkerson (1931–2011), an Assemblies of God pastor from Pennsylvania, began a ministry among the gangs of New York City from 1958 onwards, where he found the power of the Holy Spirit to be effective even among often violent young people.[31] His gripping book describing his experiences on the streets of New York made a classic Pentecostal understanding of the Holy Spirit more widely acceptable among a variety of Christian constituencies, from Roman Catholics in Duquesne University in 1967 (this was the genesis of charismatic renewal in the Catholic Church in the USA) to traditional evangelicals in Britain. It appealed especially to young people in British evangelical churches in the 1960s and 1970s. At first its message was regarded as so controversial that the book was sold under the counter by Edward England, manager of the Scripture Union bookshop in Wigmore Street in London.[32] One of the gang members converted through Wilkerson's ministry, Nicky Cruz, a Puerto Rican, visited the United Kingdom at the end of 1965 and had a considerable impact on a number of evangelical churches that became prominent in the renewal movement, such as St Andrew's, Chorleywood.

Cruz's tour in 1965 illustrates the fact that the channels of transatlantic transmission were not printed only, but also involved key individuals who crossed the Atlantic in both directions with a facility that the jet age of air travel had made possible. Frank Maguire visited Britain in May 1963, and spoke at a London meeting attended by, among others, John Stott and Martyn Lloyd-Jones. He was followed later that year by both Agnes Sanford and Larry Christenson; the latter visit was seminal for Michael Harper's reception of the gift of tongues.[33] Another visitor to Britain in the autumn of 1965 was Dennis Bennett. His speaking tour, organized by the Fountain Trust (founded in September the previous year to promote the renewal), was the key influence in introducing to charismatic renewal the Scottish Presbyterian (later Anglican) minister and theologian Thomas A. Smail (1928–). Tom Smail became the second secretary of the Fountain Trust in 1972.[34] The founder and first

---

[31] Edith Blumhofer, *The Assemblies of God: A Chapter in the Story of American Pentecostalism*, 2 vols. (Springfield, Mo.: Gospel Publishing House, 1989), II, 140.

[32] Hocken, *Streams of Renewal*, 149, 249. England later became, as an editor at Hodder & Stoughton, one of the chief publishers of charismatic books in Britain.

[33] Hocken, *Streams of Renewal*, 119–120.

[34] Tom Smail, Andrew Walker and Nigel Wright, *Charismatic Renewal: The Search for a Theology* (London: SPCK, 1995), 7–21; Douglas McBain, *Fire Over the Waters: Renewal Among Baptists and Others from the 1960s to the 1990s* (London: Hodder & Stoughton, 1997), 70.

secretary of the Trust, Michael Harper, first visited the USA in 1965, sponsored by the Full Gospel Businessmen's Fellowship International (FGBMFI), a primarily Pentecostal organization established in southern California in 1951 by Oral Roberts and the Armenian American millionaire Demos Shakarian (1913–93).[35] The FGBMFI held a major convention in London in November 1965, and the speakers subsequently toured the United Kingdom.[36]

Through such channels of transatlantic transmission an American movement whose origins lay largely outside the evangelical fold took deep root across the Atlantic from the mid-1960s onwards, especially among Anglicans and British Baptists. In England the two most influential pioneers of renewal among Anglican evangelicals were Michael Harper and John Collins, vicar of St Mark's church, Gillingham, from 1957 to 1971, and from 1980 to 1985 vicar of Holy Trinity Church, Brompton, in London. Two of Collins's curates at St Mark's, David Watson (1933–84) and David MacInnes (1932–), were to become among the best-known figures in British evangelicalism. Watson, through his ministry in York from 1965 to 1982, first as vicar of St Cuthbert's church, and then from 1973 in a new location at St Michael's-le-Belfrey, and in his role as conductor of many university evangelistic missions, exercised an enormous influence in commending an unsectarian and intellectually credible version of renewal to the expanding Christian Unions of the British universities. MacInnes became precentor of Birmingham Cathedral (1967–78) and was from 1987 to 2002 rector of St Aldate's, a strategic student church in Oxford. Although the acknowledged leader of Anglican evangelicalism, John Stott, had delivered at the Islington conference of Anglican evangelical clergy in January 1964 a negative exegetical verdict on the charismatic understanding of the 'baptism in the Holy Spirit', many of the Anglican evangelicals whom he had mentored in the faith took a different path. Among Baptists, the most strongly evangelical of the British Free Churches, charismatic renewal was pioneered by David Pawson, who exercised influential ministries in Chalfont St Peter in Buckinghamshire and Guildford in Surrey, and by two Scots serving in English congregations, Douglas McBain and Jim Graham; by the 1980s the movement had gained the allegiance of the majority of conservative evangelical ministers in the Baptist Union of England and Wales.[37] The renewal movement had become a prominent feature of the evangelical landscape in Britain.

---

[35] See Blumhofer, *Assemblies of God*, II, 88–89.

[36] Hocken, *Streams of Renewal*, 147–148.

[37] See McBain, *Fire Over the Waters*.

The quest for a restored apostolic church (part 1): Brethren influence on charismatic origins in Britain and New Zealand

The charismatic movement in Britain thus owed much to primarily Episcopalian influences from across the Atlantic. Nevertheless, it also drew inspiration and independent momentum from sources integral to British evangelical tradition. The most important single figure in this strand of the movement was Arthur Wallis (1922–88), the second son of the evangelist Captain Reginald Wallis.[38] Both father and son were brought up among the Open Brethren but increasingly developed a wider network of Christian association. Arthur was baptized at Duke Street Baptist Church in Richmond, and had close links with Above Bar Church, a large independent evangelical church in Southampton. He was particularly influenced by the Brethren writer G. H. Lang (1874–1958). Lang had little time for the Pentecostal movement as such, yet had sufficient independence of mind to reject the standard Brethren dispensational view that gifts such as tongues had been given for the apostolic age only. Wallis became a regular visitor to Lang's home, and early in 1951 Wallis engaged him in correspondence on the question of whether believers should expect a specific enduing with the power of the Spirit, equipping them for service in the same way as Jesus had received the Spirit at his baptism: Lang encouraged Wallis to think that they should. Shortly afterwards, on 10 March, Wallis received just such an experience, which he described as 'being filled' with the Spirit, though he did not speak in tongues. In the autumn of 1951 he travelled to the Hebridean island of Lewis to see for himself the fruits of the revival that had broken out in December 1949 associated with the Faith Mission evangelist Duncan Campbell (1898–1972).[39] Wallis met Campbell, and was deeply affected by his visit. Campbell, standing in the holiness tradition, taught the baptism of the Spirit as a distinct post-conversion experience,[40] and Wallis found in him a kindred spirit.

In 1952 Wallis first met a former member of the Brethren, David Lillie,

---

[38] The account of Wallis that follows is dependent on the biography by his son, Jonathan Wallis, *Arthur Wallis: Radical Christian* (Eastbourne: Kingsway, 1991); and Roger Shuff, *Searching for the True Church: Brethren and Evangelicals in Mid-Twentieth-Century England* (Milton Keynes: Paternoster Press, 2005), 200–209.

[39] For a highly unsympathetic and probably unfair evaluation of Campbell, see John MacLeod, *Banner in the West: A Spiritual History of Lewis and Harris* (Edinburgh: Birlinn, 2008), 262–267.

[40] Ibid. 264; Andrew Woolsey, *Duncan Campbell: A Biography* (London: Hodder & Stoughton, 1974), 165.

who, to an even greater extent than Wallis, was deeply influenced by G. H. Lang's teaching on the need for a restoration of the church to its apostolic power and purity, and who had experienced the 'baptism of the Spirit' as early as 1941. Wallis and Lillie began a series of conferences on the Holy Spirit near Lillie's home at Countess Wear on the outskirts of Exeter; the speakers included some from a specifically Pentecostal background, such as Cecil Cousen. At the same time Wallis was working on a book on revival; he sent the manuscript to G. H. Lang and Leith Samuel, pastor of the Above Bar Church, and received their endorsement. *The Day of Thy Power* was published in June 1956. Duncan Campbell had agreed to write the foreword, in which he remarked that the book was 'a powerful plea for the recognition of the supernatural in the realm of revival'. In many respects Wallis's book was a classic exposition of the theme of revival from a moderate Calvinistic perspective: revival was emphatically a work of God, an outpouring of the Spirit, although granted in response to the eager expectations and prayers of God's people; the book closed by reproducing a prayer for revival by C. H. Spurgeon. Nevertheless, one of the undoubted marks of revival, according to Wallis, was a renewal of the supernatural spiritual gifts of the apostolic age, 'together with various other signs and wonders'.[41]

Wallis maintained close fellowship with evangelicals in the older churches: the service of thanksgiving for his life in September 1988 was held in Above Bar Church, not a church known for its sympathy with renewal.[42] He was a significant influence on Michael Harper, and was a frequent speaker at Fountain Trust conferences in the 1960s and 1970s.[43] Nevertheless, he was probably the most influential pioneer of that strand of the British charismatic movement which believed that God's purpose to restore his church necessitated a break with the existing denominational structures. Along with Lillie and Cousen he is recognized as one of the founding fathers of the 'new' or 'apostolic' churches (formerly known as 'house churches'), which in their various networks now form such a major feature of the religious scene in Britain, as elsewhere. The most notable networks of apostolic churches that originated in Britain are Newfrontiers (formerly spelled 'New Frontiers'), Vineyard, Salt and Light, Ichthus, Pioneer, Multiply and Ground Level. Brethren influence is

---

[41] Arthur Wallis, *In the Day of Thy Power: The Scriptural Principles of Revival* (London: Christian Literature Crusade, 1956), ix, 249, 74.

[42] Wallis, *Arthur Wallis*, 311.

[43] David Matthew (ed.), *Arthur Wallis 1922–1988: A Tribute* (Bradford: Harvestime Services, 1988), 22.

traceable in the histories of several of these: Barney Coombs, founder of Salt and Light Ministries, and Gerald Coates, founder of the Pioneer network, are both former Brethren, while Roger Forster, founder of Ichthus, was much influenced in his youth by G. H. Lang.[44]

Wallis also played a major part in the inception of charismatic renewal in New Zealand, which he visited in 1963–4. There he worked closely with Campbell McAlpine, a former member of the Brethren in Scotland, who had entered into charismatic experience in November 1954 and emigrated to New Zealand in 1959. The ministry of Wallis and McAlpine in Brethren assemblies in New Zealand over a period of twenty-one months in 1963–4, which laid emphasis on the continuing availability of the gift of tongues, aroused strong reactions, leading to a number of secessions to form new charismatic churches.[45] From the mid-1960s New Zealand became one of the main centres of the renewal movement.

The transformation of evangelical worship

New Zealand was also the source of some of the first collections of 'Scripture songs' that soon began to change the face of evangelical hymnody, though a simultaneous and ultimately more influential generator of the new contemporary style of Christian music from the late 1960s was the California Jesus movement.[46] In 1968 a New Zealand couple, Dave and Dale Garratt, produced a gramophone record entitled *Scripture in Song*, followed in 1971 by a songbook, *Songs of Praise*, and then from 1978 onwards a series of songbooks and cassette tapes, entitled *Scripture in Song*, which were distributed internationally, especially in Britain through Anchor Recordings, a firm founded

---

[44] See Andrew Walker, *Restoring the Kingdom: The Radical Christianity of the House Church Movement* (Guildford: Eagle, 1998); William K. Kay, *Apostolic Networks in Britain: New Ways of Being Church* (Milton Keynes: Paternoster Press, 2007); Peter Hocken, *The Challenges of the Pentecostal, Charismatic and Messianic Jewish Movements: The Tensions of the Spirit* (Farnham: Ashgate, 2009), 37–39; Shuff, *Searching for the True Church*, 218–220. Coombs, though from a Brethren background, was for a time in Baptist ministry at Basingstoke.

[45] Shuff, *Searching for the True Church*, 215–216; Peter J. Lineham, 'Tongues Must Cease: The Brethren and the Charismatic Movement in New Zealand', *Christian Brethren Review* 34 (Nov. 1983), 23–27.

[46] Larry Eskridge, 'God's Forever Family: The Jesus People Movement in America, 1966–1977' (University of Stirling PhD thesis, 2005), 19, 266–307.

by Arthur Wallis's elder brother, Peter.[47] Other new songbooks had more explicit links to the United States, such as *Sounds of Living Water* (1974) and *Fresh Sounds* (1976). In Britain the most popular new songbooks in the 1980s were those emanating from Spring Harvest, the annual Easter holiday gatherings of mainly charismatic Christians that started in 1979, and reached a peak aggregate attendance of between seventy thousand and eighty thousand in the early 1990s.[48] By that decade, however, songbooks were in decline, being supplanted first by overhead projectors using acetate slides and then by digital projectors. Modern technology facilitated the rapid global dissemination of new worship material. In the 1990s songs emanating from a Sydney Assemblies of God church, the Hills Christian Life Centre, became internationally popular in charismatic and evangelical churches.

The renewal and restoration of the church found expression in more subjective and explicitly experiential styles of worship that suited the expressive cultural mood of the era. In the long term this proved a more enduring transformation than the reappearance of the supernatural gifts of tongues and prophecies in services. The frequency of such phenomena in charismatic churches in the historic denominations diminished in the 1980s and 1990s, though they remained more common in the new churches. Although charismatic churches frequently tended to express their increased hunger for God by lengthening rather than shortening the duration of the sermon, the character of worship services in evangelical churches became markedly less cerebral and formal as a result of the renewal movement. Popular church music moved closer to prevailing fashions in secular musical culture, although there was often a marked time lag in the adoption of new musical styles. Guitars, electronic keyboards and drums, rather than the organ or the piano, were the dominant instruments. The leading of the congregation in often prolonged periods of consecutive singing of worship songs frequently passed from the ordained pastor to leaders of music groups, most of whom had no theological training. In Britain, to an even greater extent than in the United States, choirs, whether robed or not, had virtually disappeared from evangelical churches by the end of the century. So, in many cases, had the use of traditional hymns, although these remained more common in some sectors of American evangelicalism, such as the Southern Baptists. Many congregations with an originally liturgical tradition sat increasingly lightly to liturgical discipline, although

---

[47] Matthew, *Arthur Wallis 1922–1988*, 7; *Scripture in Song*. Vol. I: *Music*, rev. ed. (London: Marshall, Morgan & Scott, 1978), foreword.

[48] Rob Warner, *Reinventing English Evangelicalism, 1966–2001: A Theological and Sociological Study* (Milton Keynes: Paternoster Press, 2007), 67, 75–76.

in some sectors of charismatic Anglicanism renewal inspired new and creative uses of liturgy, sometimes making use of dance, and even of traditionally 'Catholic' aids to worship, such as incense. At its worst, however, charismatic worship became self-absorbed and indifferent to the needs of the world, with the intercessory dimension of prayer forgotten.[49]

The charismatic movement transformed the experience of Christian worship for many evangelicals, leading them into a new joy and liberty in their response to God, but often leaving others, particularly of an older generation, perplexed or dissatisfied with superficiality and banal repetition. The renewal movement has forged new bonds of unity between Christians of different traditions, but it has also provoked divisions. One source of such divisions has been its controversial implications for ecclesiology, particularly for churches accustomed to congregational understandings of church government.

Restoration and anointing: authority in the new charismatic churches

'When there is no anointing, democracy is probably the safest form of church government. But when God begins to give anointed leadership, democracy must make room for God to have his way.'[50] This statement from Terry Virgo, the founder of the Restorationist New Frontiers International network of 'new' churches, exemplifies a trend discernible in many neo-Pentecostal movements across the globe. Virgo came from an impeccable conservative evangelical background: a sermon by John Stott played a part in his conversion; he was raised as a Baptist at Holland Road Baptist Church in Hove, Sussex, and while a student at London Bible College from 1965 to 1968 regularly attended Martyn Lloyd-Jones's ministry at Westminster Chapel.[51] He dedicated his book *Restoration in the Church* (1985) to his former Baptist pastor, Ernest G. Rudman, in gratitude for his persistent encouragement even 'when I seem to have turned upside-down so many things which he held dear'.[52] Not least among those overturned principles was Rudman's belief as a Baptist that

---

[49]   On these and related trends see David W. Bebbington, 'Evangelicals and Public Worship, 1965–2005', *EvQ* 79 (2007), 3–22.

[50]   Terry Virgo, *Restoration in the Church* (Eastbourne: Kingsway Publications, 1985), 135, cited in *Renewal* 118 (Aug.–Sept. 1985), 24.

[51]   Kay, *Apostolic Networks*, 64–65; Atherstone, Jones and Kay, 'Lloyd-Jones and the Charismatic Controversy', in Atherstone and Jones, *Engaging with Martyn Lloyd-Jones*, 133.

[52]   Virgo, *Restoration in the Church*, opening dedication.

God guides his people through the Spirit's moving in the congregation gathered to govern the life of the church in a church members' meeting. Virgo, however, wrote of his profound shock as a young Christian at finding that the evident 'God-given anointing' of his pastor did not entitle him to any more than the one vote allowed to any other church member; in his book congregational church government is implicitly repudiated as an illegitimate invasion of the worldly principle of democracy into the realm of the Spirit.[53]

Virgo's New Frontiers network (which had as many as five hundred congregations in Britain and overseas by 2005)[54] has in fact been more moderate in the application of this understanding of authority than have some other new church networks, both in Britain and globally. Many strands of the charismatic movement have been more radical in expressing their dissatisfaction with the secularity of the values of modernity by subverting or wholly repudiating the Enlightenment's confidence in the voice of the people. They have displayed a typically Romantic (or perhaps postmodern) preference for the role of strong individual leaders. The charisma of the Spirit's wisdom, though in principle given to all God's people, has in practice often been reserved to those who have been specially anointed by the touch of God. As in traditional Catholic understandings of ministry, ecclesiastical order is founded on a disjunction between a small cadre of leaders who are acknowledged to have received the 'anointing' of the Spirit to an unusual degree, and the majority of church members, whose role is to respect that anointing and submit to the wisdom of their divinely appointed leaders.[55] One influence has been the teachings of the Chinese evangelical leader Ni Doushen, known as 'Watchman Nee' (1903–72), on the necessity of total submission to God-given authority. The writings on discipleship of the Argentinean Pentecostal Juan Carlos Ortiz (1934–), a prominent member of the Lausanne movement, have also been significant.

In some sections of the global neo-Pentecostal movement the emphasis on discipleship and its converse of 'shepherding' or 'covering' encouraged some extremely authoritarian and intrusive tendencies among church leaders. In North America the teaching of 'shepherding' was closely associated with a group known as the 'Fort Lauderdale Five', comprising Charles Simpson (originally Southern Baptist), Derek Prince (a British Pentecostal and former Fellow of King's College, Cambridge), Ern Baxter (Canadian Pentecostal),

---

[53] Ibid. 93–95.

[54] Kay, *Apostolic Networks*, 81.

[55] For an internationally influential popular exposition of the idea of anointing, though one that does not make explicit deductions in terms of ecclesiology, see Hinn, *Anointing*.

Bob Mumford (American Assemblies of God) and Don Basham (Disciples of Christ). Following mounting criticism and a very public controversy between the Five in 1975–6, the American shepherding movement lost momentum, and was formally dissolved at the end of 1986.[56] In Britain also there is evidence that many of the new churches were by the mid-1980s pulling back from the cultic tendencies of extreme or 'heavy' shepherding.[57]

Reassessing charismatic renewal, 1978–81

By the late 1970s the charismatic renewal movement had begun to penetrate the higher echelons of church leadership, especially in the Anglican communion. The Lambeth Conference in 1978 was preceded by an international conference for renewal leaders that ended with twenty-five Anglican bishops leading a dance round the altar in Canterbury Cathedral.[58] And yet there were signs of a growing volume of questioning over the future of the movement. At the end of 1978 the Temple Trust, the Australian equivalent of the Fountain Trust, announced that its national conference to be held in Sydney in January 1979 was to be the last of its kind. Alan Langstaff, its director, explained that 'It is my conviction that the charismatic renewal as we have known it is coming to an end and God is about to launch a new wave of the Spirit upon his Church and on this land.' This decision inspired *Renewal* magazine to adopt as its editorial an article submitted by Eddie Gibbs entitled 'Has the Wind Dropped?' Gibbs's answer was 'Maybe'.[59] The August–September 1979 issue of *Renewal* contained an editorial by Tom Smail observing that it was impossible to travel round Britain 'without noticing the disappointment, malaise and even measure of disillusionment that have set in where there used to be enthusiasm and expectation'. Smail concluded that 'the charismatic movement as a thing in itself is just about over'.[60] A similar verdict came from New Zealand at the close of 1981, when David Harper, the new director of the New Zealand charismatic body Christian Advance Ministries, reflected on the first decade of the organization and observed that, in the Anglican Church

---

[56] For a full account see S. David Moore, *The Shepherding Movement: Controversy and Charismatic Ecclesiology* (London: T. &. T. Clark International, 2003).

[57] Nigel Scotland, *Charismatics and the New Millennium: The Impact of Charismatic Christianity from 1960 into the New Millennium*, new ed. (Guildford: Eagle, 2000), 106–128.

[58] *Renewal* 79 (Feb.–Mar. 1979), 10–11.

[59] *Renewal* 80 (Apr.–May 1979), 3–10.

[60] *Renewal* 82 (Aug.–Sept. 1979), 2–4.

at least, enthusiasm for renewal was slackening.[61] In 1981 the Fountain Trust followed the example of the Temple Trust and dissolved itself.

Predictions of the demise of the charismatic movement were, however, premature. The quest for ever more intense and fulfilling spiritual experience had perhaps reached its natural plateau among the first generation of charismatics in Britain and Australasia. From the early 1980s, however, the movement entered a new phase that would ultimately prove even more significant for the character of world Christianity.

The internationalization of charismatic renewal

One fruit of the 1978 charismatic Anglican leaders' conference at Canterbury was the launch by Michael Harper in 1979 of SOMA, 'Sharing of Ministries Abroad'. It was a conscious attempt to export the message of charismatic renewal to Anglicans in the non-Western world. Harper commented in *Renewal* in 1987:

> For the last 12 years I have felt deeply a sense of injustice that we in the west have had so much of the Spirit's ministry, and that like Dives we have thrown out the crumbs to the spiritual Lazaruses in the world. From 1978 we have sought to change this sinful attitude and expose these acts of disobedience.
>
> In 1975 when I left the Fountain Trust my conscience would give me no peace until SOMA ministries were started. I find it impossible to live in peace with God and myself while over half the world has not yet heard the gospel and over half the church is starving spiritually while I feast, and do nothing about it.[62]

SOMA had its value, and by 1987 was ministering in all six continents, but what Harper failed to emphasize was that by then the flow of spiritual influence was not so much running from Europe or North America to the rest of the world, as in the opposite direction. In Britain immigration from the Caribbean had added black Pentecostal and charismatic varieties to the range of evangelical churchmanship. Perhaps the most important of the Afro-Caribbean churches in Britain was the New Testament Church of God, an affiliate of the Church of God, based in Cleveland, Ohio, which was introduced to Britain from Jamaica between 1953 and 1956. By the year 2000 the denomination had about twenty thousand members in England and

---

[61] *Renewal* 96 (Dec. 1981–Jan. 1982), 29–31.

[62] Michael Harper, 'To Be Real It Must Be GLOBAL!', *Renewal* 136 (Sept. 1987), 6–8.

Wales.[63] The black Pentecostal churches have had a major impact on the Evangelical Alliance; this was reflected in the appointment of Joel Edwards, a minister in the New Testament Church of God, as UK director of the Alliance in 1992 (as assistant to Clive Calver), and then as general director in 1997.

Pentecostal and charismatic churches were also flourishing in parts of Asia. In India the government clampdown on visas for missionaries in the 1960s appears to have encouraged the growth of a thoroughly indigenous Pentecostalism, especially in the southern Indian states.[64] In South-East Asia a strongly charismatic variant of conservative evangelical Anglicanism had taken root without the aid of SOMA. Charismatic renewal in Singapore first appeared among the boys of the Methodist Anglo-Chinese School in September 1972, and spread to two other schools. The crucial influences appear to have been youth rallies held by an Assemblies of God evangelist, Howard Ridings, the circulation among the schoolboys of *The Cross and the Switchblade* and Nicky Cruz's book *Run, Baby, Run* (1968), and a visit to Singapore by Ralph Wilkerson,[65] pastor of Melodyland Christian Center in Anaheim, California. A young Anglican clergyman, James Wong, was asked to counsel the high school students and ended up being baptized in the Spirit himself. In December 1972 Chiu Ban It, the Malaysian-born Anglican bishop of Singapore, attended a conference in Bangkok, convened by the World Council of Churches Commission on World Mission and Evangelism, on the theme 'Salvation Today'. The dominant understanding of salvation at Bangkok was a liberationist one, but during the conference an Indian Anglican priest from Fiji handed the bishop a copy of Dennis Bennett's *Nine O'Clock in the Morning*, and as a result he began speaking in tongues. Chiu Ban It and James Wong subsequently shared their common experience, and before long St Andrew's Cathedral in Singapore had become a major centre for renewal in the diocese of Singapore and further afield in the Anglican province of South-East Asia.[66] It was while visiting Singapore in 1973 at Chiu's invitation that the

---

[63] Nicole Rodriguez Toulis, *Believing Identity: Pentecostalism and the Mediation of Jamaican Ethnicity and Gender in England* (Oxford: Berg, 1997), 102–118; William K. Kay, *Pentecostals in Britain* (Carlisle: Paternoster Press, 2000), 31–36.

[64] Michael Bergunder, *The South Indian Pentecostal Movement in the Twentieth Century* (Grand Rapids: Eerdmans, 2008), 58 and *passim*.

[65] Ralph Wilkerson, who came from an Assemblies of God background, was no relation of David Wilkerson.

[66] The above account is based on Michael Poon and Malcolm Tan (eds.), *The Clock Tower Story: The Beginnings of the Charismatic Renewals in Singapore*, rev. ed. (Singapore: Trinity Theological College, Singapore, 2012).

well-known rector of St Aldate's church in Oxford, Michael Green, received the gift of tongues following prayer by Chiu that he should do so. As a result St Aldate's subsequently became a centre of moderate charismatic influence in the Church of England. Chiu retired in 1982 and was succeeded by Moses Tay, another committed charismatic. By 1987 the Anglican Province of South-East Asia was more thoroughly penetrated by a charismatic brand of conservative evangelicalism than was the Church of England.[67]

What was true in South-East Asia was also true on a still wider scale on the continent of Africa. Among South African Anglicans, charismatic renewal was pioneered by Bill Burnett (1917–94), bishop of Bloemfontein and later of Grahamstown, and from 1973 primate of the Church of the Province of South Africa. But of far wider significance were indigenous African Pentecostal movements, especially in West Africa. The August–September 1985 issue of *Renewal* reported in passing the ministry at an Assemblies of God conference in Minehead, Somerset, of Benson Idahosa, 'the Pentecostal archbishop from Nigeria'.[68] Idahosa (1938–98) was converted in the early 1960s through an Assemblies of God pastor in Benin City in southern Nigeria, and was also influenced by a missionary of the Apostolic Church, S. G. Elton, and by the prosperity teaching of the independent American Pentecostal evangelist T. L. Osborn.[69] By January 1987 Idahosa featured on the front cover of the magazine, which printed an article about him by Edward England, describing his international evangelistic ministry and labelling him as 'one of the most anointed men of this generation'.[70] If there was one epicentre of the Pentecostal movement in the English-speaking world, it was now located in Nigeria. West African Pentecostalism has multiple origins, some of them dating from the early twentieth century and being indirectly related to J. A. Dowie's Zion City in Illinois.[71] However, to understand the roots of the neo-Pentecostalism that has been so influential in Nigeria and Ghana in recent decades we must go back in time to the 1960s, and to the process of internationalization of the Scripture Union movement described in chapter 3.

---

[67] Michael Green, *Asian Tigers for Christ* (London: SPCK, 2001).

[68] *Renewal* 118 (Aug.–Sept. 1985), 41.

[69] Ogbu Kalu, *African Pentecostalism: An Introduction* (Oxford: Oxford University Press, 2008), 91–92.

[70] *Renewal* 128 (Jan. 1987), 11–13.

[71] Many of the links can be traced through the influence in Nigeria and Ghana of Faith Tabernacle, Philadelphia, originally an affiliate of Dowie's Christian Catholic Church; see Adam Mohr, 'Out of Zion and into Philadelphia and West Africa: Faith Tabernacle Congregation, 1897–1925', *Pneuma* 32 (2010), 56–79.

Nigeria and the origins of the new African Pentecostalism, 1964–70

In West Africa the most important watershed between a predominantly non-charismatic mission-controlled evangelicalism and the development of an indigenized and explicitly Pentecostal style of African evangelicalism appears to have been the Biafran war of 1967 to 1970, when the largely Christian south-east of Nigeria attempted to secede from a nation that was dominated by the Muslim north. To the dismay of the Igbo Christians in the south-east, Britain and other 'Christian' countries in the northern hemisphere backed the federal government, provoking the secessionist Igbo government to lambast the mission churches as unpatriotic. In this context of armed conflict, massive dislocation of population and widespread disillusionment with supposedly Christian Britain, indigenized expressions of Christianity took off.

In November 1964 the first Scripture Union travelling secretary to be appointed to the Eastern Region of Nigeria, Bill Roberts, arrived at the SU office at Umuahia in the heart of Igboland.[72] Roberts was an Anglican who had found evangelical faith as a teenager in 1954, and at Cambridge had been a member of the CICCU. The outbreak of the Biafran war at the end of June 1967 immediately affected his work in a variety of ways. A number of Igbo university students had been compelled to migrate, first from the University of Ibadan and other western Nigerian universities to the University of Nigeria at Nsukka, where they had reinforced the infant SU group, and then, following its closure due to the war, to Umuahia. Here they assumed important leadership roles in the SU movement.[73] All secondary schools had been closed because of the war, and accordingly Roberts transferred the focus of SU work to extramural activities. Refugees poured into Umuahia, and many of those who had been involved in SU groups gravitated towards the SU headquarters at the Mission Hill Chapel, impressed that Roberts, unlike many European missionaries, had decided to remain at his post despite the outbreak of war. Most were Anglicans or Methodists, the predominant Protestant denominations in Igboland, and found the SU fellowship in Umuahia a source of spiritual renewal and encouragement. Roberts instituted a regular programme of Sunday afternoon Bible studies, plus a twice-weekly diet of Bible teaching, prayer and worship, followed by games. Monthly evangelistic services were also held, always with an African preacher. These attracted growing numbers, and Roberts's prayer letters reported an acceleration in the rate

---

[72] See Bill Roberts, *Life and Death Among the Ibos* (London: Scripture Union, 1970).

[73] Richard Burgess, *Nigeria's Christian Revolution: The Civil War Revival and Its Pentecostal Progeny (1967–2006)* (Carlisle: Paternoster Press, 2008), 55–56, 87–88.

of conversions. The reputation of the Umuahia fellowship spread and its example was followed, as young people formed themselves into bands for prayer, village evangelism and hospital visitation. On his return from a short period of home leave in the second half of 1968 Roberts became involved in relief efforts, and was appointed as Field Officer of the Protestant relief team in the eastern province. He also discovered on his return that the movement of spiritual renewal at Umuahia had acquired a new emphasis: 'Everyone', recalls Roberts, 'was talking about the Holy Spirit and longing to be filled with Him.'[74] There were reports of speaking in tongues and healings. Roberts was supportive, but warned against excesses.

The deepening revival at Umuahia came to an abrupt end in April 1969, when the town fell to the federal army, and the growing community of evangelical students centred on the SU House was dispersed to villages throughout Igboland, as well as to the major urban centres of Onitsha, Enugu and Aba. However, this enforced dispersal proved a strategic means of mission in a manner that reminded many involved of the scattering of the first Jerusalem church as recorded in Acts 8. Over the next six months the number of SU groups in Igboland multiplied from twenty-five to eighty-five.[75] In the town of Ufama, Roberts established contact with three young men – Stephen and Rafael Okafor and Arthur Orizu – who were prominent in one of the Aladura 'prayer houses'. Through his witness they were converted to evangelical faith and formed The Hour of Freedom Evangelistic Association. From its base in Onitsha, a strategic town on the banks of the river Niger, the 'Hour of Freedom' became a powerful force for radical charismatic evangelism throughout Igboland, attracting many members of SU groups and other young people to its prayer and evangelistic bands. The war ended in January 1970, but the growing charismatic revival in Igboland continued through the 1970s, and spread to university students and others in the south-west and north of Nigeria. From that time on the voice of Nigerian Protestant Christianity increasingly carried a Pentecostal tone, and by the 1980s, through figures such as Idahosa, it was being heard on an international stage. Southern movements of the Spirit were beginning to shape northern-hemisphere evangelicalism. Nowhere was this more apparent than at Fuller Theological Seminary.

---

[74] Roberts, *Life and Death*, 69.
[75] Ibid. 79; Burgess, *Nigeria's Christian Revolution*, 89–90.

'Signs and wonders' and the Toronto Blessing

After studies at Fuller Theological Seminary, C. Peter Wagner served as a missionary in Bolivia from 1956 to 1971, initially with the South American Indian Mission, and then with the Bolivian Indian Mission, which later became the Andes Evangelical Mission. As one reared on a dispensationalist diet from the Scofield Bible he had little or no sympathy for the Pentecostals whom he encountered in Bolivia or in neighbouring Chile. However, in 1967–8 he spent a furlough taking a degree in missiology under Donald McGavran at Fuller's newly established School of World Mission. McGavran and his pragmatic theories of church growth made a great impression on Wagner. Wagner also impressed McGavran, who invited him to join the Fuller faculty. Wagner did not accept the invitation immediately, but eventually moved to Pasadena in 1971. There the compelling logic of McGavran's theory confronted him with the need to identify what were the ingredients of church growth among the fastest growing churches in Latin America, which were, of course, the Pentecostal churches. Increasingly Wagner found himself driven to the conclusion that a Pentecostal approach to mission that expected the preaching of the gospel to be confirmed and validated by signs and wonders might be the key to rapid church growth, at least among 'primal' peoples who had no doubt of the reality of evil spirits. With some trepidation, in January 1982 he invited his old friend John Wimber to teach a course at Fuller entitled 'The Miraculous and Church Growth'.[76]

John Wimber (1934–97) was a former rock musician and producer converted in 1963. His early Christian and pastoral experience was in an evangelical Friends' (Quaker) congregation at Yorba Linda in California. In 1975 he enrolled as a part-time student at Fuller Seminary, taking a course on church growth taught by Wagner. Under influence from Wagner, and shaped by his reading of writers such as Agnes Sanford, the charismatic Episcopalian Morton Kelsey and the English Pentecostal Donald Gee, Wimber became convinced that effective preaching of the gospel depended on confirmatory miraculous signs, as in the ministry of Jesus. He taught these principles to a fellowship that began in his own home in 1977, which was at first affiliated to Chuck Smith's Calvary Chapel group of churches, whose growth was closely associated with the Jesus movement among members of the California counter-culture.[77] However, earlier in 1982, when he began to teach at Fuller,

---

[76] C. Peter Wagner, 'My Pilgrimage in Mission', *International Bulletin of Missionary Research* 23 (1999), 164–167.

[77] Eskridge, 'God's Forever Family', 129–140.

Wimber's increasing emphasis on use of the gifts of the Spirit in worship and his cultivation of a relaxed style of mystical intimacy in worship (the Quaker influence is clear) led him and his congregation to sever his links with Calvary Chapel. He formed a new affiliation to a small network of congregations, known as the Vineyards, established in 1974 by Kenn Gulliksen, a member of the Jesus movement and friend of the celebrated songwriter and singer Bob Dylan. Wimber's congregation in Anaheim became known as the Vineyard Christian Fellowship.[78]

Although it is clear that Wagner's increasing sympathy with Pentecostal emphases was itself a major influence on Wimber, Wagner has written that he and his Fuller colleague the anthropologist Charles Kraft initially attended Wimber's lectures with some hesitation, but that before long they both testified to 'a life-changing paradigm shift that caused us to be open to the contemporary, immediate ministry of the Holy Spirit'.[79] From that time on the Fuller course on 'Miracles and Church Growth' taught by Wimber, with growing participation by Wagner, placed increasing emphasis on healing and the casting out of demons, which actually took place in the seminary classrooms; the course became extraordinarily popular, with enrolment reaching three hundred students. Promoted to the Donald MacGavran chair of church growth at Fuller, Wagner became a major influence on evangelical missiology, taking a leading role in the Lausanne movement and the AD 2000 movement.[80] An overtly Pentecostal approach to Christian mission, leading Christians to expect 'signs and wonders' as a normal accompaniment of the preaching of the word, had finally penetrated the heart of the American evangelical establishment, hitherto resistant to much of the charismatic movement. In the course of the 1990s Wagner devoted increasing attention to the exploding global phenomenon of what he variously termed 'the Third Wave' of the Spirit, or 'the new apostolic reformation', in which radically new patterns of church were emerging beyond the confines of the traditional denominations, and characterized by the expectation that 'signs and wonders' should accompany the proclamation of the gospel and hence release a baptism in the Spirit that should be coincident with, rather than subsequent to, conversion.[81]

---

[78] Scotland, *Charismatics and the New Millennium*, 199–218; Hilborn, *'Toronto' in Perspective*, 134–135.

[79] Wagner, 'My Pilgrimage in Mission', 166.

[80] The AD 2000 movement (later rebranded as the 'AD2000 and Beyond Movement') was established in 1989 with the aim of reaching every people group with the gospel by the year 2000.

[81] Wagner, 'My Pilgrimage in Mission', 164–167; John Wimber, *Power Evangelism: Signs*

One important segment of 'the new apostolic reformation' was the network of Vineyard churches that was rapidly proliferating from California. By 1986 Wimber's Anaheim Fellowship had grown to some five thousand members, and he was being prepared by Gulliksen to assume the leadership of the Vineyard network. The Vineyard churches spread from the United States to Britain (from September 1987 onwards) and to other countries, and by the end of the century numbered some nine hundred congregations worldwide. The number of Vineyard churches in Britain grew from five in 1990, with an aggregate attendance of 2,025, to seventy-five in 2000, with an aggregate attendance of 9,700.[82] This was a relatively small percentage of the aggregate membership of the 'new churches' in Britain at that date, which was between two hundred thousand and four hundred thousand.[83] However, Wimber's influence in Britain extended well beyond the Vineyard churches. At the invitation of David Watson he visited Britain for the first time in 1981, ministering in some of the leading charismatic Anglican churches, including Holy Trinity, Brompton, the London church that was fast becoming the 'cathedral' of charismatic Anglican evangelicalism. He made the first of three visits to South Africa in 1981, ministered in New Zealand in 1986, Australia in 1990 and again in Britain in 1984, 1986, 1987, 1990 and 1991; in the two latter countries he had a particularly marked impact on Baptist and 'new' church pastors. He also formed connections for a time with a group called the 'Kansas City prophets', whose most prominent figure, Paul Cain, had in the 1950s been an associate of William Branham.[84]

The Toronto Airport Vineyard church was formed in 1987, but did not join the Vineyard network until 1991.[85] In January 1994 the congregation began to experience phenomena in worship services of 'holy laughter', bodily prostration and other physical expressions of what became known as 'drunkenness in the Spirit'. Such manifestations were not new, having close precedents in the ministry of John Wesley, for example. Since 1989 they had also been a marked feature of the ministry in Orlando, Florida, and elsewhere of the South

---

and Wonders Today (London: Hodder & Stoughton, 1985), 11, 50–51; see also Wagner's Churchquake! How the New Apostolic Reformation Is Shaking up the Church as We Know It (Ventura, Calif.: Regal Books, 1999).

[82] Cory E. Labenow, Evangelicalism and the Emerging Church: A Congregational Study of a Vineyard Church (Farnham: Ashgate, 2009), 7.

[83] Compare the estimates in Anderson, Introduction to Pentecostalism, 157; Scotland, Charismatics and the New Millennium, 25; and Kay, Pentecostals in Britain, 176.

[84] Hilborn, 'Toronto' in Perspective, 136–142.

[85] Eskridge, 'God's Forever Family', 379.

African Pentecostal and prosperity gospel advocate Rodney Howard-Browne (1961–). The stimulus to the Toronto outbreak was a visit by Randy Clark, a Vineyard pastor from St. Louis, Missouri, who had been deeply affected by attending a series of meetings in Tulsa, Oklahoma, conducted by Howard-Browne. Another indirect influence was Claudio Freidzon, pastor of the Rey de Reyes (King of Kings) church in Buenos Aires. John Arnott, the pastor of the Toronto Vineyard church, had visited Argentina in November 1993 to investigate reports of revival there, and had attended some of Freidzon's meetings. Within four months, attendance at Arnott's church multiplied fourfold to one thousand. The numbers were swelled by 'evangelical tourists' from overseas: by August 1994 visitors from over 1,500 British churches had been recorded.[86] One of those was Eleanor Mumford, a member of staff with her husband, John, at the first London Vineyard church in Putney. John Mumford had previously been an Anglican clergyman in London, and the couple maintained close links with charismatic Anglican leaders in London. On Eleanor's return from Toronto she invited a number of pastors to her home, including Nicky Gumbel, curate at Holy Trinity, Brompton, who later became an international figure as coordinator of the highly successful 'Alpha' course for enquirers into Christianity. As a result, similar phenomena spread to the staff and subsequently the congregation of Holy Trinity, Brompton. Other churches in the London area, notably Baptist and 'new' churches, experienced parallel happenings as a result of visits by their church leaders to Toronto. By June the spread of the 'Blessing' to Britain was attracting widespread attention in both the church press and the secular media. Evangelicals were deeply divided in their responses, some seeing the movement as the herald of a great revival, and others dismissing it as mere hysteria. The movement also spread to parts of the United States, New Zealand, Australia, South Africa and beyond the English-speaking world.[87]

Even within the Vineyard movement the Toronto Blessing was not universally accepted as a mighty outpouring of the Spirit. From mid-1995 another revival outbreak, focused on the Assemblies of God church at Brownsville, Pensacola, Florida, competed for the attention of charismatics. At the end of 1995, the Association of Vineyard Churches withdrew its endorsement from the Toronto church, which continued as an independent church, the Toronto Airport Christian Fellowship. By 1996 the Toronto Blessing was cooling. Its most important long-term effect may have been in preparing the soil for the

---

[86] Scotland, *Charismatics and the New Millennium*, 232.

[87] The best treatments of the Toronto Blessing are Hilborn, *'Toronto' in Perspective*, and Jürgen Römer, *The Toronto Blessing* (Åbo: Åbo Academi University Press, 2002).

remarkable growth of the Holy Trinity, Brompton, Alpha course, which took off, first in Britain, and then internationally, in the wake of the Blessing.[88] By the end of the decade the Alpha course was claiming a global harvest of over two million Christian converts.[89]

Conclusion: movement of the Spirit or movement of culture?

Between 1945 and 2000 the theological orientation of world evangelicalism shifted markedly. The classic evangelical emphasis on the Bible as the Word of God was supplemented and at times supplanted by a focus on the gifts of, and direct revelation from, the Holy Spirit. The reorientation irreversibly weakened the historic connection of evangelicalism with the intellectual legacy of the European Enlightenment, with its innate suspicion of all human claims to divine authority, and its preference for the acquisition of knowledge from written texts over untested intuition or illumination. Those who found their devotional lives and experience of Christian worship rejuvenated by charismatic renewal were in no doubt that they were the beneficiaries of a decisive movement of the Spirit, opening up the hardened arteries of evangelical faith and restoring Christian confidence in the continuing capacity of God to transform human lives in ways that were no less dramatic than those recorded in the pages of the New Testament. Those who stood outside the movement, or who became progressively disillusioned with it, were more likely to be attracted to academic explanations that analysed the movement in cultural terms, as a readjustment of the evangelical tradition to the philosophical and cultural mood of a postmodern age that privileged experience over dogma, self-expression over decorum, and fluidity over structure.[90]

As with every movement of renewal or revival in Christian history, the dichotomy between confessional and social explanations is ultimately a false one. Mid-twentieth-century evangelicalism had undoubtedly reacted to the ascendancy of Protestant liberalism with a form of defensive textual

---

[88] Hilborn, 'Toronto' in Perspective, 321–322, 324; Scotland, Charismatics and the New Millennium, 250.

[89] Michael Green, Adventure of Faith: Reflections on Fifty Years of Christian Service (Harrow: Zondervan, 2001), 184.

[90] For one such early academic interpretation of the charismatic movement see David W. Bebbington, Evangelicalism in Modern Britain: A History from the 1730s to the 1980s (London: Unwin Hyman, 1989), 229–248. It should be noted that what Bebbington terms 'Modernist' has subsequently become known as 'postmodernist'.

scholasticism that left too little room for the freedom and enjoyment of the Spirit. As western, and increasingly also global, societies espoused post-Enlightenment values of freedom of expression and plurality of form, the cultures of Christian communities moved with them. The global evangelical family gained much-needed spiritual vitality as a result, but also found its cohesion weakening as evangelicals disagreed on where to strike the balance between Word and Spirit. It is not the role of the Christian historian to attempt to disentangle the continually interwoven strands of Spirit and culture, but simply to enable readers to discern, and interpret, those strands for themselves.

8. HERMENEUTICS, GENDER AND SEXUAL ETHICS

Evangelical Christians have always been distinguished by the seriousness of their commitment to make the teaching of Scripture their absolute norm of faith and conduct. They have further tended to maintain that the essential message of Scripture is, through the illumination of the Holy Spirit, plain and accessible to ordinary believers. Although some strands of the evangelical movement, notably those in the Presbyterian tradition, have emphasized the teaching authority of a learned ministry, evangelicals have customarily held that neither priest nor theologian is essential for the Word of God to be communicated effectively to believers. If it can be established 'what the Bible says' on a particular matter, that has been regarded as in principle sufficient to settle any argument. Yet most evangelicals who have participated in mission or other Christian activities that have brought them into contact with fellow-evangelicals from different church or cultural backgrounds have been confronted with the stark reality that evangelical faith does not in fact guarantee unanimity of view on 'what the Bible says'. On such matters as the extent of the atonement, or church order, or the proper subjects and mode of baptism, evangelicalism from its very origins has had to cope with deep-rooted disagreement within its ranks. For most of its history the evangelical movement has sought to interpret such disagreement as the consequence of partial vision in biblical exegesis, and the hope has often been expressed that, by the application of more thorough and insightful methods of exegesis of the relevant texts, the scope of disagreement might be minimized or even eliminated.

In the period covered by this book, three significant and to some extent

interrelated trends can be observed in the sphere of evangelical biblical interpretation. One is an increasingly common appeal to the evidence of personal
spiritual experience as a decisive argument in the endeavour to establish how
the biblical text should be applied today. This appeal was most widely made
within the rapidly expanding constituency of Pentecostal or charismatic
Christianity.

The second is a growing awareness that the task of biblical interpretation
involves more than simply trying to establish what the text says. The course
of European theology and especially German philosophy since the early
nineteenth century had concentrated attention on the fact that the original
authorial intention of a text does not necessarily correspond to what it 'meant'
for its original readers or hearers, still less to what it 'means' for those who
read or hear it in a different age or cultural context. In the period after 1945,
in response to the growing influence of the so-called 'new hermeneutic' associated with such figures as Ernst Fuchs, Gerhard Ebeling and Hans-Georg
Gadamer, the focus of applied biblical study moved progressively from exegesis to hermeneutics. For scholars committed to an evangelical understanding
of biblical inspiration, ascertaining what the text was originally intended to
convey, and what it meant to its original audience, necessarily remained para-
mount, but for a growing number it no longer constituted the entire interpretative task: the subsequent stage of endeavouring to establish what that text
means for us in our very different context increasingly became the focus of
debate. The growing salience of hermeneutics in the global evangelical community in this period was uneven: for many African Christians, for example,
the affinity between their own cultures and the cultural world of the Old
or New Testaments was so close that the questions of what the text originally meant and what it meant for them in their contemporary context were
virtually the same question.[1] For late twentieth-century evangelicals living
in the religiously plural and increasingly secularized cultures of the northern
hemisphere, on the other hand, the issues of biblical hermeneutics could no
longer be confined to the university or seminary lecture room, and increasingly intruded themselves even into the Sunday sermon or the midweek Bible
study. This was in part because of the third development apparent in the
history of evangelical biblical interpretation in the second half of the twentieth
century.

The third trend identifiable in the period from 1945 onwards is that the
question of how to interpret the authority of Scripture for today became

---

[1] See Philip Jenkins, *The New Faces of Christianity: Believing the Bible in the Global South*
(New York: Oxford University Press, 2006), ch. 2.

focused on two successive areas of highly contentious debate that contemporary social trends forced onto the agenda of all churches: the first, which acquired growing prominence in the period up to the 1980s, was the role of women in church leadership and particularly ordained ministry; the second, which gradually came to rival and arguably even eclipse the former theme from the 1980s onwards, and has continued to grow in prominence among all Christians, evangelicals included, to this day, was the question of the moral status of homosexual practice. Although there were obviously other major issues of sexual ethics on which it would be highly illuminating for primary research to trace the sometimes unpredictable trajectories of evangelical opinion during that period – abortion being the most obvious[2] – a chapter in an introductory survey such as this book cannot attempt to deal adequately with these. The discussion of the application by evangelicals of biblical teaching to the realm of gender and sexuality will instead be confined to the two areas mentioned.

This chapter will therefore attempt to summarize these three concurrent trends, beginning with the first. Discussion of these three interconnecting trends will, however, be to some extent interleaved, rather than strictly sequential in approach.

The Spirit falls on all flesh: the ministry of women in Pentecostal Christianity

Among the increasingly diverse expressions of evangelical Christianity apparent in the second half of the twentieth century, Pentecostal and charismatic churches stand out by virtue of the highly visible role that women have frequently assumed in forms of public ministry. As the prophet Joel, and the apostle Peter on the Day of Pentecost, proclaimed, the Spirit falls on all flesh, without differentiation of gender. Women, no less than men, have been prominent in the exercise of the distinctively charismatic gifts of prophecy, healing and speaking in tongues. Nevertheless, Pentecostal and neo-Pentecostal churches have tended to be quite literal in their interpretation of Scripture, and have therefore sought to adhere scrupulously to New Testament teaching on the place of women in the church. Scholarship on Pentecostalism,

---

[2] Alister Chapman, *Godly Ambition: John Stott and the Evangelical Movement* (New York: Oxford University Press, 2012), 124–125, comments on the fact that John Stott's position on abortion became noticeably more conservative over the years, in contrast to his gradual liberalization on some other issues, such as the ordination of women.

whether in its North American or its global manifestations, has been inclined to emphasize either one side or the other of this paradox, so that Pentecostal churches can equally be applauded by secular scholars as agents of female liberation or lambasted as arenas in which the patriarchal dominance of the pastor has been more absolute than in more traditional denominations.[3] In practice within the movement, this tension between the sublime indifference of the Holy Spirit to gender distinctions and the apparently continuing validity of such distinctions in New Testament teaching on ministry and church order has been negotiated, if never entirely resolved, by an appeal to the power of individual spiritual experience.

Thus an academic study of Pentecostal women preachers in a deeply con- servative rural area of central Missouri in the 1980s found that, though both male and female members of Pentecostal churches in this region held very traditional views of appropriate gender roles in family, church and society, a surprising number of women functioned not merely as itinerant preachers but even on occasion as de facto pastors of congregations. The women involved justified their leadership role in response to frequent criticism by making reference to Joel 2 and Acts 2, but also by pointing to the ultimately unan- swerable evidence of the blessing of God upon their ministries: if God had blessed, he must have called, and the only appropriate response to a divine call is obedience.[4]

Studies of Ghana's proliferating neo-Pentecostal movement have similarly emphasized both the prevalence of patriarchal attitudes among the churches as a whole and the salience of some individual congregations where women have assumed prominent positions of leadership, grounding their role in the empirical evidence supplied by the apparent extraordinary outpouring of the Spirit on them. Frequently, such positions are those of assistant pastor, some- times with the husband occupying the role of senior pastor. In these cases, the pastor's wife and/or assistant pastor is often styled as 'Mummy', and hence benefits from the immense respect given to mothers in West African cul- tures.[5] Occasionally, however, Ghanaian Pentecostal churches have women in the role of senior pastor. The most notable example is the Solid Rock Chapel

---

[3] For a balanced assessment of both sides of the paradox in relation to Pentecostalism in the USA see Grant Wacker, *Heaven Below: Early Pentecostals and American Culture* (Cambridge, Mass.: Harvard University Press, 2001), 158–176.

[4] Elaine J. Lawless, *Handmaidens of the Lord: Pentecostal Women Preachers and Traditional Religion* (Philadelphia: University of Pennsylvania Press, 1988).

[5] Jane Soothill, *Gender, Social Change and Spiritual Power: Charismatic Christianity in Ghana* (Leiden: E. J. Brill, 2007), 121.

International in Accra, founded in 1994, whose pastor is the Rev. Christie Doe Tetteh, known popularly as the 'Spiritual Bulldozer'. Brought up as a Catholic, Tetteh was converted through a crusade conducted in Accra in 1977 by the Nigerian Pentecostal Benson Idahosa, for whom she went to work as his secretary and pastoral assistant. She was sent for leadership training at the Haggai Institute in Singapore and returned to Ghana in 1992 convinced of the calling of God to a ministry in her own right: 'I saw specifically what God had for me to do. God blessed me with the ministry of signs and wonders. Whenever I stood to minister there were outstanding testimonies of instant healing and deliverance in the lives of people.'[6] Tetteh, most unusually for a mature African woman, is single, but her authority over the Solid Rock congregation is often defined in explicitly maternal terms: its members are viewed as her spiritual children.[7] It has been cogently argued by Jane Soothill that what distinguishes Ghanaian Pentecostal discourse on gender roles from that of the mainline churches is not that Pauline teaching on the submission of women is repudiated, but rather that it is conjoined to a strongly individualistic ethic of divine blessing, manifested in success that is both spiritual and material. Submission to one's husband in marriage, and to male leaders within the Pentecostal movement as a whole, is commended as a guarantee of the blessing of God on one's life, and, paradoxically, as the best way to get one's husband or the men in one's congregation to do exactly what one wants: submission to male headship is thus presented as the road that leads to female power and prosperity.[8] Although the prosperity gospel raises serious theological questions of its own, Pentecostal varieties of evangelicalism in Africa may have found an ingenious way to combine conventional exegesis of the Pauline texts on the submission of women to male authority with a practical hermeneutic that empowers and inspires women.

The churches and the ministry of women in the post-war era

In 1945 very few churches, whether evangelical or not, ordained women to Christian ministry. The United Church of Canada, one of the few that did

---

6 Cited in Brigid M. Sackey, *New Directions in Gender and Religion: The Changing Status of Women in African Independent Churches* (Lanham, Md.: Lexington Books, 2006), 96.

7 Soothill, *Gender, Social Change and Spiritual Power*, 169–172.

8 Ibid. 103–136; Jane Soothill, 'The Problem with "Women's Empowerment": Female Religiosity in Ghana's Charismatic Churches', *Studies in World Christianity* 16 (2010), 82–99.

(it had done so since 1936), had a weak evangelical presence. In the Anglican communion much controversy had been generated by the unilateral decision in 1944 of R. O. Hall, bishop of Hong Kong, to ordain to the priesthood an Anglican deaconess, Florence Li Tim Oi, in the extraordinary wartime circumstances that threatened to deprive the Anglican community in Macao of eucharistic ministry. The manifest disapproval of Hall's fellow-bishops in China and of Geoffrey Fisher as archbishop of Canterbury led Li Tim Oi in 1946 to offer, and Hall to accept, her resignation from her priesthood.[9] No other woman would be ordained to the Anglican priesthood until 1971, when, again in the diocese of Hong Kong, Jane Hwang, who had for long been in charge of a Hong Kong parish, and Joyce Bennett, a missionary of the Church Missionary Society, were ordained as priests.

The only churches in which women were generally prominent in leadership in the immediate post-war period were either those without a distinct ordained ministry, such as the Society of Friends, or those with a wholly non-sacramental understanding of ministry, such as the Salvation Army, or those at the radical end of the theological spectrum, such as the Unitarian and Universalist churches. In the United States examples can be found of women pastors in fundamentalist and Pentecostal churches from the early twentieth century.[10] In Britain two of the historic Free Churches, the Congregational Union of England and Wales and the Baptist Union of Great Britain and Ireland, had ordained women since 1917 and 1918 respectively, but the numbers actually ordained since then had been small: by 1946 they totalled twenty-seven in the former case, and only four in the latter; the few ordained Baptist women were, moreover, until 1957 designated as 'women pastors' rather than as ministers.[11] Similarly, though the Maritime Baptist Convention in Canada ordained a woman minister as early as 1954, majority opinion among Canadian Baptists remained strongly opposed to women's ordination for long afterwards.[12] The Methodist Church of Great Britain did not agree

---

[9] Jacqueline Field-Bibb, *Women Towards Priesthood: Ministerial Politics and Feminist Praxis* (Cambridge: Cambridge University Press, 1991), 84–85, 134–135, 327.

[10] Mark A. Noll, *American Evangelical Christianity: An Introduction* (Oxford: Blackwell, 2001), 89–93.

[11] F. D. Bacon, *Women in the Church* (London: Lutterworth Press, 1946), 100, 134–135; J. H. Y. Briggs, 'She-Preachers, Widows and Other Women: The Feminine Dimension in Baptist Life Since 1600', *Baptist Quarterly* 31 (1986), 346–347.

[12] P. Lorraine Coops, '"Shelter from the Storm": The Enduring Evangelical Impulse of Baptists in Canada, 1880s to 1990s', in George A. Rawlyk (ed.), *Aspects of the Canadian Evangelical Experience* (Montreal: McGill-Queen's University Press, 1997), 221.

to accept women as candidates for the ministry until 1973; the Church of Scotland did not do so until 1968.[13] In the United States the Northern Baptist Convention (known from 1950 to 1972 as the American Baptist Convention) had ordained significant numbers of women ministers from the late nineteenth century onwards, whereas in the much more conservative Southern Baptist Convention it was 1964 before the first woman – Addie Davis in Durham, North Carolina – was ordained to the ministry, though it is noteworthy that she had to go to the north to find a congregation (and, moreover, one affiliated to the American Baptist Convention) that was willing to call her.[14] The Methodist Church (which became the United Methodist Church in 1968) admitted women as supply pastors and 'ordained local preachers', but not until 1956 were they given full clergy status.[15] The Presbyterian Church (USA) had ordained women as elders since 1930, but once again it was 1956 before they could be ordained as ministers of Word and sacrament.[16]

In the southern hemisphere New Zealand was by some distance the most 'advanced' nation on this issue. Here an approximate, but not total, inverse correlation can be observed between the strength of evangelicalism in the denomination and the rapidity with which it moved to admit women to the ordained ministry: Congregationalists ordained women from 1951 onwards, Methodists from 1959, Presbyterians from 1965, Baptists from 1973, and Anglicans (most of whom were Anglo-Catholic) from 1977. The first Anglican woman diocesan bishop anywhere in the world, Penny Jamieson, was consecrated in Dunedin diocese in 1990; she was not an evangelical, and her diocese was traditionally Anglo-Catholic.[17] In Australia the predominantly liberal Uniting Church, formed in 1977 from a union of Congregational, Methodist

---

[13] Field-Bibb, *Women Towards Priesthood*, 66, 117.

[14] David W. Bebbington, *Baptists Through the Centuries: A History of a Global People* (Waco: Baylor University Press, 2010), 173; H. Leon McBeth, *The Baptist Heritage: Four Centuries of Baptist Witness* (Nashville: Broadman Press, 1987), 690; Nancy Tatom Ammerman, *Baptist Battles: Social Change and Religious Conflict in the Southern Baptist Convention* (New Brunswick, N.J.: Rutgers University Press, 1990), 91.

[15] Field-Bibb, *Women Towards Priesthood*, 55.

[16] See http://www.witherspoonsociety.org/2006/women's_ordination.htm (accessed 30 July 2012).

[17] Field-Bibb, *Women Towards Priesthood*, 50, 55; Ian Breward, *A History of the Churches in Australasia* (Oxford: Oxford University Press, 2001), 323–324, 385; Allan K. Davidson and Peter J. Lineham (eds.), *Transplanted Christianity: Documents Illustrative of New Zealand Church History* (Auckland: College Communications, 1987), 362; Kevin Ward, *A History of Global Anglicanism* (Cambridge: Cambridge University Press, 2006), 295.

and Presbyterian traditions, ordained women from its inception. Although the Australian Baptists, a mainly evangelical denomination, ordained their first woman minister in 1978, the Anglican Church of Australia, a denomination with a very strong conservative evangelical presence in the dioceses of Sydney and Melbourne, did not do so until 1992.[18]

Despite the paucity of churches in 1945 that were prepared to ordain women, the post-war years saw an intensifying debate in different denominations about the continuing justification for the exclusion of women from the Christian ministry. In many countries the Second World War, like the First, had thrust women into roles in public life that were normally closed to them, and the churches were not immune from the lasting impetus thus given to women's aspirations. In February 1949 an article appeared in the Australian evangelical journal the *Reformed Theological Review* that noted 'the emerging question whether women should be admitted to the Holy Ministry' as one example of the sorry divisions arising in the churches over questions of exegesis. The author, Donovan F. Mitchell, a one-time Baptist minister now in pastoral charge of St Stephen's Presbyterian Church, Surrey Hills, Melbourne, concluded that a more rigorously scientific exegesis was not in itself the answer to this uncertainty: the remedy lay instead in a renewed dual emphasis on 'Apostolic Tradition' and the 'Law of Nature'. By both criteria, Mitchell argued, women were debarred from the public Christian ministry. The growing pressure on the churches to abandon this position could be traced ultimately to the godless egalitarianism of the French Revolution and the philosophy of Rousseau. In such conditions, pronounced Mitchell, 'blessed is the exegete who can interpret and decide by the authority of the Apostolic Tradition. For he can withstand the surrounding pressures by means of the authority of the Apostolate.'[19] Here was an evangelical recognizing that sound exegesis in itself was inadequate to stem the tide of pagan egalitarianism, and appealing for assistance to an essentially Catholic understanding of the authority of tradition. Mitchell's article made an immediate impression on Donald W. B. Robinson, who later, in 1982, became Anglican archbishop of Sydney and as such led the robust campaign of Sydney Anglican evangelicals against the ordination of women in the Anglican Church

---

[18] Bebbington, *Baptists Through the Centuries*, 173; Stuart Piggin, *Evangelical Christianity in Australia: Spirit, Word and World* (Melbourne: Oxford University Press, 1996), 203–221.

[19] Donovan F. Mitchell, 'Women and the Ministry: Whither Exegesis?', *RTR* 8 (1949), 1–11; see Ian Breward, 'From Baptist Leader to Presbyterian Leader: The Rev. Donovan Mitchell (1890–1954)', in David W. Bebbington and Martin Sutherland (eds.), *Interfaces: Baptists and Others from the Seventeenth to the Twenty-First Centuries* (Milton Keynes: Paternoster Press, forthcoming).

of Australia, an outcome they proved ultimately unable to prevent when it narrowly passed the General Synod of the Church in November 1992. As late as
1985 Robinson referred to Mitchell's essay as an 'article I regard as the most
important I have ever read on the topic'.[20]

Mitchell, and Robinson after him, responded to the weight of secular egalitarian pressure by attempting to reinforce dangerously pliable 'pure exegesis'
with the steel of apostolic tradition. However, more characteristic of many
Protestants in the decades that followed 1949 was an alternative response,
one that explored the resources of the new biblical science of hermeneutics.
The trigger for this alternative response was the debate in 1957–8 over the
ordination of women in the established Lutheran Church of Sweden, a church
that had a degree of intercommunion with the Church of England and whose
stance on women's ministry was therefore watched keenly by both conservatives and progressives in England. In 1957 the Swedish Church Assembly had
voted 63 to 62 against allowing ordination, but a year later the vote was 69 to
27 in the other direction, thanks in large part to a decisive lay vote in favour.
In between the two votes, Krister Stendahl, a clergyman of the Church of
Sweden then teaching at Harvard University, published an essay in Swedish
arguing that the real issue was one of hermeneutics. In 1966 Fortress Press in
Philadelphia published a revised version of his essay in English.[21] Observing
that in 1951 all except one of the New Testament teachers in the Swedish universities had issued a statement declaring that the proposal to ordain women
to the priesthood faced 'grave exegetical obstacles', Stendahl countered that
the issue at stake was not the exegesis of texts so much as the hermeneutics of
scriptural authority. He observed that any idea of a priestly caste was noticeably absent from New Testament teaching on ministry. Rather than expounding a theology of priestly office, the biblical texts justified their position on the
subordination of women in both church and society by appeal to the original
order of God's creation. It was hence inconsistent for Christians to accept the
emancipation of women in society while denying it within the church, which
was supposed to be the embodiment of the new order of God's kingdom.
If biblical teaching on the subordination of women were to be accepted as
normative for today, then Christians ought logically to resist equality between
the sexes in political and civic affairs, and not simply in matters of church
governance.[22]

---

[20] Piggin, *Evangelical Christianity in Australia*, 206.

[21] Krister Stendahl, *The Bible and the Role of Women: A Case Study in Hermeneutics*
(Philadelphia: Fortress Press, 1966).

[22] Ibid. 39–40, 42–43.

Stendhal's argument was ingenious and, by appearing to make an insistence on biblical authority absurd, was not calculated to win the support of evangelicals. Nevertheless, it was a powerful one that was to appear increasingly in evangelical writing over the next two decades.[23] By July 1973, when a Tyndale Fellowship New Testament Study Group assembled in Cambridge to address the topic of the interpretation of the New Testament, it is noteworthy that the paper on the authority of the New Testament, given by Robin Nixon, then a staff member of St John's College, Durham, cited Stendahl's booklet when raising the question 'What sort of cultural transposition do we have to make [in applying Pauline teaching about the order of creation] and is it so great that we may almost have to demythologize the biblical doctrine of creation?'[24] When these papers were published in 1977 it is not surprising that the executive of the Theological Students' Fellowship raised the question of whether the stance of some of the contributors was compatible with the doctrinal basis of the Tyndale Fellowship.[25]

The evangelical discovery of hermeneutics

The hermeneutical point made by Krister Stendahl may not have attracted much attention from evangelicals when it was first made in English in 1966. But in the course of the next two decades the currents of the new hermeneutic propelled a growing number of conservative scholars in directions that challenged traditional evangelical understandings not simply of the role of women, but even, in some cases, of the nature of biblical authority itself. The co-author of an Anglican booklet published in 1973 on the subject of 'Evangelicals and the Ordination of Women' observed that the number of Anglican evangelicals favouring the ordination of women had multiplied from a mere handful five or ten years previously to what was now a sizeable minority; he went on to note that the Pauline passages taken by many to rule out the admission of women to ordained ministry 'were regarded by almost all evangelicals not so long ago as enforcing still the wearing of hats in church', or by an earlier generation as a reason for denying women the vote (which was precisely Stendahl's

---

[23] E.g. Colin Craston, *Biblical Headship and the Ordination of Women*, Grove Pastoral Series 27 (Bramcote: Grove Books, 1986), 5, 19.

[24] R. E. Nixon, 'The Authority of the New Testament', in I. H. Marshall (ed.), *New Testament Interpretation: Essays on Principles and Methods* (Exeter: Paternoster Press, 1977), 346.

[25] T. A. Noble, *Tyndale House and Fellowship: The First Sixty Years* (Leicester: Inter-Varsity Press, 2006), 174–175.

point).[26] Indeed, it should be remembered that well into the 1970s and beyond there were sections of the evangelical community, such as many of the Christian Brethren, for whom the Pauline injunction in 1 Corinthians 11 to women to keep their heads covered in public prayer was still regarded as absolutely requiring all women to wear hats in church.[27] Nevertheless, evangelicals were beginning to approach such questions with a much greater awareness of hermeneutical issues than their predecessors had shown.

In the Church of England it became apparent in 1982–3 how great was the potential of the new approach to hermeneutics to create divisions within the evangelical community. In that year James D. G. Dunn, a prominent member of the Tyndale Fellowship, published a long article in the Anglican evangelical journal *Churchman* on 'The Authority of Scripture According to Scripture', which attacked the Warfield view of scriptural inerrancy as 'exegetically improbable, hermeneutically defective, theologically dangerous, and educationally disastrous'. Dunn insisted that 'It is only when we properly recognize the historical relativity of Scripture that our ears can be properly attuned to hear the authoritative Word that God speaks to us in the words of Scripture here and now.'[28] The reverberations of this article were such that in March 1983 the Church Society,[29] the proprietor of the journal, forced the resignation both of the editor, C. Peter Williams, and his editorial board. Williams was replaced by a more conservative scholar, Gerald L. Bray, and a new editorial board was appointed. In response a new 'open evangelical' Anglican journal, *Anvil*, was set up under Williams's editorship. Although Dunn's article was by no means the only cause of the split, the division was a symbolic episode that signalled the growing divergence between Reformed and 'open' evangelicals in the Church of England. Hermeneutics was at the heart of the argument.[30]

---

[26] Colin Craston, Joyce Baldwin and J. I. Packer, *Evangelicals and the Ordination of Women*, Grove Booklet on Ministry and Worship 17 (Bramcote: Grove Books, 1973), 3. It should be noted that J. I. Packer, unlike his two fellow-authors, here argued (25–26) that the ordination of women to the presbyterate, though not absolutely prohibited by Scripture, would be 'decidedly inexpedient'.

[27] Neil Dickson, 'Worn Symbols: Women's Hair and Head-Coverings in Brethren History', unpublished paper given at Charlotte Chapel, Edinburgh, 8 Oct. 2011.

[28] James D. G. Dunn, 'The Authority of Scripture According to Scripture', *Chm* 96 (1982), 104–122, 201–225 (quotations at 118, 214).

[29] The Church Society was formed in 1950 by a union between the Church Association (founded in 1865) and the National Church League (founded in 1906).

[30] For a full account see Andrew Atherstone, *An Anglican Evangelical Identity Crisis: The Churchman – Anvil Affair of 1981–1984* (London: Latimer Trust, 2008).

The new salience of hermeneutics in scholarly debate among evangelicals owed a good deal to the work of Anthony C. Thiselton. Thiselton's book *The Two Horizons* seems not to have attracted much attention from evangelicals when it first appeared in 1980, but its significance in the longer term for evangelicalism was immense. Thiselton had been a leading Anglican member of the Tyndale Fellowship since 1967, and was a contributor to the Tyndale Fellowship Study Group on the interpretation of the Bible in July 1973. The book was a revision of a University of Sheffield PhD thesis, which one of the examiners, J. B. Torrance, described as 'one of the most competent dissertations I have ever read'.[31] Thiselton's exploration of the philosophical hermeneutics of Heidegger, Bultmann and Wittgenstein was dense and demanding. His central argument was that the application of modern philosophical categories to biblical interpretation, far from being an illegitimate imposition on 'pure' biblical exegesis, was in fact a defence against interpreters so reading the scriptural text that they merely hear echoes of their own attitudes or pre-judgments.[32] Only those who have been made aware of their own 'pre-understanding' (or hermeneutical horizons) can engage perceptively with the different hermeneutical horizon of an ancient biblical text. Thiselton anticipated, no doubt correctly, that this argument would not endear itself to the disciples of Cornelius Van Til, for whom any attempt to utilize insights from philosophies that are not distinctively Christian was illegitimate.[33] He also by implication criticized the Warfield–Packer view of biblical authority as being too propositional and 'abstract'. For Thiselton, the authority of the Bible, though a quality independent of the faith of the hearer or reader, is *experienced* dynamically only 'when some kind of correspondence or inter-relation occurs between the situation addressed by the biblical writer and the situation of the modern reader or hearer'.[34]

A lecture on hermeneutics by Thiselton at the second National Evangelical Anglican Congress at Nottingham in 1977 became the main talking point of the congress.[35] After Thiselton, evangelical biblical scholars, theologians and ethicists would find it much more difficult to write as if the exegetical task were a self-sufficient, closed enterprise, quite independent of the cultural

---

[31] Preface by J. B. Torrance to Anthony C. Thiselton, *The Two Horizons: New Testament Hermeneutics and Philosophical Description with Special Reference to Heidegger, Bultmann, Gadamer, and Wittgenstein* (Exeter: Paternoster Press, 1980), xii.

[32] Ibid. xx, 225.

[33] Ibid. 9.

[34] Ibid. 434–437.

[35] Alister E. McGrath, *To Know and Serve God: A Life of James I. Packer* (London: Hodder & Stoughton, 1997), 215–216.

context and limitations of the exegete. The same gradually became true of the most discerning evangelical preachers also. By 1981 John Stott could write in his diary, 'It is increasingly clear to me that hermeneutics is Issue No.1 in the church today, & not least for evangelical Christians. Our differences are largely due to different ways of reading and understanding Scripture.'[36] Other evangelical Anglican leaders, however, such as Jim Packer and Dick Lucas, the rector of St Helen's, Bishopsgate, worried that the new fashion for hermeneutics would prove to be a Trojan horse that would smuggle a new liberalism into the evangelical camp.[37]

Thiselton's influence is clear in the two volumes of systematic theology published in 1991 and (posthumously) in 1996 by Paul King Jewett of Fuller Theological Seminary. Jewett (1919–91) had been taught by Gordon H. Clark at Wheaton College and was at one time a member of the Evangelical Theological Society. He dedicated the first volume of his systematic theology *God, Creation, and Revelation* to his 'Former Colleague and Esteemed Friend' E. J. Carnell.[38] Jewett had first come to general notice following the publication in 1975 of *Man as Male and Female*, a work that attracted the gunfire of his former Fuller colleague Harold Lindsell, in *The Battle for the Bible*.[39] Jewett had argued that the apostle Paul was torn between his training in rabbinic exegesis and his distinctively Christian vision, as expounded in Galatians 3:28, that in Christ any distinction of status between male and female had been abrogated. Occasionally, Jewett implied, the former influence had got the upper hand, as when Paul in 1 Corinthians 11 taught female subordination on the basis of the accepted rabbinic interpretation of the second creation narrative of Genesis 2.[40] In *God, Creation, and Revelation* Jewett drew directly from Thiselton and the 'new hermeneutic', in his insistence that the hermeneutical task 'cannot be limited to the question of what the text meant when it was written'; but must also include asking 'what it means now when it is preached'; interpreters should not follow an Enlightenment path of trying to close the gap between the biblical world and our own 'by simply making

---

[36] Cited in Chapman, *Godly Ambition*, 105.

[37] McGrath, *To Know and Serve God*, 218–219; D. W. Bebbington, *Evangelicalism in Modern Britain: A History from the 1730s to the 1980s* (London: Unwin Hyman: 1989), 269.

[38] Paul King Jewett, *God, Creation, and Revelation: A Neo-Evangelical Theology with Sermons by Marguerite Shuster* (Grand Rapids: Eerdmans, 1991).

[39] Harold Lindsell, *The Battle for the Bible* (Grand Rapids: Zondervan, 1976), 117–121; see George M. Marsden, *Reforming Fundamentalism: Fuller Seminary and the New Evangelicalism* (Grand Rapids: Eerdmans, 1987), 280–282.

[40] Paul King Jewett, *Man as Male and Female: A Study in Sexual Relationships from a Theological Point of View* (Grand Rapids: Eerdmans, 1975), 112–122, 134.

the text over in our image'.[41] What this meant in practice for the interpretation of biblical teaching in the field of gender and sexuality became fully clear only in Jewett's second volume, *Who We Are: Our Dignity as Human: A Neo-Evangelical Theology*, which was two-thirds completed at the time of his death, and was brought to press by Marguerite Shuster, his pastor at Knox Presbyterian Church in Pasadena. We shall return to this volume in a later section.

Egalitarians and complementarians

During the 1980s the question of the role of women in Christian ministry emerged as the chief test case for the increasingly divergent ways in which evangelicals were applying biblical teaching to the contemporary context. Since the late 1950s, in a cultural climate increasingly affected by the women's liberation movement, the majority of Christian denominations in the western world had been compelled to reassess and eventually abandon their historic opposition to the ordination of women. Although evangelicals were not prominent in the decisions of the mainline American Protestant denominations taken from the late 1950s onwards to ordain women, during the 1970s a significant body of opinion emerged in North America that came to be known as 'evangelical feminism'.[42] The Chicago Declaration of Evangelical Social Concern in 1973 included the statement 'We acknowledge that we have encouraged men to prideful domination and women to irresponsible passivity. So we call both men and women to mutual submission and active discipleship.'[43] One consequence of that commitment was the organization at the second conference of Evangelicals for Social Action in November 1974 of a seminar on women's equality. This led to the formation in January 1975 of the Evangelical Women's Caucus, whose inaugural conference in Washington in November that year attracted over four hundred women from the United States and Canada, drawn from eighteen different denominations. For many within this emerging movement Jewett's *Man as Male and Female* was a foundational source of scholarly inspiration and encouragement.[44]

---

[41] Jewett, *God, Creation, and Revelation*, 154; see n. 65, citing Thiselton, *Two Horizons*, 60–61, and n. 66 on p. 155.

[42] See Pamela D. H. Cochran, *Evangelical Feminism: A History* (New York: New York University Press, 2005).

[43] The Chicago Declaration of Evangelical Social Concern, cited in ibid. 14.

[44] Cochran, *Evangelical Feminism*, 15–16, 24–25; Virginia Ramey Mollencott, 'Evangelicalism: A Feminist Perspective', *USQR* 32 (1977), 95–103.

There was also a growing company in North America and elsewhere of those, including male evangelicals, who did not own the label 'feminist', but who were convinced that the fundamental equality of women and men within the new humanity that Christ came to establish was intrinsic to the biblical witness. However, probably larger still in the United States was the number of those evangelicals who responded to the rise of evangelical feminism by re-asserting their belief that the Scriptures taught a complementarity of distinct roles between men and women, with the roles of headship in the family, church life and (by ultimate implication) society at large, being reserved to men. The fundamental nature of the divergence between these two camps became clear at the 1986 meeting of the Evangelical Theological Society, where the theme of the meeting was 'Male and Female in Biblical and Theological Perspective'. Two opposing coalitions were organized: the egalitarians formed Christians for Biblical Equality, and the complementarians the Council on Biblical Manhood and Womanhood.[45] These two coalitions have continued to argue their corner ever since. Complementarians such as John Piper (pastor of Bethlehem Baptist Church, Minnesota, since 1980) and Wayne Grudem (for many years a member of faculty at Trinity Evangelical Divinity School, Illinois) have argued that the Bible teaches that there are permanent and distinct qualities of 'manhood' and 'womanhood' that should be replicated in the structures of church and family life in all cultures.[46] In contrast, evangelical feminists, such as the British Anglican Elaine Storkey, have repudiated the idea of unchanging opposing 'es-sences' of the two sexes as being more Greek than biblical. They have argued instead for a theology of gender that models its understanding of all persons and their mutual relations on the pattern of God who is three persons in non-hierarchical and eternally loving interrelationship.[47]

In the United States the evangelical presence in the mainline denomin-ations was generally too weak to hold these churches back from ordaining women from the 1970s onwards. In more conservative denominations com-plementarian opinion was either strong enough to ensure that moves to ordain women were blocked, or that in practice little progress was made towards the official recognition of the ministry of women. Thus the Synod of the Christian

---

[45] Stanley J. Grenz, *Women in the Church: A Biblical Theology of Women in Ministry* (Downers Grove: InterVarsity Press, 1995), 14–15.

[46] John Piper and Wayne Grudem (eds.), *Recovering Biblical Manhood and Womanhood: A Response to Biblical Feminism* (Wheaton: Crossway, 1991).

[47] Elaine Storkey, 'Evangelical Theology and Gender', in Timothy J. Larsen and Daniel J. Trier (eds.), *The Cambridge Companion to Evangelical Theology* (Cambridge: Cambridge University Press, 2007), 161–176.

Reformed Church voted in 1990 to allow congregations to ordain women to all church offices, but the 1992 Synod refused to ratify the decision; the 1993 Synod voted to open the door once more to women's ordination, only for the 1994 Synod to repeat the cycle by declining to endorse the decision; in 1995 a compromise solution was eventually reached that allowed each district of the church to make its own decision on the matter.[48] In the Church of England, by contrast, the stance taken by Anglican evangelicals was to prove decisive in removing the obstacles to the ordination of women.

Evangelical Anglicans and the ordination of women in the Church of England

On 11 November 1992 the General Synod of the Church of England voted by the necessary two-thirds majorities in the three houses of bishops, clergy and laity to ordain women to the priesthood (women had been ordained to the diaconate since 1987). The vote was close, particularly in the House of Laity, where the measure would have been lost if two members had voted in the contrary direction.[49] The majority of those voting against were from the Anglo-Catholic wing of the Church; for them the issue was whether women could legitimately represent the male Christ when performing the sacerdotal mystery of the eucharistic sacrifice. Some Anglican evangelicals also voted against, believing that the measure contravened biblical teaching on male headship and female submission, but a larger number voted alongside more liberal Anglicans in favour of the measure. It was widely observed that it was these evangelical votes, especially in the House of Laity, that had secured the narrow victory. Some of the evangelicals who spoke in the debate testified that they had changed their position. Thus Pete Broadbent, a London vicar, referred to an essay he had written as a theological student at St John's College, Nottingham, in the 1970s, arguing strongly against the ordination of women on the basis of the New Testament texts that appeared to teach the headship of the male. It was only during his first curacy, at St Nicholas's Church in Durham from 1977 to 1980, where his vicar was George Carey, later archbishop of Canterbury and a strong supporter of women's ordination, that Broadbent came to the conclusion that the headship texts would not bear the weight that the opponents of ordination placed on them. He went on to outline to the

---

[48] Grenz, *Women in the Church*, 30–31.

[49] Sean Gill, *Women and the Church of England: From the Eighteenth Century to the Present Day* (London: SPCK, 1994), 257–259.

Synod Krister Stendahl's argument that if the headship argument were valid, it had to be applied to society as a whole, and not merely to the church.[50] One of those whose opinion had changed in this way was John Stott. In an article written in 1963 he had stated baldly that Scripture did not permit women to exercise authority over men. By 1984 he had declared himself in favour of the ordination of women, though not of women ministers being in sole pastoral charge or being bishops. By 2006 he appears to have accepted that there was no a priori reason why women should not serve as bishops.[51]

Some eighteen months after the crucial debate in General Synod, in March 1994, one leading Anglican evangelical New Testament scholar, Dick France, observed in a sermon preached in Wycliffe Hall chapel in Oxford that 'Had the Synod vote taken place twenty years ago, I guess that most evangelicals would have voted against the ordination of women to the presbyterate. I would have done so myself.'[52] France went on to argue that the change of mind of many evangelicals on this matter should not be interpreted as a mere capitulation to the secular mood of the age. Rather, he maintained, it was evidence of the impact on evangelicals of a new appreciation of hermeneutics:

> We have now learned to recognise the distance between the 'two horizons' of the biblical author's world and our own, and to ask difficult questions about how what is said in the one horizon can be applied in the other. We have learned, I hope, to be more aware of the whole scriptural context within which a given text comes to us, and to be suspicious of interpretations which fail to set a text in its wider context, both in its historical situation and in its place within the canon of Scripture.[53]

A slippery slope? From the ministry of women to the homosexual debate

Although France's Oxford sermon did not explicitly cite Anthony Thiselton's work, the allusion was clear. The contemporary milieu of feminist and egalitarian

---

[50] *The Ordination of Women to the Priesthood: The Synod Debate 11 November 1992: A Verbatim Record* (London: Church House Publishing, 1993), 44.

[51] Chapman, *Godly Ambition*, 123–124, 204–205.

[52] R. T. France, '"It Seemed Good to the Holy Spirit and to Us"? Some Thoughts on Decision-Making in the Church, and on Christian Disagreement, in the Light of the Decision of the Church of England to Ordain Women to the Presbyterate', *Chm* 108 (1994), 234–241 (quotation at 237). France (1938–2012) was then principal of Wycliffe Hall.

[53] Ibid. 238.

thought may indeed have prompted evangelicals to re-examine the scriptural evidence, but, in France's view, it was the new science of hermeneutics that was crucial in persuading them to change their position. He developed his argument in a Grove booklet published in 2000, in which he surveyed the apostle Paul's list of twenty-seven of his colleagues in ministry in Romans 16, ten of whom were women, and one of whom, Junia, Paul significantly denominates as an apostle. France readily conceded, however, that the New Testament evidence was ambiguous: some passages, such as 1 Timothy 2:11–15, appear to restrict the role of women in at least certain spheres, while others, such as Romans 16, unashamedly celebrate their role in ministry and leadership. He noted that the 1992 decision had polarized opinion among evangelical Anglicans, as witnessed by the formation in February 1993 of the conservative pressure group 'Reform'.[54] Making appeal to the plain teaching of Scripture, Reform opposes not the ministry of women as such but rather their ordination to any role that would give them primary teaching authority, either as incumbents in a parish congregation or as bishops presiding over a diocese. Reform advocates are profoundly unsympathetic to the weight now being given by evangelicals to hermeneutics, and appeal in a fashion that has a long history within evangelicalism to 'basic common-sense rules' of textual exegesis: establishing the original intention of the biblical writer is all that is required to discover the relevant application for today.[55] France's *Churchman* article in 1994 elicited an immediate published reply by Melvin Tinker, a Hull vicar and a prominent member of Reform. Tinker cited with approval the complaint of a leading Sydney evangelical, John Woodhouse of Moore Theological College, that evangelicals had widely succumbed to a 'developmental hermeneutic', which so emphasized the relevance of the changing cultural situation that biblical principles were being 'applied' in a way that subverted the original intention of the biblical teaching.[56] Tinker recruited the unlikely figure of Paul King Jewett to his cause, citing (with no reference to his overall argument) Jewett's statement in *Man as Male and Female* that in 1 Corinthians 11 Paul teaches that 'The subordination of the woman to man is an essential part of the hierarchy which God himself has established to ensure a proper order in the relationships of life.'[57]

---

54 R. T. France, *A Slippery Slope? The Ordination of Women and Homosexual Practice – A Case Study in Biblical Interpretation*, Grove Biblical Series 16 (Cambridge: Grove Books, 2000).

55 Jonathan Fletcher, 'Interpreting the Bible', http://reform.org.uk/download-file/downloads/interpreting.pdf (accessed 5 June 2012).

56 Melvin Tinker, '"It Seemed Good to the Holy Spirit and to Us"? A Reply to Dick France', *Chm* 108 (1994), 242–246 (quotation at 245).

57 Jewett, *Man as Male and Female*, 57, cited in Tinker, 'It Seemed Good', 245.

The central and most disturbing accusation of Tinker's article was that the evangelical adoption of developmental hermeneutics had set evangelicals sliding down a slippery slope that was bound, sooner or later, to lead those who employed these methods to endorse homosexual practice. The arguments used by Dick France in support of a rereading of the texts on the role of women were, Tinker claimed, precisely the same as those used by those who attempted to explain away the clear biblical prohibition of homosexual practice.[58] France's 2000 Grove booklet was his considered reply to Tinker. His response was that, while it was undeniable that the pressure of the age had been the trigger forcing evangelicals to re-examine the scriptural teaching on the ministry of women, and was indeed now compelling a similar scrutiny in relation to homosexuality, it did not follow that the result of the re-examination would be the same regarding the thorny issue of homosexuality. The New Testament textual evidence on the ministry of women was indeed mixed, and could lead different evangelicals in all integrity to reach mutually contradictory conclusions. There was no such ambiguity, however, on homosexual practice: an honest re-examination of the biblical evidence, France insisted, led to the conclusion that on this question the traditional Christian position was the only admissible one.[59]

Evangelicals and homosexuality

Was Tinker correct to argue that evangelical revisionism on the interpretation of New Testament teaching on the role of women in church leadership was bound in due course to lead to a similar reversal of stance on the more foundational moral issue of homosexuality? As a partial answer to that question we shall return to the second volume of Paul King Jewett's systematic theology, *Who We Are: Our Dignity as Human*, published posthumously in 1991, in which Jewett addressed at considerable length the subject of human sexuality. His central argument was that, according to Genesis 1, to be created in the image of God is to be created as male and female in mutual relationship. The first creation narrative was unambiguous in teaching that 'the man–woman relationship should be one of equality and complementarity in all of life'.[60] This understanding, however, had become obliterated in Jewish tradition by the

---

[58] Tinker, 'It Seemed Good', 245.

[59] France, *A Slippery Slope?*, 22–23.

[60] Paul King Jewett, *Who We Are, Our Dignity as Human: A Neo-Evangelical Theology* (Grand Rapids: Eerdmans, 1996), 149.

patriarchal culture of ancient Israel. Christians were no more obliged to absolutize patriarchy as found in the social order of the Old Testament than they
were to absolutize monarchy as found in its political order. The clear teaching
of Jesus, and Paul's insistence in Galatians 3 that in Christ all hierarchical
divisions between men and women were abrogated, represented a recovery of
God's original creative purpose for men and women.[61]

In an extended addendum to the book Jewett applied these theological
principles to the subject of homosexuality.[62] If Scripture as a whole presents
the relationship between man and woman as fundamental to God's creative
purpose for humanity, then, he contended, evangelicals were simply not at
liberty to approach the topic of homosexuality as if this unified biblical testimony did not exist, however deep their sympathy might be for those whose
inclination was homosexual. Jewett could thus find no scriptural warrant for
the statement in the bylaws of the homosexual group 'Evangelicals Concerned'
that homosexuality is 'part of God's created order'.[63] He confessed that 'we
have not seen our way clear to attributing homosexuality to the creation side
of the ledger rather than to the effects of the Fall'.[64] Nevertheless, Jewett
went on to expound his conviction that within the fallen estate of humanity
the legitimacy of committed same-sex relationships may on occasion have
to be conceded as the lesser of two evils, just as within marriage relationships Christians sometimes have to accept a divorce as the lesser of two
evils. While churches should not bless or celebrate homosexual partnerships,
they should in certain circumstances accept them. Jewett readily acknowledged that this position was in some ways unsatisfactory, yet insisted that the
witness of Scripture, while it provided no basis for the inordinate horror with
which homosexuality had been conventionally regarded by Christian tradition,
equally afforded no basis for a theological position that presented homosexual
relationships as congruent with God's created order and purpose.[65]

Jewett's exposition of the biblical case for grounding human identity in a
relationship between the sexes that was characterized by both equality and
complementarity thus prevented him from giving any principled endorsement
to homosexual relationships. A similar argument was independently advanced
in 1998 by the Vancouver-based Baptist theologian Stanley J. Grenz, in
Welcoming but Not Affirming. Grenz, as will be noted in the next chapter, has

---

[61] Ibid. 149–167.

[62] Ibid. 290–350.

[63] On 'Evangelicals Concerned' see below, 232.

[64] Jewett, *Who We Are*, 330, 340.

[65] Ibid. 341–350.

been labelled by some conservative evangelicals as a 'post-evangelical', but his stance on this issue was unambiguous: he too insisted that 'we discover God's intention for us to be the divine image bearers – and hence our full humanness – through our interaction with one another as male and female'.[66] Grenz, like Jewett, argued that evangelical churches should nevertheless accept homosexuals into church membership, though he sounded a more conservative pastoral note than Jewett in stressing that homosexuals, no more or less than heterosexuals, should remain subject to loving church discipline in their sexual practice.[67]

The willingness of Jewett and Grenz to concede a place to homosexuals within the life of the church was strictly limited and grounded not on any appeal to the created order, but rather on recognition of how relationships might be structured according to principles of grace within a fallen world. Their arguments, though equally unacceptable both to strict conservatives and to evangelical advocates of homosexuality, went beyond mere proof-texting to serious endeavours to provide a solid theological basis for pastoral practice. In their central affirmations that same-sex relationships did not conform to God's creative purpose, Grenz and Jewett were more con-servative in their conclusions than their nearest British equivalent, Michael Vasey, a tutor in liturgy at the Anglican evangelical college Cranmer Hall in Durham, who in 1995 published *Strangers and Friends*. Vasey employed Anthony Thiselton's insistence on the importance of taking into account a writer's cultural horizon to advance the startling suggestion in relation to the apostle Paul that 'There is certainly an argument to be made that the man we know from his letters might be more at home today in gay rather than non-gay society.'[68] Vasey employed an essentially situational ethic to claim that in the Bible

> sexual behaviour derives its meaning from the social order of which it is a part. This emerges clearly in the case of the prohibition of adultery in the Ten Commandments: what is forbidden is not certain physical acts that are intrinsically wrong but sexual acts which threaten social relationships that are central to the ordering of society.[69]

---

[66] Stanley J. Grenz, *Welcoming but Not Affirming: An Evangelical Response to Homosexuality* (Louisville, Ky.: John Knox Press, 1998), 104.

[67] Ibid. 132–136.

[68] Michael Vasey, *Strangers and Friends: A New Exploration of Homosexuality and the Bible* (London: Hodder & Stoughton, 1995), 133.

[69] Ibid. 231.

Paul in Romans 1 was not condemning homosexual acts per se, but only what he saw in the world of his day, namely exploitative relationships associated with idolatry, slavery and social domination.[70] Some readers may feel that Tinker's 'slippery slope' is rather more applicable to Vasey than to Grenz or Jewett.

From the 1980s onwards the question of homosexuality came to rival, and eventually to replace, that of the ministry of women at the head of the list of controverted ethical questions preoccupying evangelicals. The first signs of dissent from the overwhelmingly conservative stance of evangelicals on the acceptability of homosexual practice became apparent from the late 1970s onwards. Even before then, in October 1968, Troy Perry, a graduate of Moody Bible Institute and a former pastor in the Church of God of Prophecy, had founded the openly pro-gay Metropolitan Community Church in Los Angeles. However, although this new and radically post-denominational church soon established branches throughout the USA and internationally, it maintained only sporadic connections with the evangelical community.[71] In contrast, Dr Ralph Blair, an evangelical psychotherapist from New York City, established 'Evangelicals Concerned' in February 1976 at a meeting in Washington D.C. that was provocatively held over the street from the conference of the National Association of Evangelicals, whose delegates were given leaflets advertising the new organization. Blair's movement founded regional groups, or linked together in a loose coalition already existing evangelical gay and lesbian groups, mainly on the west coast of the USA.[72] In the later stages of the Jesus Movement on the west coast homosexuality became an issue through the colourful and controversial figure of Lonnie Frisbee (1949–93). Frisbee, of whom it has been said that he 'put the freak in Jesus freak', was a close associate of Chuck Smith of Calvary Chapel and later of John Wimber in the Vineyard movement, but combined his spectacular 'signs and wonders' evangelistic ministry with a lifestyle that was subsequently revealed to be both homosexual and promiscuous.[73]

In Britain the Gay and Lesbian Christian Movement, formed in January

---

[70] Ibid. 132.

[71] See http://en.wikipedia.org/wiki/Troy_Perry (accessed 5 June 2012).

[72] See http://www.evangelicalsconcerned.org (accessed 5 June 2012) and http://www. ecwr.org/about-us/who-we-are/history.html (accessed 5 June 2012); on Frisbee's role in the Jesus Movement see Larry Eskridge, *God's Forever Family: The Jesus People Movement in America* (New York: Oxford University Press, 2013), ch. 3.

[73] See http://www.inplainsite.org/html/vineyard_lonnie_frisbee.html (accessed 21 Dec. 2011).

1976, included an evangelical fellowship within its ranks from May 1979 onwards. However, it remained very small, with only about a hundred members in 1991.[74] A more conservative British network, Courage, was founded in May 1988 by Jeremy Marks. Intended originally to provide support and counselling for gay and lesbian evangelicals, Courage was affiliated to the Evangelical Alliance, but at the close of the 1990s moved its position to one that affirmed the legitimacy of stable and loving same-sex relationships. As a result, affiliation to the Alliance was discontinued in March 2002.[75] One of those who identified himself with the new approach adopted by Courage was Dr Roy D. Clements, pastor of a large student congregation in Cambridge, Eden Baptist Church, from 1979 to 1999, and one of the most influential and intellectually gifted figures in British evangelicalism during that period. Following his resignation from his pastorate, Clements made public that he was gay and subsequently left his wife and family; it was an episode that caused great distress to many British evangelicals. Clements later published some of his private correspondence with John Stott conducted during August 1999, in which he debated with Stott over the compatibility of homosexual relationships with an evangelical view of scriptural authority. He assured Stott that he did not accept the 'polyvalent indeterminacy in biblical hermeneutics which is characteristic of extreme postmodern critics like Derrida and Rorty', but had nonetheless reached the conclusion that on this issue, as with other issues in earlier periods of history, Bible-believing Christians had simply been in serious error in their interpretation of Scripture.[76] Once again, hermeneutics was located at the centre of a contemporary evangelical debate.

The cases of evangelical leaders such as Lonnie Frisbee or Roy Clements understandably attracted considerable publicity. It would be wrong to imply, however, that by the end of the century there were clear signs of a significant shift of evangelical opinion on the gay issue. Surveys conducted in 1996 suggested that 96% of members of conservative evangelical churches in England regarded homosexual practice as incompatible with Christian profession, in contrast to only 52.5% of members of the Church of England's General Synod.[77] Although evangelical statements on the question issued during the 1990s became noticeably more pastorally sensitive and more theologically

---

[74] Sean Gill (ed.), *The Lesbian and Gay Christian Movement: Campaigning for Justice, Truth and Love* (London: Cassell, 1998), 34–35, 73.

[75] See http://www.courage.org.uk/articles/eapressrelease.shtml (accessed 5 June 2012).

[76] Clements to Stott, 20 Aug. 1999, at http://www.courage.org.uk/articles/article. asp?id=142 (accessed 21 Dec. 2011).

[77] Gill, *Lesbian and Gay Christian Movement*, 109.

reflective, their essential moral position had not changed. The Church of England Evangelical Council, for example, issued a statement drawn up by seven evangelical scholars on St Andrew's Day (30 November) in 1995 which concluded that the church was not entitled to confer moral legitimacy on alternatives to the two vocations of marriage between a man and a woman or celibate singleness. However, in terms somewhat similar to those employed by Paul King Jewett, the statement also stressed that a measure of flexibility was appropriate in pastoral care, and that all who seriously desired to follow Christ within the fellowship of his church should be encouraged, even if they did not conform to either of these two vocations.[78] In the non-Western world, in much of which homosexuality continued to be regarded with unqualified abhorrence, evangelical statements on the gay issue tended to be considerably less nuanced. Within the Anglican communion, and especially at the 1998 Lambeth Conference, evangelical bishops from Nigeria and Uganda were in the vanguard of opposition to the preparedness of the Episcopal Church of the USA to ordain practising homosexuals to the priesthood and even conse-crate them as bishops.[79]

By the end of the century it was clear that this issue, more than any other, was likely to be the major symbolic fault-line dividing conservatives from liberals in twenty-first century Christianity. Evangelicals had been compelled to reassess their principles of biblical interpretation, both by the currency in intellectual circles of the 'new hermeneutic', and by the increasingly sharp dissonance between traditional Christian stances and the norms of the age on matters of gender roles and sexual ethics. In the former area the majority of evangelical scholars, and a substantial proportion of those who had received formal theological education, reached the conclusion that their traditional understanding of how the teaching of the Bible should be applied to questions of the eligibility of women for church leadership had been in error. Whether the bulk of lay evangelicals had reached the same conclusion by the year 2000 is considerably more doubtful. Even in the new Pentecostal churches of Africa, despite the priority given to individual spiritual experience, the over-whelming majority of those in pastoral leadership remained male. In the field of sexual ethics, however, although the pressure of the gay and lesbian lobby had forced evangelical theologians and ethicists to re-examine the scriptural evidence, no such sea change in evangelical moral convictions was apparent by the end of the century.

---

[78] The St Andrew's Day Statement, at http://www.aco.org/listening/book_resources/ docs/St%20Andrew%27s%20Day%20Statement.pdf (accessed 5 June 2012).

[79] See Ward, *History of Global Anglicanism*, 306–315.

9. EVANGELICALISM: DIFFUSION OR DISINTEGRATION?

Trends from 1945 to 2000

Evangelical expressions of Christianity were by 2000 far more prominent within the world Christian movement than they had been in 1945. In the United States the 'new evangelicals' of the late 1940s were a marginal group struggling to differentiate themselves from the intellectually despised fundamentalists. Although they had many supporters within the historic denominations, they were decidedly not 'the mainline'. By 2000 the 'mainline' of liberal Protestantism had declined into numerical and perhaps even social marginality, whereas evangelicals of many different kinds now occupied the centre stage of American Protestantism.[1] In Britain, Canada and Australasia the weak and isolated conservative evangelicalism of 1945 had made deep inroads into the ranks of the ordained ministry and the leadership of the major denominations. On both sides of the Atlantic, new churches, many identified with migrant ethnic communities, and many others appealing to younger people whom the established denominations had failed either to reach or to hold, were legion: almost all were evangelical in theology and ethos. On a global stage, Pentecostal styles of Christianity, which scarcely any academic commentators deemed worthy of notice in 1945, were by the end of the century the fastest growing of all

---

[1] See D. Michael Lindsay, *Faith in the Halls of Power: How Evangelicals Joined the American Elite* (New York: Oxford University Press, 2007).

sectors of the world church, and attracting the attention of a host of scholarly monographs. Although the new Pentecostalism of the majority world cannot be properly understood without appreciating its deep indebtedness to indigenous world views, the fact of the global diffusion of a style of Christianity in the course of the second half of the twentieth century that exhibits many, if not all, of the classic marks of evangelicalism is beyond dispute.

The key question to ask is whether this numerical and geographical diffusion has been accompanied by, and indeed has engendered, a diffusion of identity and theological coherence. In Britain, for example, there is considerable evidence of broadening evangelical diversity to such an extent that by the end of the century the fractures within the evangelical movement were more evident than any continuing sense of pan-evangelical unity.[2] These fractures no longer followed the historic fault-line between Anglicanism and the Free Churches, but to a greater extent than hitherto ran across denominational lines, reflecting deep-seated theological and cultural divergences. Thus evangelicals in the Church of England now fell into three distinguishable though sometimes overlapping categories, both on a national scale and even within some individual parishes. 'Open' evangelicals were characterized by progressive stances on biblical hermeneutics, support for women clergy and the prospect of women bishops, and a willingness to engage constructively with non-evangelicals both within the Church of England and outside it; they are now mostly affiliated to 'Fulcrum', a body formed in 2003.[3] 'Reformed' evangelicals held to a more Calvinistic theology of the priority of biblical preaching, opposed women exercising any headship role within the church, and remained generally wary of ecumenical involvement; their interests were represented by the Church Society (founded in 1835) and Reform (1993). Charismatic evangelicals sat loosely to Anglican liturgy, tended to value Spirit-filled worship more highly than thorough biblical exposition, and often associated more with non-Anglican charismatics than with non-charismatic Anglicans; they were often affiliated to organizations that transcended Anglican boundaries, such as 'Alpha' and 'New Wine' (whose origins go back to 1989).[4] Parallel alignments may also be found in other parts of the Anglican communion, such as in Australia, where

---

[2] David W. Bebbington, 'Evangelical Trends, 1959–2009', *Anvil* 26 (2009), 93–106.

[3] For the origins of Fulcrum see Graham Kings, 'Founding of Fulcrum', *Fulcrum Newsletter* (Aug. 2006), at http://www.fulcrum-anglican.org.uk/news/2006/newsletter09.cfm?doc=137 (accessed 9 July 2012).

[4] Graham Kings, 'Canal, River and Rapids: Contemporary Evangelicalism in the Church of England', *Anvil* 20 (2003), 167–184. For the history of 'New Wine' see http://www.new-wine.org/home/about-us/our-history (accessed 9 July 2012).

the diocese of Sydney has exhibited the predominance of Reformed evangelical Anglicanism, while the diocese of Melbourne has reflected a more 'open'
stance.[5] Similar categorizations could also be applied to evangelicals in other
denominational families: the majority of British Baptists, for example, could
equally be classified using the three labels of open, Reformed and charismatic
evangelicals, although again it must be emphasized that these labels represent
tendencies rather than mutually exclusive parties.

In the radically plural and voluntaryist religious context of the United
States, the evangelical family has always been more ecclesiastically diverse
than in Britain, but even in the United States broadly similar trends can be discerned, with some evangelicals by the 1990s pursuing strategies of witness and
worship premised on varying degrees of accommodation with postmodern
cultural motifs, while others maintained stalwart opposition to any dilution
of emphasis on the preached Word and a propositional understanding of
biblical truth. In the light of such diversity within the camp, *Christianity Today*
in December 1999, as part of its regular review of the state of evangelicalism
at the end of the decade and its predictions of the course of the new century
about to dawn, cited some words of Billy Graham: 'We seem to be confused,
bewildered, divided, and almost defeated in the face of the greatest opportunity and responsibility, possibly in the history of the church.'[6] There might
appear to be more than enough evidence in this book to justify this pessimistic verdict, and this chapter may seem to add further weight to the case that,
by the end of the twentieth century, evangelicalism, for all of its remarkable
numerical and geographical expansion since 1945, had become so diffuse as to
be theologically unstable and incapable of definition.

Nevertheless, it is part of the vocation of the church historian to remind
Christians who may be depressed about the current condition of the church
that states of division and uncertainty are the norm rather than the exception
in Christian history. It should be noted that Graham's comment, cited by
Christianity Today as relevant in 1999, was in fact uttered in 1955 on the occasion of the founding of the magazine. The perceptive editorial comment in
1999 was that 'though the specifics may have shifted since Graham's 1955
speech, evangelicals are still confused about their role in society, divided as
a body, and even bewildered about what *evangelical* means'.[7] In the late 1980s

---

[5] Stuart Piggin, *Evangelical Christianity in Australia: Spirit, Word and World* (Melbourne:
Oxford University Press, 1996), 193–194, 204.

[6] *CT*, 6 Dec. 1999, 36, cited in Stanley J. Grenz, *Renewing the Center: Evangelical Theology
in a Post-Theological Era* (Grand Rapids: Baker Academic, 2000), 11.

[7] Ibid. (italics original).

and 1990s evangelical theologians such as David F. Wells deplored with good reason the lack of theological cohesion and cultural captivity of contemporary evangelicalism, and tended to look back wistfully to the united evangelical front of the 1950s and 1960s.[8] However, chapter 2 has shown that the 'new evangelical' consensus constructed in the United States out of the husks of the inter-war fundamentalist controversies was fragile and short-lived, while in Britain in the same period the meaning of the label 'evangelical' was still remarkably elastic, embracing some of quite liberal sentiments who would within a few years no longer be generally recognizable as belonging to the evangelical family. The impression that evangelicalism in Britain in 2000 was much more diverse and less cohesive than it was in 1945 arguably rests on the doubtful premise that those in the immediate post-war years whose evangelicalism was of a liberal or even 'centrist' kind should not be counted in the comparison.[9] That many in this category had by the 1960s abandoned essential evangelical commitments is not in dispute, but the historian must beware the temptations of hindsight. The conservative evangelicals who remained after these secessions from the margins largely succeeded in establishing their credentials as the authentic representatives of evangelicalism, but for much of the 1950s those credentials had been contested. While there seems little doubt that the 1990s ushered in a new phase of realignment and redefinition within large sections of what formerly styled itself as conservative evangelicalism, it is not necessarily the case that this phase heralds the disintegration of the evangelical movement; indeed, analysis of earlier periods in the history of the movement that witnessed similar realignments, such as the 1830s, the 1910s or the 1950s, would tend to suggest that the movement has the capacity to survive significant secessions from the margins and even realignments of the centre without succumbing to the disintegration that its most pessimistic adherents or unsympathetic critics have predicted. There is also the danger of universalizing on the basis of evangelical trends in the two nations that dominate the literature: the United States and the United Kingdom. The Canadian experience, for example, suggests that where secularizing tendencies in public life have progressed much further than in the USA, evangelicals may have

---

[8] David F. Wells, '"No Offense: I Am an Evangelical": A Search for Self-Definition', in A. James Rudin and Marvin R. Wilson (eds.), *A Time to Speak: The Evangelical–Jewish Encounter* (Grand Rapids: Eerdmans, 1987), 36; *No Place for Truth, or Whatever Happened to Evangelical Theology?* (Grand Rapids: Eerdmans, 1993), 127–136.

[9] I am following here the terminology used by David Bebbington in *Evangelicalism in Modern Britain: A History from the 1730s to the 1980s* (London: Unwin Hyman, 1989), 251–253.

found it easier to maintain a strong sense of common identity across denominational and ethnic boundaries.[10] The British example, on the other hand, shows that there is no necessary correlation between a more radically secular society and the cohesion of the evangelical community.

Even if the pessimists turn out to be correct so far as the evangelical movement in its historic northern heartlands is concerned, it seems manifestly improbable that the burgeoning evangelical Christianity of the southern hemisphere will follow a similar trajectory. Nevertheless, it is this Christianity that poses perhaps the most important question of all. Is the prominence of the Spirit in the Pentecostal movements of the majority world so pronounced that the centrality of the Word – that grounding of all Christian experience in the authority of Scripture, which has been a defining characteristic of evangelicalism from its beginnings in the 1730s – is in peril? To put the question in its bluntest form: How much of the global neo-Pentecostal movement – whose internal diversity must be stressed – may meaningfully be characterized as evangelical?

It is likely to be many decades before a conclusive verdict on questions as far-reaching as these can be offered, but this final chapter briefly considers at least some of the evidence. While predictions of the disintegration of evangelicalism may be premature, it is, nevertheless, imperative that serious attention is paid to those trends apparent by the end of the century that appeared to have corrosive potential for the durability of the evangelical movement. The first of these was the occurrence of secessions from the evangelical fold, particularly from its charismatic wing. Although more numerous in the United States than elsewhere, such secessions never represented more than a minority trend. Nonetheless, they included some high-profile figures and tended to point towards areas of theological weakness or instability within the structures of evangelical theology.

The quest for a restored apostolic church (part 2): charismatic evangelicals and the appeal of sacramental traditions, 1973–2000

Intrinsic to the charismatic movement surveyed in chapter 7 was a concern for the spiritual renewal of not simply the individual believer but also the church as a whole. Charismatic leaders, both inside and outside the historic denominations, believed that the Spirit was restoring a doctrinally compromised and evangelistically enfeebled church to its apostolic pattern of purity

---

[10] I owe this point to the Revd Dr Bruce Milne of Vancouver.

and power. Evangelical movements that seek to restore the church to its supposed primitive state have often displayed more or less marked elements of congruence with Catholic or Orthodox strands of Christian tradition. This was true in the 1830s and 1840s, when the Christian (Plymouth) Brethren and Oxford (Tractarian) movements shared certain key ecclesiological features in common, notably the insistence on the centrality of the Lord's Supper, known in these two traditions respectively as the Breaking of Bread and the Eucharist. A similar parallelism is observable in the last two decades of the twentieth century, when some evangelicals, especially those from a charismatic background, began to seek an integration or self-styled 'convergence' of evangelical, charismatic and sacramental traditions. An important source of the convergence movement were the later writings of Dr Robert E. Webber (1933–2007), reared as a fundamentalist Baptist and formerly a professor at Wheaton College, which called evangelicals to return to conformity to patristic traditions of worship. In 1985 Webber published a book, *Evangelicals on the Canterbury Trail*, recounting his own pilgrimage, and the parallel pilgrimages of several fellow-evangelicals, towards a more liturgical and sacramental expression of the Christian faith as found in the Protestant Episcopal Church.[11] The 'convergence' movement culminated in the formation of two new Christian communions. The Communion of Evangelical Episcopal Churches was formed in Fredericksburg, Virginia, in 1995.[12] More radical in its departure from historic Protestant positions was the Charismatic Episcopal Church, formed in California in June 1992 under the primacy of Randolph Adler, one-time pastor of the charismatic Stone Mountain Church in Laguna Hills; Adler had been influenced first by the Christian reconstructionist movement, which sought to apply biblical law to secular society, and then increasingly by sacramental and liturgical Christian traditions.[13] As happened in the early nineteenth century with former Anglican evangelicals such as John Henry Newman or H. E. Manning, the quest for apostolicity led in some cases away from the evangelical fold. However, in the late twentieth century the main beneficiary of such pilgrimage was not the Roman Catholic Church but the Eastern Orthodox Church.

In 1973 Peter Gillquist, a graduate of Dallas Theological Seminary and

---

[11] Robert E. Webber, *Evangelicals on the Canterbury Trail: Why Evangelicals Are Attracted to the Liturgical Church* (Harrisburg, Pa.: Morehouse Publishing, 1985); see his obituary in *CT*, Apr. 2007, 1–2; see also Peter Hocken, *The Challenges of the Pentecostal, Charismatic and Messianic Jewish Movements: The Tensions of the Spirit* (Farnham: Ashgate, 2009), 71–73.

[12] See http://www.theceec.org (accessed 5 July 2012).

[13] See http://www.cec-na.org/aboutus/history.html (accessed 5 July 2012).

Wheaton College, and a former staff member of Campus Crusade for Christ, together with several former Campus Crusade colleagues established a network of house churches, strongest in Berkeley, California, and in the Chicago area, known as the New Covenant Apostolic Order. A number of its prominent members, including its other main leader, Jack Sparks, had been active in the Jesus movement in California, and their educational backgrounds included such well-known conservative evangelical institutions as Westminster Theological Seminary, Asbury Theological Seminary, Oral Roberts University and Trinity Evangelical Divinity School.[14] The concern of Gillquist and Sparks's group to restore a primitive form of Christianity led them to study the patristic writings. The pattern of worship of the Order became increasingly liturgical, with a growing emphasis on the need for apostolic succession and authority. In 1979 the Order was reconstituted as the Evangelical Orthodox Church. In the spring of 1987 the eighteen congregations of this church, comprising nearly two thousand members, joined the Antiochian Orthodox Church, initially under the banner of 'the Antiochian Evangelical Orthodox Mission', and from 1995 as fully integrated parishes of the Antiochian branch of the Orthodox Church.[15] In 1990 Francis Schaeffer's son, Frank (Franky), was received into the Greek Orthodox Church. He published a book, *Dancing Alone*, recounting his spiritual pilgrimage, and subsequently an autobiography that was damaging to his father's memory, accusing him of a lack of intellectual integrity.[16] A one-time Presbyterian and later pastor in the Vineyard movement, Charles Bell, set out in 1993 to respond to Schaeffer, but to his surprise found that he was convinced by his studies of early Christian tradition, and himself became a well-known Orthodox priest,

---

[14] Larry Eskridge, 'God's Forever Family: The Jesus People Movement in America, 1966–1977' (University of Stirling PhD thesis, 2005), 342–344; Michael Harper, *True Light: An Evangelical's Journey to Orthodoxy* (London: Hodder & Stoughton, 1997), 148; http://cdn.calisphere.org/data/13030/w8/kt6z09r9w8/files/kt6z09r9w8.pdf (accessed 5 July 2012).

[15] See http://www.antiochian.org/node/17756 (accessed 5 July 2012); Peter E. Gillquist (ed.), *Coming Home* (Ben Lomond, Calif.: Conciliar Press, 1992); *Becoming Orthodox: A Journey to the Ancient Christian Faith* (Ben Lomond, Calif.: Conciliar Press, 1992).

[16] Frank Schaeffer, *Dancing Alone: The Quest for Orthodox Faith in the Age of False Religion* (Brookline, Mass.: Holy Cross Orthodox Press, 1994); *Crazy for God: How I Grew up as One of the Elect, Helped Found the Religious Right, and Lived to Take All (or Almost All) of It Back* (New York: Carol & Graf Publishers, 2007); see Os Guinness, 'Fathers and Sons: On Francis Schaeffer, Frank Schaeffer, and *Crazy for God*', *Books and Culture*, Mar.–Apr. 2008, at http://www.christianitytoday.com/bc/2008/marapr/1.32.html (accessed 5 July 2012).

Father Seraphim Bell, taking his Vineyard church with him into Orthodoxy.[17] In 1998 Jean Stone (who had undergone a divorce and remarried as Jean Stone Willans), who was identified in chapter 7 as one of the earliest and most influential publicists of charismatic renewal in the United States, followed the example of her new husband in being ordained within the Syrian Orthodox Church in Hong Kong, where the couple had worked, particularly among drug addicts, since 1968.[18]

The North American evangelicals who seceded to Eastern Orthodoxy were not all charismatics, but their example proved highly significant for Michael Harper. Harper's first real contact with Orthodoxy was in Finland in January 1990, where he was seeking to recruit Orthodox representatives to an international charismatic conference on world evangelization that took place in Brighton in July 1991. Another significant influence was an American Antiochian Orthodox priest, Michael Keiser, who visited Britain in January 1993; Keiser was in close touch with many conservative Episcopalians who were abandoning the increasingly liberal Protestant Episcopal Church for a spiritual home in Orthodoxy. Michael Harper had been dismayed by the decision of the Church of England General Synod in November 1992 to ordain women to the priesthood, and began to explore other branches of the Christian church. In June 1993 he published an article in the *Church of England Newspaper* entitled 'The Orthodox Option', which described the formation of the Antiochian Evangelical Orthodox Mission, and opined that 'I believe the time has come for a major revival of the Orthodox Church in Britain among British people'. Harper's article led to the formation of a group of like-minded Anglican clergy that assumed the title 'Pilgrimage to Orthodoxy'.[19] Later that year Gillquist and several of the other American evangelical converts to Orthodoxy came to Britain, and visited Michael and Jeanne Harper, among others, making a profound impact on them. On 15 March 1995 the Harpers were both received into the Orthodox Church at the Antiochian Orthodox Cathedral in London, and a few months later Michael was ordained as a priest of the Antiochian Orthodox Church.[20] Under his new title of 'Father Michael

---

[17] Hieromonk Alexios Karakallinos, 'Contours of Conversion and the Ecumenical Movement: Some Personal Reflections' (1994), http://www.orthodoxinfo.com/inquirers/fralexistalk.aspx (accessed 5 July 2012); *CEN*, 5158 (4 June 1993), 7.

[18] Stanley M. Burgess (ed.), *The New International Dictionary of Pentecostal and Charismatic Movements* (Grand Rapids: Zondervan, 2002), 1197.

[19] *CEN*, 5158 (4 June 1993), 7.

[20] Michael Harper, *True Light: An Evangelical's Journey to Orthodoxy* (London: Hodder & Stoughton, 1997), 4–5.

Harper' he remained as an editorial consultant for *Renewal* magazine.[21] In an article published in *Renewal* in January 1996 Harper surveyed the thirty-year history of the journal and of the charismatic renewal movement as a whole. While he pronounced as mistaken the scepticism of those who had predicted in the late 1960s that the renewal movement would soon die out, he was equally clear that it had not led to the widespread transformation of church life or revival that had been widely hoped for. Harper's explanation for the comparative failure reflected both his roots in the All Souls, Langham Place, tradition, with its appeal to biblical authority, and his new ecclesiastical allegiance:

> The spirit of compromise is prevalent. And what is more serious is the under-valuing and lack of respect for leadership which is endemic in the church scene. Equality grips the intellects of people, and the concepts of 'rule' and 'authority', so deeply embedded in both the Old and the New Testaments, are ignored in both church and family.
>
> Leaders cannot function any more as they used to, because people neither want them to nor truly value them.[22]

'Post-evangelicalism' and 'post-conservatism'

A second potentially corrosive influence, closely allied to the first, was the emergence of those who either chose to label themselves as 'post-evangelicals' or were labelled as such by others. In the United States the most-influential 'post-evangelical' has been Brian McLaren (1956–), the founding pastor of Cedar Ridge Community Church in Spencerville, Maryland, and a leading figure in the emerging church movement. McLaren's commitment to post-modern epistemology would eventually (through publications that appeared mainly after 2000) lead him to repudiate classic evangelical doctrinal positions. In Britain few British evangelical Anglicans accompanied or followed Michael Harper in his journey to Eastern Orthodoxy, perhaps because ecclesiological awareness was rather more highly developed among British than North American evangelicals. More common in Britain as the renewal movement entered the 1990s was a piecemeal dispersion of some prominent leaders of more or less 'renewed' evangelicalism into a variety of spiritual homes, some within Anglo-Catholicism, and others into various expressions

---

[21] *Renewal* 230 (July 1995), 3–4.
[22] *Renewal* 336 (Jan. 1996), 12.

of 'post-evangelicalism'. One high-profile example in the former category was Nick Mercer, a Baptist minister, vice-principal of the London Bible College (now the London School of Theology) and a leading light at Spring Harvest, who became an Anglo-Catholic priest in 1995. This was no sudden decision, but the culmination of a long process in which Mercer had come to recognize himself as 'theologically a Baptist, but aesthetically an Anglo-Catholic', and in which the spiritual aesthetics increasingly began to trump the evangelical Baptist theology.[23]

In the second category belonged Dave Tomlinson, a prominent leader in the new 'apostolic' churches in Britain and another Spring Harvest luminary, who published a book, *The Post-Evangelical*, in 1995, whose title was largely responsible for provoking a debate about the emergence of the phenomenon of 'post-evangelicalism'. Tomlinson propounded a distinctly postmodern understanding of theology; the parallel with postmodernity was clear: 'a post-evangelical consciousness of truth', he affirmed, 'is to be found less in propositional statements and moral certitudes and more in symbols, ambiguities and situational judgments'. Tomlinson advocated a doctrine of Scripture that was closer to Barth than to historic evangelicalism, proclaiming that 'the notion that everything can be reduced to an exact statement of words is a distinctly Enlightenment perspective, based on a subject–object relationship'.[24]

Tomlinson's book provoked considerable debate and self-questioning, especially among those at the charismatic end of the British evangelical spectrum, where more discerning participants were by the 1990s beginning to question the triumphalism and self-importance that had characterized sections of the charismatic movement.[25] Although largely unknown in North America, *The Post-Evangelical* did attract the attention of an American-born but Canada-based Baptist theologian who had become increasingly dissatisfied with the dependence of much evangelical apologetic in North America on a propositional and rationalistic view of truth. In his *Renewing the Center* (2000) Stanley Grenz (1950–2005) neatly summed up the awkward challenge posed

---

[23] See his 'Living Intimately with Strangers – a Postevangelical Pilgrimage?', in Graham Cray, Maggi Dawn, Nick Mercer, Michael Saward, Pete Ward and Nigel Wright, *The Postevangelical Debate* (London: SPCK, 1997), 57–74 (quotation at 69).

[24] Dave Tomlinson, *The Post-Evangelical* (London: SPCK, 1995), 90.

[25] For a perceptive and critical analysis of the movement by a former insider, British Baptist minister and former Spring Harvest platform speaker, see Rob Warner, *Reinventing English Evangelicalism, 1966–2001: A Theological and Sociological Study* (Milton Keynes: Paternoster Press, 2007).

by Tomlinson: Was it in fact the case that 'postmodern sensitivities will quite readily lead to a post-evangelical ethos, just as evangelicalism was in a certain sense a product of modernity'?[26] Grenz was sympathetic to certain elements of postmodernity, but did not accept the corollary that the demise of evangelicalism itself was imminent. Although biblical orthodoxy was intrinsic and necessary to the story that evangelicals as gospel people had to tell of their own experience of God, the heart of evangelical faith, Grenz contended, lay not in adherence to formal doctrinal statements, but in what he termed the 'convertive piety' that animated the eighteenth-century evangelical revivals. Evangelicals have always disagreed on some quite fundamental matters of theology, but they have been united in their testimony to having been radically transformed by the redeeming grace of God in Christ and the renewing power of the Spirit. In a postmodern age, evangelical 'foundationalism' (the post-Enlightenment quest for epistemological certitude via propositional statements) was in his view in terminal decline, but the challenge and opportunity facing evangelicals was how to renew or 're-imagine' the abiding reality of evangelical faith for the new cultural climate in which Enlightenment norms were no longer generally accepted.[27]

Grenz's endeavours to effect at least a partial reconciliation between evangelical faith and postmodern cultural perspectives were directed more at an American theological audience than a Canadian one, and his influence was undoubtedly stronger south of the frontier. The American Baptist theologian Roger E. Olson includes Grenz, alongside other like-minded theologians, such as the Canadian Baptist Clark H. Pinnock, in the company of those whom he approvingly terms 'postconservatives': they may be classified as such because of their commitment to 'ongoing reform of evangelical life, worship and belief in the light of God's word'.[28] Such commitment is radical in its preparedness to question the biblical basis of certain positions that had been widely accepted in evangelical tradition (e.g. the certainty of eternal damnation for all those who had never heard the gospel), but should not, according to Olson, thereby be denominated as 'liberal'. A similar and still more influential

---

[26] Grenz, *Renewing the Center*, 167; for a similar question from an influential British charismatic Anglican see Graham Cray's opening essay in Cray et al., *Post Evangelical Debate*, 1–18.

[27] Grenz, *Renewing the Center*, 325–351.

[28] Roger E. Olson, 'Postconservative Evangelical Theology and the Theological Pilgrimage of Clark Pinnock', in Stanley E. Porter and Anthony R. Cross (eds.), *Semper Reformandum: Studies in Honour of Clark H. Pinnock* (Carlisle: Paternoster Press, 2003), 16–37 (quotation at 36).

'post-conservative' evangelical has been the British Anglican New Testament scholar N. T. Wright (1948–). Tom Wright, who as a student at Oxford at the start of the 1970s was president of the Oxford Inter-Collegiate Christian Union, has been strongly influenced by the so-called 'New Perspective' on Paul pioneered by E. P. Sanders. His consequent reinterpretation of the central thrust of the epistle to the Romans (as having to do with the broad scope of God's saving purpose and not merely with the substitutionary atone-ment) has aroused the opposition of some conservative evangelicals, though many others have found his lucid exposition of New Testament eschatology, for example, transformative and inspirational for commitment to action on environmental issues.

For post-conservatives such as Grenz or Wright, post-conservatism is emphatically not to be equated with post-evangelicalism, and neither should its emergence be seen as a sign of the impending dissolution of the global evangelical community. For others of more conservative inclination, on the other hand, there is and can be no clear distinction between a post-conservative and a post-evangelical: to modify any major tenet of conservative evangelicalism is to identify oneself with the essentially self-contradictory and evanescent phenomenon of 'liberal evangelicalism', and hence to stand on the slippery slope that leads to liberalism pure and simple. Hence Don Carson of Trinity Evangelical Divinity School, Illinois, who since the 1980s has been the most consistently prolific and skilful of theological apologists for a strongly conservative evangelical position, in a published review of *Renewing the Center* criticized Grenz for domesticating the gospel to a postmodern world view; the clear implication of the review was that Grenz had, in effect, become a post-evangelical: 'Grenz's reformulation of the doctrine of Scripture is so domesticated by postmodern relativism that it stands well and truly outside the evangelical camp.'[29] Grenz, however, remained until his death a faithful member of First Baptist Church, Vancouver, under the conservative exposi-tory ministry of Bruce Milne, and left instructions that Milne should preach at his funeral.[30] Assessments of the state of evangelicalism can be misleading if they focus exclusively on academic theological arguments and neglect the evidence of spirituality and church life.

---

[29] D. A. Carson, 'Domesticating the Gospel: A Review of Stanley J. Grenz's *Renewing the Center*', available at http://www.sbts.edu/resources/files/2010/07/sbjt-064_win02-carson.pdf (accessed 5 July 2012; quotation at 94).

[30] Personal information from the Revd Dr Bruce Milne, senior pastor of First Baptist Church, Vancouver, for eighteen years until his retirement in 2001.

The future of evangelicalism and the challenges of the twenty-first century

At the end of our period post-conservatives and conservatives in the North were tussling, just as liberal evangelicals and fundamentalists had done before them, over how to reconcile aspects of the legacy of the European Enlightenment (in this case, in its 'late modern' or postmodern form) with the faith once delivered to the saints. These arguments within the theological community of evangelicals in the northern hemisphere have their importance, and show no sign of abating in the twenty-first century. They are, however, unlikely in the long run to determine the future of evangelicalism. If the global diffusion of evangelicalism proves eventually to have transmuted into the global disintegration of evangelicalism, it will not be because of the philosophical and hermeneutical boldness of a few post-conservative evangelical theologians in the North. It will rather be because in the explosive popular Christianity of the southern hemisphere the balance will have been tipped away from a Bible-centred gospel that, while being properly holistic, still holds to the soteriological centrality and ethical normativity of the cross, towards a form of religious materialism that subordinates the cross to a crude theology of divine blessing reduced to the promise of unlimited health and wealth here and now. In the majority world the sharpest challenge confronting believers in the message of the atoning power of the cross derives not from Enlightenment scepticism but from the daily realities of endemic poverty, hunger, pandemic disease and structural injustice. In cultures in which the traditional role of religious rituals and specialists was to provide power to ward off sickness and evil, Pentecostal versions of evangelicalism that give central place to the victory of Christ and the power of the Spirit have proved immensely attractive. The question is whether such deeply inculturated variants of Christianity will succeed in grounding the message of the victory of Christ over the powers of darkness in a biblical eschatology that recognizes that the full establishment of the kingdom of God is still to come.[31] The battle for the integrity of the gospel in the opening years of the twenty-first century is being fought not primarily in the lecture rooms of North American seminaries but in the shanty towns, urban slums and villages of Africa, Asia and Latin America.

---

[31] For a controversial argument that African Christianity has already lost a proper sense of the world to come, see Paul Gifford, 'African Christianity and the Eclipse of the Afterlife', in Peter Clarke and Tony Claydon (eds.), *The Church, the Afterlife and the Fate of the Soul*, SCH 45 (Woodbridge: Boydell & Brewer for the Ecclesiastical History Society, 2009), 413–429.

SELECT BIBLIOGRAPHY

Primary periodicals

Christian Century
Christian Record
Christianity Today
Church of England Newspaper
Church Times
Crusade
IFES Journal
International Review of Mission
Moody Monthly
Newsweek
Renewal
Sunday School Times
The Times
Third Way
Time

Reference works

Burgess, Stanley M. (ed.) (2002), *The New International Dictionary of Pentecostal and Charismatic Movements*, Grand Rapids: Zondervan.

Crockford's Clerical Directory, London: Oxford University Press.

Garraty, John A., and Mark C. Carnes (eds.) (1999), *American National Biography*, 24 vols., New York: Oxford University Press.

Larsen, Timothy, David Bebbington and Mark A. Noll (eds.) (2003), *Biographical Dictionary of Evangelicals*, Leicester: Inter-Varsity Press.

Who Was Who, 1971–1980 (1989), 2nd ed., London: A. & C. Black.

Willimon, William H., and Richard Lischer (eds.) (1995), *Concise Encyclopedia of Preaching*, Louisville, Ky.: John Knox Press.

Other primary and secondary works

Adeyemo, Tokunboh (ed.) (2006), *Africa Bible Commentary*, Nairobi: WordAlive Publishers.

Adogame, Afe (2011), *Who Is Afraid of the Holy Ghost? Pentecostalism and Globalization in Africa and Beyond*, Trenton, N.J.: Africa World Press.

Adogame, Afe, and James Spickard (eds.) (2010), *Religion Crossing Boundaries: Transnational Religious and Social Dynamics in Africa and the New African Diaspora*, Leiden: E. J. Brill.

Ammermann, Nancy Tatom (1990), *Baptist Battles: Social Change and Religious Conflict in the Southern Baptist Convention*, New Brunswick, N.J.: Rutgers University Press.

——(ed.) (1993), *Southern Baptists Observed: Multiple Perspectives on a Changing Denomination*, Knoxville: University of Tennessee Press.

Anderson, Allan (2004), *An Introduction to Pentecostalism*, Cambridge: Cambridge University Press.

Anderson, Allan, and Edmond Tang (eds.) (2005), *Asian and Pentecostal: The Charismatic Face of Christianity in Asia*, Oxford: Regnum Books, 2005.

Appasamy, A. J. (1965), *Write the Vision! Edwin Orr's Thirty Years of Adventurous Service*, London: Marshall, Morgan & Scott.

Asamoah-Gyadu, J. K. (2009), 'Bediako of Africa: A Late 20th Century Outstanding Theologian and Teacher', *Mission Studies* 26, 5–16.

Atherstone, Andrew (2008), *An Anglican Evangelical Identity Crisis: The Churchman – Anvil Affair of 1981–1984*, London: Latimer Trust.

——(2011), 'The Keele Congress of 1967: A Paradigm Shift in Anglican Evangelical Attitudes', *Journal of Anglican Studies* 9, 175–197.

Atherstone, Andrew, and David Ceri Jones (eds.) (2011), *Engaging with Martyn Lloyd-Jones: The Life and Legacy of 'the Doctor'*, Nottingham: Apollos.

Bacon, F. D. (1946), *Women in the Church*, London: Lutterworth Press.

Bacote, Vincent, Laura C. Miguélez and Dennis L. Okholm (eds.) (2004), *Evangelicals and Scripture: Tradition, Authority and Hermeneutics*, Downers Grove: InterVarsity Press.

Bahnsen, Greg (1986), 'Pressing Toward the Mark: Machen, Van Til, and the Apologetical Tradition of the OPC', at http://www.cmfnow.com/articles/PA064.htm.

Baker, Deane-Peter (2007), *Tayloring Reformed Epistemology: Charles Taylor, Alvin Plantinga and the de jure Challenge to Christian Belief*, London: SCM.

——(ed.) (2007), *Alvin Plantinga*, Cambridge: Cambridge University Press.

Barbour, Robin (2000), *J. S. Stewart in a Nutshell*, n.p.: Handsel Press.

Barclay, Oliver R. (1997), *Evangelicalism in Britain 1935–1995: A Personal Sketch*, Leicester: Inter-Varsity Press.

Barclay, Oliver R., and Robert M. Horn (2002), *From Cambridge to the World: 125 Years of Student Witness*, Leicester: Inter-Varsity Press.

Barr, James (1977), *Fundamentalism*, London: SCM Press.

——(1984), *Escaping from Fundamentalism*, London: SCM Press.

Bebbington, David W. (1989), *Evangelicalism in Modern Britain: A History from the 1730s to the 1980s*, London: Unwin Hyman.

——(2003), 'Evangelism and Spirituality', in Alan P. F. Sell and Anthony R. Cross (eds.), *Protestant Nonconformity in the Twentieth Century*, Carlisle: Paternoster Press, 184–215.

——(2005), *The Dominance of Evangelicalism: The Age of Spurgeon and Moody*, Leicester: Inter-Varsity Press.

——(2006), 'The Place of the Brethren Movement in International Evangelicalism', in Neil T. R. Dickson and Tim Grass (eds.), *The Growth of the Brethren Movement: National and International Experiences: Essays in Honour of Harold Rowdon*, Milton Keynes: Paternoster Press, 241–260.

——(2007), 'Evangelicals and Public Worship, 1965–2005', *EvQ* 79, 3–22.

——(2009), 'Evangelical Trends, 1959–2009', *Anvil* 26, 93–106.

——(2010), *Baptists Through the Centuries: A History of a Global People*, Waco: Baylor University Press.

Bebbington, David W., and Martin Sutherland (eds.) (forthcoming), *Interfaces: Baptists and Others from the Seventeenth to the Twenty-First Centuries*, Milton Keynes: Paternoster Press.

Beckwith, Roger (1990), 'Philip Edgcumbe Hughes', *Chm* 104, 351–352.

Bediako, Kwame (1989), 'World Evangelisation, Institutional Evangelicalism and the Future of the Christian World Mission', in Vinay Samuel and Albrecht Hauser (eds.), *Proclaiming Christ in Christ's Way: Studies in Integral Evangelism*, Oxford: Regnum Books, 52–68.

——(1992), *Theology and Identity: The Impact of Culture upon Christian Thought in the Second Century and Modern Africa*, Oxford: Regnum Books.

——(1994), 'Jesus in African Culture: A Ghanaian Perspective', in William A. Dyrness (ed.), *Emerging Voices in Global Christian Theology*, Grand Rapids: Zondervan, 93–121.

——(1995), *Christianity in Africa: The Renewal of a Non-Western Religion*, Edinburgh: T. & T. Clark.

Begbie, Jeremy (1991), *Voicing Creation's Praise: Toward a Theology of the Arts*, Edinburgh: T. & T. Clark.

Bennett, Dennis (1970), *Nine O'Clock in the Morning*, Plainfield, N.J.: Logos International.

Bennett, John C. (1954), 'Billy Graham at Union', *USQR* 9, 9–14.

Bergunder, Michael (2008), *The South Indian Pentecostal Movement in the Twentieth Century*, Grand Rapids: Eerdmans.

Berlet, Chip, and Matthew N. Lyons (2000), *Right-Wing Populism in America: Too Close for Comfort*, London: Guilford Press.

Blumhofer, Edith (1989), *The Assemblies of God: A Chapter in the Story of American Pentecostalism*, 2 vols., Springfield, Mo.: Gospel Publishing House.

——(1993), *Restoring the Faith: The Assemblies of God, Pentecostalism, and American Culture*, Urbana: University of Illinois Press.

Bowen, Roger (1996), 'Rwanda: Missionary Reflections on a Catastrophe', *Anvil* 13, 33–44.

Boyd, Robin (2007), *The Witness of the Student Christian Movement: 'Church Ahead of the Church'*, London: SPCK.

Bratt, James D. (1984), *Dutch Calvinism in Modern America: A History of a Conservative Subculture*, Grand Rapids: Eerdmans.

Brencher, John (2006), *Martyn Lloyd-Jones (1899–1981) and Twentieth-Century Evangelicalism*, Carlisle: Paternoster Press.

Breward, Ian (2001), *A History of the Churches in Australasia*, Oxford: Oxford University Press.

Briggs, J. H. Y. (1986), 'She-Preachers, Widows and Other Women: The Feminine Dimension in Baptist Life Since 1600', *Baptist Quarterly* 31, 337–352.

Bromiley, G. W. (1947), 'The Authority of the Bible: The Attitude of Modern Theologians', *EvQ* 19, 127–136.

Brown, Callum G. (2006), *Religion and Society in Twentieth-Century Britain*, Harlow: Pearson Longman.

Bruce, F. F. (1947), 'The Tyndale Fellowship for Biblical Research', *EvQ* 19, 52–61.

——(1980), *In Retrospect: Remembrance of Things Past*, Glasgow: Pickering & Inglis.

Burgess, Richard (2008), *Nigeria's Christian Revolution: The Civil War Revival and Its Pentecostal Progeny (1967–2006)*, Carlisle: Paternoster Press.

Callen, Barry L. (2003), 'Clark H. Pinnock, His Life and Work', in Stanley E. Porter and Anthony R. Cross (eds.), *Semper Reformandum: Studies in Honour of Clark H. Pinnock*, Carlisle: Paternoster Press, 1–15.

Cameron, Nigel M. de S., and Sinclair B. Ferguson (eds.) (1986), *Pulpit and People: Essays in Honour of William Still on his 75th Birthday*, Edinburgh: Rutherford House Books.

Carnell, Edward J. (1948), *An Introduction to Christian Apologetics: A Philosophic Defense of the Trinitarian-Theistic Faith*, Grand Rapids: Eerdmans.

——(1957), *Christian Commitment: An Apologetic*, New York: Macmillan.

——(1959), *The Case for Orthodox Theology*, Philadelphia: Westminster Press.

Carpenter, Humphrey (1978), *The Inklings: C. S. Lewis, J. R. R. Tolkien, Charles Williams and Their Friends*, London: George Allen & Unwin.

Carpenter, Joel (1997), *Revive Us Again: The Reawakening of American Fundamentalism*, New York: Oxford University Press.

Carson, D. A. (1996), *The Gagging of God: Christianity Confronts Pluralism*, Grand Rapids: Zondervan.

——(2000), 'Domesticating the Gospel: A Review of Stanley J. Grenz's *Renewing the Center*', originally published in *Modern Reformation*, available at http://www.sbts.edu/resources/files/2010/07/sbjt-064_win02-carson.pdf.

Carson, D. A., and J. D. Woodbridge (eds.) (1986), *Hermeneutics, Authority and Canon*, Leicester: Inter-Varsity Press.

——(1993), *God and Culture: Essays in Honor of Carl F. H. Henry*, Grand Rapids: Eerdmans.

Carson, D. A., R. T. France, Alec Motyer and Gordon J. Wenham (eds.) (1994), *New Bible Commentary 21st Century Edition*, Leicester: Inter-Varsity Press; Downers Grove: InterVarsity Press.

Chadwick, Owen (1990), *Michael Ramsey: A Life*, Oxford: Clarendon Press.

Chapman, Alister (2008), 'Anglican Evangelicals and Revival 1945–59', in Kate Cooper and Jeremy Gregory (eds.), *Revival and Resurgence in Christian History*, SCH 44, Woodbridge: Boydell & Brewer for the Ecclesiastical History Society, 307–317.

——(2012), *Godly Ambition: John Stott and the Evangelical Movement*, New York: Oxford University Press.

Chester, Timothy (1993), *Awakening to a World of Need: The Recovery of Evangelical Social Concern*, Leicester: Inter-Varsity Press.

Chestnut, R. A. (1999), 'The Salvation Army or the Army's Salvation? Pentecostal Politics in Amazonian Brazil, 1962–1992', *Luso-Brazilian Review* 36, 33–49.

Church, J. E. (1981), *Quest for the Highest: An Autobiographical Account of the East African Revival*, Exeter: Paternoster Press.

Church of England, Archbishops' Commission on Evangelism (1945), *Towards the Conversion of England*, Westminster: Press and Publications Board of the Church Assembly.

Clark, Gordon H. (1963), *Karl Barth's Theological Method*, Nutley, N.J.: P. & R. Publishing.

Cochran, Pamela D. H. (2005), *Evangelical Feminism: A History*, New York: New York University Press.

Colquhoun, Frank (1955), *Harringay Story: The Official Record of the Billy Graham Greater London Crusade 1954*, London: Hodder & Stoughton.

Coomes, Anne (1990), *Festo Kivengere: A Biography*, Eastbourne: Monarch.

——(2002), *African Harvest: The Captivating Story of Michael Cassidy and African Enterprise*, London: Monarch.

Craston, Colin (1986), *Biblical Headship and the Ordination of Women*, Grove Pastoral Series 27, Bramcote: Grove Books.

Craston, Colin, Joyce Baldwin and J. I. Packer (1973), *Evangelicals and the Ordination of Women*, Grove Booklet on Ministry and Worship 17, Bramcote: Grove Books.

Cray, Graham, Maggi Dawn, Nick Mercer, Michael Saward, Pete Ward and Nigel Wright (1997), *The Post Evangelical Debate*, London: SPCK.

Crowe, Philip (ed.) (1967), *Keele '67: The National Evangelical Anglican Congress Statement*, London: Falcon Books.

Cruz, Nicky (1968), *Run, Baby, Run*, Plainfield, N.J., Logos International.

Curtis, Heather D. (2007), *Faith in the Great Physician: Suffering and Divine Healing in American Culture, 1860–1900*, Baltimore: Johns Hopkins University Press.

Davidson, Allan K., and Peter J. Lineham (eds.) (1987), *Transplanted Christianity: Documents Illustrating Aspects of New Zealand Church History*, Auckland: College Communications.

Davidson, F. (ed.), assisted by A. M. Stibbs and E. F. Kevan (1953), *The New Bible Commentary*, London: Inter-Varsity Fellowship.

Dillistone, F. W. (1980), *Into All the World: A Biography of Max Warren*, London: Hodder & Stoughton.

Douglas, J. D. (ed.) (1975), *Let the Earth Hear His Voice. International Congress on World*

Evangelization Lausanne, Switzerland: Official Reference Volume: Papers and Responses, Minneapolis: World Wide Publications.

Downs, Frederick S. (1971), *The Mighty Works of God: A Brief History of the Council of Baptist Churches in North East India: The Mission Period, 1836–1950*, Gauhati: Christian Literature Society.

Dudley-Smith, Timothy (1999), *John Stott: The Making of a Leader*, Leicester: Inter-Varsity Press.

——(2001), *John Stott: A Global Ministry*, Leicester: Inter-Varsity Press.

Dunn, James D. G. (1982), 'The Authority of Scripture According to Scripture', *Chm* 96, 104–122, 201–225.

Ellison, H. L. (1954), 'Some Thoughts on Inspiration', *EvQ* 26, 210–217.

——(1958), *From Tragedy to Triumph: The Message of the Book of Job*, London: Paternoster Press.

Enns, James (2012), 'Saving Germany – North American Protestants and Christian Mission to West Germany, 1945–1974', University of Cambridge PhD thesis.

Eskridge, Larry (2005), 'God's Forever Family: The Jesus People Movement in America, 1966–1977', University of Stirling PhD thesis.

——(2013), *God's Forever Family: The Jesus People Movement in America*, New York: Oxford University Press.

(n.d. [1947]), *Evangelical Essentials: Report of the 113th Islington Clerical Conference, Held in the Church House, Westminster, January 14th, 1947, Under the Chairmanship of the Rev. HUGH R. GOUGH, O.B.E., M.A.*, London: Church Book Room Press.

(1948), *Evangelicals Affirm in the Year of the Lambeth Conference: The Proceedings of the Congress Held in London, April 13th–14th, 1948*, London: Church Book Room Press.

Ferdinando, Keith (2004), 'The Legacy of Byang Kato', *International Bulletin of Missionary Research* 28, 169–174.

Field-Bibb, Jacqueline (1991), *Women Towards Priesthood: Ministerial Politics and Feminist Praxis*, Cambridge: Cambridge University Press.

Fletcher, Brian (2004), 'The Diocese of Sydney and the Shaping of Australian Anglicanism 1940–62', in Geoffrey R. Treloar and Robert D. Linder (eds.), *Making History for God: Essays on Evangelicalism, Revival and Mission in Honour of Stuart Piggin*, Sydney: Robert Menzies College, 111–132.

Frady, Marshall (1979), *Billy Graham: A Parable of American Righteousness*, Boston, Mass.: Little Brown.

Frame, John M. (1995), *Cornelius Van Til: An Analysis of His Thought*, Phillipsburg: P. & R. Publishing.

France, R. T. (1994), '"It Seemed Good to the Holy Spirit and to Us"? Some Thoughts on Decision-Making in the Church, and on Christian Disagreement, in the Light of the Decision of the Church of England to Ordain Women to the Presbyterate', *Chm* 108, 234–241.

——(2000), *A Slippery Slope? The Ordination of Women and Homosexual Practice – A Case Study in Biblical Interpretation*, Grove Biblical Series 16, Cambridge: Grove Books.

Freshwater, Mark Edwards (1988), *C. S. Lewis and the Truth of Myth*, Lanham, Md.: University Press of America.

Freston, Paul (2001), *Evangelicals and Politics in Asia, Africa and Latin America*, Cambridge: Cambridge University Press.

Frizen, Edwin L., Jr. (1992), *Seventy-Five Years of IFMA, 1917–1992: The Nondenominational Missions Movement*, Pasadena, Calif.: William Carey Library.

Frykenberg, R. E. (2008), *Christianity in India from Beginnings to the Present*, Oxford: Oxford University Press.

Gatu, John G. (2006), *Joyfully Christian + Truly African*, Nairobi: Acton Publishers.

George, Timothy, James Earl Massey and Robert Smith, Jr. (eds.) (2010), *Our Sufficiency Is of God: Essays on Preaching in Honor of Gardner C. Taylor*, Macon, Ga.: Mercer University Press.

Gibbard, Noel (2002), *The First Fifty Years: The History of the Evangelical Movement of Wales, 1948–98*, Bridgend: Bryntirion Press.

Gifford, Paul (1998), *African Christianity: Its Public Role*, London: Hurst.

——(2004), *Ghana's New Christianity: Pentecostalism in a Globalising African Economy*, London: Hurst.

——(2009), 'African Christianity and the Eclipse of the Afterlife', in Peter Clarke and Tony Claydon (eds.), *The Church, the Afterlife and the Fate of the Soul*, SCH 45, Woodbridge: Boydell & Brewer for the Ecclesiastical History Society, 413–429.

——(2009), *Christianity, Politics and Public Life in Kenya*, London: Hurst.

Gill, Sean (1994), *Women and the Church of England: From the Eighteenth Century to the Present Day*, London: SPCK.

——(ed.) (1998), *The Lesbian and Gay Christian Movement: Campaigning for Justice, Truth and Love*, London: Cassell.

Gillquist, Peter E. (1992), *Becoming Orthodox: A Journey to the Ancient Christian Faith*, Ben Lomond, Calif.: Conciliar Press.

——(ed.) (1992), *Coming Home*, Ben Lomond, Calif.: Conciliar Press.

Girolimon, Michael T. (1995), '"The Charismatic Wiggle": United Methodism's Twentieth-Century Neo-Pentecostal Impulses', *Pneuma* 17, 89–103.

Glover, Willis B. (1954), *Evangelical Nonconformists and Higher Criticism in the Nineteenth Century*, London: Independent Press.

——(1954), 'The Old Evangelicalism and the New', *Religion in Life* 23, 286–296.

Goodhew, David (2003), 'The Rise of the Cambridge Inter-Collegiate Christian Union, 1910–1971', *JEH* 54, 62–88.

Graham, Billy (1997), *Just as I Am: The Autobiography of Billy Graham*, London: Harper Collins.

Grass, Tim (2011), *F. F. Bruce: A Life*, Milton Keynes: Authentic Media.

Green, Michael (2001), *Adventure of Faith: Reflections on Fifty Years of Christian Service*, Harrow: Zondervan.

——(2001), *Asian Tigers for Christ*, London: SPCK.

Grenz, Stanley J. (1995), *Women in the Church: A Biblical Theology of Women in Ministry*, Downers Grove: InterVarsity Press.

——(1998), *Welcoming but Not Affirming: An Evangelical Response to Homosexuality*, Louisville, Ky.: John Knox Press.

——(2000), *Renewing the Center: Evangelical Theology in a Post-Theological Era*, Grand Rapids: Baker Academic.

Grubb, Norman P. (1952), *Continuous Revival*, London: Christian Literature Crusade.

——(1969), *Once Caught, No Escape: My Life Story*, London: Lutterworth Press.

Guinness, Os (2008), 'Fathers and Sons: on Francis Schaeffer, Frank Schaeffer, and *Crazy for God*', *Books and Culture* (Mar.–Apr.), online at http://www.christianitytoday.com/bc/2008/marapr/1.32.html.

Gundry, Robert H. (1982), *Matthew: A Commentary on His Literary and Theological Art*, Grand Rapids: Eerdmans.

Guthrie, D., and J. A. Motyer (eds.) (1970), *The New Bible Commentary Revised*, London: Inter-Varsity Press.

Hanciles, Jehu (2008), *Beyond Christendom: Globalization, African Migration, and the Transformation of the West*, Maryknoll: Orbis Books.

Hankins, Barry (2008), *Francis Schaeffer and the Shaping of Evangelical America*, Grand Rapids: Eerdmans.

Harper, Michael (1997), *True Light: An Evangelical's Journey to Orthodoxy*, London: Hodder & Stoughton.

Harrell, D. E. (1975), *All Things Are Possible: The Healing and Charismatic Revivals in Modern America*, Bloomington: Indiana University Press.

Hart, D. G. (1999), 'Evangelicals, Biblical Scholarship and the Politics of the Modern American Academy', in David N. Livingstone, D. G. Hart and Mark A. Noll (eds.), *Evangelicals and Science in Historical Perspective*, New York: Oxford University Press, 306–326.

Hebert, Gabriel (1957), *Fundamentalism and the Church of God*, London: SCM Press.

Hennell, Michael (1973), 'An Episode in Twentieth Century Church History', *Theology* 76, 480–483.

Henry, Carl F. H. (1946), *Remaking the Modern Mind*, Grand Rapids: Eerdmans.

——(1947; new ed. 2003), *The Uneasy Conscience of Modern Fundamentalism*, Grand Rapids: Eerdmans.

——(1976–83), *God, Revelation and Authority*, 6 vols., Waco: Word Books.

——(1986), *Confessions of a Theologian: An Autobiography*, Waco: Word Books.

Henry, Carl F. H., and W. Stanley Mooneyham (eds.) (1967), *One Race, One Gospel, One Task: World Congress on Evangelism Berlin 1966: Official Reference Volumes: Papers and Reports*, 2 vols., Minneapolis: World WidePublications.

Hession, Roy (1996), *My Calvary Road: One Man's Pilgrimage*, Fearn: Christian Focus.

Hession, Roy and Revel (1950), *The Calvary Road*, London: Christian Literature Crusade.

Hickin, Leonard (1978), 'The Revival of Evangelical Scholarship', *Chm* 92, 125–133.

Hilborn, David (ed.) (2001), *'Toronto' in Perspective: Papers on the New Charismatic Wave of the Mid-1990s*, Carlisle: Paternoster Press.

Hinn, Benny (1992), *The Anointing*, Milton Keynes: Word.

Hocken, Peter (1986), *Streams of Renewal: The Origins and Early Development of the Charismatic Movement in Great Britain*, Exeter: Paternoster Press.

——(2009), *The Challenges of the Pentecostal, Charismatic and Messianic Jewish Movements: The Tensions of the Spirit*, Farnham: Ashgate.

Hooper, Walter (ed.) (1979), *They Stand Together: The Letters of C. S. Lewis to Arthur Greeves (1914–1963)*, New York: Macmillan.

Howard, David M. (1986), *The Dream That Would Not Die: The Birth and Growth of the World Evangelical Fellowship 1846–1986*, Exeter: Paternoster Press.

Hughes, Philip Edgcumbe (1962), 'Editorial', *Chm* 76, 131–135.

Hutchinson, M., and O. Kalu (eds.) (1998), *A Global Faith: Essays on Evangelicalism and Globalization*, Sydney: Centre for the Study of Australian Christianity.

Hutchinson, M., and J. Wolffe (2012), *A Short History of Global Evangelicalism*, Cambridge: Cambridge University Press.

Hylson-Smith, Kenneth (1988), *Evangelicals in the Church of England 1734–1984*, Edinburgh: T. & T. Clark.

Inter-Varsity Fellowship (1935), *Evangelical Belief*, London: Inter-Varsity Fellowship.

Jacobs, Donald R. (1992), 'My Pilgrimage in Mission', *International Bulletin of Missionary Research* 42, 146–149.

Jenkins, Philip (2006), *The New Faces of Christianity: Believing the Bible in the Global South*, New York: Oxford University Press.

——(2011), *The Next Christendom: The Coming of Global Christianity*, 3rd ed., New York: Oxford University Press.

Jewett, Paul King (1975), *Man as Male and Female: A Study in Sexual Relationships from a Theological Point of View*, Grand Rapids: Eerdmans.

——(1991), *God, Creation, and Revelation: A Neo-Evangelical Theology with Sermons by Marguerite Shuster*, Grand Rapids: Eerdmans.

——(1996), *Who We Are, Our Dignity as Human: A Neo-Evangelical Theology*, Grand Rapids: Eerdmans.

Johnson, Douglas (1979), *Contending for the Faith: A History of the Evangelical Movement in the Universities and Colleges*, Leicester: Inter-Varsity Press.

Johnson, Todd M., and Kenneth R. Ross (eds.) (2009), *Atlas of Global Christianity*, Edinburgh: Edinburgh University Press.

Kalu, Ogbu (2008), *African Pentecostalism: An Introduction*, Oxford: Oxford University Press.

Karakallinos, Hieromonk Alexios (1994), 'Contours of Conversion and the Ecumenical Movement: Some Personal Reflections', online at http://www.orthodoxinfo.com/inquirers/fralexistalk.aspx.

Kay, William K. (2000), *Pentecostals in Britain*, Carlisle: Paternoster Press.

——(2007), *Apostolic Networks in Britain: New Ways of Being Church*, Milton Keynes: Paternoster Press.

Kendall, Elliott (1978), *The End of an Era: Africa and the Missionary*, London: SPCK.

Kessler, J. B. A., Jr. (1968), *A Study of the Evangelical Alliance in Great Britain*, Goes, Netherlands: Oosterbaan & Le Cointre.

Kings, Graham (2003), 'Canal, River and Rapids: Contemporary Evangelicalism in the Church of England', *Anvil* 20, 167–184.

——(2006), 'Founding of Fulcrum', *Fulcrum Newsletter* (Aug.), at http://www.fulcrum-anglican.org.uk/news/2006/newsletter09.cfm?doc=137 (accessed 9 July 2012).

Krueger, Myles S. (2009), *James S. Stewart*, Cambridge: James Clarke.

Labenow, Cory E. (2009), *Evangelicalism and the Emerging Church: A Congregational Study of a Vineyard Church*, Farnham: Ashgate.

Laird, John (1981), *No Mere Chance*, London: Hodder & Stoughton and Scripture Union.

Larsen, Timothy J., and Daniel J. Trier (eds.) (2007), *The Cambridge Companion to Evangelical Theology*, Cambridge: Cambridge University Press.

Lawless, Elaine J. (1988), *Handmaidens of the Lord: Pentecostal Women Preachers and Traditional Religion*, Philadelphia: University of Pennsylvania Press.

Lehtonen, Risto (1998), *Story of a Storm: The Ecumenical Student Movement in the Turmoil of Revolution, 1968–1973*, Grand Rapids: Eerdmans; Helsinki: Finnish Society of Church History.

Lewis, C. S. (1942), *The Screwtape Letters*, London: Geoffrey Bles, Centenary Press.

——(1955), *Surprised by Joy: The Shape of My Early Life*, London: Geoffrey Bles.

——(1956), *Mere Christianity*, London: Collins.

——(1961), *Reflections on the Psalms*, new ed., London: Fontana.

——(1965), *Screwtape Proposes a Toast*, London: Fontana.

Lindsay, D. Michael (2007), *Faith in the Halls of Power: How Evangelicals Joined the American Elite*, New York: Oxford University Press.

Lindsell, Harold (1976), *The Battle for the Bible*, Grand Rapids: Zondervan.

——(1979), *The Bible in the Balance*, Grand Rapids: Zondervan.

Lineham, Peter J. (1977), *There We Found Brethren: A History of Assemblies of Brethren in New Zealand*, Palmerston North: G. P. H. Society.

——(1980), *No Ordinary Union: The Story of Scripture Union Children's Special Service Mission and Crusader Movement of New Zealand, 1880–1980*, Wellington: Scripture Union in New Zealand.

——(1983), 'Tongues Must Cease: The Brethren and the Charismatic Movement in New Zealand', *Christian Brethren Review* 34 (Nov.), 23–27.

Logan, George R. (1956), 'A Memoir of Dr Lamont's Life', in Daniel Lamont, *Studies in the Johannine Writings*, London: James Clarke, 7–62.

Lowman, Pete (1983), *The Day of His Power: A History of the International Fellowship of Evangelical Students*, Leicester: Inter-Varsity Press.

Ludwig, Frieder, and J. Kwabena Asamoah-Gyadu (eds.) (2011), *African Christian Presence* in the West: New Immigrant Congregations and Transnational Networks in North America and Europe, Trenton, N.J.: Africa World Press.

McBain, Douglas (1997), Fire Over the Waters: Renewal Among Baptists and Others from the 1960s to the 1990s, London: Hodder & Stoughton.

McBeth, H. Leon (1987), The Baptist Heritage: Four Centuries of Baptist Witness, Nashville: Broadman Press.

McDermott, Gerald R. (2010), The Oxford Handbook of Evangelical Theology, New York: Oxford University Press.

McGrath, Alister E. (1997), To Know and Serve God: A Life of James I. Packer, London: Hodder & Stoughton.

——(1999), Thomas F. Torrance: An Intellectual Biography, Edinburgh: T. &. T. Clark.

——(2009), The Open Secret: A New Vision for Natural Theology, Malden, Mass.: Blackwell.

MacLeod, A. Donald (2007), C. Stacey Woods and the Evangelical Rediscovery of the University, Downers Grove: IVP Academic.

McLeod, Hugh (2007), The Religious Crisis of the 1960s, Oxford: Oxford University Press.

MacLeod, John (2008), Banner in the West: A Spiritual History of Lewis and Harris, Edinburgh: Birlinn.

McMahon, Robert J. (1970), To God Be the Glory: An Account of the Evangelical Fellowship of India's First Twenty Years, 1951–1971, New Delhi: Christian Literature Institute.

MacMaster, Richard K., with Donald R. Jacobs (2006), A Gentle Wind of God: The Influence of the East Africa Revival, Scottdale, Pa.: Herald Press.

Manley, G. T. (ed.), assisted by G. R. Robinson and A. M. Stibbs (1947), The New Bible Handbook, London: Inter-Varsity Fellowship.

Marsden, George M. (1981), Understanding Fundamentalism and Evangelicalism, Grand Rapids: Eerdmans.

——(1987), Reforming Fundamentalism: Fuller Seminary and the New Evangelicalism, Grand Rapids: Eerdmans.

Marshall, I. H. (1982), Biblical Inspiration, London: Hodder & Stoughton.

——(ed.) (1977), New Testament Interpretation: Essays on Principles and Methods, Exeter: Paternoster Press.

Martin, Linette (1979), Hans Rookmaaker: A Biography, London: Hodder & Stoughton.

Martin, William (1991), A Prophet with Honor: The Billy Graham Story, New York: William Morrow.

Marwick, Arthur (1998), The Sixties: Cultural Revolution in Britain, France, Italy and the United States, c. 1958–1974, Oxford: Oxford University Press.

Matthew, David (ed.) (1988), Arthur Wallis 1922–1988: A Tribute, Bradford: Harvestime Services.

Maxwell, David J. (2006), African Gifts of the Spirit: Pentecostalism and the Rise of a Zimbabwean Transnational Religious Movement, Oxford: J. Currey; Harare: Weaver; Athens, Ohio: Ohio University Press.

Mews, Stuart (1982), 'The Revival of Spiritual Healing in the Church of England

1920–26', in W. J. Sheils (ed.), *The Church and Healing*, SCH 19, Oxford: Blackwell, 299–331.

Michaels, J. Ramsey (1981), *Servant and Son: Jesus in Parable and Gospel*, Atlanta: John Knox Press.

Miller, Steven P. (2005), 'Billy Graham, Civil Rights, and the Changing Postwar South', in Glenn Feldman (ed.), *Politics and Religion in the White South*, Lexington: University Press of Kentucky, 157–186.

Mitchell, Donovan F. (1949), 'Women and the Ministry: Whither Exegesis?', *RTR* 8, 1–11.

Moberg, David O. (1972), *The Great Reversal: Evangelism Versus Social Concern*, Philadelphia: Lippincott; London: Scripture Union.

Mohr, Adam (2010), 'Out of Zion and into Philadelphia and West Africa: Faith Tabernacle Congregation, 1897–1925', *Pneuma* 32, 56–79.

Mollencott, Virginia Ramey (1977), 'Evangelicalism: A Feminist Perspective', *USQR* 32, 95–103.

Moore, S. David (2003), *The Shepherding Movement: Controversy and Charismatic Ecclesiology*, London: T. & T. Clark International.

Morgan, Jill (1951), *A Man of the Word: Life of G. Campbell Morgan*, London: Pickering & Inglis.

Murray, Iain H. (1990), *David Martyn Lloyd-Jones: The Fight of Faith 1939–1981*, Edinburgh: Banner of Truth Trust.

——(2000), *Evangelicalism Divided: A Record of Crucial Change in the Years 1950 to 2000*, Edinburgh: Banner of Truth Trust.

Nelson, Rudolph (1987), *The Making and Unmaking of an Evangelical Mind: The Case of Edward Carnell*, Cambridge: Cambridge University Press.

Newbigin, Lesslie (1966), *Honest Religion for Secular Man*, London: SCM Press.

——(1983), *The Other Side of 1984: Questions for the Churches*, Geneva: World Council of Churches.

——(1986), *Foolishness to the Greeks: The Gospel and Western Culture*, London: SPCK.

——(1989), *The Gospel in a Pluralist Society*, London: SPCK.

——(1993), *Unfinished Agenda: An Updated Autobiography*, Edinburgh: St Andrew Press.

Nicholls, Bruce (ed.) (1986), *The Church: God's Agent for Change*, Exeter: Paternoster Press for the World Evangelical Fellowship.

Noble, T. A. (2006), *Tyndale House and Fellowship: The First Sixty Years*, Leicester: Inter-Varsity Press.

Noll, Mark A. (1991), *Between Faith and Criticism: Evangelicals, Scholarship, and the Bible*, 2nd ed., Leicester: Apollos.

——(1994), *The Scandal of the Evangelical Mind*, Grand Rapids: Eerdmans; Leicester: Inter-Varsity Press.

——(2001), *American Evangelical Christianity: An Introduction*, Oxford: Blackwell.

Noll, Mark A., David W. Bebbington and George A. Rawlyk (eds.) (1994), *Evangelicalism:*

Comparative Studies of Popular Protestantism in North America, the British Isles, and Beyond 1700–1990, New York: Oxford University Press.

The Nottingham Statement: The Official Statement of the Second Evangelical Anglican Congress Held in April 1977 (1977), London: Church Pastoral Aid Society.

Oakes, Peter (2004), 'F. F. Bruce and the Development of Evangelical Biblical Scholarship', *BJRL* 86, 99–124.

O'Brien, Peter T., and David G. Peterson (eds.) (1986), *God Who Is Rich in Mercy: Essays Presented to Dr. D. B. Knox*, Homebush West, NSW: Lancer Books.

Olson, Roger E. (2003), 'Postconservative Evangelical Theology and the Theological Pilgrimage of Clark Pinnock', in Stanley E. Porter and Anthony R. Cross (eds.), *Semper Reformandum: Studies in Honour of Clark H. Pinnock*, Carlisle: Paternoster Press, 16–37.

Omenyo, Cephas (2008), 'In Remembrance of the Late Professor Dr. Kwame Bediako', *Exchange* 37, 387–389.

Opp, James (2006), *The Lord for the Body: Religion, Medicine, and Protestant Faith Healing in Canada, 1880–1930*, Montreal: McGill-Queen's University Press.

The Ordination of Women to the Priesthood: The Synod Debate 11 November 1992: A Verbatim Record (1993), London: Church House Publishing.

Orr, J. Edwin (1975), *Evangelical Awakenings in Southern Asia*, Minneapolis: Bethany Fellowship.

Packer, J. I. (1958), *'Fundamentalism' and the Word of God: Some Evangelical Principles*, London: Inter-Varsity Fellowship.

Padilla, C. René (ed.) (1976), *The New Face of Evangelicalism: An International Symposium on the Lausanne Covenant*, London: Hodder & Stoughton.

Padilla, C. René, and Chris Sugden (eds.) (1985), *Texts on Evangelical Social Ethics 1974–1983 (i)*, Grove Booklet on Ethics 58, Bramcote: Grove Books.

Patterson, Bob E. (1983), *Carl F. H. Henry*, Waco: Word Books.

Piggin, Stuart (1996), *Evangelical Christianity in Australia: Spirit, Word and World*, Melbourne: Oxford University Press.

Pinnock, Clark H. (1967), *A Defense of Biblical Infallibility*, Nutley, N.J.: P. & R. Publishing.
——(1984), *The Scripture Principle*, San Francisco: Harper & Row.

Piper, John, and Wayne Grudem (eds.) (1991), *Recovering Biblical Manhood and Womanhood: A Response to Biblical Feminism*, Wheaton: Crossway.

Plantinga, Alvin (1967), *God and Other Minds: A Study of the Rational Justification of Belief in God*, Ithaca, N.Y.: Cornell University Press.
——(1974), *The Nature of Necessity*, Oxford: Clarendon Press.
——(1977), *God, Freedom and Evil*, 2nd ed., Grand Rapids: Eerdmans.
——(2000), *Warranted Christian Belief*, Oxford: Oxford University Press.

Pollock, John C. (1958), *Shadows Fall Apart: The Story of the Zenana Bible and Medical Mission*, London: Hodder & Stoughton.
——(1965), *Billy Graham: The Authorized Biography*, New York: McGraw-Hill.

Poon, Michael, and Malcolm Tan (eds.) (2012), *The Clock Tower Story: The Beginnings of the Charismatic Renewals in Singapore*, rev. ed., Singapore: Trinity Theological College, Singapore.

Porter, Andrew (1996), 'Empires in the Mind', in P. J. Marshall (ed.), *The Cambridge Illustrated History of the British Empire*, Cambridge: Cambridge University Press, 185–223.

Price, Robert M. (1983), 'Inerrant the Wind: The Troubled House of North American Evangelicals', *EvQ* 55, 129–144.

Ramm, Bernard L. (1983), *After Fundamentalism: The Future of Evangelical Theology*, San Francisco: Harper & Row.

Randall, Ian M. (1995), 'Conservative Constructionist: The Early Influence of Billy Graham in England', *EvQ* 95, 312–318.

——(1996), 'Schism and Unity: 1905–1966', in Steve Brady and Harold Rowdon (eds.), *For Such a Time as This: Perspectives on Evangelicalism, Past, Present and Future*, London: Evangelical Alliance; Milton Keynes: Scripture Union, 163–177.

——(2000), *Educating Evangelicalism: The Origins, Development and Impact of London Bible College*, Carlisle: Paternoster Press.

——(2005), *The English Baptists of the Twentieth Century*, Didcot: Baptist Historical Society.

——(2005), *A School of the Prophets: 150 Years of Spurgeon's College*, London: Spurgeon's College.

——(2008), *Spiritual Revolution: The Story of OM*, Milton Keynes: Authentic Media.

Rawlyk, George A. (ed.) (1997), *Aspects of the Canadian Evangelical Experience*, Montreal: McGill-Queen's University Press.

Reed, Colin (2007), *Walking in the Light: Reflections on the East African Revival and Its Link to Australia*, Brunswick East, Victoria: Acorn Press.

Rees, Jean (1971), *His Name Was Tom: The Biography of Tom Rees*, London: Hodder & Stoughton.

'A Response to Lausanne' (1974), *IRM* 63, 574–576.

Robert, Dana (2006), 'World Christianity as a Women's Movement', *International Bulletin of Missionary Research* 30:4 (Oct.), 180–188.

Roberts, Bill (1970), *Life and Death Among the Ibos*, London: Scripture Union.

Robbins, John W. (1993), 'An Introduction to Gordon H. Clark', *Trinity Review* (July–Aug.), 1–10; online at http://www.trinityfoundation.org/PDF/101a-AnIntroductiontoGordonHClark.pdf.

Römer, Jürgen (2002), *The Toronto Blessing*, Åbo: Åbo Academi University Press.

Russell, C. Allyn (1981), 'Donald Grey Barnhouse: Fundamentalist Who Changed', *Journal of Presbyterian History* 59, 33–57.

Ryken, Philip G., Derek W. H. Thomas and J. Ligon Duncan III (2003), *Give Praise to God: A Vision for Reforming Worship: Celebrating the Legacy of James Montgomery Boice*, Phillipsburg: P. & R. Publishing.

Sackey, Brigid M. (2006), *New Directions in Gender and Religion: The Changing Status of Women in African Independent Churches*, Lanham, Md.: Lexington Books.

Samuel, V., and C. Sugden (eds.) (1983), *Sharing Jesus in the Two-Thirds World*, Bangalore: Partnership in Mission-Asia.

Sanford, Agnes (1949), *The Healing Light*, Evesham: Arthur James.

Sangster, Paul (1962), *Doctor Sangster*, London: Epworth Press.

Schaeffer, Francis A. (1982–5), *The Complete Works of Francis Schaeffer*, 5 vols., Wheaton: Crossway Books.

Schaeffer, Frank (1994), *Dancing Alone: The Quest for Orthodox Faith in the Age of False Religion*, Brookline, Mass.: Holy Cross Orthodox Press.

——(2007), *Crazy for God: How I Grew up as One of the Elect, Helped Found the Religious Right, and Lived to Take All (or Almost All) of It Back*, New York: Carol & Graf Publishers.

Scotland, Nigel (2000), *Charismatics and the New Millennium: The Impact of Charismatic Christianity from 1960 into the New Millennium*, new ed., Guildford: Eagle.

Sherrill, John L. (1964), *They Speak with Other Tongues*, New York: Revell.

Shuff, Roger (2005), *Searching for the True Church: Brethren and Evangelicals in Mid-Twentieth-Century England*, Milton Keynes: Paternoster Press.

Simmons, Martha, and Frank A. Thomas (eds.) (2010), *Preaching with Sacred Fire: An Anthology of African American Sermons, 1750 to the Present*, New York: W. W. Norton.

Smail, Tom, Andrew Walker and Nigel Wright (1995), *Charismatic Renewal: The Search for a Theology*, London: SPCK.

Soothill, Jane (2007), *Gender, Social Change and Spiritual Power: Charismatic Christianity in Ghana*, Leiden: E. J. Brill.

——(2010), 'The Problem with "Women's Empowerment": Female Religiosity in Ghana's Charismatic Churches', *Studies in World Christianity* 16, 82–99.

Stackhouse, John G., Jr. (1993), *Canadian Evangelicalism in the Twentieth Century: An Introduction to Its Character*, Toronto: University of Toronto Press.

Stanley, Brian (1978), 'The East African Revival: African Initiative Within a European Tradition', *Chm* 92, 6–22.

——(1990), *The Bible and the Flag: Protestant Missions and British Imperialism in the Nineteenth and Twentieth Centuries*, Leicester: Apollos.

——(ed.) (2003), *Missions, Nationalism, and the End of Empire*, Grand Rapids: Eerdmans.

——(2009), *The World Missionary Conference, Edinburgh 1910*, Grand Rapids: Eerdmans.

Stendahl, Krister (1966), *The Bible and the Role of Women: A Case Study in Hermeneutics*, Philadelphia: Fortress Press.

Still, William (1991), *Dying to Live*, Fearn: Christian Focus Publications.

Stockwell, A. J. (2008), 'Leaders, Dissidents and the Disappointed: Colonial Students in Britain as Empire Ended', *Journal of Imperial and Commonwealth History* 36, 487–507.

Stott, John R. W. (1956), *Fundamentalism and Evangelism*, London: Crusade Booklets.

——(1958), *Basic Christianity*, London: Inter-Varsity Fellowship.

——(1975), 'The Significance of Lausanne', *IRM* 64, 288–294.

——(1986), *The Cross of Christ*, Leicester: Inter-Varsity Press.

Sylvester, Nigel (1984), *God's World in a Young World: The Story of Scripture Union*, London: Scripture Union.

Thiselton, Anthony C. (1980), *The Two Horizons: New Testament Hermeneutics and Philosophical Description with Special Reference to Heidegger, Bultmann, Gadamer, and Wittgenstein*, Exeter: Paternoster Press.

Thomas, Jacob (2003), *From Lausanne to Manila: Evangelical Social Thought*, New Delhi: ISPCK.

Tinker, Melvin (1994), "'It Seemed Good to the Holy Spirit and to Us'? A Reply to Dick France', *Chm* 108, 242–246.

Tizon, Al (2008), *Transformation After Lausanne: Radical-Evangelical Mission in Global–Local Perspective*, Oxford: Regnum Books.

Tomberlin, James E., and Peter Van Inwagen (eds.) (1985), *Alvin Plantinga*, Dordrecht: D. Reidel Publishing.

Tomlinson, Dave (1995), *The Post-Evangelical*, London: SPCK.

Torrance, Thomas F. (1941), *The Modern Theological Debate: Notes of Three Addresses Delivered at the T.S.P.U. Conference, Bewdley, Dec. 30–Jan. 2, 1941*, London: Theological Students' Prayer Union of the Inter-Varsity Fellowship.

Toulis, Nicole Rodriguez (1997), *Believing Identity: Pentecostalism and the Mediation of Jamaican Ethnicity and Gender in England*, Oxford: Berg.

Treloar, Geoffrey R. (forthcoming), *The Disruption of Evangelicalism: The Age of Mott, Machen and McPherson*, Leicester: Inter-Varsity Press.

Triton, A. N. [Oliver R. Barclay] (1970), *Whose World?*, London: Inter-Varsity Press.

Van Til, Cornelius (1967), *The Defense of the Faith*, 3rd ed., Philadelphia: P. & R. Publishing.

Vasey, Michael (1995), *Strangers and Friends: A New Exploration of Homosexuality and the Bible*, London: Hodder & Stoughton.

Virgo, Terry (1985), *Restoration in the Church*, Eastbourne: Kingsway Publications.

Wacker, Grant (2001), *Heaven Below: Early Pentecostals and American Culture*, Cambridge, Mass.: Harvard University Press.

Wagner, C. Peter (1999), *Churchquake! How the New Apostolic Reformation Is Shaking up the Church as We Know It*, Ventura, Calif.: Regal Books.

——(1999), 'My Pilgrimage in Mission', *International Bulletin of Missionary Research* 23, 164–167.

Wainwright, Geoffrey (1976), *Lesslie Newbigin: A Theological Life*, New York: Oxford University Press.

Walker, Andrew (1988), *Restoring the Kingdom: The Radical Christianity of the House Church Movement*, Guildford: Eagle.

Wallis, Arthur (1956), *In the Day of Thy Power: The Scriptural Principles of Revival*, London: Christian Literature Crusade.

Wallis, Jim, and Joyce Holladay (eds.) (1991), *Cloud of Witnesses*, Maryknoll: Orbis Books; Washington, D.C.: Sojourners.

Wallis, Jonathan (1991), *Arthur Wallis: Radical Christian*, Eastbourne: Kingsway.

Walls, Andrew F. (2008), 'Kwame Bediako and Christian Scholarship in Africa', *International Bulletin of Missionary Research* 32, 188–193.

Walls, Andrew F., and Wilbert R. Shenk (1990), *Exploring New Religious Movements: Essays in Honour of Harold W. Turner*, Elkhart, Ind.: Mission Focus.

Ward, Kevin (2006), *A History of Global Anglicanism*, Cambridge: Cambridge University Press.

——(2008), 'The East African Revival of the Twentieth Century: The Search for an Evangelical African Christianity', in Kate Cooper and Jeremy Gregory (eds.), *Revival and Resurgence in Christian History*, SCH 44, Woodbridge: Boydell & Brewer for the Ecclesiastical History Society, 365–387.

Ward, Kevin, and Emma Wild-Wood (eds.) (2012), *The East African Revival: History and Legacies*, Farnham: Ashgate.

Ward, Michael (2008), *Planet Narnia: The Seven Heavens in the Imagination of C. S. Lewis*, New York: Oxford University Press.

Warner, Rob (2007), *Reinventing English Evangelicalism, 1966–2001: A Theological and Sociological Study*, Milton Keynes: Paternoster Press.

Watford, Jack D. (1995), *Yesterday and Today: A History of Crusaders* (n.p. [Crusaders Union]).

Webber, Robert E. (1985), *Evangelicals on the Canterbury Trail: Why Evangelicals Are Attracted to the Liturgical Church*, Harrisburg, Pa.: Morehouse Publishing.

Wells, David F. (1987), '"No Offense: I Am an Evangelical": A Search for Self-Definition', in A. James Rudin and Marvin R. Wilson (eds.), *A Time to Speak: The Evangelical–Jewish Encounter*, Grand Rapids: Eerdmans, 20–44.

——(1993), *No Place for Truth, or Whatever Happened to Evangelical Theology?*, Grand Rapids: Eerdmans.

Wenham, John W. (1998), *Facing Hell: An Autobiography 1913–1996*, Carlisle: Paternoster Press.

Weston, Paul (comp.) (2006), *Lesslie Newbigin, Missionary Theologian: A Reader*, London: SPCK.

Wilkerson, David (1963), *The Cross and the Switchblade*, New York: B. Geis Associates.

Wilson, A. N. (1991), *C. S. Lewis: A Biography*, new ed., London: Harper Collins.

Wimber, John (1985), *Power Evangelism: Signs and Wonders Today*, London: Hodder & Stoughton.

Wirt, Sherwood E. (1968), *The Social Conscience of the Evangelical*, New York: Harper & Row; London: Scripture Union.

Woolsey, Andrew (1974), *Duncan Campbell: A Biography*, London: Hodder & Stoughton.

Wright, David F. (1980), 'Soundings in the Doctrine of Scripture in British Evangelicalism in the First Half of the Twentieth Century', *TynB* 31, 87–106.

Wuthnow, Robert (1988), *The Restructuring of American Religion: Society and Faith Since World War II*, Princeton: Princeton University Press.

Yeh, Allen (2008), '*Se hace camino al andar*: Periphery and Center in the Missiology of Orlando Costas', University of Oxford DPhil thesis.

Websites

http://cdn.calisphere.org/data/13030/w8/kt6z09r9w8/files/kt6z09r9w8.pdf

http://christianmusic.suite101.com/article.cfm/stuart_hine_how_great_thou_art

http://en.wikipedia.org/wiki/Anglican_Diocese_of_Sydneyhttp://www.witherspoonsoc
    iety.org/2006/women's_ordination.htm

http://en.wikipedia.org/wiki/Troy_Perry http://www.etsjets.org/about/constitution

http://gospel-culture.org.ukhttp://www.ibr-bbr.org/brief-history-ibr

http://reform.org.uk/download-file/downloads/interpreting.pdf

http://thefellowship.info/cbf/files/29/2982b463-235d-43ad-9173-917ee67d6b8b.pdf

http://www2.wheaton.edu/bgc/archives/docs/Berlin66/stott3.htm

http://www.aco.org/listening/book_resources/docs/St%20Andrew%27s%20Day%20
    Statement.pdf

http://www.alliancenet.org/CC_Content_Page/0,,PTID307086_CHID798774_CIID,00.
    html

http://www.alliancenet.org/partner/Article_Display_Page/0,,PTID307086_CHID58134
    8_CIID1907714,00.html

http://www.allianceofbaptists.org

http://www.antiochian.org/node/17756

http://www.artscentregroup.org.uk/about_history.php

http://www.cec-na.org/aboutus/history.html

http://www.courage.org.uk/articles/article.asp?id=142

http://www.courage.org.uk/articles/eapressrelease.shtml

http://www.ecwr.org/about-us/who-we-are/history.html

http://www.evangelicalsconcerned.org

http://www.gocn.org

http://www.inplainsite.org/html/vineyard_lonnie_frisbee.html

http://www.jedwinorr.com/bio.htm

http://www.langhampartnership.org/about-us/history

http://www.lausanne.org/all-documents/lop-3.html#9,

http://www.lausanne.org/documents/lau2docs/294.pdf

http://www.lausanne.org/en/documents/lops/79-lop-21.html http://www.lausanne.org
    /en/documents/manila-manifesto.html

http://www.lausanne.org/en/gatherings/cape-town-2010.html

http://www.manhattan-institute.org/html/_chicsuntimes-hollywood.htm

http://www.new-wine.org/home/about-us/our-history

http://www.oac.cdlib.org/data/13030/w8/kt6z09r9w8/files/kt6z09r9w8.pdf

http://www.presaffirm.org.nz

http://www.theceec.org

http://www.wheaton.edu/bgc/archives/bgeachro/bgeachrono2.htm

http://www.yuricareport.com/Dominionism/HansRookmaakerAndSchaefferInArt.html

INDEX

Aalders, G. C., 100
Abdul-Haqq, Akkbar, 69, 70, 157
abortion, 213
Above Bar Church, Southampton, 193, 194
Adeyemo, Tokunboh, 119
Adler, Randolph, 240
Adogame, Afe, 18
Africa
    evangelicals in, 74–75
    traditional religion, 118
Africa Bible Commentary, The (2006), 120
Africa, East (*see also* East African Revival),
    15
Africa Inland Church, Kenya, 74
Africa Inland Mission (AIM), 74
Africa, sub-Saharan, 15, 19
Africa, West (*see also* Ghana; Nigeria), 15,
    89–90, 202, 214–215
African Enterprise, 85
African Pentecostal movements, 202
Akrofi-Christaller Institute, Ghana, 119
All Souls, Langham Place, London, 41, 42, 82,
    114, 189, 190, 243
Allan, Tom, 47
Alliance of Baptists, 111
Alliance of Confessing Evangelicals, 113
Alpha course, 208, 209, 236
Amerding, Hudson, 170
American Academy of Religion, 97
American Council of Christian Churches,
    30, 134
American Scientific Affilation, 124
Ammermann, Nancy Tatom, 110, 111, 217
Andersen, Francis I., 58, 97
Anderson, Allan, 186, 207
André, Jean, 163
Anglican Evangelical Group Movement,
    41
Anglican Prayer for Revival, 190

Anglicanism
    in Australia, 57–59, 115–116, 218–219,
        236–237
    in New Zealand, 59
Anglo-Catholicism, 240, 243, 244
Antiochian Orthodox Church, 241, 242
Anvil journal, 221
apologetics, 24, 121–124, 131–139
Apostolic Faith Mission, 185
apostolic (new or house) churches, 194–195,
    206, 207, 235, 241
apostolic tradition, appeal to, 218, 219, 240
Appasamy, A. J., 80, 187
Archer, Gleason L., 131
Ariko, Reuben, 88
Aristotle, 128
Arnold, Matthew, 148 'On Dover Beach'
Arnott, John, 185, 208
Arts Centre Group, London, 138
arts, the, 137
Asa-Ludwig, Frieder
Asamoah-Gyadu, J. K., 18, 119
Asia, South-East, 15, 201–202
Association Biblia Universitaria Argentina, 158
Association of Evangelicals of Africa and
        Madagascar (AEAM), 21, 74, 118
Atherstone, Andrew, 44, 50, 52, 189, 197, 221
Audu, Ishaya, 87
Australia
    Anglicans in, 57–59, 115–116, 218–219,
        236–237
    Baptists in, 218
    Billy Graham crusades, 53, 66
    charismatic movement/renewal (neo-
        Pentecostalism), 182
    Children's Special Service Mission (CSSM),
        54
    Crusaders Union movement, 57
    divine healing, 183